Africa in the New Millennium

ABOUT THIS SERIES

The books in this new series are a new initiative by CODESRIA, the Council for the Development of Social Science Research in Africa, to encourage African scholarship relevant to the multiple intellectual, policy and practical problems and opportunities confronting the African continent in the 21st century.

CODESRIA in association with Zed Books

Already published:

African Intellectuals: *Rethinking Politics, Language, Gender and Development*
    Edited by Thandika Mkandawire

Urban Africa: Changing Contours of Survival in the City
    Edited by A. M. Simone and A. Abouhani

Titles in preparation:

Africa and Development Challenges in the New Millennium: The NEPAD Debate
    Edited by J. O. Adesina, A. Olukoshi and Yao Graham

Liberal Democracy and Its Critics in Africa: Political Dysfunction and the Struggle for Social Progress
    Edited by Tukumbi Lumumba-Kasongo

Negotiating Modernity: Africa's Ambivalent Experience
    Edited by Elísio Salvado Macamo

Insiders and Outsiders: Citizenship and Xenophobia in Contemporary Southern Africa
    Francis B. Nyamnjoh

About CODESRIA

The Council for the Development of Social Science Research in Africa (CODESRIA) is an independent organization whose principal objectives are facilitating research, promoting research-based publishing and creating multiple forums geared towards the exchange of views and information among African researchers. It challenges the fragmentation of research through the creation of thematic research networks that cut across linguistic and regional boundaries.

CODESRIA publishes a quarterly journal, *Africa Development*, the longest-standing Africa-based social science journal; *Afrika Zamani*, a journal of history; the *African Sociological Review*, *African Journal of International Affairs* (AJIA), *Africa Review of Books* and *Identity, Culture and Politics: An Afro-Asian Dialogue*. It co-publishes the *Journal of Higher Education in Africa*, and *Africa Media Review*. Research results and other activities of the institution are disseminated through 'Working Papers', 'Monograph Series', 'CODESRIA Book Series', and the CODESRIA Bulletin.

ABDOUMALIQ SIMONE &
ABDELGHANI ABOUHANI | editors

Urban Africa

Changing contours of survival in the city

CODESRIA Books
DAKAR

in association with

Zed Books
LONDON | NEW YORK

University of South Africa Press
PRETORIA

Urban Africa: changing contours of survival in the city was first published
by Zed Books Ltd, 7 Cynthia Street, London N1 9JF, UK and Room 400,
175 Fifth Avenue, New York, NY 10010, USA in 2005
www.zedbooks.co.uk

and in South Africa by UNISA Press, PO Box 392, Pretoria RSA 003
www.unisa.ac.za

in association with CODESRIA, Avenue Cheikh Anta Diop, X Canal IV,
BP3304 Dakar, 18524 Senegal
www.codesria.org

CODESRIA would like to express its gratitude to the Swedish International
Development Cooperation Agency (SIDA/SAREC), the International Develop-
ment Research Centre (IDRC), Ford Foundation, MacArthur Foundation,
Carnegie Corporation, the Norwegian Ministry of Foreign Affairs, the Danish
Agency for International Development (DANIDA), the French Ministry of
Cooperation, the United Nations Development Programme (UNDP), the
Netherlands Ministry of Foreign Affairs, Rockefeller Foundation, FINIDA,
NORAD, CIDA, IIEP/ADEA, OECD, IFS, OXFAM America, UN/UNICEF and the
Government of Senegal for supporting its research, training and publication
programmes.

Cover designed by Andrew Corbett
Set in Arnhem and Futura Bold by Ewan Smith, London
Index: ed.emery@britishlibrary.net
Printed and bound in Malta by Gutenberg Press Ltd

Distributed in the USA exclusively by Palgrave Macmillan, a division of
St Martin's Press, LLC, 175 Fifth Avenue, New York, NY 10010.

A catalogue record for this book is available from the British Library.
US CIP data are available from the Library of Congress.

CODESRIA edition   ISBN 2 86978 142 3
Zed Books edition   ISBN 1 84277 592 8 cased
                    ISBN 1 84277 593 6 limp

Contents

Tables and figure | vii Acknowledgements | viii
Abbreviations and acronyms | ix

1   Introduction: urban processes and change   1
    ABDOUMALIQ SIMONE

one | Making urban politics

2   Urban policies in Cairo: from speeches on new cities to
    the adjustment practices of ordinary city dwellers   29
    BÉNÉDICTE FLORIN

3   Feasts: panoramas in town – the spaces and times of the
    moulids of Cairo   68
    ANNA MADOEUF

4   Kisangani: a city at its lowest ebb   96
    JEAN OMASOMBO

5   The city centre: a shifting concept in the history of Addis
    Ababa   120
    BAHRU ZEWDE

6   At the limits of possibility: working notes on a relational
    model of urban politics   138
    EDGAR PIETERSE

two | Urban practices

7   Life in a high-density urban area: Anguwar Mai Gwado
    in Zaria   177
    MOHAMMED-BELLO YUNUSA

8   Ethnicity and the dynamics of city politics: the case of Jos   206
    VICTOR A. O. ADETULA

9 Urban development and urban informalities: Pikine,
Senegal   235

MOHAMADOU ABDOUL

10 Formal and decentralized financing of housing:
Operation 200,000 Houses, Marrakesh   261

MOHAMED GHERIS

Contributors | 295
Index | 298

Tables and figure

Tables

4.1	The first five cities of Congo according to urban population	102
7.1	Proportions of respondents involved in various categories of activities	196
7.2	Mean hours spent by respondents on various activities per day by sex	197
7.3	Mean hours spent by respondents on various activities per week by age	198
7.4	Mean hours spent by respondents on various activities per week by levels of education	199
7.5	Mean hours spent on various activities by respondents by households per week	200
10.1	Size of households by 2010	269
10.2	Trend in number of authorized houses in Marrakesh	269
10.3	Total number of units built by ERAC-Tensift	272
10.4	Work done by each developer	274
10.5	Breakdown of the programmes completed by *préfecture* or province	275
10.6	Distribution of surface area of utilities by activity and sector	276
10.7	Level of satisfaction in the neighbourhood	277
10.8	Nuisances in the neighbourhood	277
10.9	Surface area of houses	278
10.10	Modifications made	278
10.11	Home buyers' opinion of bank loans	279
10.12	Went to the *tontine*	279
10.13	Status of occupation before the purchase of the house	280
10.14	Evaluation of pseudo-mortgage rates	280
10.15	Appreciation of the accessibility of pseudo-mortgage	281

Figure

6.1	Dimensions of political engagement in the city	145

Acknowledgements

The editors gratefully acknowledge the generous and patient support of present and former staff members of the Council for the Development of Social Science Research in Africa (CODESRIA). Particular acknowledgement is made of the critical engagements of Francis Nyamnjoh, Bruno Sonko, Sheila Bunwaree, Ebrima Sall, Achille Mbembe, Mahmood Mamdani, Adebayo Olukoshi, Thandika Mkandawire and Mamadou Diouf.

Gratitude is also extended to Okwui Ewenzor for the opportunity to present this work as part of the Documenta 11 process. This volume also celebrates the memory of one of the working group's original members and one of Africa's great urbanists, Tshikala Kayembe Biaya.

Abbreviations and acronyms

ACCT	Agence de Coopération Culturelle et Technique
ADIE	Association pour le Développement de l'Information Environement
ANC	African National Congress
ANHI	Agence Nationale de Lutte Contre l'Habitat Insalubre
ANI	Agence Nationale d'Immigration
ASC	Cultural and Sports Associations
BCM	Banque Commerciale du Maroc
BCP	Banque Centrale Populaire
BECO	Berom Educational and Cultural Organization
BESM	Bulletin Économique et Social
BHP	Berom Historical Publications
BIROMC	Berom Intellectual Revival Organizational Movement Club
BWA	Berom Women's Association
BYM	Berom Youth Movement
CDG	Caisse de Dépôt et de Gestion
CDS	city development strategy
CEDEJ	Centre d'Études et de Documentation Économique, Juridique et Sociale
CEPED	Centre Population et Développement
CESHS	Centre d'études en sciences humaines et sociales
CIH	Crédit Immobilier et Hôtelier
CNRS	Centre National de Recherche Scientifique
CNRSC	Centre National de Recherches Sociales et Criminologiques
CODESRIA	Council for the Development of Social Science Research in Africa
COWAN	Country Women's Association of Nigeria
CRERI	Centre de Recherches et d'Études en Relations Internationales
ECA	Economic Commission for Africa
ECOWAS	Economic Community of West African States
EHESS	L'École des Hautes Études en Sciences Sociales
EIC	East India Company
EMAM	Équipe Monde Arabe Méditerranée
EPRP	Ethiopian People's Revolutionary Party
ERAC	Economic Recovery and Adjustment Credit
FCFA	Franc Communauté Financière Africaine
FOMWAN	Federation of Muslim Women's Associations in Nigeria

GEAR	Growth, Employment and Redistribution
GIE	Economic Interest Groups
GRA	Government Reservation Area
IAURIF	Institut d'Aménagement et d'Urbanisme de la Région Île de France
ICA	Igbo Cultural Association
IDP	integrated development plan
IFAN	Institut Fondamental d'Afrique Noire
INEC	Independent National Electoral Commission
IRMC	Institut de Recherche sur le Maghreb Contemporain
ISTED	Institut des Sciences et des Techniques de l'Équipement et de l'Environnement
Jef PADS	Jef Parti Africain pour la Démocratie et le Socialisme
JMDB	Jos Metropolitan Development Board
JNI	Jama'atu Nasri Islam
KASUPDA	Kaduna State Urban Planning and Development Authority
LGC	Local Government Council
MOST	Management of Social Transformations Programme
NCNC	National Council of Nigeria Citizens
NCWS	National Council of Women's Societies
NGO	non-governmental organization
NPC	Nigerian People's Congress
OAU	Organization of African Unity
OECD	Organization for Economic Co-operation and Development
OPU	Owo Progressive Union
ORSTOM	Office de Recherche Scientifique et Technique Outre Mer
PAC	Pan-African Congress
PDS	Parti Démocratique Sénégalais
PS	Parti Socialiste
SAP	Structural Adjustment Programme
SDAU	schéma directeur d'aménagement et d'urbanisme
SNEC	Société Nationale d'Études et de Construction
SYBA	Sidi Youssef Ben Ali
TAC	Treatment Action Campaign
TACA	Tiv Development and Cultural Association
TWA	Tiv Women's Association Congress
UMBC	United Middle Belt Progressive Union
UMR-CITERES	Centre Interdisciplinaire Cités Territoires Environnement et Sociétés
UNCHS	United Nations Centre for Human Settlements
URBAMA	Urbanisation du Monde Arabe
UREF	Université des réseaux d'expression française

1 | Introduction: urban processes and change

ABDOUMALIQ SIMONE

A problematic urban reality

Urban Africans have long made lives that have worked. There has been an astute capacity to use thickening fields of social relations, however disordered they may be, to make city life viable. This book is dedicated to this long-term effort on the part of Africans from many different walks of life to make cities in which they not only survive but use as a platform to consolidate particular approaches to engaging a larger world.

For this purpose, this book focuses on notions of urban change, on the city as a laboratory of change, rather than simply an embodiment of accommodation, social engineering or the spatial fix of economic growth. It emphasizes the resilience and resourcefulness displayed by African cities, qualities drawn upon for local survival, but difficult to mobilize on a larger stage. With this emphasis on the process of change, the ways in which urban life is concretized across the region are thus seen not as history or as a series of policies gone wrong; rather, we wish to emphasize the determination of urban Africans to find their own way.

If the primary resource that urban Africans have had to draw upon to make their cities has essentially been themselves, then the process of configuring an urban public life is crucial to this story. If an accelerated differentiation of social practices and organization has had to compensate for the long-term absence of investment, infrastructure development, formal employment and multiplex economic articulations with the larger world, how are the ensuing complex social fields managed? How do residents construct the various survival strategies, specializations and social identities necessary for urban life and yet maintain their roots in cultures traditionally valuing a sense of personal stability, mutuality and social balance?

For this reason, many of the papers focus on the elaboration or disintegration of urban public life, as well as on the intricacies of sustaining traditional modes of sociality through periods of economic and political crisis. The critical emphasis here is on what residents actually do in order to enlarge their spaces of operation or, conversely, to demarcate territories of habitation that are livable, and where the negative impacts generated by the undermining of local livelihoods by global economic processes might be partially mediated. This is a book, then, that seeks to valorize urban Africa's own agency, its own constructive powers.

It is true that African cities have been an ambivalent refuge when economic survival was no longer possible in rural areas. It is true that these cities most visibly serviced the agendas of external interests, and that those interests shaped the physical and social terrain in ways that constrained a broad range of uses and developmental possibilities. It is true that these cities reflect a certain marginalization from the prevailing trajectories of urbanization that emphasize capital intensity and technological innovation. The costs of this history have been high.

Urban growth rates in Africa remain high, at nearly 5 per cent on aggregate. Growth rates for Southern African nations with a high urban population as a percentage of total population, such as Zambia and South Africa, have slowed considerably, while traditionally non-urbanized societies, such as Mozambique and Tanzania, are experiencing urban growth rates of over 7 per cent. Dar es Salaam and Maputo are two of the fastest growing cities on the continent, but cities simply cannot keep up with the demands placed upon them. Africa's population base remains young; life expectancy remains under fifty years and is declining with the impact of HIV/AIDS, and fertility rates are declining. Sixty-four per cent of African household income is spent on food, as the poorest 20 per cent of the population controls only 6 per cent of national incomes. Despite urban growth rates, on aggregate, access to clean water and sanitation facilities has not improved in twenty years, with a statistical majority of the region's population still without basic amenities (World Bank 2002).

Urban projects in Africa

Cities are the places where Africans have been most intensely engaged in the conflicts precipitated by their own convictions, their political and economic practices and their heterogeneous, often contradictory, representations of outside worlds. Cities are also places where Africans' own struggles and deliberations about present and future ways of living are most rigidly structured by the constantly changing demands of external powers. Even today, the common assumption prevails that Africa is a rural continent. While conceding the fact that cities have grown enormously, large sectors of the international development community may concede that many Africans are urban residents, but that they are not truly *urbanized*. But what does this purported absence of urbanization mean? That rural orientations still largely persist? That African cities exemplify a truncated modernization? Here, the absence of a historical perspective results in a structural invisibility as to the multiple ways through which viable cities have been and can be made. Across Africa, a new urban infrastructure is being built with the very bodies and life stories of city residents, but what kind of city is being put together is not clear. This ambiguity is not only a reality that urban residents must face but also one which they must apparently instigate. In many cities, this process of making urban life opaque is reflected in the architecture: the layout of many quarters is designed to confound those who try to make clear statements about what is going on or formulate clear plans for how these quarters should operate.

This infrastructure is also temporal. What appears to be stasis, with nothing apparently accomplished, may actually be the highly intricate engineering of interactions among different events, actors and situations. In such occurrences, events, actors and situations may 'pass through' each other and take notice of each other without conditions actually changing discernibly. It is precisely these possibilities – of different actors and situations dealing with each other without apparent ramifications – that make African cities appear dynamic and static at the same time. Conversely, things can happen very fast, where nothing has been done in a particular setting. In other words, sometimes conditions change with remarkable speed – structures of authority, alignments of loyalty and collaboration, mobilization of money and resources – where it is not readily apparent what is going on and who is contributing what to these changes.

Nevertheless, the conditions that have been relied upon hitherto to sustain both dynamic and stable urban quarters – fraught though most have been with major problems concerning urban services and ineffective management – are becoming increasingly strained. These strains are sometimes political, as quarters are given more official responsibility to manage different urban services (Brett 1996). This responsibility generates new modalities of collaboration, but also intensifies competition (Schübeler 1996). In some instances, communities have become polarized along lines of social stratification that were more open-ended and interconnected in the past (Al-Kenz 1995; Devisch 1995; Diouf et al. 1999).

The strains are also economic in that employment of any kind – formal and informal – is increasingly difficult to access (Collier and Gunning 1998; International Labor Organization 1998). As a result, formerly highly elaborated extended family and residential support systems find themselves overburdened (Kanji 1995; Harts-Broekhuis 1997; Robertson 1997). It is estimated that roughly 75 per cent of basic needs are provided informally in the majority of African cities, and that processes of informalization are expanding across discrete sectors and domains of urban life (Van Arkadie 1995; King 1996). Whereas unemployment has long been a persistent reality for African cities, available compensations now require more drastic

3

action (Lugalla 1995; Emizet 1998; Roitman 1998). Floods of cheap imports made possible through trade liberalization are shrinking local production systems (Mkandawire and Soludo 1998). At the same time, various components of economic rationalization have opened up possibilities for the appropriation of formerly public assets – land, enterprises, services – by private interests, particularly for the emerging elite, well positioned in the apparatuses managing structural adjustment.

Given these difficult conditions, the prevailing common assumption is that urban development in Africa can proceed only through a more proficient mobilization, organization and deployment of local resources and resourcefulness. Such mobilization is best accomplished through a comprehensive decentralization of governmental authority and financial responsibility to the municipal level. Only when urban citizens take responsibility for the management of their political affairs will they feel secure enough to become proficient entrepreneurs and forward-looking in their individual and collective initiatives.

The elaboration of a political framework for the more proficient management of urban spaces will then facilitate the creation of economies of agglomeration – i.e., basically taking what exists and finding new ways to organize, link and capacitate it. Targeted investments in human capital creation, employment and entrepreneurship, largely managed outside of the public realm, will result in better health and living conditions. Improvement in these conditions will result in a more solid base of human capital.

There has been an enormous range of studies on African urban informal economic sectors, land markets and livelihoods, but most of this work has focused on informalities as a compensation for the lack of successful urbanization, particularly in terms of deferring heightened levels of spatial, economic and social integration within the city. Other studies have looked at informal or 'real' economies as instruments through which sustainable and viable processes of a 'normative' urbanization might be consolidated. For the most part, they have not examined the ways in which such economies and activities themselves might act as a platform for the creation of a very different kind of sustainable urban configuration from those currently generally seen.

For this reason, this book focuses on two primary themes: social practices and urban public life. We are interested in what people are doing to deal with both the constraints and possibilities, and most particularly how apparent constraints can point to unforeseen possibilities in livelihood and in the elaboration of vibrant urban cultures.

4

Making urban publics

In cities that grow more fragmented, dispersed and outward-looking, the concept of the 'public' is put into question. For at its core, the 'public' refers to open-ended flows of communication that enable socially distinct actors positioned in different social networks, territories and organizations to formulate collective orientations and generate working alliances in pursuit of influence over issues of common concern.

Governing the 'public' results from a wide range of transactions among varied interests, where functional compromises are negotiated and re-negotiated. Theoretically, multiple and varied partnerships among diverse sectoral and institutional players constitute the locus of decision-making, enlarging the space of local political action and, at best, adding greater flexibility, creativity and efficiency to provisioning and planning. Urban governance results from a wide range of transactions among varied interests, where functional compromises are negotiated and renegotiated. Such bargaining provides new opportunities for the marginalized in society to play a more significant role in local development, as well as threatening to subsume such development into the agendas of those with more substantial resources and power.

Currently, there is a severe lack of bargaining space throughout most African cities. In part, new local authorities are overwhelmed by the degree of technical frameworks to which they must adhere. Even if those frameworks require a broad range of community consultations as part of integrated development planning, there are few resources and capacities, and little willingness, to engage in the kinds of broad-based interactions that might generate both a more comprehensive knowledge of local realities and an ability to work in collaboration. As such, a rethinking and reactivating of public life are critical.

Yet spaces of habitation and livelihood formation are apparently becoming more opaque and impenetrable. This is the inverse result of new forms of publicity and integration being fostered by various trajectories of contemporary globalization. As large numbers of urban residents no longer have access to either 'traditional' or 'modern' modalities of social reproduction, they come to rely on *provisional* actions, identities and social composition. Without structured responsibilities and certainties, the places they inhabit and the movements they undertake become instances of disjointed histories and highly inchoate environments. As a result, many places in the city seem far removed from the trajectories of development that obtain in the rest of the world, as if there is little connection, or few possibilities of interaction, between them. Whether these places are 'falling off the map' or not, however, they are part of the larger world and, even if

5

that world is largely indifferent to them, these urban places do have some kind of significance.

As the practices of different localities and regions intersect, new, provisional and often ephemeral 'publics' can be made. In fact, 'governing' – i.e., co-ordinating or steering – the intersection itself demands new forms of regulation (Jessop 1999),[1] but these issues have been neglected, most usually in favour of trying to bring government closer to the people and making it more local. At times, the preoccupation with locality, as the most appropriate level at which to ensure democracy, participation, voice and equality, represents a lingering obsession with finding the right form with which to realize the self-actualization of specific societies. In such pursuit, an organic community of a people is still thought to persist separately from the instruments of government that serve as the means or instrument for making such a community visible and viable in a world essentially hostile to it.

State institutions, economic regimes and policies, as well as global accords, provide the terms through which specific societies, groupings or peoples are recognized, where a collective subject becomes visible. This visibility is the product of unyielding argumentation and provisional settlements, of constant negotiation. In other words, the process of making 'publics' is not about reconciling or providing representative platforms for pre-existent fixed and unchanging social and cultural identities. Nor is the making of an effective 'public' something that reaches a definitive culmination. There is always conflict in cities, and this conflict will continue, but how the conflict is waged, how it is communicated or 'argued', how arguments and those who conduct them become visible and legitimate, itself constitutes the shaping of public life. Who listens to whom, under what circumstances, who does what with whom – all of these considerations are the activation of the 'public'.

Ordinary citizens? These are precisely the questions that Bénédicte Florin tackles in her chapter on the development of new satellite cities in Greater Cairo. The question here is the extent to which and in what form the residents of these new cities, which for them embody the possibilities of new ways of life, can represent these aspirations in the formation of the cities themselves. What kinds of possibilities and constraints are embedded in the morphology of these developments, as well as in their governance structures, that facilitate the construction of particular points of view – of a *being in common* that has little reference to the past? For only in a process able to assimilate the heterogeneity of encounters in everyday life within a domain capable of being the recipient and consolidation of the formation

6

of a common sense derived from these encounters can an effective public discourse take place.

Without such opportunities, how do residents avoid the factors – architectural, territorial, morphological and economic – that interfere with the reformulation of social solidarity, and thus active citizenship, among a large population separated from the mores, practices and public spheres that once characterized their residence in the older parts of Cairo? Many residents seek to disassociate themselves from what are often seen as a series of claustrophobic obligations and constricting everyday social surveillance. To what extent, however, is this aspiration forcibly channelled into an existence of relative social isolation that renders the financial, decision-making and management processes of these cities increasingly opaque and removed from public accountability?

Even if these new cities are part and parcel of the broad agenda of global neo-liberal reform, the ways in which these reforms are engaged, interpreted and practised within specific national contexts are rarely consonant with the mechanisms either specific to or implied by the various policies constituting such reform. In other words, economic reform in Egypt has largely been attained by actively suppressing the visibility of highly skewed transfers of capital, highly distorted concentrations of investment in speculative activities, manipulating national accounts and, most importantly, presenting the rapidly accelerating consumption powers of a few as representative of national economic capacity (Mitchell 1999).

The problem is compounded by the extent to which the proceeds of speculation are placed in operations on physical environments – real estate, infrastructure – which tend to 'cover up' both the often 'extra-legal' character of circulating capital and the appearance of diminishing economic capacity on the part of the majority. The national economy thus becomes increasingly a patchwork of highly informalized and disconnected activities that provide an important underpinning – not only of ordinary livelihoods, but of the increasing wealth of the few.[2] Critical transactions – and thus intersections – among social classes, domestic and transnational private entrepreneurial networks, and public officials – increasingly take place out of view.

Does this informalization of urban development on a large scale, then, require increased informalization on the part of 'ordinary citizens'? Having lost their sense of *ordinariness*, are they then forced into either the self-production of more compatible forms of urban life or into a range of micro, and superficially destructive, operations on these newly built environments? Florin explores the range of choices available for trying to reconcile the need for housing, its relationship to forging new ways of life, and the structural conditions necessary for the constitution of urban citizens having a collective voice through which to represent their own imaginaries and needs.

Urban horizons Anna Madoeuf takes us back to the older quarters of Cairo and the annual celebration of the birthday of the Prophet Muhammad. In urban quarters, with their separation of public and private, the religious and the entrepreneurial, and other bifurcations of territory, the ritual of the feast offers a sanctioned bridging of these divides. In the organization of urban life that appears as the contiguity of differentiated domains, proximate yet far, the feast and other modalities of public celebration act to place these distinct realms face to face with each other, so that their interdependencies can be directly experienced rather than remain an abstraction. In its double status as both an established social event and an instance of social discontinuity, the feast embodies the desire for togetherness of the city. As there are a number of potential ways for people to be together, that must be both concretized and limited, the feast is at once capable of unstitching the prevailing fabric of togetherness to potentially subversive and heretical expressions, and of providing an arena of stability and familiarity.

As Madoeuf describes it, the feast constitutes a horizon, simultaneously nothing and everything, where participants can reimagine what is possible, where the 'real can be recontextualized'. In this way, the time of celebration is a living time. For the feast is not simply a reiteration of ritual and gesture. Rather, it is a venue to which a multiplicity of aspirations are 'sent', have an opportunity to intersect with one another. Identities, normally constrained by gender, class and occupation, can experience each other in different ways, as everyone witnesses the fleeting nature of the established hierarchy of human valences. Even if everything remains the same, that reality only now resembles what existed before, as individuals have the sense of having taken that reality somewhere else, connecting it to a state of being long desired, even if these connections are only fleeting ones.

In cities where livelihood, mobility and opportunity are produced and enacted through the very agglomeration of different bodies marked and situated in diverse ways, how can permutations in the shifting juxtapositions of their given physical existence, their stories, networks and inclinations, produce specific value and capacity? If the city is a huge intersection of bodies in need and with desires in part propelled by the sheer number of them, how can larger numbers of bodies sustain themselves by asserting themselves at critical junctures, whether these junctures are discrete spaces, life events, sites of consumption or production? What kinds of urban objects, or quasi-objects as Serres would call them, elicit – not the social capital of trust with its overextended metaphors of solidarity – but an

8

ability to operate in concert, without representation, without frameworks of conviction? This is the facet of the urban that the feast mobilizes.

Such celebrations invoke the city as the conjunction of seemingly endless possibilities of remaking. With its artifice of architectures, infrastructures and sedimentation channelling movement, transaction and physical proximity, bodies are constantly 'on the line' to affect and be affected, 'delivered up' to specific terrain and possibilities of recognition or coalescence (Cheah 1999). Take precarious structures – roads, often flooded and pot-holed; areas often inaccessible, torn shacks – plus fragile businesses, hawkers and tailors etc. brought together in provisional locations and then dispersed. Even in their supposedly depleted condition, all are openings on to somewhere. They are the products of specific spatial practices and complex interactions of variously located actors that reflect manoeuvres on the part of city residents continuously to resituate themselves in broader fields of action (Weiss 2002).

All cities are places of multiple intensities and layers. These layers and intensities pass through, settle, consolidate and disperse across the diverse spaces to which their various intersections themselves give rise. These intensities include populations, sounds, machines, roads, discourses, buildings, grids of water and electricity, organizational forms and sites, nurturing and dispossessions, as well as the emanations of nature, to name a few.

The intersection of intensities is not that of fixed objects and identities with clear boundaries. Rather, it is an intersection that 'frees' pieces of objects and identities from specific constitutive enclosures, opening them up to new layers and formations. Since there is no 'real' difference between multiple formations and the crisscrossing of intensities – dividing up or connecting with other intensities – the multiplicities grow only by changing their nature (Sawhney 1997). For the 'event' of this convergence of multiple intensity expresses itself only as that which is subject to variation (Canning 1994). A series of these variations is held together and set apart momentarily from a larger environment through enfolding connections and implications. The convergence of exteriors that do not belong together at a paradoxical element is an intensity opened to increasing stratification, ordering and dispersion.

So at this intersection or coexistence of intensities in urban Africa, the discernible decline of living standards, the incessant politics of emergency and social dissipation and the emergence of singular capacities, of social cohabitation and general intellect, take on and configure new conditions of possibility. In the midst of every city, there is a substantial and groundless complexity of arrangements and interactions – among people, objects,

9

territories, climates – that take that city outside of its confines. To draw upon this capacity is not an act of a particular remembering. It is not an act of repositioning or relinking an observer to a more perspicacious line of sight (Rajchman 1998). Rather, such complexity is revealed in those moments like the feast in which a place is 'blown apart' – the convergence of trajectories (movements, folds, expulsions, gatherings) linked in an apparent impossibility – and thus redistributing what has come before and opening up to what is yet to come.

Cosmopolitan cities and the need for a political project Jean Omasombo's sometimes frightening presentation on the ruination of Kisangani emphasizes the thin line that distinguishes a city's strengths from its vulnerability. The city was geographically positioned at a crossroads, facilitating not only a cosmopolitan urban composition of diverse histories, peoples, religions and trades, but the possibility that those diversities could reconfigure themselves with an enhanced autonomy of development and operation. This same structural flexibility, however, could be readily expropriated as a means of narrowing the city's urban economy to that of an *entrepôt* of extraction, forcing the majority of the population into diffuse informal economic activities difficult to consolidate into more efficient production networks. The heterogeneity and rapid turnover of livelihood strategies become increasingly dependent upon the mobilization of physical labour, and thus more prone to manipulation and distortion by the convergence of the increased privatization of force and the elaboration of cross-border trade in diamonds, ivory, gold, cobalt and coltan. An active disinvestment in urban infrastructure facilitates the parasitical orientation of this trade. As livelihood becomes more informalized, Omasombo points out, so does the logic and form of governance.

In its long turbulent history, Kisangani shows just how the process of adapting to the city entailed a great deal of trial and error and on making mistakes that were sometimes tolerated and which, at other times, became the occasion for argument. In fact, tolerance and dispute were both necessary for adaptation. The character of quarters and their contributions to the overall urban system were quite heterogeneous. For example, in the study of Valdo Pons that Omasombo cites, a large number of the residents in one quarter, known as Avenue 21, came from ethnic groups without close rural–urban links and low fertility rates. As a result, most social interaction was not subject to pressures or controls from networks of well-defined institutional relations, either within or beyond the city. This is not to say that these social relations did not pay attention to these established networks. Indeed, residents would usually claim that what they did was in adherence to the norms of these networks. Because their adherence was, for the most part, simulated, the quarter could operate according to norms that were in reality much more flexible than the established ones and open to various interpretations.

Variability thus played a big part in generating the agreed-upon principles and meanings which pieced together local urban culture. The variations in what different residents knew about that culture and in their judgements about what aspects of their lives this culture affected were also significant. Quarters were not closed systems removed from each other. Thus, the emerging distinctions in character among quarters became resources for the working out of various everyday life dilemmas faced by different sets of residents living in different kinds of quarters.

During the colonial period, immigrants largely settled in locations approximating where they first arrived in the city. Accordingly, the ethnic composition of some quarters was clearly associated with social features and patterns of behaviour that had become factors of internal differentiation for the country as a whole. As Omasombo points out, both Islam and Christianity stopped in Kisangani. This is particularly the case in situations where an urban labour force was recruited from specific regions, or where certain opportunities in the city were cultivated on the basis of what local societies were doing or subjected to in their regions of origin.

For example, mineworkers may have been drawn from specific regions and assigned specific quarters in the city based on this occupation. Small-scale traders in food may have come from other regions, carrying out their activities on the periphery of the city. Administrators and police were often drawn from still other regions, and assigned to specific residential zones. This process of territorialization was then reinforced by the selective ways the city acted upon different regions.

The colonial city consolidated different functions, characters and operating practices within different quarters. It then attempted to regulate the interactions among them. In some instances, fostering homogeneous ethnic quarters facilitated the carrying out of specific urban functions. This was especially the case where colonial administrators did not want workers to settle in the city on a permanent basis. In other instances, it was more important to dilute ethnic solidarity and emphasize occupational and/or social class identities. Space had then to be cultivated for an intermixing of people from different regions and ethnic groups.

The relative importance of ethnicity, class, assimilation and urbanization thus depended on the places and situations where these attributes were invoked and supported. Additionally, different attributes could be mobilized as ways of countering the territorial arrangements imposed by

11

colonial administrations, or as ways of breaking up settlements established autonomously by Africans. Different instruments of identity had different spaces and occasions of operation. Differences in the degree to which affiliations and everyday practices were determined by ethnic consolidation were contingent upon several factors. These factors included the following: the historical circumstances under which specific migrants came to the city; the degree to which ethnic groups are dispersed across the city; the character of urban–rural linkages; and the position of migrants and ethnic groups within the labour system and urban economy.

Even here, a particular constellation of factors did not necessarily produce the same outcome. The process of identity making and exchange as fundamental aspects of emerging urban social relations was just that: a continuous process of making and exchanging. Yes, people had their identities. Different moral regimes, governance systems and economic practices were associated with different quarters. Still, the urbanizing experiences of everyday life were not brought under the complete control of these regimes, systems or practices. Residents from all walks of life increasingly 'tried out' different ways of being and doing things in the city. Regularities were sought and often institutionalized. At the same time, very little that was tried was completely discarded or given up.

Operational memory was thus spatialized. In other words, residents came to work out specific places and domains for being specific things and for working out what were often contradictory needs and aspirations. There were places to 'keep tradition alive' and there were places to be 'modern', places to be a 'kinsman' and places to be a cosmopolitan urban 'dweller', as well as more textured and subtle combinations of these primarily artificial polarities. This process of spatializing memory, options and alternatives had a large effect on making African use of the city as dynamic as possible.

There were limits on how strict or thorough such spatializing could be. After all, different facets of African everyday life and identity had to nurture each other under often rigid colonial and post-colonial controls and economic limitations. Urban quarters across the region continue to express concerns that to de-link religious life from the political, the political from the entrepreneurial, or the familial from the public, may weaken African urban societies. In cities facing many different kinds of crises, this interdependency means that the resolution of any particular difficulty within one sector is potentially availed the influences and resources of any other.

On the other hand, as Omasombo forcefully explains, the intermeshing of sectors may not create sufficient space for changes to take hold in how individual spheres of activity operate, be they religious, political, economic, familial and so forth. Without this space and an overall political project to construct it, it may be difficult to generate new forms of independent action and innovation that could be brought to the larger public sphere. If changes in how local politics operate are seen as having substantial effects on how religion, business, family life and community affairs are practised, people will be cautious about bringing about such political change. This is because too many dimensions of life may be at stake. It becomes difficult for residents to spatialize their life prospects – what should they do, where are the real powers coming from. Accordingly, independent action is limited, and thus residents are left vulnerable to the manipulations of their collective frames of reference by manipulative political regimes and economic syndicates.

Dispersing the centre Bahru Zewde's incisive short history of Addis Ababa conveys how it is possible for a process of urbanization to defer crystallizing the important economic, cultural and political activities in a defined centre. Instead, Addis historically exemplified dispersed gravitational pulls. While perhaps not fitting into the polycentric models that characterize many contemporary cities, Addis did reflect a structural accommodation of a plurality of imaginaries, powers and political and economic agendas brought to bear on the city. Articulations among the church, the monarchy, the trading class and the brief incursions of colonial administration were worked out through the maintenance of clear spatial distance. Competition for predominance did exist, but without the sustained and forceful imposition of external administrative structures capable of usurping the ways in which urban residents nested their lives in highly differentiated domains and space, spanning both the country and city, there was little need for a univocal centre.

Even under the Derg, when all urban land and property became wards of the state, Addis remained largely an assemblage of localities and concentrations. While clearly informed by its own particular concatenation of political power, religion and economy, Addis still, nevertheless, points to what might have been possible urbanizing processes and morphologies had the bulk of African urbanization not been largely driven by the requirements of colonial economies and administration.

Despite the fact that there is a general narrowing of the space in which critical formal economic activities take place – i.e. a kind of recentralization within more sharply defined territories separated from the bulk of urban life – many of the former centres of African cities have been frayed and dismantled. This may primarily reflect a deepening of economic crisis and marginalization. But it also points to the artifice of centrality within urban

13

economies that have largely grown through elaborating a heterogeneity of residential and economic opportunities marked spatially as a means of fostering the intertwining of distinction and complementarity.

Towards a new urban politics Edgar Pieterse explores the outlines of a possible urban politics in Cape Town capable of creating new forms of the public. Instead of viewing politics as managing the representation of discrete identities and interests, Pieterse focuses on politics as a practice of constituting new spaces, forms of speech and identities. This is not a matter of attaining consensus among defined interests – for consensus 'reduces people to the sum of the parts of the social body and the political community to the relationship of interests and aspirations of these different parts' (Ranciere 2001: 34). Rather, Pieterse takes off from Étienne Balibar's (2003) point that if politics is about equality, it is about the common practice of both the included and excluded, and that the political confrontation with social and political exclusion is the foundational moment of citizenship. Accordingly, political community cannot be given in advance because the constitution of this community must always trangress its own limits, pushing them beyond any institutional pattern of inclusion and exclusion, or the distribution of mutually exclusive identities.

Only in this sense can cities come to grips with the management of complex and incessant trade-offs that must be made by all cities in a context of fierce and painful global exposure. The trade-offs concern to what extent, for example, fiscal soundness takes precedence over the equitable delivery of urban services, or the extent to which managerial proficiency supersedes expanded popular participation in decision-making. The critical issue is how these trade-offs are defined. Who is involved in negotiating them? What are the appropriate forms of community organization and mobilization in a context where urban government is increasingly less capable of meeting the demands of all citizens?

How does one combine, relate and balance different forms of participation, negotiation, contestation and partnership to ensure vibrant politics and constructive collaboration to solve real problems. How can forms of political community be reimagined, especially in a temporal period where the contradictions of expanding global capitalism are more extensively imbricated in local urban life? How can such political community be reimagined in a context where the rearticulation of the economic and the political dissipates formerly valued modalities and practices of social cohesion, as well as the territorial parameters through which cohesion is recognized and performed? (Jessop 2000).

As Pieterse indicates, these difficult questions are at work in the present global preoccupation with issues of urban *governance*. For governance essentially concerns the nature, quality and purpose of the totality of relationships (both formal and informal) that link various institutional spheres – the local state, civil society and the private sector – in cities. The prevailing need is not so much to generate specific techniques for managing these relationships or subsuming them to particular objectives and frameworks. Rather, as Pieterse points out, the need is to come up with tactical orientations to these relationships, which provide increased space for them to work out and revise, more plural, yet articulated, instrumental arrangements. So, in part, urban politics must construct occasions that enable inter-relating actors to experience a measure of clarity in the midst of highly diffuse and contradictory processes of economic reorganization under way. This politics must also construct occasions where actors can flexibly, even ambiguously, shift the positions, terms and identities through which they navigate these seemingly incessant scalar recompositions while, at the same time, maintaining a coherent sense of where they are located and what it is possible for them to do.

At the grassroots, people need to have greater confidence in their ability to determine and affect the instruments of power and control that curtail their actions and that define the limits of what is possible and what is not. People need to know precisely what to do to exert influence, to make their voices heard and to deal with specific problems that arise. In theory, these needs inform the structure of urban government, with its clearly demarcated administration and representatives. But as we have seen, this popular 'need' is partially deceptive, and does not tell the entire story. In urban Africa, the capacity of communities to influence and shape cities has required a continuous oscillation between stability and the undoing of stability and between clear demarcations of what is going on and an intentional muddying of the waters. For clarity is a construction of governmentality. It is not the fundamental condition upon which manoeuvrability and the ability to make things happen ultimately rest.

Accordingly, we can expect urban *government* to do no more than occasion opportunities for associations, institutions and social groups to account for their activities in terms broadly communicable to various sectors of the larger society and to continuously anchor their operations in popularly deliberated frameworks and agendas. Regardless of whether this concretization of identities and operations is indeed representative of what associations and social groups actually do, and how they operate, urban government largely exists to institutionalize, for a moment, a reality where sectors, accountabilities, functions and actors are clearly defined and organized. But it is important to understand that urban government does this,

15

not because sectors and groups are in reality well defined and organized, but because such concretization operates as a political methodology. It is a political methodology for ensuring that governance partnerships do not result in everybody doing the same, limited, thing, everybody doing a little bit of everything, nor everybody holding on to their different specialization and doing nothing else.

For government does not exist to reduce the actual complexities involved in how communities piece together a workable sense of what they are, how they function, what they need, how they address those needs, and how those needs fit in with an overall understanding of where they are going. Rather, government institutes a process of 'rationalization' as an enabling environment for complexity – i.e. as a stage on which complexity can operate. While the state may consolidate, social groups and associations – so-called 'civil society' – may dissemble and diversify, and each process is an essential aspect of the other. The challenge for the broad range of associations, groups and institutions making up 'civil society' is to forge ways of creating, taking up and working on issues and activities without crystallizing themselves into clearly identified agendas, purviews and criteria.

Thus, associations and institutions must continue constantly to experiment with different tasks, networks, powers and conditions as long as they productively interact with the complexities generated by the everyday practices of communities themselves. They need not embody, nor represent, these community complexities in any juridical or formal sense, but provide a conduit for different communities to interact with each other and produce 'alternative or possible local realities' for all – i.e. maximize access and opportunity across a broad range of actors and groupings.

Reciprocity and exchange are required for such interchange to work. These are best cultivated in contexts where there are a lot of incentives but a minimum of judgements and exclusions. Accordingly, the potential significance of contributions made by diverse actors and sectors cannot be determined or assessed in advance. Rather, there should be room for multiple interpretations. In other words, the task of forums that might be organized to bring different actors together should not focus on trying to harness the diverse and potential contributions of different segments of the community to a specific objective. The aim should be to sustain an ongoing discussion about what different actors might accomplish through working together. The idea is to explore how different backgrounds and skills might find different ways of expressing themselves. Just because a farmer farms, or a taxi driver drives, does not mean that they have to represent or carry out those activities within a larger development agenda.

Tight-knit, cohesive local communities are probably a thing of the past. Often groups within the community are more comfortable engaging with 'like-minded' or similarly configured identities at great distances rather than the 'differences' who live or operate 'next door'. Yet, if such localities remain salient units for governance and planning, what is the common discourse or process through which diverse local networks or sub-communities, forced to pursue highly independent agendas and practices, can manage a collectively shared municipal space? As Pieterse indicates, how such differentiation is marked and balanced become the critical challenges for urban governance and planning.

Urban social practices

Passing the time In Mohammed-Bello Yunusa's explorations of popular neighbourhoods in Zaria there is an important recognition of the temporal dimensions of urban life. How do people spend their time? How is time stretched across a series of daily routines in such a way as to modulate the potential turbulence that might ensue from a dense agglomeration of people with disparate access to resources of all kinds? How is time deployed as a resource for structuring a wide range of actual and potential social encounters in a context where official regulatory systems struggle to maintain their salience?

In exploring these temporal dimensions, it becomes clear that complex local management processes are continuously being reworked and reapplied. As the municipality provides few efficient urban services, the task of maintaining a viable physical environment, of securing basic education, of mobilizing labour for construction and livelihood activities, and of co-ordinating ensuing interdependencies among family, kin, neighbours and other affiliates requires a great deal of time and effort. As Yunusa points out, the engineering of social relationships to be effective for these tasks cannot usually be forced. What then looks like 'wasted' time is often a necessary punctuation in a field of overtaxing mutual obligations, a space where new encounters are possible and, concomitantly, a new resourcefulness is made available.

Local association and struggles over place In Victor A. O. Adetula's discussion on the history of social associations in the Nigerian city, Jos, it becomes clear just how problematic conventional wisdom concerning the role of associational life as an instrument of urban democratization actually is. For associations serve as arenas through which often highly contested notions of what particular territories can be used for are elaborated, defended and reworked. With highly differentiated networks of access

17

to heterogeneous flows of goods, information and capital, residents in physically proximate relationship with each other must work out largely agonistic relationships with each other, employing different tools ranging from economic complementarities, well-cohered external articulations, to displays of physical force.

As Adetula so adeptly demonstrates, attempts to forge superseding claims of indigeneity usually devolve into periodic cycles of violence. Rather than embodying particular interests and aspirations, the viability of local cohesion depends on how well local associations can generate forms of negotiation capable of managing conflicting micro-worlds that come to share the same turf. Rather than implying a set notion of political practices, local associations come to operate most effectively when they are loci of experimentation with what counts as politics, and by identifying specific issues and domains of collaboration as accomplishments for the reiteration of particular social identities.

Political formations and local economies Mohamadou Abdoul explores how a local state still attempts to shape what acceptable forms of popular participation will look like. This occurs just as formerly marginalized groups, such as women and youth, take advantage of new economic openings, some of them occasioned by political reform, to forge new forms of social subjectivity that remain difficult for the local state to apprehend. In his discussion of women's entrepreneurial groups in the Santhiaba quarter of Pikine, Abdoul contrasts the normative political geographies through which we tend to valorize the autonomy of specific groups of local actors with those spaces configured by local residents themselves. These latter both accommodate prevailing traditions of power and chart out activities that avoid them, if not necessarily challenge them, altogether.

Development inputs and their management change the character of a community. They change the nature of what residents have to consider in order to have access to water or lighting. Successful access not only then concerns appropriate social considerations, but technical ones as well – and these considerations require specific levels of education. Traditional authorities frequently lack the education even to understand many of these basic technical considerations, let alone read or write. They are thus frequently threatened when critical features of community life seem to 'pass' from their competence and control.

Those local actors with sufficient education can then use their technical assurance to shape the community in ways that exceed the once reliable social norms and hierarchies. At the same time, as new modalities of resource and service provision can alter these social hierarchies, they must also be respected in order to prevent subterfuge or, alternatively, to convince people to change their behaviour in ways better suited to the service provided. Improved service also means that people must pay for it, and therefore be persuaded that its benefits outweigh the sacrifices entailed in mobilizing scarce resources for maintaining it. In localities where improvements in living conditions tend to centre on various locally initiated projects and the mobilization of local funds, a saturation point is frequently reached, where the costs of attempting to sustain these initiatives are seen as too high.

At the same time, the more 'modern' associations are concerned that it may take some time before the new patterns of social behaviour and co-operation – which are necessary in order to make the most beneficial use of new levels of service provision and access to resources – establish themselves. In the interim, the lingering power of customary authorities could be mobilized around these new development inputs to reiterate and entrench inequitable patterns of access and use. These inequities could be particularly unfavourable to the women and youth whose activism and role in environmental management have been most critical. In these circumstances, it is important to establish some mechanisms of financial autonomy.

The exertion of real local political power, then, largely rests with those who have the ability to participate in or engineer networks of relations that cut across wards, municipalities and other larger boundaries. Yet there is little systematic mobilization of these capacities for generating some kind of overview, let alone systematic planning and a co-ordinated administration of development inputs, for Pikine city as a whole. This does not mean that crosscutting collaboration does not take place. It does, but it has to be managed in very delicate ways and through small actions.

For example, if a group of residents, or youth, or women in a particular quarter want to start some kind of a project, they must always consider very carefully with whom they speak about it or go to for advice. Any such initiative must take into consideration who the actors are who dominate access to outside political influence, to connections with NGOs, to local public authorities or to traditional authorities. If such a group secures links to an outside Senegalese NGO, it has to think about what other links might be disrupted by virtue of such a partnership. In sum, any such initiative has to make something happen without alienating people, without 'calling up' blockages of all kinds. The configuration of authority and politics inside quarters and wards usually means that any initiative is likely to stir up a host of blockages from somewhere – and this sometimes cannot be anticipated in advance, no matter how carefully preparations have been made.

19

Abdoul's discussion of women's and youth groups in Santhiaba is a useful case of how these issues can be effectively negotiated, and how the value of development assistance often rests in its attunement to the intricacies of local politics rather than in the implementation of specific development projects.

The complexities of land and housing Perhaps the major challenge related to the financial sustainability of cities entails the conceptualization and disposition of urban land, who has access to it, for what purpose, and under what circumstances. Concomitantly, what kind of valuation is attached to its status and use, and under what circumstances can rents be appropriated from it? All of these questions have proven to be particularly intricate political, cultural and administrative challenges in most African urban contexts. After all, land still remains the most important resource and source of status and wellbeing for most residents. As such, it is a key site and locus of urban contestation. The state has frequently tried to minimize land disputes by putting all land in its hands (Peil 1991).

In most of Africa, land persists in being viewed largely as a public good. It is to be collectively owned by those who use it and can elaborate a social history on the basis of it. As colonization became the dominant force engineering urbanization on the continent, specific discourses of land management were introduced and enforced as law. In other words, the access to urban land, the ways in which it could be used, claimed, divided and participate in other exchanges became the purview of codification and law. While 'law' was certainly not a notion foreign to most African societies, subsuming relationships to land within legal frameworks was largely viewed as a distortion of the status and meaning of land within these societies.

Efforts to regularize land tenure and shelter systems in African cities took place within a complex tension between forging cities that were 'conversant' with the larger urban world, but also 'conversant' with local inclinations about land and sociality. In addition to mediating this tension, there were also difficulties involved in accommodating the large influx of rural dwellers in the city. Urban population sizes are now such that even as inward migration abates, internal population growth overtaxes the availability of land, to say nothing of services. Formerly, land belonged neither to the state nor to private ownership. As such, access to land and plotted domains in most cities have been subject to substantial speculation and irregularity.

Even when lands came under direct state control during periods of nationalization, they could be sold several times over through a variety of land agents. Land settlements served to constitute emerging patronage systems. While governments usually made some efforts to regularize tenure, the articulation of local, largely non-statutory, authority to competing national political groupings impeded regularization.

The way in which most popular neighbourhoods were once settled and organized is no longer accessible to most low-income urban households today. This is due, in part, to the very rationalization in land markets and policies that has been progressively introduced in recent years. Many popular neighbourhoods were situated on private or communally owned land. The land was developed and serviced outside legal channels. While the sale of property itself may be legal, either the substandard nature of construction and provision, or the absence of permits allowing letting or authorizations for habitation, may make the marketing of a particular built environment illegal.

While land sub-markets in Africa are often varied and opaque, a few generalizations are possible. As has been indicated, individual ownership of land does not run deep in African societies – a precept which is, by now, a well-worn stereotype. The ability to dispose land was not the same thing as owning it. Customary political authorities might bestow land or distribute rights of tenure to groups and individuals, but in the 'name' of some larger group. In Islamic societies, land was largely accorded *wakf* status, to be held in trust for the general welfare of the community.

Land was often subject to an intricate web of complementary and competing claims. These gave rise to multiple genealogies which, in turn, anchored the intersection of overlaying collective identities. Thus, land was not readily available to being marketized. Within urban contexts, land sub-markets were complicated by various patterns of co-ownership, customary and colonial frameworks. Municipal and national authorities were often bogged down trying to unravel different logical and historical forms of documentation to piece together workable land transactions (Durand-Lasserve 1994).

The difficulties in such land brokering eventually led half of Africa's states (with 75 per cent of the region's population) to assume some form of control over land ownership and/or disposition (Mabogunje 1994). What ensued varied greatly: from comprehensive and exclusive nationalization; to reparcelling of land; or to private ownership according to standardized regulatory frameworks. Yet, in almost all policy environments, the provision of land in urban sub-markets remained exceedingly problematic. It was complicated by the pursuit of rent-seeking strategies by most African regimes.

Additionally, as the poor require immediate occupation of space and access to construction at variable standards, national land policies were

21

seldom able to circumvent widespread informalized practices of land disposition. Even with widespread decentralization and the proliferation of municipal governments, land disposition remains almost exclusively a matter of national regulation and action. One of the common areas of contestation between municipal and national governments is over the control of the cadastral – i.e., over who gets to control documentation regarding land registration and about who lives where.

Many Africans exist in an incessant state of tenure insecurity. In many situations, powerful individuals could flaunt various land and building regulations at will, putting up poorly designed structures in areas not appropriate or zoned for residential use. Regulations and zoning laws would then have to be reformulated in order to accommodate this situation. Poor areas have been frequently subject to slum clearance. Policy-makers tended mistakenly to believe that these areas were composed solely of marginalized and homogeneous socio-cultural groups. As a result, it was assumed that these communities could replicate themselves intact under better circumstances somewhere else. It was also assumed that they had to be dispersed and integrated into the larger urban society. In almost all instances of slum clearance, resettlement schemes were badly planned and woefully underfinanced. Settlements grew whose conditions were worse than the original ones or brought greater density to already dense areas (Campbell 1994; Stren 1978). The legal accommodation of irregular building activity on the part of the elite and the frequently illegal break-up of poor settlements usually served to deepen a dual form of urban land development.

Currently, opportunities for shelter are becoming increasingly limited. Municipalities are under both national and external pressures to demonstrate the operations of functional regulatory frameworks. Accordingly, they are trying to demonstrate such competencies through compulsory land registration and by curtailing the development of new informal settlements. Repatriated income from migrants is increasingly invested in the acquisition and development of land otherwise potentially available for informal settlement.

There is very limited knowledge of how land transactions actually take place in the bulk of urban land sub-markets. It is often not clear, particularly to municipal authorities, where the money goes, or who, precisely, gains or loses (and in what ways) from various routes to land and property valorization. In the light of these ambiguities, it is not clear whether even today's preferred strategy of land development sequencing, beginning with the regularization of existing tenure, will provide more opportunities for shelter and security.

Repeatedly we have seen substantial disjunction between the logic of real habitat formation and the range of urban policies brought to bear in efforts to structure the city. Mohamed Gheris attempts to explore how marketized relationships in Marrakesh are unable to deal with the heterogeneity of settlement arrangements. Given extensive sub-parcelling of plots, the substantial absence of land registration and complicated relationships of subletting and household composition, large-scale publicly supported housing developments have produce limited results. Standard market assumptions that savings promotion through advantageous interest rates will consolidate greater investment in housing production have not proven correct. Gheris points out the difficult dilemmas faced by a state that built nearly a quarter of a million houses, many of which they presently are unable to sell, and which now encourages greater involvement from the private sector. At the same time, the reliance on self-construction discourages the industrialization of the housing sector.

The logic of habitation, the means of financial mobilization and the objects of investment all reflect what Gheris calls a 'solidarity economy'. This solidarity is characterized by interpersonal relationships that are, in part, cemented through interdependencies in access to land and shelter. Instead of imposing normative economic principles on such heterogeneous situations, Gheris concludes that it is necessary to develop a notion of the economy of the site. Just as there is a mixture of the informal and the formal, the public and the private, and social and individual entrepreneurship, housing financial frameworks must reflect an assemblage of mechanisms that better targets the production process to the livelihood practices deployed by the urban majority.

Concluding note

It is clear from this collection of texts that new trajectories of urban mobilization are taking place in the interstices of complex urban politics. Distinct groups and capacities are provisionally assembled into surprising, yet often dynamic, intersections outside any formal opportunity the city presents for the interaction of diverse identities and situations.

Across urban Africa, there is persistent tension as to what is possible within the city and the appropriate forms of social connections through which such possibilities can be pursued. Increasingly, more ephemeral forms of social collaboration are coming to the fore, and more effective formal governance partnerships often succeed to the degree to which they can draw on them. This emergence is a means of circumventing the intensifying contestation as to what kinds of social modalities and identities can legitimately mobilize resources and people's energies. To point out such dynamism is not to minimize the risks or underplay the suffering that

23

most urban residents experience. Making lives from the provisional is an essentially unstable process, and such instability can produce enormous creative change, but also devolve into spreading violence.

Throughout these efforts lingers the question as to how urban residents reach a 'larger world' of operations, and this concerns the present and future place of African cities within a larger global urban world. What happens within the domain of the city itself that allows urban actors, often highly rooted in specific places and ascription, to operate outside these confines? How are apparent realities of social coherence and cohesion maintained while opportunities, which would apparently demand behaviours and attitudes antithetical to the sustainability of such cohesion, are pursued?

Urban Africans are increasingly on the move, and the ability to move, either through their quarters, cities or among cities, must draw on a capacity to see themselves as more than just marginal to prevalent global urban processes. Residents must see that deteriorating urban conditions do not simply mean that they become farther removed from where the real power or opportunities lie, and that access to expanded domains of operation is not fixed to specific 'development trajectories', institutional memberships or transportation circuits. However desperate the conditions they face and no matter how physically stuck urban residents might be, they have to retain some conviction that there is something they can do. They must remain convinced that there are multiple spaces of opportunity pieced together and navigated through the particular ways in which they make connections among themselves and the ways in which these connections are folded across the mundane, improvised and often weary interactions of day-to-day life.

Notes

1 This notion of 'steering' is related to the problematic raised by Bob Jessop. He asks how socially embedded and regularized economic processes, via social practices, organizations and institutions having specific structurally inscribed temporal and spatial forms, can be steered into forms of mutual understanding and co-evaluation, and into new horizons of action.

2 These tendencies contribute to the intensifying impoverishment of Africa in several ways: a) labour immobility removes a major mechanism for wage equalization; b) the urban poor suffer most in the widening income gaps produced by uneven, episodic growth – which tends to favour larger shares of income being deployed for profit (where rates of return required for investment in risky environments increase substantially) rather than on absorbing surplus labour (which forces the poor into compensatory strategies, e.g., drawing on savings, borrowing, which makes it difficult for them to take advantage of periods of growth); and c) wage depreciation, which stems from wholesale trade liberalization undertaken before upgrades and restructures

in production, financial liberalization, where escalating rates of interest make up an implicit transfer of income from the poor to the rich, and agricultural liberalization, which often transfers profits from the public to the private sector.

References

Al-Kenz, A. (1995) 'Youth and Violence', in S. Ellis (ed.), *Africa Now: People, Places and Institutions*, The Hague: DGIS.

Balibar, E. (2003) *We the People of Europe? Reflections on Transnational Citizenship*, Princeton, NJ and London: Princeton University Press.

Brett, E. (1996) 'The Participation Principle in Development Projects: The Costs and Benefits of Participation', *Public Administration and Development*, 16, pp. 5–19.

Campbell, J. (1994) 'Urbanization, Culture and the Politics of Urban Development in Ghana 1875–1985', *Urban Anthropology*, Vol. 23, No. 4, pp. 409–50.

Canning, P. (1994) 'The Crack of Time and the Ideal Game', in C. V. Boundas and D. Olkowski (eds), *Gilles Deleuze and the Theater of Philosophy*, New York and London: Routledge.

Cheah, P. (1999) 'Spectral Nationality: The Living On [*sur-vie*] of the Postcolonial Nation and Neocolonial Globalization', *Boundary*, Vol. 2, No. 26, pp. 225–52.

Collier, P. and J. W. Gunning (1998) 'Explaining African Performance', WPS/97-2.2, Working Paper Series of the Centre for the Study of African Economies, University of Oxford.

Devisch, R. (1995) 'Frenzy, Violence, and Ethical Renewal in Kinshasa', *Public Culture*, 7, pp. 593–629.

Diouf, M., H. M. Fotê and A. Mbembe (1999) 'The Civil Status of the State in Africa', *Codesria Bulletin*, 1 & 2, pp. 39–47.

Durand-Lasserve, A. (1994) 'Researching the Relationship Between Economic Liberalisation and Changes to the Land Markets and Land Prices', in G. Jones and P. A. Ward (eds), *Methodology for Land and Housing Market Analysis*, London: UCL.

Emizet, K. (1998) 'Confronting the Apex of the State: The Growth of the Unofficial Economy in Congo', *African Studies Review*, 41, pp. 99–137.

Harts-Broekhuis, A. (1997) 'How to Sustain a Living: Urban Households and Poverty in a Sahelian Town of Mopti, Africa', *Africa*, 67, pp. 106–31.

International Labor Organization (1998) *Jobs for Africa: A Policy Framework for an Employment-Intensive Growth Strategy*, Geneva: International Labor Organization.

Jessop, B. (1999) 'The Dynamics of Partnerships and Governance Failure', in G. Stoker (ed.), *The New Politics of Local Governance in Britain*, Oxford: Oxford University Press.

— (2000) 'The Crisis of the National Spatio-Temporal Fix and the Tendential Ecological Dominance of Globalizing Capitalism', *International Journal of Urban and Regional Research*, 24, pp. 323–60.

Kanji, N. (1995) 'Gender, Poverty, and Economic Adjustment in Harare, Zimbabwe', *Environment and Urbanization*, 7, pp. 37–55.

King, K. (1996) *Jua Kali Kenya: Change and Development in an Informal Economy 1970–95*, Nairobi: East African Educational Publishers.

Lugalla, J. (1995) *Crisis, Urbanization and Urban Poverty in Tanzania: A Study of Urban Poverty and Survival Politics*, Laham, MD, London: University Presses of America.

Mabogunje, A. (1994) 'Urban Land and Urban Management Policies in Sub-Saharan Africa', *Urban Perspectives*, 4, pp. 27–42.

Mitchell, T. (1999) 'Dreamland: The Neoliberalism of Your Desires', *Middle East Report*, 29, pp. 28–33.

Mitullah, W. and K. Kibwana (1998) 'A Tale of Two Cities: Policy, Law, and Illegal Settlements in Kenya', in E. Fernandes and A. Varley (eds), *Illegal Cities: Law and Urban Change in Developing Countries*, London and New Jersey: Zed Books.

Mkandawire, T. and C. Soludo (1998) *Our Continent, Our Future: African Perspectives on Structural Adjustment*, Dakar: CODESRIA; Trenton, NJ: Africa World Press.

Peil, M. (1991) *Lagos: The City is the People*, Boston, MA: G. K. Hall and Co.

Rajchman, J. (1998) *Constructions*, Cambridge, MA: MIT Press.

Ranciere, J. (2001) 'Ten Theses on Politics', *Theory and Event*, 5, pp. 8–15.

Robertson, C. (1997) *Trouble Showed the Way: Women, Men and Trade in the Nairobi Area 1890–1990*, Bloomington, IN: Indiana University Press.

Roitman, J. (1998) 'The Garrison-Entrepôt', *Cahiers d'Études africaines*, 150–2, pp. 297–329.

Sawhney, D. (1997) 'Palimpsest: Toward a Minor Literature in Monstrosity', in K. A. Pearson (ed.), *Deleuze and Philosophy: The Difference Engineer*, London and New York: Routledge.

Schübeler, P. (1996) *Participation and Partnership in Urban Infrastructure Management*, Washington, DC: Urban Management Program, World Bank.

Stren, R. (1978) *Housing the Urban Poor in Africa: Policy, Politics and Bureaucracy in Mombasa*, Berkeley: University of California Institute of International Studies.

Van Arkadie, B. (1995) 'The State and Economic Change in Africa', in H.-J. Chang and R. Rowthorn (eds), *The Role of the State in Economic Change in Africa*, Oxford: Claredon Press.

Weiss, B. (2002) 'Thug Realism: Inhabiting Fantasy in Urban Tanzania', *Cultural Anthropology*, 17, pp. 1–32.

World Bank (2002) *African Development Indicators 2002*, Washington, DC: World Bank.

ONE | **Making urban politics**

2 | Urban policies in Cairo: from speeches on new cities to the adjustment practices of ordinary city dwellers

BÉNÉDICTE FLORIN

In Egypt the new desert towns were home to some 300,000 inhabitants at the latest census in 1996. According to some people, the forty-four new towns already built or to be built throughout the country will house some 20 million Egyptians by 2020. The figures on this implausible pharaonic project, however, hardly matter given the powerful image of these new towns, an image concerned with new lifestyles and new ways of living in the city.

The purpose of our research is twofold: first, to analyse the relationship between urban policies and housing – particularly policies concerning these new towns which are the centrepiece thereof – as well as the discourse that accompanies and justifies these policies; and, second, to examine the relationship between the way some of the inhabitants of these new towns receive and interpret such discourse and the adaptation practices to which they resort in an attempt to address the dichotomy between discourse on the new towns – presented as an ideal housing model and way of living – and the reality of these towns, that is, the way their inhabitants see them.

Existing bibliography on the new Egyptian towns essentially concerns the determinants that led to their establishment, the technical mechanisms and institutional machinery behind development policies (El Kadi 1990; Jossifort 1998) or the obstacles to the success of these towns, such as the issue of transport and commuting or that of economic autonomy and industrial development (Serageldin 1997). Except for some considerations on the aesthetics of the new towns, there is little on the process that leads to the choice of a type of housing and, to a larger extent, of an urban model based on considerations of urban functionalism and socio-spatial zoning. Similarly, to the best of our knowledge, no study has been devoted to the speeches made by decision-makers, developers, town planners, researchers or journalists with regard to the new towns, either in the press or at special events (CNRSC 1987). Finally, it seems to us that the analysis of the relationship between the discourse 'from above' – public and official – and the way such discourse is received and reformulated 'at the bottom' – that is, by ordinary citizens – the examination of adjustment practices in the face of a new situation and the requisite skills for adapting these estates on the part of these same city dwellers, constitute an innovative approach.[1]

Besides, the questions that arose at the end of the 1980s and during the early 1990s concerning, in the main, stances taken with respect to the anticipated success or the expected failure of the new towns are no longer raised in the same terms today. The issue is no longer so much that of pointing out obstacles to settlement in these towns or seeking the rationale behind them as that of observing and understanding what goes on therein. As a matter of fact, although the 'desert rush' – which some people compared to the conquest of America by the pioneers – did not take place, the fact remains that the lure of these new towns is felt ever more strongly among the inhabitants of the capital.

So, to what extent does the discourse that tends to compare the new towns with the best they hold in store – in all their 'modernity' – with the old towns, the so-called 'spontaneous' neighbourhoods and 'wild' zones, influence choice of residence and, more generally, ideas and practices relating to habitat among city dwellers? From this working hypothesis, how is the discourse on the new behavioural standards to be adopted in the new towns – the old sea serpent: 'change towns, change lives' – as conveyed by the media, interpreted by the inhabitants of these towns? What are the forms of social interaction in these new towns where the terms and conditions for access to housing bring together very different social classes? And, similarly, how does one explain the forms of socio-spatial segregation, hitherto unknown in Egypt, when, for instance, private and exclusive neighbourhoods for the rich spring up in some of these new towns – a new phenomenon akin to the American gated communities.

Review of urban policies in Cairo since 1952: context of development of the new towns and establishment of a new urban model

We do not intend to give a detailed account of developments in urban policies as regulated and implemented through master plans. Several works referred to in this chapter have already set forth these policies. The idea here is to place the choice of creating the new towns in a context that can shed light on their origin and the conditions of their development, a background that reveals a certain view of urban development. This context is closely linked to apprehensions arising from population forecasts and projections – sometimes uncertain – which led to the establishment of a specific *urban model*: that of the new town.

New towns, satellite towns, urban extensions or new settlements: these are the terms urban development experts, through successive master plans, used to make fundamental distinctions with respect to the geographical location of these new towns, their degree of autonomy with regard to the capital and their design. Yet, from the new independent or satellite towns made up of collective housing units of the council-flat type to the new settlements on the outskirts of Cairo which, in the original project, were intended to provide the underprivileged with serviced plots on which to build with government assistance, the aim of the promoters remains finding solutions to the 'housing crisis', proposing alternatives to the 'infringement' of farmland by the so-called 'wild' urban expansion and saving the capital from an imminent 'explosion'.[2]

The 1956 Master Plan and the Nasserite cities of the sixties: middle-class housing There are really no traces in Egyptian towns of a social housing policy prior to the 1952 revolution except for some resettlement operations for families from unhygienic neighbourhoods in Alexandria. In Cairo social housing consists basically in building small housing estates for railwaymen, workmen, employees or civil servants. It was born of the obligation for the state to finance the construction of social housing units and the necessity to subsidize them. Law No. 206 of 1951 provided a legislative and executive framework for a real social housing policy and several social housing operations were carried out. Due to the insolvency of the beneficiaries, however, there was a change of orientation in social housing policy. From the operations of the 1950s, through the 'Nasserite cities', and even to the new towns of today, the beneficiaries of social housing have always been the middle classes and never the destitute (Volait 1991).

The 'Nasserite years' were, from the outset, marked by state intervention in the area of urban development through the 1956 Master Plan, but in the area of housing, it was not until the sixties that major social housing projects were implemented – projects christened *masâkin cha'biyya*, 'working-class housing', for the middle classes that were the mainstay of the new regime.

The significant development of these 'Nasser years' lies in the number of projects and the size of some settlements. In Cairo, for instance, twenty-nine 'mass social housing' operations delivered a total of 1,722 apartment blocks and close to 50,000 housing units, which accommodated 310,000 inhabitants by the end of the 1980s. From the 1960s, which is the period of 'Nasserite cities', to 1974, when Sadat (president from 1970 to 1981) instituted economic liberalization – *Infitah* – the number of houses built in Egyptian towns by the public sector was slightly above 135,000 units (Hanna 1992). The *Infitah* brought an end to the social housing policy and ushered in building co-operatives leveraged by public loans. From the

31

1980s, these co-operatives took over the building of the new towns situated in the desert. They came up with the so-called economic housing, but its functioning broke with what obtained during the Nasserite era, namely rent subsidies, which gave access to social housing for families that otherwise would not have had it.

The 1970 Master Plan: the choice for the new desert towns The new Master Plan designed as from 1965 by the Haut Comité de Planification du Grand Caire was drawn up in the context of 'critical circumstances' – unrestrained increase in public spending, tension in the rural areas and labour movements in towns, routing of the Egyptian army in Yemen and then against Israel – and was the result of an 'alarming discovery' (El Kadi 1990). Statistics from the 1966 population census revealed that the population of Greater Cairo stood at slightly above 5 million inhabitants, whereas the 1956 Master Plan had predicted 4 million inhabitants by the year 2000. The consequences of this unforeseen population growth were manifold: population density was very high in the old town where buildings had become derelict and sometimes collapsed; electricity, water supply and sewage disposal network capacities became inadequate in the central neighbourhoods and did not even exist in many suburban neighbourhoods; the road network was totally congested.

Based on a new projection of the population of Greater Cairo that turned out to be exaggerated this time around,[3] the proposals of the 1970 Master Plan centred mostly on the creation of satellite towns on desert lands close to the capital intended to accommodate 5 million inhabitants by the year 2000. The new towns project took shape as from the mid-1970s. The plan for the first town, Dix de Ramadan, situated to the north east of the capital, was designed in 1976 and construction work started in 1977. In 1979, the promulgation of Law No. 59 laid down the legal and geographical framework for these towns that had to be situated away from the farmlands of the Nile valley in order to preserve them. (The surface area of useful farmland is evaluated at 4 per cent of the entire Egyptian territory.) Thereafter, decrees of implementation set in motion the construction of the new towns under the management of a public body, the New Community Authority, attached to the Ministry of Housing and Reconstruction. In the Greater Cairo region, Dix de Ramadan, Al-Sâdât, Al-Badir and Al-Amal were new independent towns, far away from Cairo, whereas Six Octobre, Quinze Mai and Al-Ubûr were new satellite towns linked to the capital. Thus, the independent towns were located more than 50 kilometres away from Cairo and had to provide jobs, housing and services in order to be totally independent. With respect to satellite towns, located close to the capital, the developers distinguished Quinze Mai (a residential town intended primarily to accommodate the Hewan industries workforce) from Six Octobre and Al-Ubûr, where the rationale was based on the availability of economic activities on the spot. These two satellite towns were expected to acquire a high degree of autonomy through the establishment of industrial zones – facilitated by various incentives – that were going to provide jobs for future inhabitants.

In the area of housing, the provision of urban housing units by the public sector was considerably reduced as compared with the previous period. On the one hand, the 'Nasserite cities' experience – already limited by investments relating to industrialization policy and by the construction of the Aswan Dam – ended with the Six-Day War of 1967 and the ensuing economic recession. On the other hand, the October 1973 war and the need for rapid reconstruction of the towns of the Suez Canal delayed the implementation of the new housing policy and, more generally, the urban development policy which entailed the construction of new towns. Finally, the *Infitah* or 'economic liberalization' also spelt the withdrawal of the state from the provision of public housing. The public sector resumed the provision of housing as from 1977, when construction work for the first new towns actually started.

The 1981 Master Plan: the fear of 'explosion' and the choice for the new settlements The third Master Plan was drawn up as from 1981 by the Omnium Technique de l'Urbanisme et de l'Infrastructure which is associated with the Institut d'Aménagement et d'Urbanisme de la Région Île de France. A new report done for the entire region warned of the threat of urban development (which was progressing at an 'annual rate of 500 hectares' west and north of the capital, absorbing villages) to farmlands as well as the housing problems for a 'population likely to rise annually, up to the year 2000, by 350,000 inhabitants, 100,000 of them being rural migrants' (Becart and Pages 1985).[4]

The main thrust of the 1981 Master Plan was the establishment of *new settlements*. These settlements were not meant to call into question the construction and settlement schedule of the new towns but were rather intended to accommodate 2 million additional Cairo inhabitants.

As opposed to the new towns that were located far away from the capital, the new settlements had to be situated on the desert outskirts of the city, along 'development corridors', and had to be linked to it through new transport infrastructure in order to break with uncontrolled urban development. Above all – and this last aspect appears fundamental to the development experts – through their design, these new urban settlements, which were going to offer satisfactory levels of employment, infrastructure and services, were to be reserved for middle- and low-income classes. At the dawn of the 1990s, construction work for seven new settlements was under way and, by 1993, the first inhabitants settled in Qattamiya, new settlement number three, to the south east of the capital. Construction work for the *new settlements* came some years after that of the 'urban extensions', which were new estates not provided for in the 1981 Master Plan.

State intervention in the area of housing for low-income classes and young couples With effect from the 1990s, housing policy was characterized by two types of intervention. The political choice underpinning these forms of intervention derives, at least in part, from the strong criticism levelled by politicians, researchers and journalists concerning empty houses in the new towns, the impossibility for some classes to have access thereto, the housing crisis in the country, etc. These criticisms were all the more scathing as they made capital out of popular discontent during events such as the earthquake of 12 October 1992.

The first type of state intervention involved the granting of loans to regions and building co-operatives linked to particular groups (army, police, professional trade unions, etc.). These co-operatives took over the construction of many housing units in the new towns. The second type of intervention involved the granting of loans to specific household categories. Thus, 1996 saw the launching of the Mubarak Project, which targeted young couples and large families. By September 1997, 39,000 apartments were already allotted to these young couples, although most of them had not yet been built. Another project, named *Les Logements de l'Avenir* (Homes for the Future or *Iskân al-Mustaqbal*), was launched in 1997. It also had to do with housing units in the new towns intended for 'young'' and 'low-income' persons. The allotment conditions for the apartments were 'draconian': beneficiaries were to be aged between thirty and forty-five years, which is the Egyptian age for marriage; they had to be covered by social insurance to guarantee the housing ministry payment of the advances provided for. Applicants for housing had to make a down payment of £E1,000 and, finally, really had to be homeless, and should never have been granted a loan or a plot of land through the body in charge of urban areas or any state co-operative or through any private-sector organization. It should be noted that following criticism over these very stringent requirements for access to housing – over-restricted age group and down payment too high for the destitute – *Al Ahram* reported that President Mubarak asked the housing ministry to review the requirements and make them more flexible.[5]

On the whole, except for the construction of some emergency estates in the 1960s, state intervention in the area of housing construction for the most underprivileged classes has been virtually non-existent since the 1970s. Housing units in the new towns, just like those built during the Nasserite period, remained *a priori* accessible only to the middle and wealthy classes. Still in the area of construction of housing units, the withdrawal of the state in favour of the private sector should be placed within a broader withdrawal context linked to the liberal orientations of the economic policy of the *Infitah*, the structural adjustment plans that came up from the 1980s or the privatization of public-sector enterprises.

Paradoxically, even as the state withdrew from the construction of social housing units, there was talk justifying its action in this domain. While encouraging the private sector to take over the construction of housing units for low- and middle-income classes, this talk was also targeted to these classes. Admittedly, a small portion of the population of the new towns received state assistance to obtain a new house, but this was never the 'low-income group'. In point of fact, it was, above all, the consequences of the earthquake of 12 October 1992 and the population evacuation following the major works undertaken in the capital that brought about the resettlement, willy-nilly, of a low-income population in the new towns and new settlements. The ability to make down payments and the monthly terms and conditions of access to ownership of apartments in these new towns, however, are still a problem because of the modest means of a good number of these families.

Discourse on the new towns and new settlements: creation of a myth

New towns: 'change towns, change lives' An appreciation of a first dichotomy, that between the new towns as they were designed and built from the 1970s and the discourse thereon, built on culture- and identity-based arguments aimed at justifying the choice of an urban model 'specific' to the Egyptian context, sheds more light on the process of creation of a mythical image of the new town. This urban model, founded on the principles of urban functionalism and socio-spatial zoning, became the choice tool of a large-scale political project intended not only to transform the organization of the territory and the distribution of its population, but also to change the whole of Egyptian society.

The urban model of the new town, on account of the intrinsic architectural and urban qualities that it sought to promote, could have the potential to reform and even to modernize, given that the discourse compared it with the 'traditional' town, the society as a whole as well as the persons who make up society. In this regard, the model of the new town makes it possible to draw up, if not decree, new behavioural standards that present and future inhabitants of these new urban centres will have to adopt. Coming from town planners as well as from a good number of researchers, and conveyed by the media, the discourse on the new towns, whose actual model was hardly called into question, did not belie the undeniable difficulties encountered by their inhabitants.

Our intention is not to judge the relevance or aesthetics of the urban model – be it with regard to the new towns here or, subsequently, with regard to the suburban estates, 'urban extensions' or the new settlements – but rather to understand how the discrepancy (and this is where the second dichotomy lies) between the mythical image of the new town and the reality of the vast suburban estates is perceived. Through the methods of adapting to this new situation and the ownership practices, which, to a certain extent, shape the milieu, we will proceed to show that, through their actions, the inhabitants try to address this discrepancy.

The design of these new towns – an outside model drawn, in part, from the works of foreign experts (French, German, Swedish, etc.) – was unquestionably based on zoning, particularly socio-spatial zoning. The idea was to offer, in well-distinguished neighbourhoods, several types of housing accessible to the various population categories, rich or middle-class in the broadest sense of the word, but excluding the more underprivileged classes and households with unstable incomes or precarious situations.

As an illustration, the satellite town of Six Octobre, where construction started in the early 1990s and which was planned over a surface area of 2,688 hectares, is mapped out into twelve districts or neighbourhoods (*hayy*) corresponding to these various target groups. These districts are, in turn, split into neighbourhood units (*mugâwirah*). One of these districts, the 'special district', is made up of plush villas with gardens reserved for the very rich classes. Another residential area, which corresponds to district numbers one, two and three in the initial development plan, consists of small estates under construction and many villas. In 1993, at the time of our first surveys, these units were still uninhabited but in 1995, and again in February 2000, some of them seemed to be inhabited occasionally during holidays. These neighbourhoods of small buildings or 'luxury' villas were the result of private real estate promotion operations that thus took advantage of state-funded infrastructure. District number 7 is made up of identical four-storey buildings with well-kept lawns in the centre and the surroundings as well as basic facilities (mosques, primary and secondary schools, small shopping malls, business outfits, banks, etc.). The inhabitants are rich families and, here, one can find, for instance, former Gulf expatriates who say they are here for 'peace and fresh air'.

The other more crowded districts that take up most of the town have apartment buildings of much lower quality that deteriorate rapidly (poor workmanship, cracks, leakages, etc.). In these districts, basic public facilities are rare and the management of the landscape seems to have been left to the inhabitants. Each *mugâwirah* is made up of a tiny central square surrounded by five- and four-storey buildings of similar shapes and sizes. These housing units are intended for the 'middle classes' – civil servants and members of professional trade unions.

Finally, during our last visit in February 2000, the extension of the town of Six Octobre had gathered considerable momentum. Many neighbourhoods made up exclusively of villas with gardens and, sometimes, swimming pools were under construction. Most of them are private real estate promotion initiatives, completely fenced off with a single entrance kept by security guards. The rates given by the officials we met on the spot show that these villas were meant for the wealthy, indeed very wealthy, classes.

Thus, the distinctions between the various neighbourhoods appear, first of all, in the urban landscape through differences in building quality, level of equipment and management of public areas. These differences are all the more glaring as some of these residential areas are several kilometres of desert apart. Selection conditions for access to housing complete this socio-spatial zoning. For inhabitants of the new towns, the price tag for owning a dwelling varies with the size and status of the apartments and, therefore, their location in the new town. Similarly, the exorbitant rates of down payments to be made to obtain the keys and the monthly instalments to be paid for these housing units over long periods of time – twenty to thirty years – before securing ownership automatically exclude the poor from housing in the new towns. Although, in 1987, the minister in charge of urban development, Hassab Allah al-Kafrawi, indicated at the opening session of the colloquium on the new towns organized by the CNRSC that 10 per cent of the housing units of the satellite town of Quinze Mai was earmarked for victims of unforeseen social situations, requiring emergency measures (demolition of homes, for instance), or for families of modest means, and although some of the victims of the 12 October 1992 earthquake were resettled in Six Octobre and in other 'urban extensions', the issue of the ability to come up with the down payment and honour the monthly instalments is still pending.

Several surveys conducted before the resettlement of the earthquake victims, while sometimes coming up with different findings, generally provide – without distinguishing between the various districts – information on the socio-professional situations of the inhabitants of the new towns that confirms the exclusion of the economically destitute classes. In this

37

regard, K. Atteya states that in Dix de Ramadan and Quinze Mai respectively, 76 per cent and 66 per cent of the inhabitants have completed secondary school as against 1.7 per cent and 7.8 per cent of illiterate inhabitants. For her part, M. Serageldin notes that average income levels for labour, both resident and non-resident, in Dix de Ramadan in 1987 were higher than the national average by 2 per cent. In 1989, another survey carried out by N. Fahmy in the same town of Dix de Ramadan revealed that the level of the population was still clearly higher than the national average, since only 3.3 per cent of the inhabitants earned less than £E50 per month and half of the inhabitants had a monthly income ranging from £E100 to 200.

The extension of construction schedules, the slow pace of settlement in the new independent or satellite towns, the initial reluctance of some entrepreneurs to set up businesses, the profits – considered as more or less justified – made by these entrepreneurs as well as speculation on vacant plots and houses, have been extensively documented and criticized by Egyptian and foreign journalists or researchers.

Altogether, this discourse, be it from official or journalistic sources, helps to build a mythical image of the new town that is inextricably linked to the urban model it offers. In purely descriptive terms, or – on a more complex level – in cultural or ideological terms, this discourse has an impact or even an efficacy that can be found both in the difference between this mythical image of the new town and the reality of the 'urban extensions' and in the voluntary residential itineraries it influences. This impact is equally felt both at the level of the representations of the inhabitants of the cities when they reinterpret the discourse on the new towns and, finally, at the level of the new behavioural patterns that individuals must adopt when they take up residence in these new towns – or, indiscriminately, in the new settlements and 'urban extensions'.

Descriptions of the new towns are akin to two sub-types of message that sometimes appear contradictory even though they are linked. Thus, the official tendency to exaggerate the effective number of inhabitants aims to offset, if not refute, the criticisms levelled in the press against the new towns, which, in a word, are described as 'ghost towns'.

The various assessments made by the population, however, whether the tendency is to overestimate or, less frequently, to underestimate, assume a completely different dimension when seen in the light of discourse of a different nature, which we could refer to as 'cultural specificity'. Such discourse is based on a pre-established perception of the nature of the entire Egyptian people – without regard to the possible components that could make up that society – a nature that would prevent them, essentially, from settling in the desert towns. Thus, in an article published on 24 October

1993 by the *Progrès Egyptien* captioned 'Flourishing Ghost Towns', Six Octobre is specifically described as a 'ghost town' and its 80,000 inhabitants are virtually invisible in a setting designed to accommodate 250,000. This, according to the author, explains the feeling of isolation experienced by the inhabitants, which feeling he epitomizes in the term *ghorba*. *Ghorba* is a key word in explaining one of the hindrances to the development of the industrial towns. *Ghorba* is this mixture of feelings that overwhelm exiles, ranging from nostalgia and boredom to loneliness and sometimes insanity. Egyptians suffer seriously from this syndrome, which inhibits in them any desire to escape, any attempt at geographical movement. Another journalist, whose article, captioned 'These So-called New Towns', carries a photograph captioned 'Avenue in the town of Six Octobre: new town, ghost town', reiterates in a different manner, but still from a cultural point of view, the idea of this difficulty – indeed impossibility – of movement faced by people as home-loving as those of the capital. Hence the need to 'convince' them to inhabit the new towns. In a presentation at the colloquium organized by the CNRSC on the new towns, a professor of economics and regional planning expressed the same opinion in these terms:

> The 'desert rush' is necessary, even if one may think, at first sight, that Egyptians unconsciously tend to follow a traditional pattern of settlement (around the river) and so the success of the new towns will depend on their capacity to modify this tendency [...] The fear of the desert that every Egyptian harbours must be overcome before the territorial distribution of the population can be changed. What is needed is a steady and continuous policy of movement towards the desert, after millennia of life in the valley. (Al-Maqsud 1987)

In another more recent article titled 'These New Towns Turned Suburbs', a journalist reflects on the 'pioneer spirit' which is 'lacking' in the case of new towns while at the same time shifting the focus of the debate. Thus, it is no longer the Egyptians who, intrinsically, are to blame for the loss of affection for, and abandonment of, the new towns but the towns themselves which, by their design, account for these two ills:

> Those who move to the new towns have specific and down-to-earth demands: bigger apartments than those in the big towns, more greenery and better facilities. That is the dream, but the reality is something else. What is a new town in terms of living standards? Often a sorry sight. And forests of council flats. Clean, but gloomy, sad and monotonous [...] For sure, the new towns are not attractive. But does this mean that they are ghost towns? In spite of everything, urban development experts remain optimistic. (*Al-Ahram*, 22–28 January 1998)

In spite of, or rather concurrently with, the criticism relating mainly to the low population as compared with the stated targets (even when the figures are exaggerated), the costliness of the apartments, the absence or shortcomings of facilities and, very rarely – as above – the type of architecture (council flats), the rationale of the new towns does not raise any particular questions and has never been put to question since – backed by figures and disquieting descriptions, especially with regard to the capital – the new towns aim to resolve the problems 'of [old] towns confronted with urgent demographic and social problems' (*Al-Ahram*, 22–28 January 1998). In this sense, the views of journalists concur with those of politicians and a good number of researchers.[6] This rhetoric comprises several registers which, when juxtaposed, lend to the new towns their full legitimacy. To begin with, it is a political option that seeks to repair 'the present situation [which] results from an accumulation of thirty-year-old errors' and, in particular – 'foremost among the blameworthy' – the socialist policy of the 1960s (*Al-Ahram*, 1–18 June 1996). This political option is then presented as a society option or, to be more precise, an option that aims to transform or reform the society as well as – and this is the last register – the individuals of which it is composed. 'In conclusion,' says the above-mentioned professor of economics and regional planning,

> it is our conviction that development constraints warrant a change in the values of the society. These values today represent aspects of economic, social and cultural development reflected in mentalities, attitudes and practices, in spite of the existence of a strong desire to achieve economic growth. Towns and urban development can be an instrument for effectively changing the traditional values of developing countries; they can bring people to accept new values and to meet the challenges of development, growth and prosperity. (Al-Maqsud 1987)

More specifically, it is the new towns – as opposed to the old towns, which are supposed to be depositories of 'traditional values' – that must be the driving force behind a more profound change. 'The new towns policy is not an end in itself; it should go beyond the towns themselves to touch Egyptian society as a whole, the priority goals being national economic growth, striking a better balance between rural and urban areas and, lastly, increased political stability' (Fahmy 1987). This opinion on the role of the new towns, whether it is expressed by the policy-makers or by researchers, is conveyed in the press. 'These settlements, according to urban development experts, are supposed to bring about social stability and economic prosperity by providing areas of demographic attraction outside existing towns' (*Al-Ahram*, 5–11 October 1994).

This aspect of transforming society and its inhabitants justifies the intervention of the state which, according to a lecturer in the Cairo Faculty of Economics and Political Sciences, 'must play an affective role in establishing regional balance, thereby, crowning regional development efforts with success', through a 'national development and town planning policy whereby urban communities will constitute a lasting solution to this problem [of population explosion]' (Nassar 1987). This equally requires the active participation of the population. 'The migration from the valley towards the desert is, first, a political problem before being a delicate technical one. It should, therefore, be resolved within a strong political framework that enables migrants to appreciate the development problems of the Egyptian society as a whole and to work towards a grand national renaissance' (Fahm 1986).[7]

At a different level, the architectural and urban design of the new towns – or what could otherwise be termed the housing model and the urban model – becomes the spatial incarnation of this momentous project aimed at reforming society and its members, and echoes the conviction that, when rationally chosen, some principles of space management can determine social organization in terms of social stability and peace which would add to the 'economic prosperity' and 'political stability' arising from this grand 'national renaissance project'.

In this light, according to Noha Fahmy, director of research at the CNRSC, if the choice of model devolves upon architects and town planners, it is because they know the desires and resources of their fellow citizens and the future inhabitants of the new towns.

Urban development choices are a reflection of the spectrum of conceptions the various Egyptian social classes have of urban life, the way this population relates to built-up real estate and their needs in terms of comfort and harmony in the urban environment. As artefacts, that is, as products of human workmanship, the new towns were born of the desire of urban development experts and planners to make optimum management and use of space to ensure that towns fulfil the functions assigned to them while meeting the material needs of future inhabitants according to their cultural and economic levels.

It is such discourse that begot the opinion that on account of the Egyptian 'specificities' mentioned above – notably that concerning the 'fear' of the desert – the imported and, therefore, exogenous model, particularly that of the new western towns – which are the subject of numerous references – cannot be applied to the Egyptian context. The same researcher, Noha Fahmy, carries on:

41

As sociologists, we cannot overemphasize the need for the urban development experts and planners charged with the design of the new towns to be Egyptians themselves, for who, better than an Egyptian, can know how to transform virgin geographical space into a vibrant and concrete entity that specifically reflects the national identity as well as the customs and traditions of Egyptians? Furthermore, the importance of the complex nature of the urban environment cannot be overemphasized. Architectural forms convey certain symbolic values; they express status, habits and lifestyles, representing some kind of abstract communication between the project managers and the users. It is the personality of the project manager that transforms buildings into symbols while the user translates the symbols and makes them function in daily life. Thus, if the implicit concepts are not clearly defined or assimilated, what follows is a series of problems leading to faulty use with its attendant economic, psychological and social repercussions (Fahmy 1987).

In other words, the conception and perception *sui generis* of the society calls for the choice of a specific model suited to local realities.

This school of thought gives rise to two points of view, both of which are culture- and identity-related, though built on separate and distinct explanatory models. The first point of view shows that the new models are unsuitable – as urban models – to the Egyptian context.

The failure of the new towns is due to a fundamental reason: the urban development process based on the European model fails to take into account the real dynamics of informal settlement on farmlands. That is why, in spite of their remarkably rapid operational implementation, the new towns will continue to develop very slowly if they persist in ignoring the social, cultural and, especially, economic practices of the country. (Becart 1987)

This point of view, expressed by a French IAURIF expert, explains the design of *new settlements* based on the principle of privately built houses with government assistance. We will come back to this project later. More rarely is the opinion expressing the unsuitability of the urban model conveyed in some press write-ups dwelling on the monotony of 'forests of council flats' and on the 'conformism' of housing units which 'is at the root of the feeling of non-belonging harboured by inhabitants of the new estates'. To this, Milad Hanna, an urban development expert regularly quoted in the press, responds: 'A great number of houses is needed because there is a great number of inhabitants. The emphasis, therefore, should be on quantity, not quality' (*Al-Ahram*, 22–28 January 1997).

The second point of view seeks to investigate the aptitude and ability of the new inhabitants to live in the new towns and to understand the behaviour that the urban model requires and which should, therefore, be adopted. This interrogation is sometimes formulated in such a way that the answers are self-evident, tending to show that what is unsuitable is not so much the model of the new towns as the inhabitants thereof. And, to come full circle, this unsuitability of the inhabitants reflects, more or less clearly, the dichotomy between the urban models of the new and the 'old' towns – and, *ipso facto*, between what these two environments entail in terms of contradictory and incompatible behaviour.

Thus, according to the sociologist, S. Yussuf, the new towns intrinsically or essentially encompass 'common cultural values' – which are, however, neither specified nor defined – that are strange to many of their new inhabitants because of their residential and social origins.

The lifestyle in Dix de Ramadan is directly linked to the circumstances of migration from one social environment to another, which is culturally different. Immigrants, therefore, have to adapt to a new lifestyle that does not correspond to their habits. This situation generates conflict between the traditional habits and practices of the immigrants and the conditions that come with a new environment and system [...] but these workers have formed a heterogeneous cultural group which has not created a social system and homogeneous values. It is, therefore, difficult to identify the types of social relationships. This new society is characterized by individualism, lack of social cohesion or refusal to share common cultural values that are specific to the town [...] No social transformation takes place and the residents have not contributed to forging a common cultural model. Each person has preserved his/her original cultural and social identity.

The author continues with the appearance of 'some forms of deviant behaviour and moral depravity, as evidenced by the fact that workers meet at night and spend their free time consuming narcotics. This phenomenon is the result of the sudden and unusual freedom given to town workers, a phenomenon which was not envisaged by the authorities' (Yussuf 1987).

Thus, in spite of the 'cultural values' specific and inherent to the new town model – values that ought to take into account principles both of social organization and social homogeneity – the new inhabitants, on account of their geographical and social origins, prove to be unsuited (in terms of what is required for the smooth functioning of the envisaged model), thereby placing the peace in jeopardy. From another standpoint it could be the strategies of business enterprises established in the new towns, which, in spite of the benefits they enjoy – cheap plots, tax exemptions, etc. – run contrary to one of the main goals of the developers, namely, having employees move in and embrace the new towns.

The majority of employees thus remain in their towns of origin and commute every day. The daily comings and goings are considerably tiring, resulting in worker instability at work. This instability in turn seriously affects their behaviour and output. As they do not feel secure, they often change jobs and their sense of belonging to an enterprise or to a town remains nil [...] The high rate of turnover and job instability can also be attributed to a regular policy adopted by several enterprises to check payroll and weed out militant workers. Most enterprises do not have trade union committees charged with defending the basic rights of workers. (*Al-Ahram*, 16–22 August 1996).

But the disparity between, on the one hand, the intentions and the expectations of the developers of a political project transcending the intrinsic qualities of the chosen urban model and, on the other hand, the many 'wanting' attitudes and practices of the inhabitants, workers and entrepreneurs – attitudes that betray a form of dereliction of the new citizenship thus proposed and their reluctance to participate in this grand national project – is never analysed in terms of calling into question the principles that underpin these new towns.

In other words, it is the adaptation – effective or expected – of some inhabitants of new towns that will justify the choice of the model. Thus, Manal, a resident of Six Octobre and who had initially suffered from *ghorba* – the feeling of loneliness and 'strangeness' that sometimes leads to insanity – 'admits to being a privileged person' with 'more or less the same standard of living as any young wife in a western country, whereas, in Cairo, because of a host of financial and material reasons, this would not have been possible'. Similarly, there is enough reason to hope in the new generation 'which, from every indication, will some day refuse to withstand the pollution and overcrowded streets of Cairo and other Egyptian towns'. The proof is that for this resident of Cairo working in Six Octobre and wishing to acquire a house there, 'with respect to the children, the talk is different. They will live here; they will like Six Octobre in the same way I like el Hussein (in the old town)' (*Le Progrès Égyptien*, 24 October 1993). So, the new towns, as one urban development expert hopes, may, with time, 'become a city of the future [...] As a matter of fact, given that most people in the towns are newcomers, it is normal that they should at least have a sense of belonging to Cairo. But for their children, born in the city, the situation will be different. They will have the feeling of really belonging to the town' (*Al-Ahram*, 6–14 August 1997).

In the same vein, the services-related problems expounded upon in the press should equally peter out with time. 'Faced with these complaints the government explains that a town is not built in a year and that the 26 July highway that links these new towns to Cairo will solve the problem [of transportation]. Transport infrastructure should be upgraded and a subway system built ... ' (Al-Ahram, 2–8 October 1998). Another envisioned project as affirmed by the minister for housing, the new 26 July highway which runs from the Mûhandisîn neighbourhood in Cairo, should contribute to the 'development of all the new towns along the desert highway between Cairo and Alexandria' for, as this journalist who supplements his write-up with a picture showing a deserted avenue in Six Octobre puts it, ' by linking up the new town with the capital more easily, the new road will enliven the streets of Six Octobre' (Al-Ahram, 6–12 August 1997).

Although there is abundant criticism of the inadequacy of the services that ought to be offered by the new towns, particularly the inadequacy of transport infrastructure, the antithesis between the image conveyed and disseminated by the media with regard to the best-built and best-developed neighbourhoods – that of the most 'fashionable' and the greenest neighbourhoods – of the new towns and Cairo is equally recurrent. One of the categories of argument that underpin this discourse has to do with the environmental qualities of the new town. These new urban centres provide the 'latest in modern luxury: silence and fresh air'. Thus, in Six Octobre, 'the climate, even in the midst of a heat wave, is pleasantly dry and some degrees lower than that of the capital [...]. Young trees have been planted everywhere'; in this way, the 'children will grow in the dry and wholesome climate of the desert' (Le Progrès Égyptien, 24 October 1993). The new town is 'relatively calm, clean and beautiful. As opposed to Cairo, green areas can be found here' (Al-Ahram, 16–22 August 1995). By contrast, Cairo inhabitants suffer from 'ills' such as 'congestion, overpopulation, noise and pollution'. And it is said that the inhabitants of Dix de Ramadan 'all came for one thing: to raise their standards of living and flee from the pollution and the chaos of big cities' (Al-Ahram, 5–11 October 1994).

Advertising campaigns through the press or television initiated by private real estate promoters – out to sell apartments and villas in the new towns – equally contribute to build up this image. In the press, advertisements of Western-style villas – which would not be out of place in a rich American suburb – sometimes feature what is supposed to be a 'model family' – parents, a boy and a girl, whose nationality is not specified (it could very well be a European family). Pictures and drawings illustrate texts with a mixture of direct interjections in Egyptian dialect – 'New al-Qahîra al-Gadîda neighbourhood (New Cairo): all in it is attractive' or, again, 'Do you remember the beautiful memories of the past [...] The Sulimaniya Golf Village brings to mind the memories of the past', complete with practical

45

information on the prices of plots and houses. The advantages of these neighbourhoods stand out clearly: drawings highlight the greenery while the text specifies the surface area reserved for green spaces.

Underlying these environmental assets of the new town, there is a second category of argument that contrasts the 'disorder' – the 'chaos' – brought about by overpopulation in the capital, with the 'orderliness' of the new urban model. This latter attribute echoes the above-mentioned discourse referring to the social stability and economic prosperity inherent in the chosen model.[8] Thus, the inhabitants of the new towns enjoy a certain comfort that is absent in the 'working-class neighbourhoods' and 'wild zones' of Cairo (Al-Ahram, 22–28 January 1997). From time to time, as articles come up in the press, one has the impression that architecture contributes to build up this image of the new towns. This is the case with the 'Houses of the Future', 'these beautiful apartments, lined up, with pleasant colours, are an ideal solution for young couples' (Al-Ahram, 2–8 October 1998); or, again, as a journalist puts it: 'it takes about an hour to get to the New Cairo road [that is Quinze Mai] in front of well lined up buildings with pleasant colours. The apartments are well built: two bedrooms, a lobby, a kitchen and a bathroom. This does not make young couples any more enthusiastic' (Al-Ahram, 27 August–12 October 1997).

Sometimes, illustrated with pictures, the architectural and urban virtues of the new towns, such as the alignment and colour of the buildings, the straightness and broadness of the avenues, are contrasted with descriptions of 'informal zones', 'wild zones', 'cancerous housing' and 'cancerous cities'. The array of services and equipment available in the new towns equally forms part of the image conveyed by this category of argument. In Dix de Ramadan, according to a young wife who is here to 'raise her standards of living', 'the services are impeccable, from potable water to electricity […]; we are no longer subjected to administrative red tape; the town is new and the number of inhabitants limited. That is why the services are efficient.' In the same vein, for another inhabitant, security is guaranteed and each town has facilities such as amusement centres, public libraries, theatre hall, cinema hall, parks and video clubs (Al-Ahram, 5–11 October 1994). Hence, the lifestyle of the inhabitants of new towns can be compared with that of Western countries – it has the 'same standard', even though it is certain that because of delays and shortcomings the inhabitants are still hoping for 'better days [as well as] the town lights' (Al-Ahram, 22–28 January 1997).

Other symbols of modernity are cinema studios and halls, amusement parks – 'Crazy Waters', 'Magic Land', 'Geroland', 'Dream Park' – sports clubs, private clinics and, in preparation, 'the biggest cardiac surgery centre of the entire Middle East'; in Six Octobre language schools and private universities are already in place or in the pipeline – facilities and services that contribute fully towards building the image of new towns which offer the inhabitants and their children – or will offer in the near future – leisure outfits, quality health and education, things that the decrepit public service cannot, or can no longer afford to, offer to the inhabitants of the capital. The contribution made by private investors in Six Octobre towards the building of collective infrastructure, namely the new 26 July highway that links the capital to the new town, is one of the most tangible signs of this trend as it confirms the more general tendency for the private sector to minister to the needs of the community.

The mythical image of the new towns – mythical in the sense that it concerns only a tiny part of operational structures reserved for privileged residents – becomes the symbol of an urban model that intrinsically harbours a new model of urbanity – in the quasi-literal sense of the word – and of 'city-dwellership'. This environment, which is gradually raised to a housing ideal, can be compared or even contrasted with the working-class districts of the old town of Cairo or the so-called 'spontaneous' districts on the outskirts of the capital, as well as the behavioural patterns of their respective inhabitants.

This image, along with the discourse that builds and accompanies it, assumes all its efficacy when it is accepted and reinterpreted by the inhabitants of Masâkin al-Zilzâl, some of whom have their roots in the old town. Its meaning and scope also come across through the perceptions the inhabitants have of their living environment, despite the discrepancy between the reality of the city and the new town image, as well as through the behaviour and practices they adopt in a bid to reduce this discrepancy.

At the same time, the dissemination of this image and the way it is received – through the representations of the individuals who espouse and reinterpret it – play a vital role in the implementation of localization strategies and, to a larger extent, residential strategies determined by a consideration which seems more and more decisive: that of the mode of occupancy of the housing unit, namely: ownership.[9] Settling in a new town can, in fact, be an answer to a residential aspiration – which is sometimes social in nature when it is associated to the acquisition – coveted or express – of a new status, even though this aspiration remains extremely limited by the constraints of an intra-urban housing market that excludes the poor classes and a sizeable part of the middle classes, owing to the limited range of possibilities as well as impossibilities. Thus, for many young households which, for want of resources, have access neither to downtown luxury apartments nor to those in plush neighbourhoods constructed through private real estate promotion initiatives, households which cannot live in the self-built suburban districts either, because their image is too degrading, moving to a new town is one of the rare options left.

New settlements: the myth of privately built 'but controlled' housing We have already mentioned the new settlements as designed by French experts of the IAURIF in collaboration with Egyptian experts of the General Organization for Physical Planning and considered as the cornerstone of the 1981 Master Plan.[10] In the original project these settlements were a new generation of housing estates situated within the immediate desert vicinity of Cairo – at a shorter distance from its centre than the satellite cities – that is, areas where land constraints were theoretically absent since the land was state-owned. Town planners had designed the new settlements as 'real urban oases' surrounded by 'green belts' acting as 'buffer zones' between them and the capital. Each new settlement had to accommodate a population of about 200,000 persons by 2002; it was equally envisaged that 2 million inhabitants would ultimately settle in the new residential areas (it should be recalled that at the time the Master Plan was being drawn up, the experts were hypothesizing that rural exodus and population growth would remain high). For its part, the state provided basic infrastructure, the necessary facilities and services, while ensuring that there was enough employment for the residents to guarantee the autonomy of these new neighbourhoods. The proximity of the new settlements to the industrial zones of the new towns was intended to find solutions to the housing problems of workers of these industries and, conversely, employment for the new settlement residents.

Above all, the new settlements, which were ten in number in the initial programme, were based on a new concept which consisted in offering serviced, low-cost plots to low- and medium-income classes in order to encourage privately built housing. It was envisaged that the urban sprawl observed on farmlands would be transferred to the plots of the new settlements. In other words, the idea was to encourage 'the massive transfer of demand for farmlands' to the new settlements, which would grow thanks to the development of private investment that was currently being carried out on farmlands, for the low-income clientele. With regard to the private construction of houses – from three to eight storeys – it had to take place on plots carved out by town planners taking into consideration the topographical constraints of the site. Construction could be phased in depending on the means of the inhabitants. Each neighbourhood, made up of several apartment blocks and intended to accommodate about 15,000 people, was to be equipped with two primary schools, several public utility services (post office, police station, dispensary etc.) and a public park. To these were to be added commercial or craft activities established on large plots as well as shops that could be opened on the ground floor of residential buildings.

In the initial project, the new settlements were mainly intended for 'a resource-poor population', but the examination of a 'pilot project' shows that although the town planners devoted half of the surface area of the new settlements to plots of 80 to 250 square metres for low- or middle-income households which accounted for about 70 per cent of the total population, the other half made up of plots of 400 to 800 square metres was, from the outset, intended for 'richer neighbourhoods' which would accommodate the remaining 30 per cent of the population. But, whereas one can imagine that relatively well-to-do households would have the means to build their own houses – supposing that such households have the desire to live in the new settlements, which is quite another issue – it seems more difficult to imagine that a really poor population would be able to settle in the same new settlements without receiving substantial financial assistance to build their own houses. And yet, no such help has ever been provided for in the project, except in the form of the low cost of acquisition of the plot.

In fact, an examination of the urban sprawl on farmlands which town planners claim inspired them to raise it almost to a model shows that the issue is less about privately built housing than private urban production.[11] There are several categories of stakeholders involved in urban production. Foremost among these are the 'professional' realtors and the very well-organized promoters, not the 'resource-poor' classes. The issue here, therefore, is one of commercial real estate promotion – which some would describe as capitalist – which, in the event, rules out the poorest people. If the latter manage to find accommodation, it is thanks more to their illegal occupation of desert state land or graveyards than building or staying in houses built on farmlands. And even if, for some time, building private houses was actually the main method of settlement on desert land, this method too is becoming more and more complex and has given way to realtors and organized entrepreneurs.

In a nutshell – assuming that this could actually be possible – access to the new *settlements* plots for the poorest classes would probably have led to a very precarious housing system, at least initially – and not 'small buildings' – hardly compatible with the desired presence of the middle classes and, without doubt, hardly acceptable to the public authorities.

Whatever their feasibility status, the new settlements, as initially designed by urban development experts, never saw the light of day. Although their fundamental principles – *inter alia*, that of privately built houses

– were approved at the highest levels of the state as far back as 1983, the urban policy later adopted by successive Egyptian governments led to a different reality even though the term 'new settlement' and the location as laid down in the Master Plan were maintained. The opposition of political leaders to the involvement of actors such as real estate agents and entrepreneurs and, to a greater extent, the participation of inhabitants through privately built houses can be explained, on the one hand, by the impossibility for the authorities to 'delegate a large portion of their responsibilities' to non-institutional actors – and at the expense of building sector companies which are very powerful in Egypt – and, on the other hand, by the 'technical modernization ideology obtaining in power circles' (Jossifort 1995: 38).

Construction work for the first new settlements – Qattamiya and Al-Churuq (new settlements numbers two and three respectively) – then that for new settlement number 6 to the north of Six Octobre and number seven south of the same town started in the early 1990s. Initially, the housing model chosen for these new settlements was a replica of that of the districts for the less well-to-do classes in the new towns, that is, collective housing in almost identical blocks, densely laid out, with poor-quality construction and finishing. As a result, in the Quattamiya new settlement, for instance, 129 housing units constructed after 1987 by a public corporation, the Société générale pour le logement préfabriqué (Prefabricated Housing Corporation), were found to be below standard and had to be demolished, forcing the state, which had ordered the construction, to pay £E400 million as damages. As more and more new settlements came up, however, finer distinctions introduced new shades into the image of residential areas made up of essentially identical apartment blocks. Levels of advancement, population growth and equipment differed from one settlement to another. In addition, new development options were adopted for some of them. For instance, in Qattamiya, a 25-hectare real estate project was under way in 1995, implemented in conformity with the 'proposals made in this regard by the town planners who designed the project', while in the same new settlement, other luxury real estate promotion programmes were on offer. Cordoning off a green golf course adorned with several private swimming pools, a crown of villas each valued between £E300,000 and £E700,000 made up the ethereal landscapes of an enclosed neighbourhood of about 60 hectares. The prices of villas in these new oases were twenty to forty times higher than those of the collective housing units for low- and medium-income classes. The advertisement campaign that accompanied the public presentation of these projects matched the ambition of their promoters. Full-page adverts in the major Egyptian newspapers and magazines, television publicity slots and the presentation of models in a major hotel in Cairo all conjured up confidence in the future of these changing towns or suburbs – the new settlements (Jossifort 1995: 39).

The 'urban extensions', which are almost contemporaneous with the new settlements (construction kicked off towards the end of the 1980s), differ from the latter by their location as they form a continuation of existing urban areas, as it were, whereas the new settlements are clearly separated from the capital by arid lands. Like the new settlements, however, these 'urban extensions' are established on desert state land, but they consist, in the main, of collective poorly constructed residential areas. As opposed to new towns like Six Octobre or Dix de Ramadan, these new residential areas are intended to house low- and middle-income classes. Consequently, the socio-spatial hierarchy imposed by the different types of neighbourhood and housing units, very apparent in the landscape of the new towns – villas, imposing buildings or 'low- and middle-income buildings' – is hardly noticed in the 'urban extensions'. In the same vein, the internal layout of these urban settlements differs from that of the new towns by the absence of an industrial zone and the absence of well-distinguished 'districts', 'neighbourhoods' and 'neighbourhood units' which, at least in the minds of the planners, contribute to space management in the new towns. Similarly, the 'business district', 'downtown', 'neighbourhood centres', 'sports clubs', 'parks', 'open spaces',' tourist areas' and 'green belts' found in these new towns, or at least in the development plans of the towns, do not exist – and are not provided for in the plans – in the urban extensions.

This description of the new settlements and 'urban extensions' reflects the gap (which can be heard in the speeches, read in the urban development plans and seen when the site is visited) between these new settlements and the new towns both at the level of management projects and that of choices and objectives in matters of urban policy regarding the adopted urban and housing model, the population categories concerned, or again, the degree of autonomy in relation to the capital. The main, if not the sole, role that planners and policy-makers assigned to the 'urban extensions' and, to a lesser extent, to the new settlements is that of housing. If the new settlements have, at times, been referred to as 'dormitory towns' the same judgement obviously applies to the urban extensions – even if far beyond plans, the practical reality of inhabitants both in the new towns and in the new settlements and urban extensions cannot be reduced to, or summarized by, the description 'dormitory town', a simplistic term which, to us, does not mean much here. The way the inhabitants of these estates assume ownership of their environment, the adaptation strategies they adopt, or again, the social relationships that develop here – issues we will examine later – all suggest that these cannot be mere 'dormitory towns'.

Despite the differences between these three urban models, however, there is abundant discourse on the new towns, whereas little or nothing exists on the new urban extensions. The abundant talk on the urban model of the new town tends to produce a univocal and 'generic' viewpoint, bridging the gap that exists between the different chosen models while precisely highlighting the virtues of the new towns, without mentioning the other residential models.

Although the way in which this talk is received, espoused or assimilated, interpreted and reformulated, varies according to the social categories to be accommodated in these estates and, beyond these categories, according to each inhabitant who has the leeway to weave his/her own real perception of the town into this discourse, the fact remains that the discourse, to a certain extent, influences residential aspirations and, *ipso facto*, itineraries.

Thus, the itineraries of the Masakin al-Zilzal urban extension inhabitants are partly linked to the assimilation of this discourse. To some of them, taking up residence in the area is tantamount to the acquisition – coveted or effective – of a new residential status, closely determined by access to ownership. For the other inhabitants who constitute the majority of the Masakin al-Zilzal population, moving house is linked to a crisis – that which followed the earthquake of 12 October 1992 and which led to their resettlement, willy-nilly. But irrespective of which group we take, the gap between the mythical image of the new town and the reality of this residential area remains wide.

Adjustment practices of residents of a suburban residential area: Masakin al-Zilzal or the 'earthquake housing estate'

Masakin al-Zilzal: an uncompleted housing estate On 12 October 1992, an earthquake (*zilzal*) measuring 5.9 on the Richter scale killed 561 people and injured 9,922 in the Cairo area. In addition to the death toll, 211 mosques, more than a thousand schools and more than five thousand houses collapsed. Also affected were more than 11,500 buildings, 9,000 of them on the right bank of the Nile: the old town was terribly hit. After a long period of uncertainty with regard to the resettlement of displaced persons (some families were lodged by friends, others in military tents, some by the Red Crescent; others remained in the streets, some for more than a year) several families were resettled, most of them in 1993, in an urban extension on the outskirts of Cairo.

This housing estate, made up of 1,000 identical buildings with some 31,000 apartments, was still under construction when the first victims of the earthquake moved in. At that time, the estate did not have a name, so the inhabitants called it 'Masakin al-Zilzal', the 'earthquake estate'. The buildings had been erected but there was no pipe-borne water, no electricity and no sewage system. The streets and paths were not paved and most of them were riddled with potholes and littered with various items of garbage, gravel and building machines. At the time, there were no commercial activities apart from traders of an 'informal' market; there were no facilities, no public services (schools were still being built), no telephone, no post office, etc. Only two bus lines were immediately opened up to enable residents of the estate, situated some 15 kilometres east of the main city, to go to work. During our subsequent visits in 1996 and 2000, private and public facilities had considerably improved. This time, there were several public bus lines and private minibuses; some telephone lines had been installed; there were several private clinics and a public dispensary, paved roads, household waste collection services, etc. Water, electricity and sewage systems, despite several breakdowns and shortcomings, were now operational. Also, whereas up to 1995 the estate was occupied, in the majority, by approximately 10,000 disaster-stricken families, 'young households' were gradually moving in to the vacant apartments and enjoying better conditions of access to housing. By 2000, virtually all the apartment blocks were occupied.

Town dwellers' skills at work: use of premises – from the strictly private to the fully public In the new towns and, even more so, in the suburban extensions such as Masakin al-Zilzal where the developers left a lot of leeway to inhabitants in matters of estate use and management, there are many forms of adaptation and transformation of private and public premises.

There is a range of practices in this respect, including:

- improvements to houses (moving or erecting partitions, replacing doors and windows), often in a bid to make the house more personal and distinct from the others;
- modifications relating to the separation of strictly private premises (apartment) from entirely public areas: these have to do with creating transitional space between the interior and the exterior in buildings where the 'passage' from private to public quarters is too abrupt, especially for the inhabitants of the ground floors;
- activities concerning public premises only (without any apparent link with housing).

Here we are going to discuss only the last two types of transformation concerning public premises, although they are sometimes associated with private quarters. On the one hand, the remodelling of built-on estate, at times through collective effort, modifies public space and changes its use. On the other hand, the unequal, gradual and diverse action of inhabitants on initially undefined 'interstitial' space (neither private nor public) attributes properties, meanings and uses to the space.

A SYMBOLIC EXAMPLE: THE QUASI-PUBLIC PARKS OF THE SUBURBAN NEW TOWNS In new towns and urban extensions, faced with the absence of common green space ('forgotten' in the development plans) and where the presence of the desert is undesirable, the creation of quasi-public parks symbolizes the will of the residents to settle here but equally echoes the 'urban attributes' of the new towns or, at least, those these cities should have like any other new town and which, in theory, should be provided by the state.

The processes of adaptation of public areas – or their confines – which demonstrate some of the skills of the city dwellers at work are, on the one hand, associated with the image of the new towns – even though the perceptions of the latter differ – and, on the other hand, a result of the fact that these estates are uncompleted. These adaptation processes are of two distinct types but both contribute to the metamorphosis of the residential areas. Whether we are looking at the construction of kiosks in the streets or at small squares, the conversion of balconies into stores or services offered by some inhabitants to their fellow citizens (either by setting up shop in public areas or hanging billboards on buildings), or considering the construction of small mosques, the installation of a 'public' lighting system in certain areas or the creation of quasi-public parks, it all has to do with adapting to a new situation as well as to the practices relating to production *in*, and *of*, the city. Both demonstrate the ability – and sometimes the claim – of the inhabitants to be full-fledged city dwellers despite the obstacles they encounter in these uncompleted residential areas and the feeling of relegation.

Thus, the inhabitants of Masakin al-Zilzal hope and plan for public parks in varying degrees. This is part of the image of the new town and their creation is the responsibility of the 'authorities' of the residential areas or the 'government'; just like some activities which cannot be left to the inhabitants (providing security, paving and lighting the streets, building public facilities etc.). Yet the gap between what the inhabitants expect from the 'authorities' and what they know these authorities can actually provide becomes a reason to act, forestall, replace or circumvent a state which, besides, is omnipresent and omnipotent, but whose action in daily life remains, most often, invisible to the inhabitants.

In Masakin al-Zilzal, most small parks designed by the inhabitants testify to the relative individualization of space – the fence constitutes private space; the greenery strengthens the protection of private space – but the fact remains that, in some cases, the parks are quasi-public even if they were developed by private individuals. These types of parks do not divide buildings and, as opposed to private parks (whose surface areas correspond to the length of the ground-floor apartment and an unequal width of 1 to 4 metres, depending on the degree of encroachment on the road), they are larger in size.

Situated in the middle of alleys between buildings or on small squares, their surface areas are sometimes limited only by the space left on both sides for pedestrians. These parks are not an extension of the housing unit and so can equally be designed by inhabitants of the upper floors and no longer those of the ground floor only. Some inhabitants have also taken up small patches of land dividing the small rocky parks of this same estate and have transformed them into several small parks whose boundaries are often marked off by pickets, bits of plastic material or cloth so as to keep children and other inhabitants off. Of course, these parks are not entirely public. These are not places where people can sit down, stay for a while, or where children can play. But we consider this type of park as semi-public because, as opposed to private parks, their fences – often quite light – are intended only to mark off boundaries and protect the lawns rather than create private space or protect the entrances to ground floors. These are more marks on the ground than fences as such. Moreover, according to the inhabitants, these gardens are designed with a view to making the estate 'beautiful'.

ALLOCATING, IDENTIFYING AND CLASSIFYING AREAS 'WITHOUT PROP-ERTIES' Quasi-public parks are only one example of collective activities that transform the physiognomy of the residential area and attribute a role and a use for the space outside the areas that are actually inhabited. The market, qualified 'informal' by the police chief, which was set up as soon as the first inhabitants arrived, is another example. The market is made up of a group of stalls owned by many traders selling a wide variety of items to the residents. It is situated around the geographical centre of the residential area and, more than any 'street' or 'avenue' (if the spaces separating the rows of the buildings can be referred to as such), it is actually a central public area. To many people, it is a vital stopover on the way home and also a major meeting point. It is all the more important as, contrary to the new towns, where a centre is provided for in the Master Plan, urban extensions such as Masakin al-Zilzal do not have any 'centre' or a similar place provided for in one way or another by the developers, either on their plans or in reality.

The use of space in the residential area and some aspects of its layout (probably well beyond the projections of the developers and construction engineers, assuming that they made projections) show how a built-up area which, at first sight, appears very stiff and restricting can become a resource in its own right. For instance, if balconies on the ground floor can pose a problem to some inhabitants (which explains why some are sealed off), to others they constitute a wonderful opportunity, as they can be transformed into small shops. In the same vein, some people do not like to live on the ground floor because the apartment can be seen from the street and, even more so, there is no transition between the interior and the exterior. But this same openness to the street is put to good use when part of the apartment is transformed into a small shop or a services outfit. The reinforcements and recesses for the windows provided by the architecture of the buildings certainly reinforce partitions between neighbours, but the way these micro-spaces are used shows both how the constraint can be circumvented and the variety of uses to which they can be put: climbing plants, small gardens, kiosks, coffee shops, etc.

The discontinuities, passageways, the few square metres of rocky terrain at the foot of buildings are, *prima facie*, only undefined interstitial spaces (neither completely private nor entirely public). They are not allocated; they do not have any particular purpose – spaces without description and without properties. It is the practices and the way the inhabitants use these interstices that determine properties and uses. But these urban interstices are of several kinds. At a different level, what was originally undefined, unoccupied no man's land, merely crossed, or not even visited, becomes, in its turn, gradually adapted, used and named. Accordingly, if some squares, small squares or pathways in the estate can be considered, for instance, as entirely public spaces, it is, first and foremost, because these areas are perceived and used as such by the inhabitants, well beyond the intentions of the initial development plan of the estate, which was only a juxtaposition of buildings. Generally, the uncompleted nature of the estate and the neglect of a large portion thereof by public authorities (and it is in this sense that these same spaces, irrespective of their scale, are interstices in and of the official, legal and controlled towns) allow for and encourage the emergence of ordinary or new activities and normal or abnormal forms of use. These activities and uses modify the physiognomy of the estate by transforming the 'atmosphere' and give meaning and specific practices to these areas. In this way, they participate fully in the construction of the new town.

New urban model and new model of urbanity: adjustment practices adopted by inhabitants

As a result of the heterogeneous social fabric of suburban residential areas due to the variety of means of access to housing,[12] there arises a residential proximity between neighbours – often not well appreciated – which has to do with the decent behaviour that has to be adopted in public and that goes with living in the new town, as opposed to the attitudes that the inhabitants had in their previous neighbourhoods (especially in the old town or in the 'spontaneous' neighbourhoods). If the image of the new town appears to be a factor in the dissemination and assimilation of these new behavioural standards, the image of the estate and its inhabitants is also at stake. These new behavioural standards are generally accepted: doors have to be closed (as opposed to 'open doors' in the former neighbourhoods);[13] children should not be left to themselves in public areas (except to play ball games) and – as a general rule – privacy is sacrosanct (except during special events like weddings). Any deviation from these norms is frowned upon and severely criticized; for instance, throwing garbage on the street, leaving children to themselves, rearing chickens under the buildings, women meeting and discussing outside their block, abnormal behaviour of an individual or group, etc.

The transition from the new rules to be adapted to new behavioural standards and new ways of inhabiting and living in the residential area entail two processes, which are not mutually exclusive. On the one hand, the ability to adapt to new social relationships, which stems from the greater ability to adjust, takes the form of new socio-spatial practices such as confinement to one's privacy, even if the resultant isolation is unwelcome. In other words, being able to conform to new social rules also entails showing that one can adapt, that one can 'rise to the occasion', especially in public places. On the other hand, going from new rules to new behaviour has to do with assimilating (partially) a very authoritarian discourse which conveys and imposes its new rules, defines 'suitable' attitudes and determines ways of living 'correctly' in the new town: in a nutshell, which governs a new 'urbanity', almost in the literal sense of the word, at times, which consists of learning rules first and then applying them.

Despite the difficulties involved in settling down – at times due to the abrupt and undesirable change of residence – in the new residential areas that are most often incomplete and poorly linked to the capital, we found the ability to adjust to an entirely new situation extremely rapid and varied during our surveys. These initiatives stem from the ability to adjust, to negotiate and to innovate. The initiatives range from small business activities, run particularly by women who are held hostage in these residential

57

areas as a result of the cost of transport, to the collective efforts to reduce rents. Beyond the settling-down process which this ability to adjust constitutes for the inhabitants, it can also be seen in the light of the images and perception of the new towns, as they should be and as they are conveyed in the various pronouncements on the new towns to which we have referred above. Although the ways of receiving, espousing or assimilating, interpreting and reformulating these pronouncements vary according to the social categories for whom the houses in these residential areas are intended, and beyond these categories, according to each inhabitant who has a certain leeway to weave his own real perception of the town into such discourse, the fact remains that the impact of the discourse can be seen in the attempts made to reduce the discrepancy between the discourse and the reality of the residential areas, as perceived by the inhabitants.

In other words, we posit the hypothesis that these images and representations of the new town – with the best they are supposed to hold in store – are epitomized in one motive, to better one's living conditions, and that the skills of the inhabitants equally reveal their ability and their claim to be city dwellers, ordinary ones admittedly, but in their own right. In this light, the skills of the inhabitants also depict the relationship that exists between the city dweller and a state that, although omnipresent and omnipotent, is paradoxically absent in daily life. But, to what extent can these skills translate into recognition of the participation of the inhabitants in the life of their city and, more generally, recognition of good citizenship?

General conclusion

As the 'Nasserite residential areas' were one of the symbols of the 'Nasser years' and are today part and parcel of the very diversified urban landscape of Cairo, the building – as yet incomplete – of the new towns in the desert reflects the urban policy implemented in Egypt from the 1970s and the 1980s.

The creation of the new towns was surrounded by multi-faceted rhetoric aimed at justifying this choice. In this respect, the (political) choice of an urban model that would suit 'Egyptian specificities' was part of a bigger project – that of a 'national renaissance' intended to modernize and reform the society (CNRSC 1987). Conversely, and in a kind of retrograde process, the new towns project was intended to justify the existence and action of the state, *inter alia*, its ability 'to house the people' at the level of the capital and, beyond that, its ability to remodel the territory and redistribute its population. In this regard, the project was not only a symbolic and material marker of state action in the landscape but one of the objects – perhaps the main one – of its legitimate action. From an ideological point of view, drawing from the representations of the town and the urban society by each actor involved, this rhetoric, coming from representatives of the state, researchers or journalists and conveyed by the media, was based on reasoning built on different tenets of a culture- and identity-based nature producing a mythical image of the new towns as an ideal form of housing and ideal place in which to live: an image that concerned only the 'plush' neighbourhoods, adorned with green spaces and leisure grounds and their well-to-do inhabitants; a univocal image applied to all the new urban settlements of the Cairo suburbs irrespective of the differences that existed between them in reality and irrespective of the various target populations.

This justification process that never examines the urban model *per se*, that is, the urban and architectural design of the new towns, does not exclude criticism with regard to the problems faced by the inhabitants of these residential areas under construction, especially problems relating to the inadequacy of some services and facilities. Yet, it is not so much the material difficulties that attend any attempt to create an urban centre from scratch that come across in the discourse on new towns, as the negative conduct of those to whom this message is addressed: real estate speculation, the calculating attitude of entrepreneurs and the 'innate' reluctance of Cairo inhabitants to take up residence in the 'desert houses'. This reluctance to take up the new citizenship thus proposed is not presented in terms of buying into the chosen 'urban model'. Quite the contrary, since, in principle, this model offers all the environmental benefits, the 'order' and 'modernity' which are lacking in other Egyptian towns and especially in Cairo – a town of 'chaos' with the symptoms of 'space pathology' (Lefèbvre 1968). But beyond the recurrent contrast between the capital and the chosen urban model, which is presented as intrinsically having what it takes to transform society, guarantee the peace and ensure economic stability, there is a new form of 'city-dwellership', and literally of urbanity, that is proposed and which is to be attained by having the current and future inhabitants adapt to the new behavioural standards prescribed (or imposed?) by the urban model.

Besides, the dissemination of the mythical image of the new town and its reception play an essential role in the implementation of localization strategies and, in a broader sense, residential strategies determined by a motive that appears increasingly decisive: that of the mode of occupancy of a house, that is, ownership. Settling in a new town, therefore, can be an answer to a residential aspiration – that is sometimes social in nature when it is linked to the acquisition – covert or overt – of a new status – even though this aspiration remains stifled by the mechanisms of an intra-urban housing market which excludes the underprivileged classes and a considerable portion of the middle classes. Thus, for many young families which, for want of resources, do not have access to downtown apartments or to the 'plush' neighbourhoods developed by private real estate promoters and which cannot live in the privately built suburban neighbourhoods because of their unwholesome image, the only option left is to move to the new towns whose virtues are extolled in the media.

Also, the efficacy of discourse on the new towns lies in the fact that it can reach everybody, including the 'low-income classes', since some of the housing units in these residential areas are said to be earmarked for them. Now – and this is not the least of paradoxes – if this talk influences, more or less, the aspirations and the residential choices of some households, it is never the poorest people, those with the 'lowest incomes': simply because the cost of these houses makes their acquisition impossible – assuming that this category had the intention of settling in the new towns.

It is because of an event that lasted a few seconds, one beyond everyone's control, however, that, finally, several 'low-income' families were resettled in the new towns and new settlements. To the 30,000 families involved, the 12 October 1992 earthquake is like a major disruption of their residential life and, in a broader sense, of their life history. Thus, the transfer from the dilapidated houses of the old town and central neighbourhoods to the apartments of these new residential areas entails a profound change for families which, had it not been for the earthquake, would probably never have had access to this type of housing and many of which would have remained in their former neighbourhoods.

Notes

1 As part of our thesis research on the residential and social itineraries of the inhabitants of four working-class districts of Cairo and its outskirts, we carried out interviews of a qualitative nature in two social housing estates, one going back to the Nasserite period and the other built at the end of the 1980s and inhabited by Cairo residents from the old town who were resettled here after the earthquake that rocked the Egyptian capital on 12 October 1992. We also conducted a series of surveys in the new town of Six October, some 30 kilometres from Cairo. We published an article at the end of this exercise but did not carry on with the research thereafter. Under the CODESRIA Urban Processes in Africa programme, we returned to Cairo in February 2000 to continue our research, this time shifting the focus as indicated above and extending our surveys in the three housing estates mentioned above. Accordingly, the surveys conducted between 1992 and 1995, then in 1996 and in 2000, cover, in part, developments in the situation of the inhabitants and in their views as we 'followed' several families from one abode to the other.

2 These worries were brought out in the alarmist, if not dramatic, state-

ments made by experts, journalists and some researchers and seemed to be echoed by many inhabitants of the capital. In 1985, for instance, the governor of Cairo was calling for 'measures aimed at making Cairo a town "shut off" to internal immigration: refusal to enrol children of immigrants in schools and to issue food procurement cards, refusal of employment, housing, housing loans, etc.' Robert Ilbert, proposing a critical analysis of the thought parameters that underpin urban policy, writes:

> In point of fact, Egypt experienced what happened everywhere else: The systematic management of urban areas only started the day the city threatened to elude the control of its inhabitants and the government. As a result of population growth – which caused the transition from the millionaire town to the megapolis – the Egyptian capital [...] has become, in the very eyes of its masters, an immense, ungovernable body which everybody agrees is one of the great capitals of the Third World, and the stream of reports of international experts (19 in two years) tends to show to what extent the urban situation overwhelms us. The change of scale – and so abrupt it was! – was such that the existing frameworks for the analysis of urban changes turned out to be unusable. [...] All we have to do is prevent the rapid and total collapse of the urban system. We need a kind of emergency plan. (Ilbert 1984).

3 This projection estimated that the population of Greater Cairo would stand between 14 and 16 million by 1990.The first figures of the 1996 census supplied by E. Denis for the OUCC database reported slightly over 10 million inhabitants for the city and 13 million inhabitants for the whole region (Denis 1998).

4 The evaluation of the number of rural migrants differs from one source to another and the resultant overestimation reinforces the alarmist and ideological talk on Cairo (El Kadi 1984).

Yet migration between rural and urban areas is – in all probability – more reduced than in the past, and between 1960 and 1976, it already accounted only for an eighth of urban population growth. At the level of the capital, rural exodus seems just as timid [...] In all, migration does not seem to have played a major role in the growth of the city. It seems to have affected, in the main, the town of Chubra al-Khayma, as well as the small market towns of the region. It should be recalled that, at the level of the region, between 1966 and 1976, migration already accounted only for 10% of population growth in Greater Cairo. We can conjecture that there was no significant increase in the subsequent years. Given that back in 1976 the proportion of this growth was already two-thirds urban as against a third rural, one can reasonably imagine that – assuming that rural exodus reduced significantly – urban migration trends remained stable or even increased and account for most of the migration to the capital today.

As analysed by E. Denis, the results of the 1996 census confirm the structural compression of the population growth of the metropolitan region that started during the preceding decades. Henceforth, the growth of towns is, essentially, only the result of a natural expansion which is also on the decline. Migration no longer accounts for much. Towns are even losing inhabitants to decongestion trends and centrifugal migration towards the outskirts and satellite towns. The author equally evaluates the annual influx of inhabitants into Greater Cairo between 1986 and 1996 at 228,000 (Denis 1998). Besides, it should be noted that there are major differences in the description of the urban sprawl into farmland from one author to another.

5 It should be pointed out that this kind of stance adopted by President Mubarak is fundamental for the inhabitants of the new towns and, more generally, for many inhabitants of Cairo. In the neighbourhoods where we carried out our surveys, the inhabitants referred, first and foremost, to the statements of the head of state – sometimes in criticism – each time we discussed the problems of the neighbourhood or those of access to housing. Similarly, the inhabitants appealed to the president – and not to the minister in charge or the government – who appeared to be the sole legitimate person to solve some of their problems. One of the expressions of this relationship between the inhabitants and the president lies in the fact that he asks the housing minister, as in the example above, to ease conditions of access to housing in the new towns and, more generally, that he makes himself the advocate of the underprivileged.

6 Our intention here is not to assess the relevance or veracity of the 'urgent demographic and social problems' of Cairo or the other big towns – which are abundantly addressed in this discourse – but rather to understand the way this discourse works to achieve its ends. It should be recalled that what interests us here is precisely the relationship between this discourse on the mythical model of the new towns conveyed by the media and assimilated, to a certain extent, by the inhabitants, and the reality of housing conditions and, more generally, the living conditions of the inhabitants of the Masakin al-Zilzal urban extension.

7 The author, who is a researcher at the CNRSC, makes very concrete proposals. Thus, the choice of the population of the new communities, particularly those aimed at developing desert land, should take into account the number of young people available and the average age. The family head should be, at most, in his forties. Young couples and candidates for marriage should have priority. There should be an acceptable level of sanitation and education. Endemic diseases should be prevented. In a different context from that of the new towns of Cairo, the author adds:

> We think it is necessary for the settlers of the border regions of the Sinai peninsula to have done their military service; they should receive advanced, ongoing and regular training in the Valley, in order to reinforce the defence capacity of the inhabitants of the area close to the occupied territories of Palestine. The encouragement of migration among people who have served a prison term for blood-letting crimes such as murder committed in vengeance or to protect one's honour, and have been freed for good conduct, could go to reinforce the productive and defensive capacity of these regions. (Fahm 1986)

The first proposal concerning 'young couples' is, as we will see below, fully assimilated by the population resettled in the aftermath of the earthquake at Masakin al-Zilzal, who know that the housing units of the estate were intended for young couples and not for them. With regard to the second proposal, it seems that these are equally statements conveyed in one way or another and which we heard on several occasions, more or less distorted (for instance, the criminals who would settle in the Sinai could be joined by all the beggars in Cairo who give a bad image to the town and who are just useless parasites).

8 Apocalyptic descriptions of the capital abound in the press. Among many other examples, an article captioned 'Cairo: Complete Town' presents the 'chaos' of the capital and the population 'explosion' in these terms:

In the face of this alarming explosion, the town planners are perplexed. Some go for measures aimed at decongesting the town while others prefer a more radical solution: creating another capital. In the meantime, the city continues its mad race. Cairo is a time bomb. Overcrowded, paralysed by daily traffic jams, disfigured by the flyovers, the millennium town has become unbearable and apparently impossible to manage. The expansion of the capital undermines any form of control. Depopulating the town has become the leitmotiv of the authorities, etc.

The article also presents the point of view of several urban development experts: 'By bridging the gap between the province and the capital we will put an end to rural exodus. New settlements in the Sinai are the only way of redistributing the excess population of Cairo throughout the country. It has to do with civic responsibility. The authorities decry the ever increasing population growth rate but the figures bespeak the contrary,' etc. (Al-Ahram, 25–31 March 1998). Similarly, in the discourse referring, in broad terms, to the culture and specific identity of the Egyptian people, an identity-based sub-discourse can be distinguished, one aimed at justifying the action on the town which is said to be 'in crisis'. In this regard, in Egypt this kind of discourse frequently equates two schools of thought: on the one hand, the 'overcrowding' of the 'millennium city' caused by an external population – generally, rural migrants who, through their practices, are said to ruin the very tenets of its identity – which is said to cause 'disorder', 'chaos' and the simultaneous need to restore the historical town – but for whom? For tourists? – which explains, for example, the renovation operations in the old town. On the other hand, there is the new towns policy. This is the second variable of the equation since, in a way, it can make it possible – through the resettlement of this same population expelled from the old town – for the authorities to start again 'from scratch' and to 'reorganize' the behaviour of inhabitants found wanting in civic responsibility.

9 It should be noted here that occupation status – owner or tenant – is immaterial in itself because of the frequency of the frozen-rents system in Cairo. In working-class circles – this does not hold for the wealthy classes – this status does not reflect any particular social status necessarily higher than that of tenants, as opposed to what being an owner means in Western countries, for example. In contrast, in the case of the privately built neighbourhoods, access to ownership is ultimately a prime consideration since it makes it possible for the housing unit to be remodelled and for more than one generation to cohabit. Thus, it is not so much the status of owner that is important as the

benefits that come with it for the occupants of the housing unit. It is equally irrefutable that the relevance of occupation status develops with time. On the one hand, it is becoming difficult to obtain a cheap housing unit for rental and rent-freezing laws are increasingly called into question. On the other hand, in the new towns and urban extensions, ownership of housing – which is the general rule here – is also part of the new model referred to above.

10 The 1981 Master Plan led to the production of a very complete working document in 1985 by two of its experts: Laurent Becart and Jean-Louis Pages. It is on the basis of this document that we tackle the new settlements project as it was designed from the outset. Except otherwise stated, the quotations in italics come from this document: Becart and Pages 1985: 11–38.

11 Private construction is different from private production in that private construction is carried out by the inhabitant and the primary purpose is to accommodate this inhabitant along with his family, even if subsequently part of the building is hired out to other households, whereas private production is carried out by 'illegal' real estate promoters who want to hire out or sell the houses.

12 It should be recalled that these housing estates as well as some in the new towns provided accommodation to households that were often poor. These were families from the old town resettled here after the 1992 earthquake. But it also housed young couples who were more well-to-do and wanted ownership or, in the case of the new towns, middle- or high-income families, although in the latter case partitioning between neighbourhoods restricted contact between different social categories.

13 The closing of doors has the advantage of less social control in the estate as compared with the previous neighbourhood (less intrusion into private life), but the price for that was isolation, felt more especially by women. In the same vein, their public habits change as they take up residence in the estates. They can no longer go out alone in the evening and they are often accompanied when running an errand or going to the market.

References

Abu Al Makaram, S. (1987) 'Le rôle du Ministère des Affaires Sociales concernant les programmes de développement social : l'action menée à Dix de Ramadan', *Les villes nouvelles en Égypte*, selected contributions to CNRSC conference on the socio-economic development of new towns in Egypt, 7–10 April 1986, Dossier 2, prepared by Mercedes Volait and François Ireton, Cairo: CEDEJ, pp. 149–62.

Al-Maqsud, S. (1987) 'La politique des villes nouvelles en Égypte: tentative d'évaluation du point de vue spatial', *Les villes nouvelles en Égypte*, selected contributions to CNRSC conference on the socio-economic development of new towns in Egypt, 7–10 April 1986, Dossier 2, prepared by Mercedes Volait and François Ireton, Cairo: CEDEJ, pp. 31–51.

Becart L. (1987) 'Peut-il se développer une véritable promotion foncière et immobilière populaire sur les terres désertiques autour du Caire?', contribution to international seminar at the Harvard Aga Khan Program, roneo, pp. 1–7.

Becart, L. and J. L. Pages (1985) 'L'aménagement du Grand Caire: un projet ambitieux, une coopération exemplaire', *Cahiers de l'IAURIF*, 75, pp. 9-42.

Blin, L. (1993) *Chronique économique*, 'Le séisme du Caire, drame social plus qu'économique', *Égypte/Monde Arabe*, 12-13, Cairo: CEDEJ, pp. 399-402.

CAPMAS (1990) *The Project of Demographic Activities at Local Levels. Population and the Most Important Population Activities*, Cairo Governorate.

CNRSC (Centre National de Recherches Sociales et Criminologiques) (1976) *Opinion et préférences des ménages à revenu limité, concernant l'habitat social*, 'Journées d'Études sur l'Habitat social', Cairo.

— (1987) *Les villes nouvelles en Égypte*, selected contributions to CNRSC conference on the socio-economic development of new towns in Egypt, 7-10 April 1986, Dossier 2, prepared by Mercedes Volait and François Ireton, Cairo: CEDEJ.

Deboulet, A. (1991) 'La diversification des filières de promotion foncière et immobilière au Caire', *Revue Tiers-Monde*, XXXII, 125, January-March, Paris: IEDES-PUF, pp. 115-33.

Denis, E. (1998) 'Le Caire et l'Egypte à l'orée du XXIe siècle. Une métropole stabilisée dans un contexte de redéploiement de la croissance', *Lettre d'Information*, 48, June, OUCC, CEDEJ, pp. 4-17.

— (1999) 'La face cachée des villes nouvelles', *Lettre d'Information*, 49, OUCC, CEDEJ, pp. 38-46.

DePaule, J.-Ch. and G. El Kadi (1990) 'New settlements: une réponse à la surpopulation?', press dossier, *Égypte/Monde Arabe*, 1, Cairo: CEDEJ, pp. 171-6, 187-90.

El Kadi, G. (1984) 'Le désengagement de l'État dans la ville égyptienne', *Villes en Parallèle*, 8, June, Le logement, l'État et les pauvres dans les villes du Tiers Monde, Laboratoire de géographie urbaine de Paris X, pp. 11-35.

— (1990) 'Trente ans de planification urbaine au Caire', *Egypte: années 80. Elements pour un bilan de 'l'ouverture'*, *Revue Tiers-Monde*, 121, XXXI, January-March, Paris: IEDES, PUF, pp. 185-207.

— (1993) 'Le tremblement de terre en Égypte', *Égypte/Monde Arabe*, 14, Cairo: CEDEJ, pp.163-95.

— (1995) 'Introduction' to 'Aménagement régional et aménagement urbain en Égypte', *Les Cahiers d'Urbama*, 10, Tours, pp. i-x.

El Kadi, G. and M. Rabie (1995) 'Les villes nouvelles d'Égypte. La conquête du désert entre mythe et réalité', *Villes en parallèle*, 22, Paris and Nanterre, pp. 159-76.

Fahm, A. (1986) 'Vers des sociétés intégrées dans les déserts égyptiens: interrogations centrales', *Les villes nouvelles en Egypte*, selected contributions to CNRSC conference on the socio-economic development of new towns in Egypt, 7-10 April 1986, Dossier 2, prepared by Mercedes Volait and François Ireton, Cairo: CEDEJ, pp. 52-62.

Fahmy, A. (1986) 'Genèse et développement des villes nouvelles en Égypte. Propositions pour des solutions alternatives', *Les villes nouvelles en Egypte*, selected contributions to CNRSC conference on the socio-economic development of new towns in Egypt, 7–10 April 1986, Dossier 2, prepared by Mercedes Volait and François Ireton, Cairo: CEDEJ, pp. 13–29.

Fahmy, N. (1987) 'Formation des prix des terrains dans les villes nouvelles égyptiennes', *Les villes nouvelles en Egypte*, selected contributions to CNRSC conference on the socio-economic development of new towns in Egypt, 7–10 April 1986, Dossier 2, prepared by Mercedes Volait and François Ireton, Cairo: CEDEJ, pp. 131–45.

Florin, B. (1995a) 'Six Octobre, ville secondaire ou banlieue du Caire?', *Villes en Parallèle*, 22, December, 'Villes secondaires d'Afrique', Paris and Nanterre, pp. 179–98.

— (1995b) 'Masâkin al-Zilzâl ou la cité du tremblement de terre', *Égypte/ Monde Arabe*, 23, Cairo: CEDEJ, pp. 11–55.

— (1997) 'Savoir faire son jardin au Caire. Des espaces verts dans deux cités de logement social', *Les Annales de la Recherche Urbaine*, 74, 'Natures en villes', Paris, pp. 85–93.

— (1998) 'Appropriation d'un nouveau modèle urbain dans la périphérie du Caire', in N. Haumont and J. P. Lévy (eds), *La ville éclatée: quartiers et peuplement*, Paris: L'Harmattan, Coll. Habitat et Sociétés, pp. 89–100.

Hanna, M. (1992) *Le logement en Egypte, essai critique*, Cairo: CEDEJ.

Ilbert, R. (1984) 'Politiques urbaines, Le Caire: à la recherche d'un modèle, Politiques urbaines dans le Monde Arabe', *Études sur le Monde Arabe*, 1, pp. 245–63.

Jossifort, S. (1993) 'Les "new settlements" du Caire', Supplement to information sheet, July, 33, Cairo: CEDEJ.

— (1995a) 'L'aventure des villes nouvelles. Vingt ans après: bilan et débats', *Egypte/Monde Arabe*, 23, Cairo: CEDEJ, pp. 169–91.

— (1995b) 'Villes nouvelles et new settlements: l'aménagement du désert égyptien en question', *Les Cahiers d'Urbama*, 10, regional and urban development in Egypt, conducted by Galila el Kadi, Tours, 1995, pp. 29–43.

— (1998) 'L'aménagement de la région métropolitaine du Caire. La contribution des villes nouvelles et des new settlements du désert', Doctoral Thesis on Town Planning and Development, IUP, June.

Lefèbvre, H. (1968) *Le droit à la ville*, Paris: Point Seuil.

Meyer, G. (1989) 'Problems of Industrial Development in the New Desert Cities of Egypt', in *Applied Geography and Development, a Biannual Collection of Recent German Contributions*, vol. 34, Tübingen: Institut für Wissenschaftliche Zusammenarbeit, pp. 90–105.

Nassar, H. (1987) 'L'explosion démographique et les politiques de développement et d'urbanisation', *Les villes nouvelles en Egypte*, selected contributions to CNRSC conference on the socio-economic development of new towns in Egypt, 7–10 April 1986, Dossier 2, prepared by Mercedes Volait and François Ireton, Cairo: CEDEJ, pp. 74–93.

Serageldin, M. (1997) 'La ville de 10-de-Ramadan, en Egypte', Seminar, 'The Contemporary Urban Habitat in Islamic Cultures', Aga Khan Program for Islamic Architecture at Harvard University, 17–22 October 1993, pp. 76–83.

Volait, M. (1986) 'Le Caire: les problèmes de la croissance à la lumière du recensement de 1986', *Espaces, Populations, Sociétés*, 1988-2, pp. 213-25.

— (1991) 'De l'habitation salubre au logement de masse: l'expérimentation égyptienne en matière d'habitat économique et social', Notes on ongoing research, Bureau de la Recherche Architecturale, Ministère de l'Équipement, du Logement, des Transports et de la Mer, uncirculated provisional document, Cairo: June.

Yussuf, S. (1987) 'Les villes nouvelles entre les stratégies de planification et les réalités sociales (étude de cas: la ville de Dix de Ramadan)', *Les villes nouvelles en Égypte*, selected contributions to CNRSC conference on the scoioeconomic development of new towns in Egypt, 7-10 April 1986, prepared by Mercedes Volait and François Ireton, Cairo: CEDEJ, pp. 164-85.

3 | Feasts: panoramas in town – the spaces and times of the *moulids* of Cairo

ANNA MADOEUF

Most of the social sciences raise questions regarding the definition and existence of a town. How does a town acquire its identity and status? Answers to these questions are seemingly provided by public spaces – which are of various types and uses. For the ancient Greeks, a town gained its vitality from its agora, consisting of both form and spirit. In the Muslim tradition, a town comprises a mosque and a *souk*, while in George Amado's romanesque intuition,[1] it is a feast that institutes the town. Thus, in Brazil, it is during the celebration of the Feast of St John that Tocaia Grande, a small locality in the north east of the country, becomes 'civilized': to show that theirs is a town, its inhabitants organize a feast therein. This truly founding act unequivocally demonstrates that it has attained the status of a town. Indeed, if a town is viewed as the expression of the wish to be together, it is through the feast that this wish is confirmed. Also, the feast is the expression of what Michel Maffesoli calls 'social viscosity', this 'strange impulse that prompts people to attach themselves to others'.[2]

When it is the month of *rabî' al-thânî*, everybody in Cairo and the whole of Egypt knows that the *moulid*[3] of Husayn is around the corner. The date of this feast is determined by the Hegira calendar, but each year, it jumps ahead by ten days on the solar calendar, and thus shifts gradually from one season to the next. The *moulid* of Husayn, grandson of the Prophet, is the feast that commemorates the anniversary of the birth of this saint and festivities are organized in the mosque dedicated to him. The feasting residents are joined by pilgrims coming from all over the country in colourful celebrations that give the neighbourhood a fresh decor based on a ritual in which the codified and harmonious use of space plays a major role.

Moulids of Egypt: inconspicuous objects

The *moulids* of Egypt are a widespread social phenomenon, judging from the number of participants and the meaning given to the area concerned. Yet all the social sciences give them but scant attention and hardly explore them, with the exception of history, which mentions them especially as part of the study of Sufism and the fraternity or sainthood phenomenon.

In this context, some room is created for the contemporary practice of *moulids*, especially in the works of Pierre-Jean Luizard and Rachida Chih, two researchers who have shed new light on the contemporary fraternity networks, their role in the social and political spheres and the foothold they have gained locally. Catherine Mayeur-Jaouen's monograph, *Al-Sayyid al-Badawî*, retraces the history of this great Egyptian Islamic saint and the forms of religious worship devoted to him.

The references that can be used as baseline sources in locating and identifying *moulids* are Alî Pacha Moubarak's *Khitats* for the end of the nineteenth century and J.-W. MacPherson's study of Egyptian *moulids*, published in 1941. Nicolaas Biegman's book also provides much factual information on all the *moulids* in Egypt. Sometimes too, the accounts of travellers – especially Edward Lane or Gérard de Nerval – reveal interesting facts about the location and conduct of certain celebrations; but, all too often, they all go over the same feasts and scenes. Lastly, the writers on folklore have published many works in Egypt on the *moulids*.

True, contemporary Egyptian romantic literature (Yehia Haqqi, Naguib Mahfouz, Abdel Hakim Qassem) and autobiographies in particular (Taha Hussein, Sayyid Uways) bring out the meaning and intensity of the bonds knit with certain sacred places. But these founding themes for representations and spatial practices are only rarely mentioned and no clear reasons given for this surprising oversight. Scientific publications, though prolific and diverse in Cairo, see them as having neither visibility nor a place in the lives of the city or its inhabitants. A noteworthy exception is the essay by Jacques Berque and Mustapha Al-Shakaa on the social history of the Gamâliyya neighbourhood, which highlights the symbolic values and permanence of sacred places, and stands out as the premise for the idea of 'system', linking up functions of space and values of space. Yet not much can be learned about these events from this work. In analysing the urban, the vast domain of what is considered sacred and of the social practices that go with it remains unexplored here, whereas the urban space lends itself to manifold interpretations.[4]

In several respects, the *moulids* of Cairo could have become objects of research, particularly geographic research. For, beside religion and the conditions for its expression during which mention is made naturally thereof, pilgrimages can also be seen in the light of tourism: they confer the status of shrines of national tourism on the central neighbourhoods of ancient Cairo.

Moreover, these are pristine feasts and practices that are part of the Egyptian culture. Maybe herein lies part of the explanation: have they been relegated to the category of folklore despite their liveliness and popularity?

69

Or were they classified as archaic practices threatened with extinction, swept under the carpet and consigned to oblivion from where no one has thought of exhuming them? Perhaps their concealment stemmed from their being too short-lived and their confinement to circumscribed places in the town.

Moulids are an expression of 'traditional', popular Islam which, though ever prolific and enduring, is often obscured by the preference shown for over-represented political Islam. Besides, with the spread of Muslim reformism, Sufism came under virulent criticism and a whole culture became branded as obscurantist.

Paradoxically, *moulids* are attended by millions of Egyptians, but are still considered a marginalizing phenomenon. And it is one of the paradoxes of the celebration of a *moulid* that it is a very intense and noisy feast, but a discreet event.

In his essay on urban culture, Marcel Roncayolo urges us 'to take account of symbols and manifestations: emblems of collective rites and feasts whose importance is only being realized today' (Roncayolo 1990: 89). Speaking about cherished and much-lauded places, Gaston Bachelard remarks that, 'attached to their "positive" value of protection are other values that are imagined, and which soon become the dominant values' (Bachelard 1989: 17). The space apprehended by the imagination cannot remain indifferent, for it is peopled by experiences: 'Particularly, it attracts almost all the time.'

There are awaited and re-enacted events that require collective support and participation, and for which some neighbourhoods of the town, for a time, serve as decor. 'We need an environment which is not only well-organized but equally charged with poetry and symbolism' (Lynch 1999: 140). Festive celebrations – cyclical moments that punctuate the lives of humans and mark the symbolism and meaning of places – result from the merging and superimposition of a consecrated place with a celebrated moment. Apart from those of the Prophet and the members of His family (*ahl al-beyt*), the *moulids* of other saints are also celebrated. *Moulids* are not typically Muslim feasts, but are also Christian and Jewish, although Egyptians no longer attend the latter. Barring those of the Delta (Sayyid al-Badawî in Tantâ and Ibrâhîm al-Disuqî in Disûq), the most important feasts are held in Cairo. According to the Egyptian Ministry of *Waqfs*, there are more than forty commemorations of saints in the country, while the Sufi Council puts at eighty *moulids* at least the number of founding fraternities. Added to these are hundreds or thousands of small *moulids*. Being of unequal importance, attendance therein ranges from a few tens to several hundreds of thousands of persons.

Every village, hamlet, town in Egypt, and neighbourhood in old Cairo, has its own *moulid*. Thus, we will not be treating here the neighbourhood or local *moulids* held in the old town, but will focus on the major events of a more exceptional character which transcend the merely local sphere. We will occasionally illustrate our work, however, with examples drawn from the other *moulids*. Thus, a survey conducted during the two principal Cairo-based *moulids* – those of Husayn and Zaynab – will enable us to treat these events as the place-time of specific one-time cyclical urban practices within specific territories, asserting and confirming, both locally and nationally, the centrality of Cairo's historic sites, and highlighting their collective significance.

As adequately demonstrated by research, Cairo is a city that does not fall into the usual categories used in the definition and demarcation of urban space and whose analysis requires inputs from diverse sources. To identify and link up the diverse components of the town, we have in our possession morphological criteria and socio-economic indicators; positing our work on the premise that religious festivities are linked to networks and have secured a firm foothold in the land, however, these parameters may be introduced in the location of coherent spaces. In this respect, the *moulid* appears as an indicator of the way space is structured and perceived.

Though symbolic and abstract, these shrines mark the space with an indelible and identifiable stamp and can be rated on a scale of hierarchy. After a summary review of all the 'ritual places' in the Gamâliyya neighbourhood, Jacques Berque notes 'the extent to which sacredness abounds and is ordered according to a liturgical structure which closely fits the form and economy of the old town' (Berque and Al-Shakaa 1974: 60). From a historical perspective, Philippe Ariès prompts us 'to grasp the sacred steeped in time, but not destroyed by its passage and wherein all ages are at one'. This research adopts a geographical approach – one in which the sacred is immersed in space,[5] at the moment of its being reactivated.

The conditions for the meeting of space and time – two fundamental ingredients in the geographical approach – then find significant expression. The space implied and invested by the *moulid* can be 'broken down', and the area it occupies and over which it exerts an influence mapped out. The task here would be to identify and understand the logic underlying the distribution and allocation of space to the various stakeholders and for the different functions; to note the terms and conditions for these attributions; to compare the space of the feast, the rules governing its celebration and uses, with the space taken up in ordinary times and the practices that prevail then.

As far as the analytic side of our approach is concerned, we need to

71

state the fundamental premises of the research and the caution that goes with it. But here, we will neither, on the pretext of dealing with an exotic domain, track and highlight changeless and permanent features and relics, nor will we, while observing practices, show a partiality for Islamic views. A first pitfall would be to focus on the purely theological aspects of practice. As Catherine Mayeur-Jaouen demonstrates, nobody knows more about Badawî than that he was a saint. In this light, it would be illusory to try to sift what falls under 'established religion' from what is considered 'popular belief'. Thus, it would be preferable to consider this field as one with intersecting and dovetailing aspects.

Similarly, it would be futile to strive formally to classify what is religious and sacred, and what is festive; to establish a dichotomy using a composite set of inseparable situations and scenes. There is no *moulid* without a fraternity, just as there is no *moulid* without a fairground, attractions and trade stalls. Furthermore, rather than attempt to separate the two aspects of the feast, we will view them as merged into one whole. True, there is a logic behind the spatial distribution of these two traits and participants do not necessarily partake of the two. But the feast is a space, a system where no holds are absolutely barred and where combinations are plotted. We will deal with aspects of the festive and the sacred by presenting several different temporal and spatial sequences, and by successively or concurrently exploiting observations made in the two big *moulids* of Cairo: those of Husayn and Zaynab.

As suggested by Bernard Debarbieux, we will view the sacred place as a spatial structure built around the imagination of those who practise religion and as a real place of an 'active imaginary territorialization' (Debarbieux 1995: 878).

We should stress the fact that the *moulid* does not come 'out of the blue', but is an event linked to the knowledge and practice of the territory by the inhabitants of the neighbourhood, or where an important saint is involved, the inhabitants of a more extensive area. Everyone knows the saints of the neighbourhood and their feast days. In his study of the *hârat* al-Sukkariyya, Nawal al-Messiri Nadim notes that the quality of the tombs of saints stands as one of the most significant elements that structure the geography of feminine Cairo.

> While each woman has different social networks which put her in touch with various spots in the town, the women of the *hâra*, as a group, share the knowledge of special religious sites. Faith in the saints is an important aspect of their belief system, the neighbourhoods of the town are known to them by the name of their saints and the place where their tombs are

located. Women visit these tombs frequently, alone or in a group, depend-ing on the occasion and purpose of the visit. [...] Each saint has his specialty and powers, and is invoked accordingly. Thus, a woman who feels depressed would rather visit Sayyida Zaynab, while another who wishes to bear a child will choose to visit al-Husayn. (Al-Messiri Nadim 1979: 345).

If we view *moulids* as the space-time of vivid first-hand memory, it is necessary to recall that 'memory is a perpetually current phenomenon, a living link to the eternal present' (Nora 1984: xix).

Interest in feasts implies the availability of real time, the same time that is needed to shape one's views on the object studied in order for words, deeds and images to become clear. Since feasts are evanescent, only frag-ments are collected. Besides, during a feast everybody seems to live and act faster than usual and it thus becomes difficult to grasp the simultaneity of situations and scenes. One therefore has to make do with the instantane-ous and spontaneous and maybe see the feast in this light, accepting its immediacy, and to work under such conditions. Mention should also be made of the absence of distance, the immersion, the closeness of scenes and persons, the promiscuity, the contact with others. The usual space between individuals, particularly those of opposite sexes, is very much reduced. The crowd is thick and dense with faces close together and one is constantly meeting the same persons over and over again. Each person's pace and direction of movement is different; people cross and recross each other in infinitely variable combinations in an ever-changing landscape. The feast is unstable; it is based on perpetual, incessant movement which, however, drops in intensity towards midnight. From a particular moment, the general rhythm swings over, breaks and is reversed.

Times and places of feasts

A feast may be considered as an 'establishment', albeit a non-perennial one: a group goes to its favourite haunt, which is clearly and firmly mapped out and well surveyed and stalked; after exploring it to its outer confines, everybody turns back. One may enter and explore a territory with which one is perhaps already familiar, but here, there is a difference. The feast creates a relationship at the specific place as it is itself, with its components and boundaries, a space that superimposes itself on the neighbourhood.

The main *moulids* in Cairo – those of the Prophet (*al-Nabî*) and his grand-sons Husayn and Zaynab – attract hundreds of thousands of people every year. It is hard, if not impossible, to estimate the number of people present, coming not only from Cairo but also from the provinces. The press gener-ally estimates at a million the number of visitors to each of the three big *moulids* in Cairo; but this is a very conservative estimate. Although the majority of the visitors are, of course, from within Cairo, there is a massive influx of visitors from all over Egypt, especially coming under the banners of the multiple Sufi fraternities. These fraternities play an important role in Egypt and the number of faithful is believed to be 6 million men belonging to over 120 fraternities, seventy-three of which are official. Thus, it is a vast social phenomenon with a far-reaching geographical spread.

Many pilgrims occupy their positions during the week preceding 'the great night' (*leîla al-kebîra* or *leîla al-khatimiyya*: closing night), which is the apotheosis of the feast. The celebration and its participants congregate single-mindedly on an epicentre. Elsewhere in town, the event could go totally unnoticed, but on the spot, the approach of the feast is felt and perceived. Like everywhere else, it is the youth (children and teenagers) who first perceive the signs heralding the *moulids*; they flock to the scene to get a foretaste of the feast mood and to see stands and marquees being erected; to witness the hanging of decorations and to sample the pleasures and delights that are on hand.

The mood of anticipation, tickling the imagination, spreads. Tents are erected, pilgrims flow in,[6] there will be a huge crowd and the feast will take place at the reference place, known to all. The Al-Husayn mosque, the sanctuary that effectively is the most important and the most visited in Egypt and the rallying point for most religious ceremonies, serves as the capital's holy centre.

The neighbourhood swarms with small vans loaded with props for tents, furniture (carpets, chairs), generators, electrical installations and sound equipment, or the necessary items for everyday life (provisions, blankets, kitchen utensils, etc.). And for a few days, the landscape is one of disorder and incompleteness: vehicles are parked everywhere; reserved spaces are fenced off by heaps of materials and cartons. The stage shows tents in various phases: for some, only the frames have been erected; others, on the other hand, have been fully erected with carpets and chairs installed, and the lighting is being tested for the last time. As the hours go by, with the multiple small but combined efforts, the fairground takes its real and full shape. On the Friday night preceding the great night,[7] most tents are already up and life in the camp becomes organized. In the background, arrangements for the fun fair are nearing completion.

Tents[8] – wooden structures overlaid with stretched and predominantly red cloth, in all sorts of geometric shapes and decorated with coloured interlace designs – have been raised everywhere from the square in front of the mosque right to the neighbouring cul-de-sacs. Among all these tents, the biggest and most beautiful, meant for the ceremonies, are those situated on the square itself and within the immediate vicinity of the mosque. Further away are makeshift undecorated canvas shelters intended mainly to lodge the pilgrims. Whole families expose themselves under more precarious circumstances, armed with blankets, stoves and their cooking utensils, and set up camp on the roadway, mainly around the mosque or on its square but also in corners close to a tree or in any other suitable place that can provide temporary accommodation. Floating banners whose colours proclaim the pilgrim's membership of a fraternity[9] (black for the Rifa'iyya Order, red for the Ahmadiyya Order, green for the Burhâmiyya Order), as well as his geographic origin, the tents suggest in the heart of town the temporary representation of the provinces: 'Burhâmiyya of Disûq', 'Qâdiriyya of Mansûra', 'Ahmadiyya of Mîniyâ', 'All the saints of Louxor', etc.

'No month goes by without a feast being celebrated in Cairo and without there being a gathering to announce that: today is the day for this or that procession' (Mustafa Ali, 1599, quoted in Yerasimos 1985: 63). This remark portrays a recurrent theme cherished by foreign observers (chroniclers and travellers): the importance and multitude of feasts in Egyptian social life. This theme is often linked to the presumed personality and character of Egyptians as well as their low morals, a representation to which we made reference in our opening section. Travellers generally describe religious celebrations held in honour of 'saints' as trade fairs, presenting them as being conducted alongside secular festivities but dissociating the two facets of life. 'Religious feasts in Egypt always coincide with popular trade fairs: while some people are plunged in fervent worship, others beside them indulge in unbridled and sometimes very obscene pleasures. Thus, the huge Tantah trade fair, an immense masquerade whose folly outstrips all the orgies of antiquity, merges with the feast of a Muslim saint' (Charmes 1880).

Yet the celebration of the *moulid* is a unique multi-toned feast where mass piety does not preclude the joy of trivial entertainment and where the religious rites of the feast are performed alongside secular rites. Practices merge in a complementary whole: in Egypt, the love and devotion owed the Prophet and his relatives are synonymous with joy. Proof of this is the verse of the Qu'ran, etched on many monuments: 'No certainly, the saints of God are not subject to fear, neither do they know sadness'.[10] How better to honour them than by reproducing, if necessary, exemplary traits of their character?

The fact that old Cairo is regarded as sacred is a primordial facet of its personality, as each of the city's neighbourhoods is placed under the influence of a patron saint. This is a determining factor of its inhabitants' perception of the other residents of Cairo. One cannot talk about the *moulids* without mentioning this link. Some sanctuaries are symbols whose presence and proximity cause feelings to well up. Thus, the veneration of members of the Prophet's family bursts forth in an affective manner on places of worship dedicated to them. It is the custom to recite the *fâtiha*[11] when passing in front of the tomb of Al-Husayn; visits to his tomb (*zyâra*) are open all year round on Thursday evenings; and many *dhikrs*[12] are conducted round the mosque.

The intensity of such devotion is further heightened during the *moulid*, through ritual contact with the saint's tomb, whose *baraka*[13] is greatly enhanced on such occasions. The historic reality of the presence of relics is much debated and it is possible that Husayn, Zaynab and the other saints were not laid to rest in Cairo in the tombs consecrated to them. 'Memory fixes remembrance in the sacred, history fishes it out, it renders everything prosaic' (Nora 1984: xix). But here, we note just one reality, namely, the feelings caused by these presences and the ceremonies dedicated to them: 'The authenticity of our beliefs is not measured by the truth of their object' (Veyne 1983: 123).

Thus, representations of Cairo's emblematic saints are also found else-where: Sayyida Ruqayya, daughter of Husayn, is also buried in Damas, just as Sayyida Zaynab, who reposes in the suburb of the same town. The Omayyades mosque also hosts a sanctuary of Husayn, found also in Alep, Raqqa, Achkelon and Karbalâ. These saints, major figures of Islam, belong to the collectivity. They are international, 'capital' saints, adopted in diverse places, where they are venerated and celebrated in different ways.

The Necropolis and old neighbourhoods of Cairo, wherein many saints repose and reside through their worship, are the ideal places of expression of the major *moulids*. The 'town of the Lineage' – alluding to all the members of the Prophet's family (people of the house of *ahl al-bayt*) who have their tombs in Cairo (Husayn, Zaynab, Nafîsa, Sakîna, Ruqayya, 'Alî Zayn-al-'Abidîn, Hasan al-Anwar, 'Aîcha, Fâtima al-Nabawiyya, Fâtima, Ga'far al-Sâdiq) – has asserted itself nationwide as a pilgrimage centre, since the *moulids* of these prestigious saints attract tens and even hundreds of thousands of pilgrims from all over Egypt. Added to these major events are a multitude of commemorations of 'local' small-scale saints, the emblematic figures of a given neighbourhood.

A study, published in 1973, attributed to Cairo notes about twelve mosques dedicated to the Prophet's descendants, two to great doctors of law and fifteen to some famous Sufis. Alî Pacha Moubarak, in his *Khitat* published in 1887, identified in Cairo 102 celebrations of all types, eighty of which were *moulids*. In 1940, J.-W. MacPherson identified seventy-three *moulids* in Cairo, fifty-one of which were in the ancient town and the adjoining necropolis and sixteen in Bûlaq. These events, spread across the old town and its adjoining cemeteries, are recurrent in time and space; attendance therein depends on the importance of the saint and his *baraka*. The season for the main Cairo *moulids* sets in over a five-month period, from *rabî' thânî* to *cha'bân*.

For a time, entire neighbourhoods in the old town are blocked and rendered impassable to traffic. They are cut off from the rest of the city and life therein is tuned to the pace of the celebration. This is so with the Gamâliyya and al-Husayn neighbourhoods in the months of *rabî' al-awwal* and *rabî' al-thânî*, followed by that of Zaynab in the month of *ragab*. They fall under 'mythical' time, as referred to by Mircea Eliade.

Secular time, whose linear flow is interrupted, becomes eclipsed at the expense of sacred time, composed of sequences and rhythms, and inscribed in the surrounding space haloed by the sacredness of the saint's tomb.

Conditions for stage-managing the feast: decor, accessories and attitudes

The decor during the celebration of a saint's anniversary is composed of garlands of coloured bulbs; fabrics with brightly coloured print; pyramids of chickpeas, sugar-coated candies of many different shapes (from the small cuboid to the big doll); festive accessories (gold- and silver-gilt *tartûrs* [pointed hats], party novelties, masks and streamers), made with scrap paper, packaging paper and recycled cartons; toys and figurines made of plastic or assorted recycled materials (cans, foam, feathers etc.); painted metallic swings; marksmanship stands where a picture can be won; fifty-piastre shows or exhibitions in trailers, marquees or behind folding screens; and a wide gamut of games of skill and strength.

If the *moulid* is one of little import, like that of Cheikh Yûnis al-Sa'adî, in Bab al-Nasr, it will have, on a smaller sparingly decorated space, a few substitutes for all this. But if it is that of Husayn or Zaynab, there will be a more lavish display on a grander scale, supplemented by large wheels, bumper cars, a great diversity of attractions and the amenities that befit central neighbourhoods.

Needless to say, after outlining the elements and accessories of the celebration, that this is a popular feast. The ordinary is inflated to exceptional proportions. The town is stage-managed, made aesthetic and sublime and becomes a show in itself. Buildings are redesigned into various shapes and stylized by the addition of luminous garlands. Once every year, the grand mosque – the centre and soul of the feast – is all lighted up and reshaped by lights. According to a poetic metaphor, it is adorned and sparkling 'like a newly wed damsel' ('arûsa), sometimes becoming invisible under the cascade of dazzling lights. The neighbourhood is completely transformed in the eyes of its inhabitants; but for those who visit it only on such occasions, they go away with memories of just this unique appearance. The magical aspect of the city lends it a permanently festive look. Youssef Idris mentions this misapprehension, when a youth from the province arrives in Cairo: 'What is this kind of town where everyday is like a feast day!' (Idris 1986: 27–8).

Hangings along buildings and on arches found intermittently along the roads, a lavish display of strings of fairy lights, multi-coloured pennants and banners, a complete recursive set artfully blending draped items and lights either hide or show up boldly the features of the configuration of the premises. The old town takes on a new decor. The landscape is reordered, recomposed, and comes under the sway of a new harmony. A new ephemeral order, which modifies distances, reigns; it reorders the constituent elements of the urban set-up. Hierarchy, from the sacred to the secular, can be read from the graduated distribution of elements: the festive fairground and residential tents are in the background while the ceremonial tents of official institutions and noteworthy fraternities hug closely the front of the mosque.

The same is true of the status of spaces whose appearance, utilization and function can fluctuate from private to public. The practice of the town is thereby altered – the neighbourhood in which the *moulid* is held is open, common ground where people can move about freely everywhere. Public spaces – major squares – are restructured by the line of ceremonial tents which cut off and limit traffic areas.[14] Semi-private spaces such as cul-de-sacs and alleys are occupied by the provincial rustics and their canvas dwellings. This horizontal expansion is also coupled with occupation of private places: the fraternities not only occupy the mosques but also take up rooms in the many small fully booked hotels (*lokandas*) found in the Husayn neighbourhood, sundry premises (such as sports clubs), or apartments. Thus, every year, the *hawch* of rab' Qizlâr plays host to the pilgrims of the *moulid* of al-Rifâ'î.

Similarly, the day loses its sway to the night – the ideal time for feasting and inspiration, fanned by poetry and song. The recurrent mention of the nocturnal theme transcends a mere time period and is suggestive of a conducive climate and setting for poetry and dreaming. The night is source of inspiration, the effects of which are invoked and evoked by a multitude of songs and poetry. Thus, the *mawwâl*, an improvised chant, generally starts with 'Yâ layl, yâ 'ayn (O night, O light of the eyes). The *moulid* is a nocturnal feast. The announcement given indicates the date of the last night, which corresponds to the closing date.

78

One world is founded on another. It replicates it, borrows from it and disrupts it momentarily. The *moulid* abolishes the humdrum of everyday life, and confounds the ordinary. This festive celebration of a religious commemoration is also an interface between Cairo and the provinces, between the neighbourhood and the town, between the *baraka* and the pilgrim, and between the sacred and the secular. Contrasts, whether concurrent or successive, appear. The crowd has a heterogeneous composition: provincial people can be recognized from their dress; families try to avoid the crush; and children from the nearby neighbourhoods press around the fairground attractions, torn between the caravan of the conjurors and that of Abû Zayd, a hero of the *geste hilalienne* (an epic poem popular in the Middle Ages).

The feast brings together complementary extras without, however, really mixing them: Cairo-dwellers and provincial dwellers; men and women; youths and the elderly; the devout and the gawking onlooker; the rich and the beggar; charitable souls and pickpockets, etc. These manifold, disorderly and fortuitous encounters generate their own share of tensions. The path of the devout, *dhikrs*, in prayer, crosses the path of idle strollers and candy stalls transformed into attraction huts; the disdain displayed by some inhabitants of the neighbourhood before this influx of 'peasants' is in sharp contrast to the fervour and wonderment of the provincial rustics exclaiming 'Allah!' at the sight of the beautiful mosques and alluring shops. Participants with a role to play in the organization, co-ordination and conduct of these events fall into two categories – internal and external; on the one hand, the ordinary inhabitants and local notables and, on the other, the state institutions and Sufi fraternities, who are particularly involved in perpetuating these celebrations which are privileged moments for their exteriorization.

It is worth mentioning that, although the *moulids* are partly supervised by religious and civil authorities, they turn out, to an extent, to be places of deviant practices, for the feast itself also 'allows certain well-ordered excesses and is a solemn violation of certain taboos [...]. Excesses are an integral part of the nature of feasts: the joyful disposition is produced by the permission granted, to do what is forbidden under normal circumstances' (Freud 1965: 211).

The extraordinary festive time is a period when free rein can be given to attitudes that would be castigated or concealed outside that context, and when the control of the family/society and one's surroundings abates. The mingling, the crowd and the exceptional circumstances confer some degree of anonymity. Such moments when one is more prone to mind one's own business lead to variations in behaviour. Many deeds perpetrated in public remain unknown or are tolerated: they become acceptable at such fleeting moments and within this closed space, the ideal and arguably necessary place for transgression, exception and deregulation, under cover of religious celebration. Thus, it is possible directly to accost young girls, who may on such an occasion be strolling unaccompanied, a daring act that goes unnoticed under anonymous circumstances but which would be hard to accomplish in surroundings where she is known. Thus, Naguib Mahfouz recounts in *Le Palais du désir* how a young man succeeded in getting into a relationship with his close female neighbours on this occasion: 'And how did you meet them?' – 'In the hut of Mouled d'al-Husseïn. I accosted them boldly and kept walking along with them calmly as if we were members of the same family come to stroll at the feast!' (Mahfouz 1985–89: 93).

The same goes for carnal contact, dance, consumption of alcohol and drugs, fancy dress, the parody of events such as marriage, which are derided, etc. At Sayyida 'Aîcha, the local young men organize a cart procession in the afternoon of the last day. On these carts, they act out various scenes (featuring the coffee man, the gendarme [law enforcement officer] and the thief), and wherein, disguised as women, some of them mime and parody marriage, suggesting sundry forms of sexual intercourse. We should, however, point out that here, we are talking of rites of inversion, for such entertainment is neither systematic nor is it present in all *moulids*. Each catches its own mood. Such peculiarities are determined solely by spontaneous local initiatives. The following testimony conveys the conditions of association of a place, the neighbourhood and a time, the evening of the feast: 'If I were offered a thousand pounds to go and stage my show in a Cairo hotel on the evening of the feast, I would decline such an offer because my show is meant for the neighbourhood people who look forward to it' (words of a participant in the *moulid* of Sayyida 'Aîcha, getting ready for a chariot show).[15]

To underscore the local significance of the event, the highly improbable possibility of a tempting offer that would jeopardize the feast is simultaneously raised and immediately discarded. The *moulid*, an occasion for exteriorization, is an important moment in the life of the neighbourhood, enabling various social groups to express and assert themselves. The young men in disguise who file past in the carts procession unquestionably display provocation. Coffee men armed with loudspeakers 'grab' the right of speech as well as exclusive rights to run commentaries on the street show while also vaunting their businesses. Children, in the spotlight, become temperamental and are spoiled. Families, in their full numbers, come on an outing while young girls, who spend lavishly on toiletries, hairdressing and make-up, put their strong points to advantage and turn on their power of seduction.

Feasts, although different, look alike; superimposed over pre-existing space, they seem to absorb or partially blur it and exhibit a range of 'dominant traits' with the capacity to create an atmosphere at once unique and commonplace, a landscape both original and familiar. In this sense, going to a feast is like embarking on a journey to a surprising but reassuring world. The feast marks a discontinuity in both time and space; afterwards, everything resumes its normal course, but there has been a break or a pause.

The feast is also the occasion to treat oneself in a variety of ways: one forgets oneself, a little or much; sometimes one is not oneself any more (under the influence of drugs, dance, trance, fatigue etc.). One even lets go of oneself, leaving things to chance and wandering about aimlessly, sometimes drifting with the crowd.

Energies are bent on amusement and absorbed by much-sought-after imagination, whereas the rest of the time, people mostly operate in functional mode. There, the scale of preferences changes, based on a completely different logic: sugar is preferred to salt; one prefers the palate to nourishment; the aesthetic prevails over the practical; adults play; poetry is appreciated.

The feast is a brightly lit and noisy territory with clearly marked out places of exhibition, verges, nooks and crannies, dead-ends, areas of light and half-shadow. It ends in a blur, a space of halos (of sounds and lights), which is the transition to ordinary life.

Same feast, many atmospheres astir

The *moulid* of Zaynab is certainly the one with the widest 'spread'. Its feel extends from the Munira neighbourhood right to la Citadelle, after the Ibn Tûlûn Mosque, a linear distance of about three kilometres from west to east. From these extremities can be seen the ceremonial tents and isolated camps, the number growing significantly as one gets closer to the centre which is the Sayyida Zaynab mosque. From the square, the components of the *moulid* radiate like a halo; tents, commercial businesses and attractions fan out in different directions. The 'Abd al-Magîd al-Labbânî road is occupied mainly by tents; fairground attractions are concentrated on the Port-Saïd road; commercial businesses are found in the permanent market round the mosque, but also occupy both sides of the al-Barrâni road.

On the last evening of the *moulid* of Sayyida Zaynab, the feast, whose core is the square in front of the mosque, continues all night. Almost all

81

shops are open and illuminated; the shop-owners receive their friends then. Opposite the mosque is placed a second line of businesses – the candy stalls, flooded by the harsh glare of neon lights. Adjacent to the mosque are tents in which sheikhs, accompanied by musicians, chant, and the participants in the *dhikr* are gathered. The capacity of the tent is clearly too small for this company around whom is formed a shifting cordon of spectator-participants. The entire centre of the square from one side to the other is reserved as a passage for the extremely thick crowds moving up and down the entire area. Some twenty lines of persons squeezed together constantly cross each other; others come up again soon afterwards. While some dislike close contact with the crowd, others like it. Few are alone. A very distinct group of turbaned Sa'îdîs (inhabitants of southern Egypt), clad in *galabeyas*, can be seen walking in Indian file; sometimes, the person in the lead holds his cane up as a rallying sign. One of the nagging fears associated with the *moulid* is of getting lost, a grave cause of concern for the provincial rustic. A tent is placed at the centre of the square for receiving lost children.

Intermittently, a hooting police van or an ambulance cuts a passage through the crowds, taking advantage of the occasion; it then gets stuck behind droves of persons and ends up breaking the queues formed. Groups of very conspicuous young men, often in tracksuits topped by pointed hats, forming a train by holding themselves by the shoulder, run across the full length of the square, bumping into others. In the lead is a sturdy man who plays the locomotive. Sometimes, fights break out, caused by the jostle and bustle, taunting of some people by others, harassment of women, pickpockets, etc. These sometimes intensely violent scenes are quickly settled and the protagonists again melt into the crowd. Otherwise, when a crowd forms, police officers who are scattered in the crowds intervene.

The edges of the square are less crowded than the centre; there, one can move about more freely and visit the attractions and items on display. This is particularly appealing to families, women, the elderly as well as everyone wishing to take a calm walk. The whole square is lit by garlands of multi-coloured blinking light bulbs that crisscross the tents, shops, stalls, merry-go-round and swings and then reconnect with the mosque where a green neon light inscribes the name of God. These blinking lights end up rolled around the minaret right to its summit.

From the direction of the tents, the melody of singing, chanting, recitations of the Qu'ran or prayers is amplified by sound equipment turned outwards; traders vaunt their wares with the help of microphones; the fairground people hail passers-by; vendors of the latest variety music cassettes turn up their volume; in front of their shops, young boys sing, dance and clap their hands. Everywhere, whistle, rattle and castanet vendors test their instruments. At the core of the shattering din, the omnipresent sharp jingling of cymbal-puppets, peculiar to *moulids*, rises above the general din and sets the distinctive tone of the feasts. Away from the square, the tone of the celebration changes. The buzz of the fairground with its sound of rifles, firecrackers, the creak of see-saws, the drumming that accompanies the rotating merry-go-round, the calls of the fairground attendants all drown the sound of recitations of the Qu'ran and the music of the *dhikr*, wafting from the tents.

A confined world

The Khalwatiyya Hasâniyya[16] fraternity prides itself on being installed on the square itself, opposite the al-Husayn mosque. This privileged position within the sacred and coveted perimeter is a clear sign of the influence of the fraternity, the *baraka* and charisma of the sheikh, and stems from the fact that the fraternity is rich and generous and distributes hundreds of meals each day. The decision to allocate these positions is taken by the Sufi Council and, in general, the same positions are allocated from year to year.

The long rectangular tent, surmounted by a banner proclaiming the identity of the fraternity, opens from the front. On the frontage, adorned by a string of fairy lights, the decorative designs of the cloth are highlighted, whereas on the other frontages, it is the wrong side that is visible from outside. At the entrance, unknown entities introduce themselves; entry is restricted. The tent (*khidmâ*)[17] is a place which, quite paradoxically, appears partly a-spatial: although it is situated in the very heart of town, it is a closed, static and confined world where material as well as spiritual life is a complete intense community experience. It appears suddenly but stands as a model of functionality: 'settling on a territory is equivalent to founding a world' (Eliade 1965: 47).

Inside it are performed practices both private and public, sacred and secular. In the same space, male pilgrims sleep, eat, perform their ablutions, receive their guests, pray and practise the *dhikr*. A typically *sa'îdî* space is formed at the centre of Cairo. The pilgrims' outings are few but then they receive many Cairo-based visitors of the same geographical origin; a community atmosphere prevails. Inside, the thick coloured walls tint and filter the daylight and on the back inner wall is suspended the portrait of the fraternity's sheikh.

On the right side, close to the entrance, an area hidden from public gaze by curtains is arranged for ablutions; in the background, another is set aside for the kitchen. The floor is entirely covered by carpets and, at night, chandeliers and coloured bulbs are lighted. The pilgrims' personal belongings are put away on the sides and shoes are left at the entrance. Hassan al-Bannâ sees to everything: the reception of visitors; each and everyone's comfort; arrangements for hospitality and charity,[18] values that are essential especially during a *moulid*; and, of course, ceremonial procedures since he presides over the *dhikr*. Following the timetable, the same area is used alternately for prayer, rest and meals after a few adjustments warranted by the variations in use. A few accessories contribute to the necessary adjustments that the change of use entails. Thus, incense is burned during prayers; at mealtimes, narrow plastic mats are spread out on the entire length of the tent and disciples sit on both sides of plastic plates placed in staggered rows. After dinner, they leave quickly to allow the poor of the neighbourhood, waiting behind the entrance, to take their place. Several services can thus follow in quick succession, with the possibility of receiving some two hundred people simultaneously under the tent.

While the evenings and nights are highly animated, the day is marked by the calm of the shadowy light and sleepiness. The tents open and close alternately at regular intervals, carefully handled through the interplay of hangings. Thus, *dhikr* sessions, crucial to the celebration, are times when the fraternity withdraws within itself, a practice not common to all fraternities. But in adjacent tents, on the other hand (Burhâmiyya and Rifâ'iyya), *dhikrs*, accompanied by music, are conducted with much more ostentation and correspond to moments of intense exteriorization. Over and above being seen, what is more important for this fraternity, reputed for the beauty of its *dhikr*, is being heard. At Sayyida Zaynab, the fraternity hires a sports club, away from the road, but airs the *dhikr* through loudspeakers placed beside the road.

Coveted spaces

Moulids are important moments in the life of fraternities. The exteriorization that they foster strengthens the cohesion of disciples and encourages people to join. Major celebrations serve – at various levels – as public forums and representations. In tents privileged to be mounted on the square itself, official representations, the Sufi Council and the most prestigious fraternities – those with the most charismatic and influential sheikhs – are very conspicuous.

Unable to ban, and much less organize, such gatherings, the authorities may try to use them for political ends. Thus, the *moulid* of Sayyid al-Badawî held during the Gulf War, shortly before the assassination of the president of the chamber, was presented as a gathering of two million Egyptian anti-terrorist[19] demonstrators, an interpretation that is all the more disconcerting because in Egypt there is no space for a political demonstration of such magnitude.

In December 1994, the *moulid* of Sayyida Zaynab was used as an electoral campaign platform. Its distinguishing feature was the great number and lavish display of lights and perpetual fireworks, attributed to the extravagance of Fathi Sourour, the local MP. The fact that portraits and banners in his name featured at the feast signalled his intention to run in the forthcoming legislative elections billed for autumn 1995. It further affirmed state[20] presence and involvement in the neighbourhood since Sourour was equally Speaker of the National Assembly. The luminous splendour of the *moulid* that followed less than a year later (December 1995) was proof this time around of the MP's success at the said elections. Further proof was the banner of hearty congratulations hoisted by local traders and notables, who gave the neighbourhood a treat by financing the lighting, a show, or a *khidmâ*, with such patronage obviously translating into their increased personal prestige and publicity for themselves and their businesses: 'public feasts exalt the authorities while private feasts strengthen the clientele and social audiences' (Heers 1983: 19). As interface between the two, the *moulid* not only benefits many protagonists through interactive links, but also derives profits from such links.

Being popular festivities, *moulids* provoke a wide range of reactions – from outright lack of interest and indifference to negation and vehement denunciation. Detractors are many and varied. The main criticisms levelled against these festivities concern the forms of religious practices expressed therein, deemed unorthodox, and the roundly condemned social practices. The neighbourhoods in which they are celebrated take on a slightly 'shameful' character: it is recommended for women and mostly strangers not to go to *moulids* alone, especially during the last night. Are *moulids* not ideal locations for all sorts of brigands?

Such old and recurrent discourse, reflected in debates echoed by the press, does not in any way dampen the popularity of the phenomenon. According to a popular saying, 'everybody takes home chickpeas from the *moulid*', but the gamut of what each comes to look for is quite eclectic: animation, games, encounters, prayers, *baraka*, trance, or a dose of all of them. Can the journey symbolized by the *moulid* be construed as a simulation or a substitute to the pilgrimage to Mecca or sometimes as a complement to it?

Barring those dedicated to major, somewhat non-temporal personalities, ordinary *moulids* are subject to the vicissitudes and cycle of life. Some collapse, disappear and phase out concurrently or are reborn and given fresh impetus. Attendance too fluctuates. While devotion to some saints

85

lapses into oblivion, others gather new momentum. *Moulids* are revived when a sheikh of a fraternity dies.

Attempts have been made by public authorities to contain or direct *moulids*, because after 1952, the government put an end to all feasts during which fraternity processions were held. After 1967, these, especially the *moulid* of the Prophet, were again authorized in the al-Rifâ'î and al-Husayn mosques. A few examples in Cairo prove that, for *moulids*, the trend cannot be reduced to their decline. Thus, the *moulid* of Ahmad al-Rifâ'î, one of the most striking at the turn of the nineteenth century, described by MacPherson as moribund, is presently one of the most important. That of Nafîsa, very popular nowadays, did not exist as such in the late 1930s; during the *moulid* of Sakîna (whose tomb is close by), advantage is taken of this to pay a visit to this saint, whose shrine, at the time, was at the edge of the desert.

Meanwhile, the major Cairo-based celebrations, particularly the al-Nabî, al-Husayn and Sayyida Zaynab trio, do not come under such temporal considerations and their perpetuation seems guaranteed. Their magnetic force keeps growing. Towards the end of the 1980s, an estimated 500,000 persons attended the *moulid* of al-Husayn; in 2000, the *Al-Ahram* newspaper doubled this figure. Apart from these estimates, there are indications that attendance at the major *moulids* has greatly increased: thus, during the anniversary of Husayn in September 1995, traffic was deviated off the al-Azhar road to allow the huge crowds to pour out their feelings.

Thus, it is possible that the practice of *moulids* could have changed, with its spread extending over smaller geographic areas and concentrated around major celebrations in honour of the most charismatic and emblematic figures. Such figures whose memory is constantly kept rejuvenated can never be eclipsed. The notoriety and popularity of the *moulids* of Husayn and Zaynab, major saints and non-temporal personalities, who, in Catherine Mayeur-Jaouen's phraseology concerning Sayyid al-Badawî, 'travel across time', confer on them an exceptional character.

The feast itself is a matrix of contrasts, composed of superimposed or successive tableaus deployed and restricted in space. All *moulids* have one thing in common: the non-solemnity and density of the feast. Significant differences mark the grand *moulids* from the less grand, those of Cairo from those of the provinces, those held in the necropolis from those held in central neighbourhoods ...

One needs only attend the grand *moulids* of the Delta to observe that their atmosphere is not comparable to that of their Cairo equivalents, each of which has its own style and scope. These specificities are linked, among others, to their location in a given area (social composition, specificity and 'reputation' of the neighbourhood), the structure of public spaces, the personality of the saint, and the local stakeholders (inhabitants, traders, associations). Thus, as J.-W. MacPherson remarked earlier, the *moulid* of Sayyida Zaynab appears as one of the liveliest and one with the greatest play, partly owing to the many games and attractions featured on the wide Port-Saïd road (swings and see-saws, big wheels, conjurors' shows, bumper cars, stunt riders, display of the woman-serpent, etc.). The *moulids* of Bûlaq were reputed for being unbridled, and historians made references to attractions, games and rituals which are today a thing of the past.[21]

Novelties are introduced from one year to the next: since the appearance of the animated cartoon series *Ninja Turtles* on TV, caravans carry their effigies; new stage-managed productions come up every day; strings of blinking fairy lights produce increasingly elaborate figures within an enlarged band of colours; the echo effect diversifies the possibilities of modulating songs and the evocation of the name of God; the gamut of traditional puppets has changed with the use of diverse materials, etc. Quite obviously, the present time is there, manifest; the fairground feast, superimposed and in parallel, is an expression and reflection of the town; it is but an emanation of present-day realities.

The general atmosphere of the major *moulids* is sensitive to and permeated by cyclical uncertainties. J.-W. MacPherson and later on Nicolaas Biegman noted fluctuations in the practice of *moulids*, particularly in times of war. Furthermore, Pierre-Jean Luizard points out that significantly fewer people than usual attended the *moulid* of al-Husayn held shortly after the earthquake of October 1992. In contrast, the *moulid* of Sayyida Zaynab held at the beginning of January 1994 was particularly lively as it also fell on New Year's Day, and sundry accessories and banners were decorated using this theme (Happy New Year 1994, etc.).

The major Cairo-based *moulids*, on the other hand, are real boons for traders and are places of temptation. As the feast is prime time for consumption, pilgrims wish to take back home souvenirs from the *moulid*. They buy small objects sold close to the sanctuary (amulets, small Qu'rans, toys, sweets etc.) which bring blessings – fancy jewels, trinkets, pendants or beads. The festive climate and *baraka* sublimate the multitude of small insignificant articles. The presence of the same article everywhere, in shops, stalls, carts, seen a thousand times over and glistening in the bright light, becomes monotonous. *Moulid*-goers, most of whom are not rich, cannot indulge themselves without tremendous sacrifice. This is therefore the occasion for them to purchase objects worth a lot more than their cost price.

The influx of *moulid* attendants stretches the market around Sayyida

Zaynab to breaking point: during the day, a vast display of assorted goods – dishes, kitchen utensils, fabric and dresses – is organized. Pilgrims take advantage of their stay in Cairo to shop. Thus, *Sa'îdîs* (inhabitants of southern Egypt) make on-the-spot purchases of scarves produced in *Sa'îd* mostly on the eastern side of the al-Husayn mosque and in the Aouf shop close to Khân al-Khalîlî.

For *moulid*-goers, attending this or that celebration is subject to screening and appraisal criteria: one may choose to participate only in the feast of the Prophet, or specially to venerate a saint, or again to participate only if the *moulid*(s) is/are held in a given neighbourhood.

Big *moulids* provide the necessary forum for the rural, urban, provincial Cairo and other communities to meet around shared representations. They strengthen the cohesion and identity of the social groups present. They also help to create occasions for building and affirming the feeling of belonging to one or several communities (fraternity, village, neighbourhood, etc.), to suspend social control and to perpetuate rites. They stand as essential periods for the individual and the community. The way of life associated with the single-minded practice of *moulids*, tinged with temporal nomadism, is not a valorizing referent. For those perpetuating this tradition, the inconveniences suffered are deemed insignificant compared with the spiritual or material benefits reaped. The *moulid* is above all the space-time with boundless opportunities for intercession (*madad*), wishes and hope. It is supposed that the Prophet is present and mention is made of diverse miracles of differing magnitude ...

In contrast to many recurrent events whose past is, in accounts, steeped in nostalgia, *moulids* are seen by their practitioners as perpetuated in a continuity that precludes any comparative description. To corroborate Mircea Eliade's assertion, sacred time does not flow; it is always equal to itself, and neither changes nor runs out. Thus, by definition, a *moulid* is always a success and is generally always appraised as 'very good this year, as always'. It could possibly get better with time, if the decoration is particularly well done, for example. This fact may be noted, but in speech, the quality of the celebration cannot be assessed.

'If sacred places are perennial, it is because sacredness imbues them with a constant outpouring, in forms that are continuously being renewed' (Geoffroy 1993: 173). Celebrations – events reproduced but also moments that are readjusted and reinvented each time – induce and heighten the meaning of the old town. By dint of this repeated, collective and renewed allegiance and recognition, it asserts its undeniably conceptual permanence. The big *moulids* of Cairo confer on the central areas of the old town the identity of large-scale public and consensual spaces, or places of first-hand memory. They proclaim their cultural supremacy and heighten the significance of the space.

At the time of Lane (1834), the *moulid* of the Prophet was held in birkat Azbakiyya; then, at the end of the nineteenth century, it was located first between Cairo and Bûlâq, and then at Fum al-Khalîg (to the south of Cairo). Later, at the start of the twentieth century, the feast was held in changing locations designated each year, generally in the periphery, at Abbâsiyya. Presently, the celebration of the birth of the Prophet is organized around the al-Husayn mosque – towards which converge sundry processions (*zaffas*) – thereby enhancing its prestige. In addition to this centre, there is the al-Rifâ'î mosque in whose direction head many convoys of the *moulids* of the Khalifa necropolis, such as that of Sayyida 'Aîcha.

The contribution, coupled with the commingling, of multiple asserted or superimposed identities (social categories, sexes, generations, geographical origins, membership in fraternities, etc.) may be perceived as the channel for the constant invention and propagation of the cultural spirit. Through these factors, we are able to identify the space-time of the *moulid* as one of the manifestations of identity.

It should also be recalled that it is territory for various forms of expression: recitals, stories, tales, songs, dance, music and shows. Remember that Umm Kulthum started her career in the *moulids* of the Delta region. Sheikh Yasîn al-Tuhâmi, extremely famous in Egypt, owes his present popularity to nothing but the *moulids*. Henceforth, it is his presence that is the crowd-puller of a *moulid*. The repeated or occasional practice of *moulids* is part of a way of life, but certainly not one of its most anecdotal aspects. It thus partly transcends certain social divisions.

Lastly, the *moulid* is the place where information and relational networks are activated, mainly through fraternity circles, and which serves as a forum of integration. A young man from Louxor, member of the Khalwatiyya fraternity, explains that he came to the *moulid* of Zaynab to honour the saint, and that, while there, he tried to find work by passing round the word through the Cairo-based members and asking those present about various job opportunities. Before him, his brother had found work through the relations of the sheikh of the fraternity.

Conclusion: the feast as panorama

The day after the 'grand night', before noon, the tents, the fairground stalls, the decorations and the crowds have all disappeared. The contrast is striking indeed between the bygone period, especially the previous (exceptional) night, and the present day, the transition to ordinary everyday life. The neighbourhood looks hollow and empty; only the rubbish on the ground, the trampled lawns, the unusual odour and the presence of sweepers attest to a now past reality. The transition is fleeting, the inertia short-lived; the suddenness and intensity of the metamorphosis of the town are brutal on the new day – the celebration has come and gone. The restitution of the neighbourhood to its real inhabitants puts an end to the exteriorization of self.

Passers-by yawn. Many are those who do their errands in pyjamas or indoor garments. For a few hours, the atmosphere is laden with torpor, just time enough to kick oneself back to the pace of habit and to allow the signs of the neighbourhood's hangover to wear out. Later, in the Sayyida Zaynab neighbourhood, a 'thief's market' springs up briefly, just time enough to sell items that were lost – or stolen – during the *moulid*. Almost everywhere in Egypt, in many homes, small toys and portraits, sachets of sweets and chickpeas, beads, sticks of incense or miniature Qu'rans, and a multitude of assorted objects and ritual gifts keep alive memories of a trip to Cairo, a visit to a saint; they also dispense the *baraka* of a *moulid* now past. 'Memory entrenches itself in the concrete, in space, in gesture, in the picture and the object' (Nora 1984: xix).

There are things that are read in the town, others which are seen, some of which are spoken and others still which are known and experienced. The latter are not always the ones that are most exposed and can be identified on sight. Sufism is a way of accessing other than material reality, an invisible world. The *moulid* brings to the fore the values of the area and, for a time, enhances their visibility. The feast in honour of the saint is past, but his aura lingers on. The *moulid* is a moment of exaltation of ideological and symbolic values, which then become apparent, for they are visibly expressed and experienced. The rest of the time, however, such symbolic representations are diffuse, less legible, but always none the less present.

The feast is an awaited, much-thought-about event that is surmised, but which is devoid of unanimous and objective reality. It exists none the less and assumes the shape and function projected by everyone. The panorama is an abstract formless figure which is simultaneously all and nothing, space and time, an open limitless figure turned to all that is possible and probable. It is a ferment for the imagination and opens one's vision to an enlarged world, a reshaping of the real. This theme, often treated in many forms in fiction, is handled more explicitly in *Désert des Tartares* and *Rivage des Syrtes*.

The full existence of the feast entails preparation in three essential but unequal phases: before (expectation), during (the experience) and after (memories), with its recomposition through the piecing together of accounts and commentaries. An example of this is given by John Steinbeck with detailed narration of the episodes of one magnified and idealized night in *Tortilla Flat*.

The time of the feast is absolute and total: it has a beginning and an end. There is full knowledge that life must continue in the meantime like a summarized parody of a lifetime, but whose end-time is known. As such, it awakens strong, contradictory and clashing feelings, outbursts of joy and anguish; in short, a very special state of mind, a 'moral jumble, half-attractive, half-doleful', according to Balzac. One is not joyful all the time; but one is joyful, primarily because one is there, and because one shares with others this presence and the circumstances surrounding it. Everyone exhibits a clear and very prominent will to be there and to live these moments intensely – to be more conspicuous and more noisy, more present, more prominent in space. To that end, the 'territories of self' (Goffman 1973) will be more conspicuous and more alert. Everyone is ready and perfumed for the feast, often more agitated and noisy than in ordinary times – one speaks louder and laughs more.

By our very human condition, we are always more or less looking forward to something. It could be said that the feast provides a momentary outlet, and a break from this state. Each can condense and cause to converge on the feast his vague, confused and unexpressed wishes, aspirations, quests, expectations and desires which are projected to a time and place that are neutral and become a clearer target, even though all of this will probably remain unfulfilled. The feast, however, is ephemeral: it unfolds and breaks up; everything therein is nervousness, beginning with the participants whose frame of mind is one that carries a dose of exaltation. The time of the feast is counted, with even a countdown to the day itself; time is staked out, it flies, which implies 'syndromes', that can easily be figured out as being those of the pumpkin and the sandglass, manifested mainly through an anguish of passing time and, more specifically, the coming of dawn, the return of daylight, which will set things to normal again – the dominant binary day–night rhythm which regulates the life of men and towns.

Notes

1 Intuition corroborated by much research, which has shown that religious processions and feasts are the oldest urban activities in Brazil.

2 Which is neither verbalized nor conscious; see M. Maffesoli's interview in the 14 July 2000 issue of the journal *le Monde*, regarding the picnic organized in France on the occasion of the National Day celebration.

3 *Mawlid* (anniversary), plural *mawâlid*, is called *moulid* in Egypt. Beyond the anniversary of a precise event, a birth or a death (both cases exist), the *moulid* is simply the day devoted to a saint.

4 As attested particularly by Moussaoui's (1996) thesis on the logic of the sacred in the spatial organization of south-west Algeria, especially the chapters devoted to the *mawlid* of Kenadsa and the Gourara feasts (pp. 58–89, 275–96).

5 As suggested by Henri Chamussy (1995: 863).

6 Pilgrims bound for the *moulid* of al-Husayn on board the train were not required to pay the fare.

7 The *moulids* of Husayn and Zaynab invariably end on Wednesday's eve.

8 These tents, used during ceremonies (marriages, funerals) or public meetings (political rallies, etc.) as well as chairs, carpets and lighting equipment, are hired during such occasions. Their mere presence is therefore a sign that an event is in progress.

9 Egyptian fraternities are affiliated to orders, the main ones of which are: Khalwatiyya, Ahmadiyya, Burhâmiyya, Châdhiliyya, Rifâ'iyya and Qâdiriyya.

10 Qu'ran, Surat *Yûnis*, verse 63.

11 The opening Surat and profession of Faith in the Qu'ran.

12 The *dhikr* (remembrance), a collective exercise performed by Sufi disciples under the supervision of the Sheikh, consists in repeating the name of God in various rhythms and following special body movements.

13 *Baraka* literally means blessing; it is associated with divine grace and protection.

14 Certain spaces – out-of-bounds – are not subjected to these intense disturbances. Even when the crowd is extremely thick at the centre of the square in front of the al-Husayn mosque, fenced off by small railings guarded by agents, nobody strays into the green rectangle of the lawn.

15 Included by Hassan El Geretly in *The Mouled, Al-mûlid*, a documentary film produced by the El Warsha company of Cairo.

16 This is more precisely the Ahmadiyya branch, located in Gurna, on the western bank of Louxor, Governorate of Qena. Concerning the contemporary history of this fraternity, and the role of *moulids* in fraternity life, see Chih (2000).

17 These tents bear the name *khîmas*, but when used for celebrations, they are referred to as *khidmâ* (service). This word makes reference to their use, since it can mean both the tent and the premises where the ceremonies are held, as well as the meal served during these occasions.

18 In addition to tea offered to all visitors and the meals served in the tent to disciples and the needy, the fraternity hands out baskets of food to women who so request to be taken home to their families.

19 See Mayeur-Jaouen (1994).

20 It will be recalled that three Islamists were killed in the Sayyida Zaynab neighbourhood in February 1994, during a clash with the police.

21 See in particular Wiet (1969).

References

Abdel, Hakim Quassem (1998) *Les sept jours de l'homme (Ayyâl al-insân al-sab'a)*, Paris: Actes Sud.

Abu-Zahra, N. (1997) *The Pure and Powerful*, Berkshire, UK: Ithaca, Studies in Contemporary Muslim Society.

Al-Messiri, Nadim N. (1979) 'The Concept of the Hâra. A Historical and Sociological Study of Al-Sukkariyya', *Annales Islamologiques*, XV, Cairo: IFAO.

Amado, J. (1984) *Tocaia Grande (Tocaia Grande : a face obscura)*, Paris: Stock, Le Livre de Poche.

Arendt, H. (1972) *La crise de la culture*, Paris: Gallimard, Folio Essais.

Augé, M. (1989) 'L'autre proche', *L'autre et le semblable. Regards sur l'ethnologie des sociétés contemporaines*, Paris: CNRS.

Bachelard, G. (1989) *La poétique de l'espace*, Paris: PUF, Quadrige.

Balzac, H. (1996) *Sarrasine*, Paris: Mille et une nuits.

Bannerthe, E. (1966) 'La Khalwatiyya en Égypte', *MIDEO*, 8, Cairo: Dâr al Maaref.

Berque, J. and M. Al-Shakaa (1974) 'La Gamâliyya depuis un siècle essai d'histoire sociale d'un quartier du Caire', *Revue des Études Islamiques*, XLII-1, Cairo: Librairie Orientaliste.

Biegman, N. (1990) *Egypt. Moulids Saints Sufis*, La Haye: Gary Schwartz-SDU.

Bromberger, C., P. Centlivres and G. Collomb (1989) 'Entre le local et le global: les figures de l'identité', *L'autre et le semblable. Regards sur l'ethnologie des sociétés contemporaines*, Paris: CNRS.

Buzzati, D. (1994) *Le désert des Tartares*, Paris: Robert Laffont, Pocket.

Chamussy, H. (1995) 'Religions dans le monde', *Encyclopédie de la Géographie*, Paris: Economica.

Charmes, G. (1880) *Cinq mois au Caire et dans la Basse-Égypte*, Paris: G. Charpentier.

Chih, R. (2000) *Le soufisme au quotidien. Confréries d'Égypte au XXe siècle*, Paris: Sinbad, Actes Sud.

Debarbieux, B. (1995) 'Imagination et imaginaire géographiques', *Encyclopédie de la géographie*, Paris: Economica.

De Nerval, G. (1980) *Voyage en Orient, I*, Paris: GF-Flammarion.

Di Méo, G. (ed.) (2001) *La géographie en fêtes*, Paris: Géophrys.

Duvignaud, J. (2000) *La scène, le monde, sans relâche*, Paris: Babel, Actes Sud.

Eliade, M. (1965) *Le sacré et le profane*, Paris: Gallimard, Folio.

El-Kadi and A. Bonnamy (2001) *La cité des morts. Le Caire*, IRD-Mardaga.

Freud, S. (1965) *Totem et tabou*, Paris: Petite Bibliothèque Payot.

Frishkopf, M. (1995) 'La voix du poète: *tarab* et poésie dans le chant mystique soufi', *Égypte Monde Arabe*, 25, Cairo: CEDEJ.

Geoffroy, E. (1993) 'L'empreinte de la sainteté', *Damas, Autrement*, 65, Paris: Autrement.

Ghitany, G. (1993) *Épître des destinées*, Paris: Seuil.

Ghosh, A. (1994) *Un infidèle en Égypte*, Paris: Seuil.

Gilsenan, M. (1973) *Saint and Sufi in Modern Egypt. An Essay in the Sociology of Religion*, Oxford: Clarendon Press.

Goerg, O. (ed.) (1999) *Fêtes urbaines en Afrique. Espaces, identités et pouvoirs*, Paris: Karthala.

Goffman, E. (1973) *La mise en scène de la vie quotidienne. II Les relations en public*, Paris: éd. de Minuit.

GREPO (1977) *L'Égypte d'aujourd'hui. Permanences et changements. 1805–1976*, Paris: CNRS.

Hannerz, U. (1983) *Explorer la ville*, Paris: éd. de Minuit, Le sens commun.

Haqqi, Y. (1991) *Choc*, Paris: Denoël-Alif.

Heers, J. (1983) *Fêtes des fous et carnavals*, Paris: Fayard.

Hoffman-Ladd, V. (1992) 'Devotion to the Prophet and His Family in Egyptian Sufism', *International Journal of Middle East Studies*, 24.

Hussein, T. (1947) *Le livre des jours*, Paris: Gallimard, coll. L'imaginaire.

Idris, Y. (1986) *La sirène et autres nouvelles*, Paris: Sindbad.

Joseph, I. (1991) 'Voir, exposer, observer', *L'espace du public. Les compétences du citadin*, Paris: Plan Urbain, éd. Recherches.

Lane, E.-W. (1989) *Manners and Customs of the Modern Egyptians*, London: East-West Publications.

L'autre et le semblable. Regards sur l'ethnologie des sociétés contemporaines (1989) Paris: Presses du CNRS.

Lévi-Strauss, C. (1985) *L'identité*, Paris: PUF, Quadrige.

Luizard, P.-J. (1993) 'Un *mawlid* particulier', *Égypte/Monde Arabe*, 14, Cairo: CEDEJ.

Lynch, K. (1998) *L'image de la Cité*, Paris: Dunod.

MacPherson, J.-W. (1941) *The Moulids of Egypt. (Egyptian Saints-Days)*, Cairo: Nile Mission Press.

Mahfouz, N. (1985–1989) *Impasse des Deux-Palais, Le Jardin du passé, Le Palais du désir*, Paris: J.-C. Lattès, coll. Lettres arabes, 1985–89.

Massignon, L. (1949) 'Géographie spirituelle et pèlerinage', *Dieu vivant*, XIV.

Mayeur-Jaouen, C. (1994) *Al-Sayyid al-Badawî. Un grand saint de l'islam égyptien*, Cairo: IFAO.

— (1995) 'Gens de la maison et moulds d'Égypte', in *La religion civique à l'époque médiévale et moderne (chrétienté et islam)*, A. Vauchez (ed.), École française de Rome.

Moussaoui, A. (1996) *Logiques du sacré et modes d'organisation de l'espace dans le sud-ouest algérien*, Doctoral Thesis, Paris: EHESS.

Nora, P. (1984) 'Entre mémoire et histoire. La problématique des lieux', *Les lieux de mémoire, I. La République*, Paris: Gallimard, Bibliothèque illustrée des histoires.

Popovic, A. and G. Veinstein (eds) (1996) *Les voies d'Allah. Les ordres mystiques dans le monde musulman des origines à nos jours*, Paris: Fayard.

Ragib, Y. (1976) 'Al-Sayyida Nafisa, sa légende, son culte et son cimetière', *Studia Islamica*, XLIV.

Raymond, A. (1993) *Le Caire*, Paris: Fayard.

Reeves, E. (1990) *The Hidden Government. Ritual, Clientelism, and Legitimation in Northern Egypt*, Salt Lake City: University of Utah Press.

Roncayolo, M. (1990) *La ville et ses territoires*, Paris: Gallimard, Folio.

Schielke, S. (2003) 'On Snacks and Saints: When Discourses of Rationality and Order Enter the Egyptian mawlid', Paper presented in a public lecture at the Netherlands-Flemish Institute in Cairo, 23 January.

Singerman, D. (1995) *Avenues of Participation. Family, Politics, and Networks in Urban Neighbourhoods of Cairo*, Princeton, NJ: Princeton University Press.

Steinbeck, J. (1972) *Tortilla Flat*, Paris: Denoël, Folio.

Uways, S. (1989) *L'histoire que je porte sur mon dos – mémoires*, Cairo: CEDEJ.

Veyne, P. (1983) *les Grecs ont-ils cru à leur mythes?*, Paris: Seuil.

Wiet, G. (1966) *Les mosquées du Caire*, Cairo: Les livres de France-Hachette.

— (1969) 'Fêtes et jeux au Caire', *Annales Islamologiques*, VIII, Cairo: IFAO.

Williams, C. (1985) 'The Cult of Alid Saints in the Fatimide Monuments of Cairo', *Muqarnas*, 3.

Yerasimos, S. (1985) 'La démesure insouciante', *Le Caire. Autrement*, 12, Paris: éd. Autrement.

Young, J.-E. (1993) 'Écrire le monument: site, mémoire, critique', *Annales Économie Société et Culture*, 3.

4 | Kisangani: a city at its lowest ebb

JEAN OMASOMBO

'Tucked well inland at the bend of the great river, Kisangani came close to extinction.' (Naipaul 1982: 9)

This title refers obliquely to Joseph Conrad's celebrated *Heart of Darkness* (1899), which castigated the atrocities of the reign of the Belgian sovereign Leopold II, who became owner of the Congo after Africa was partitioned at the Berlin Conference over a century earlier. The current situation of Kisangani cannot be divorced from this historical backdrop, for the history of this regional capital is fraught with events that make it the 'martyr-town' of the Democratic Republic of Congo.

Kisangani is renowned for its recurrent crises. Since Congo gained independence in June 1960, the town has been scourged by various violent upheavals that seriously threatened its existence and the precarious livelihoods of its inhabitants, struggling to cope with the prevailing joblessness and the collapse of local capitalism. The British writer of Indian origin, V. S. Naipaul, who followed his ancestral trail to Africa, captures this very vividly in his novel entitled *At the Bend of the River*: 'To start with, the town was reborn from its ashes for it had been almost completely destroyed by the upheavals which took place at the time of independence. Then alternated the period of economic boom and the years of lawless uprisings which jeopardized the very existence of the town.'

Caught in the wake of the collapse of the Zairian state in the mid-1970s, the town is today paying a heavy toll for the protracted war that began in 1998. It remains cut off from the capital Kinshasa, whose river transport system is its only link with the outside world. With little power to protect itself, its natural resources – mainly, diamonds and timber mined and logged using very rudimentary techniques – have been subjected to large-scale plunder.

The visitor who alights in Kisangani today will immediately sense a generalized apathy, for life seems to have come to a standstill, as it does during one of the town's many equatorial downpours. When it rains in Kisangani, the picture is one of pure chaos: the town lapses into near-complete inactivity under the torrential downpour and people slump in torpor, fearing to see their houses being swept away. The only activity is from children who congregate beneath eaves to catch the cascading rainwater, who play about and bathe, raising a monumental din. While the little ones run about stark naked, the bigger ones, especially the girls, are half-clad. This joyful scene of frolicking, laughter and screaming children is but short-lived for, as soon as the rain ceases, the children disperse into a sad town.

Traces of fighting are very visible everywhere in Kisangani.[1] The latest picture is from June 2000: in a telephone conversation with the Catholic Bishop of Kisangani, who was away, the Belgian journalist Colette Braeckman (2003: 18, 14) describes the town she discovered, caught in intense fighting:

All is well, Monsignor, the pious ones have not been harmed. Your chair of truth remains intact and the church refectory is unscathed. Several hundreds of people who sought refuge in the garage and vaults of the Procure [church logistical office] are still there praying: they have lost everything except their faith. Well, that aside, the infirmary has been destroyed. The chapel no longer exists. Many rooms in the convent have been reduced to dust. [...]

You also need to know, Monsignor, that the cathedral is on fire. The church bells chime amidst acrid smoke. People run helter-skelter across town like in Europe during the Middle Ages when the Tuscan gave the warning signal.

Visiting the interior of Kisangani during a lull in the fighting, the journalist declares:

But elsewhere in town, the picture is entirely different. I realized this during a quick incursion I made in the company of a UN major. Towards the bridge over the River Tshopo, and across the dam whose knocked-off turbines used to supply electricity to the town, houses look like a thousand flattened leaves and holes on their frontage look like eyes. While some people remain glued to walls, others creep in gardens. Madmen run across the town in a zigzag pattern as if to outpace bullets. Sometimes, they break down; sometimes, they make it across to us, preceded by wild laughter. (ibid.: 18)

The primary purpose of this study is not to show the exceptional character of a town, but to highlight the exemplary side of the Congolese crisis. The town of Kisangani is an aggravated case of debilitated growth: the resourcefulness displayed in other towns of the country meets with resistance here, since conditions have also become wholly inadequate for any meaningful adaptation. Thus, Kisangani stands as the symbol of the collapse of the whole of Congo. It is significant that, in January 2004, the international community chose the town as the venue for the training of the first battalion of the new unified national army.

Kisangani

Although our choice to study Kisangani was motivated by the situation observed on the ground, the town itself is definitely of great interest. The study dwells on the prevailing conditions in the town, focusing on a number of sectors, but it begins by broaching those historical and geo-strategic aspects that explain why the town is at once so attractive and so fragile.

The town 'at the bend of the river' is ancient and strategic

The River Congo cuts right through Kisangani and divides the town in two. Flowing northwards upstream, it is at Kisangani that the river narrows markedly to barely one kilometre in width and then veers abruptly south westwards until it empties itself in the Atlantic Ocean. This is the picture conjured up by the title of V. S. Naipaul's novel *At the Bend of the River.* Indeed, the town is prisoner to this river system: it is crossed by the River Congo and restricted in its northward expansion by another river, the Tshopo, on which is built the dam that supplies it with electricity.

Ancient town Kisangani, one of the oldest towns in the Democratic Republic of Congo, was founded before the European colonization. When in 1875 H. M. Stanley, the British colonial explorer, came to the site of the present-day location of the town, preceding Tippo-Tip, the Arabo-Swahili, by a few days, he found a relatively large core population living there with organized economic activity. Stanley recounts that about a thousand fish, each weighing between two and twenty kilos, were caught daily and that the Wagenias had significant stocks of smoked fish meant for sale. Trade was not restricted to foodstuffs but also included canoes, fishing nets, pottery, wooden utensils and metallic objects made by specialized craftsmen often belonging to specific ethnic groups like the Bamangas who were renowned makers of canoes and wooden furniture (Verhaegen 1992: 34).

Kisangani is the symbolic place where the conquest of Africa – by Arab invaders coming from the coast – was halted. The tomb of Tippo-Tip, an Arab chief shot by Lippens, a Belgian sergeant, as well as the graves of his porters, is still visible at the city gates.

It is in Kisangani that two thrusts for the colonization of Africa met: the first led by the Belgians and the other by the Arabs. But the first major foreign invasion was that of the Arabs, who attacked the town in 1875, followed and ousted by the Europeans, who settled there in 1883. The town has preserved vestiges from its dual past: the urban area today is dominated by Christianity and Islam as well as by Lingala and Swahili, two languages spoken concurrently and imported from the west. From an inhabitant's religion or spoken language, one can tell his origin and where exactly he lives in the town.

If the Arab and European invaders made Kisangani their headquarters, however, they were driven primarily by economic considerations. For the Arabs, the main consideration was the collection of ivory, and secondarily the capture of slaves to transport the ivory. But under the Europeans, exploitation became more systematic. Tippo-Tip, appointed governor by Stanley on behalf of the East India Company (EIC), tells of the plunder committed under this new domination (Verhaegen 1992: 212):

> They shipped ivory every month: sometimes, they could not even cart away the whole lot. The population of Stanley Falls increasingly became white and one could buy on the spot all that one needed. Stanley Falls grew into a big port, offering all that one desired. Belgian and French companies also set up business there and factories sprang up everywhere. Each steamship that arrived left with a full cargo-load of ivory.

With the ousting of Tippo-Tip in 1890, relations between the Europeans and the Arabs turned sour. Competition between them in the collection of ivory became fiercer and was to degenerate into open conflict in 1892. Following the final defeat of the Arabs and their capitulation to the Europeans, Kisangani and its hinterlands came under intense commercial activity for nearly twenty years – tons of ivory were collected, transported and resold; thousands of foreigners (soldiers, auxiliaries, porters) flocked to Kisangani and settled there in their hundreds; caravans of several hundreds and sometimes several thousand men scoured the region in search of ivory or to occupy it militarily. They needed to be fed, their goods had to be transported and articles of trade exchanged with them. Tippo-Tip recorded in his autobiography that he went to Stanley Falls in 1883 accompanied by 'three thousand men armed with guns and six thousand unarmed' and that, upon his arrival, he marshalled some twenty caravans each with several hundred men.

In 1891, EIC, the new occupying European power, proclaimed itself owner of all natural products found on state lands, especially ivory and rubber. This state of affairs deeply hurt the people of Kisangani and 'jeopardized the economic position of the town', as B. Jewsiewicki (1978: 4) affirms: 'The outcome of the anti-Arab campaign favoured EIC and jeopardized the economic position of the town.[...] The economy of the hinterlands of Stanley Falls was doomed to stagnation by the concessionaire system and by the provision of service in kind which replaced the Swahili trade and led to a return to local self-subsistence.'

In 1897, Kisangani lost its position of economic capital of the Swahili zone and no longer served as transit point between Congo's Arabized east and its European west. It became the headquarters of the whole of Eastern

Congo, encompassing Katanga and Kivu, for some years until 1933. Yet Kisangani was no more than an underdeveloped administrative centre surrounded by some native Congolese villages. In 'According to the testimony of the age' by Jewsiewicki (1978: 10):

> The villages of the Arabs, Kisangani-Singitini, as well as those of the Wagenias and the Lokeles around the Falls appear prosperous. Yet, they remain strangers to the town and are not part of its monetary economy. Their trade with the town is limited to the exchange of foodstuffs against indigo got from soldiers. The Wagenias especially exchange fish against cloth brought by the administration or its workers.

A strategic site The economic clout wielded by Kisangani stems from two factors. First, its location in a marshy and tropical rainforest region blesses it with abundant natural resources,[2] with geography playing an important role in the exploitation of these resources. Furthermore, its position at the freight breakpoint on the watercourse makes Kisangani the point where communications and goods trans-shipment operations were controlled. From Kisangani to Kinshasa, the Congo is navigable over a distance of 1,720 kilometres. Moreover, from Kisangani a pattern of strategic earth roads fans out: one leading northwards up to Sudan and Uganda (approximately 1,000 kilometres); the other leading south eastwards up to Goma and Bukavu or Maniema, which is the junction with the industrial province of Katanga and the diamond-producing province of Kasai. In this respect, Kisangani is an essential link with the outside when it comes to mining, which makes it much-coveted territory.

Laurent Kabila came to power in May 1997 with the backing of Rwandan and Ugandan troops who, as compensation for their support, demanded control of the town of Kisangani from the Congolese authorities. Braeckman writes (2003: 24):

> for the Ugandans, the town is the key to the equatorial forest and its huge timber resources. Its location in the middle of the forest is ideal as it also represents the last lap before the plunge down to the Equator, and beyond that, toward the river basin to the Atlantic. [...] After the fall of Mobutu, one of the first projects President Museveni undertook [...] was to build a road and railway linking Kisangani to Kampala – an open artery through which could flow the lifeblood of the forest and the earth's resources. Coupled with this regional project to tap the Congolese wealth, the Eritreans were already operating several tens of trucks to link up East Africa to Kisangani.

The Rwandans put forward nearly the same arguments:

Major N'Dahiro, Director of President Kagame's cabinet, had explained to me at great length (in 2000) that for Kigali, the stakes in Kisangani are both strategic and symbolic: 'it is the third town in the country and its real political capital. Located at the bend in the river, it controls Africa's largest river basin. During the first Congolese war which brought Kabila to power in May 1997, our troops were the ones who conquered the town and shed their blood for it. The town is ours.' (ibid.: 21)

The fact is that both Rwandans and Ugandans still remembered the ancient nineteenth-century caravan routes leaving Kisangani. For, in addition to the local exchanges mentioned earlier between the river people and the forest dwellers, the lines of communication made it possible to establish medium-range contact and exchanges either through the River Congo and its main tributaries or through paths linking Kisangani with the Ueles in the north, the Ituris to the east and Opala in the south. These paths were created neither by the Arabs nor the Europeans. They existed before their arrival and are therefore ample proof that trade existed over medium distances. The conquerors did no more than intensify and diversify trade. There were ivory, slaves, arms, supplies for field troops as well as foodstuffs and handicraft products. Distances widened and long-distance trade came into being. Zanzibar and the east coast for Arabs, Kinshasa and the western ports for Europeans became centres of trade to and partially from Europe and Asia.

Colonial accounts in the mid-1930s describe Kisangani as 'the most picturesque and most important town in [Belgian] Congo': 'Avenues more beautiful than those of many European towns, lined and overhung by exquisite trees, well situated buildings surrounded by trees in bloom, well constructed residential and commercial buildings make the town very seductive. Upstream from the town are found the famous Stanley Falls' (Morinot 2001: 41).[3]

During the colonial period, the urban structure of Kisangani comprised a commercial centre and residential districts for Europeans (Belgians, Portuguese) and Asians, separated from the all-black 'indigenous camps' by green strips, schools, military barracks or playgrounds. It was in January 1959 that the official status of town was conferred on it by the Belgian colonial authority.[4] The name Stanleyville was still used in 1966, until President Mobutu changed it to Kisangani in 1970, decreeing it the headquarters of the third economic centre of Congo/Zaire, after Kinshasa and Lubumbashi. The primness and attractiveness of the town also lent it the name 'Singa Mwambe', the town with 'eight strings' to reflect its manifold charms. In the Congolese consciousness, Kisangani passed for the town of fun and jollity or 'city of free women' (Verhaegen 1990), as designated by its local pseudonym 'Boyoma'.

All has gone bust in Kisangani

In three decades, the population of Kisangani declined steadily compared with that of other Congolese towns. Whereas Kinshasa and Lubumbashi remained first and second respectively, Kisangani receded to third position in 1970, then fourth in 1984 and fifth in 1994, coming after Kolwezi, an industrial town in Katanga Province. The same was true of Kananga, another Congolese town which dropped to fifth position in 1970 and 1984 and sixth position in 1994, overtaken by Bukavu. Had this trend continued (growth in Mbuji-Mayi outpaced that in Lubumbashi), Mbuji-Mayi would now be the second largest city, well behind Kinshasa where population growth remains very high.

Kisangani had 309,971 inhabitants in 1973.[5] The active population was 37 per cent for men, 0.4 per cent for women, whereas at the global urban level, it was barely 17 per cent. In 1956, the Port of Kisangani had fourteen cranes, but only seven remained in 1975, and the eighty-four items of port-handling equipment had dropped to 72 within the same period. While the number of fork lifts and tugs, the warehouse area and wharf length remained constant, the number of pallets dropped more than threefold from 2,050 to 848. The same steady decline was observed in the transported tonnage: from 169,292 in 1954, it rose to 203,010 in 1956, and then fell to 134,607 in 1973 and 99,414 in 1975.

In 1975, Kisangani had only 14.4km of tarred roads. Most of its roads were earth roads seriously degraded by the abundant rainfall that characterizes this equatorial region. In the same year, 7,472 vehicles plied its

TABLE 4.1 The first five cities of Congo according to urban population

Towns	Posit. 1970	Pop. 1970	Posit. 1984	Pop. 1984	Posit. 1994	Pop. 1994
Kinshasa	1	1,142,761	1	2,664,309	1	4,655,313
Lubumbashi	2	318,000	2	564,830	2	851,381
Kisangani	3	216,526	4	317,581	5	417,517
Mbuji-Mayi	4	204,923	3	486,235	3	806,475
Kananga	5	203,398	5	298,693	6	393,030

Source: Association pour le Développement de l'Information Environnementale (ADIE) country report 2003: 17.

roads against 3,768 in 1969. The number of wholesale shops increased from eighteen in 1970 to thirty-six in 1974 while retail shops climbed from 129 to 135 over the same period. Small retail stores and workshops were a dominant feature in the teeming neighbourhoods of the town.

Following President Mobutu's decision (1973/74) to nationalize businesses owned by foreigners, Congo/Zaire plunged into a long crisis that was economic at the outset, but subsequently developed interminable political ramifications. But it was in the mid-1980s that Kisangani took its last drastic dive down the abyss with galloping urban unemployment: while the town had 21,834 wage-earners in 1952, 21,873 in 1959, 23,820 in 1972, 18,835 in 1973 and 19,500 in 1982, its population increased almost tenfold between 1952 and 1982 (Regional Council annual report, 1989).

In 1989, several Kisangani-based companies had no other option than to shut down. This was the case with Solbena, Alipost (a postal supply company), Innovation, Podimpex, the Mboliaka chain stores, the New-Pop Dancing Club, etc. A total of eighty-four business undertakings disappeared from the market. Others were to follow in 1990: Hassan et Frères and then Unibra. These were indeed the pillars of local capitalism.

The situation of the textiles giant, Société Textile de Kisangani (Kisangani Textile Corporation, Sotexki), the largest company in town, is a particular case in point. It did not leave town as other companies did, but by the late 1980s had joined the smart racket to fend off hardship by combining its production activities with trading which takes businessmen into the informal sector. Prior to this, foreign currency was earned through the sale of coffee; thereafter, textiles operators started selling diamonds and gold (or ivory), which were largely mined 'informally' on a small scale. This situation could not last for long, however, and its end was soon at hand. The story of this company resembles that of the town:

> Built slightly away from town, this huge factory amazes the visitor by its sheer size, its modern look, cleanliness and vast halls wherein slumber new machines meticulously serviced by workers clad in rags.
>
> Four hundred and fifty 'Picanol' jobs were brought in from Belgium and 36 'Suzers' from Switzerland. The corridors and manager's office were lined with carefully preserved photographs showing President Mobutu, at the summit of power at the time, surveying the newly completed factory with cane lifted high. The company's objective at the time was to absorb the entire cotton production of Lower Uele and Ituri, regions in the vicinity of Kisangani, and to make it possible to clothe the populations of Eastern Congo, while 'Utexafric', another company based in Kinshasa, would cater for Western Congo.

This goal was achievable since locally produced cotton was abundant and the factory sometimes processed up to 9 tons of cotton a day. At the outset, 'Sotexki' employed 1,200 workers and the number was expected to increase to 2,500. Buyers too were available. Peasant farmers brought in rice and palm oil from Kisangani by river and could obtain a new cotton fabric for two bags of rice. (Braeckman 2003: 25–6)

In 2001, the manpower of this factory dropped to fewer than 100 workers, half of whom were sentries assigned to guard vacant houses whose occupants had been laid off. The situation was as serious for the other major corporations of the town. The brewery company Bralima, which had close to 1,000 workers in 1990, now operated with 150 agents[6] and at 4 per cent of its capacity, corresponding to 1,250 man hours per day instead of 35,000. Two persons instead of twenty-five now made Penaco paint (Solidaire 1999). The soap-making factory Sorgerie could no longer sell a quarter of its production because, lacking money, people themselves engaged in the small-scale manufacture of soap which, though poor in quality, was certainly cheap.[7] The river port (fourth in the country) was completely destroyed, while the railway had no locomotive in good working order. Of the three turbines on the Tshoppo dam that supplies electricity to the town, only one remained in operation.

Yet, for all that, Kisangani is not dead but continues to live on despite its really disturbing situation. It has its share of petty thieves and street children as well as its 'successful guys' or 'young nouveaux riches'. It is also claimed, locally and elsewhere in Congo, that the town is a huge factory that churns out false rumour. Here too, stubbornly using the practical intelligence of piecing together gossip, tit-bits and snatches of conversation obtained from chance meetings, people 'spin tales' referred to as '*kosala boules*' by putting two and two together and setting their imaginations to work. So, laughter is still very much present in Kisangani, but one gets the impression that roles are consciously reversed: rather than be a laughing stock, people make fun of others, even though they eventually reap the fruits of their temerity. Yet they run the risk of gliding gradually into this status of half-madness generally conferred on village wags and which enables them to get by in their environment. Kisangani is striving to set itself right, emulating its small retailers who, lacking means to purchase a stall, join larger retailers who own one. Maybe Kisangani will make it tomorrow; but when we look today at this town, whose plight is akin to that of its latest variety of sellers – its water sellers – nostalgia brings tears to one's eyes.

This means that although Congolese towns have many points in common, they do not all have the same chance to endure within this continually disheartening context of the country's bankruptcy. Already, under Mobutu, a large chunk of the national territory had escaped the control of state services; this situation worsened after the rebellions and wars in the era of Kabila father and son. Thus, although the 'Boyomians' (inhabitants of Kisangani) dream of the lifestyle of Kinshasa or the resourcefulness of the traders *'demulu vantards'* (a slang terms for Congolese of Luba ethnic origin) of Kasai, their dreams are frustrated by the lack of business opportunities. Here, the real sluggers, the *'tout sauté'* and *'boulonneurs'*, as they are called, sweat it out for paltry results and the bold and adventurous return *'nyanyo'*, that is, 'empty-handed'. And as a Congolese saying goes, 'When you reach the bottom of the well, you can dig no more'.

Diamonds only make matters worse for the town

Kisangani is poor, yet it has rich diamond deposits, the first discovered in 1986. There is a widely held opinion that during the tarring of a road financed by the Germans and the World Bank, a diamond was unearthed by one of the civil engineering machines. From then on, many persons hitherto engaged in the ivory and coffee trade made a rush for diamonds. In 1996, there were close to 300 diamond and gold quarries around the town. A quarry is a point of mineral deposit which reverts to whoever claims to be its owner. Those who go there to dig for diamonds pass for his subjects and pay taxes levied by the 'new lord', giving hardly anything to the government (Omasombo 2001: 79–126).

The newfound diamonds of Kisangani were as easily accessible as ivory had formerly been. They thus attracted foreign buyers from West Africa (Malians, Senegalese, Guineans),[8] but mostly Lebanese as well as Congolese from other provinces of the country. For instance, thirty-six of the forty-three counters established in Kisangani in March 1994 were operated by Lebanese. These counters were offices opened to buy, from individual diggers, the stones they found and wanted to sell for cash.

The democratic transition of April 1990 ushered in a period of political openness in Zaire that in 1991 led to the transfer of the administration of Kisangani into the hands of the natives of the region. This gave the opportunity to some Kisangani officials to deal squarely with the issue of foreigners, the reason for whose presence in the region – considered as the prime cause of the decline of the town and the entire province – had been essentially to engage in the diamond trade. Lebanese and primarily natives of Kasai were singled out. But, as the political authorities were in league with the local middle class, which itself was administrative and political in origin, they had difficulties turning the situation to their own

105

advantage. Thus, the Bangelemas, a tribe on whose land many quarries had been established, were intolerant of the other natives of Kisangani, called by the generic term Abungodi which, in the Kingelema language, means stranger.

This was because the political situation that prevailed during and especially after the 1980s was indicative of the demise of the state of Zaire.

The various measures taken by the Mobutu regime in 1981 and 1982 to liberalize trade in gemstones could not adequately hide the cracks in the country's political/administrative power edifice, gutted by corruption and disorder. These measures tended to reinforce rather than obliterate the predominant patronage system, completely erasing government control over whole portions of the national territory and groups of people. In this sense, the state truly became, to quote Ilunga (1999: 410–31), the 'Zairian bog'.

The diamond economy of the Kisangani region created a climate of anarchy: every decision taken by the authorities was accompanied by a strategy to misappropriate and embezzle resources. With the discovery of diamonds in Kisangani, the town witnessed a massive seasonal influx of people heading for the quarries. Mining provided jobs for the majority of the local workforce, involving people from all walks of life – civil servants, laid-off corporate workers, small independent workers, nurses, pastors, soldiers, athletes, etc. Everyone rushed to the quarries and took up jobs as diggers, traders, porters, traffickers, commissioners and guards. At first sight, it looked as if initial capital was a decisive factor in shaping each individual's performance in business. This is not so in practice, however, as there are no holds barred: what counts is each individual's resourcefulness and abilities. Moreover, during the same year, one can move from one quarry to another and switch activities. The protagonists themselves say it all: 'One must try one's luck everywhere'.

The town earns virtually nothing from the diamond business. Once mined, the bulk of the gemstones gathered are stealthily whisked away and quickly sold to independent diggers or middlemen. During the first quarter of 1994, for instance, diamonds weighing 1,123,950.37 carats, worth an estimated US$13,021,402.15, were bought by the counters in Kisangani. All these counters put together employ no more than 200 workers. Their offices are actually rooms leased in private homes for paltry sums, since living standards are particularly low in the area. As office equipment, they have just a calculator, a scale balance for weighing diamonds, a valuation book and a magnifying glass for detecting defects (cracks, pitting, etc.) and scrutinizing colour.[9]

Before the war, taxes were paid in Kinshasa to facilitate the repatriation of hard currency via the National Bank. Expatriate residence permits were sold in Kinshasa, and the town received no share of the proceeds. Furthermore, sundry approval fees for purchase counters ($US150,000), advance annual royalties ($US100,000) and the 15 per cent export tax in US dollars were all paid in Kinshasa.[10] And in cases when, as in 1995, Kisangani was authorized to sell merchant cards, the sharing of proceeds was far from being equal. A digger's card cost $US50, while a merchant's cost $US100. Eighty per cent of this revenue had to be transferred to the National Treasury in Kinshasa, while the town and the entire province were left with the remaining 20 per cent.

When the Rwandans and Ugandans won back parts of eastern Congo in August 1998, after the second war fought while Laurent Kabila was in power, attention was immediately focused on Kisangani's diamonds:

> Officially, Rwandans and Ugandans claimed that if they intervened twice in neighbouring Congo, it was to guarantee their own security and to track down their enemies beyond their borders. This was for a long time their official position. It took the Kisangani wars to unmask the true reason for such violence: Rwanda had this longstanding dream [...] of acquiring a vast hinterland on Congolese territory where it could settle its surplus population, and Kisangani was the ideal natural frontier.
>
> However, beyond geographical considerations, there were other compelling reasons: Kisangani had also become a new Eldorado. Indeed, it is here that towards the mid-80s diamond mines richer and more promising than those of Kasai in the south of the country had been discovered. Although the town had become a quagmire in the last years of Mobutu's reign, it nevertheless experienced significant economic growth. The number of purchase counters, owned mostly by Lebanese, had multiplied. But shortly before the war of June 2000, the biggest of these diamond houses were placed under the control of Ugandan generals, especially Generals Kazini and Salim Saleh, President Museveni's stepbrother. (Braeckman 2003: 23–5)

The reason why Rwanda, backed by its local allies, fought so hard to win back Kisangani was that it also wanted to regain control over the diamond houses, whose turnover ran into several million US dollars a month. The war raged on among the plunderers in Kisangani, who were at each other's throats over sharing the booty. But Braeckman saw the siege of the town solely as a mean war pitting rival armies against each other.

In actual fact, since the beginning of the first Congolese war in 1996, the Rwandans and Ugandans, jointly at first and then separately, struggled to bring Kisangani to its knees and to again make it willy nilly part of the global trade, but on their own terms. [...] the town's new masters brutally shoved it back to its place: what mattered to them was timber, diamonds and the river. The inhabitants either had to give in ... or be eliminated.

The social organization of the town was thus dealt a serious blow. The new form of domination now in place was rooted in unchecked and wanton mining, which plunged the town into disarray, at the expense of its middle class, composed mostly of civil servants, petty traders and the like. These civil servants had lost their incomes to wage cuts or unpaid salaries, and so could not help sustain petty trade activities. Thus, earning a daily livelihood became a nagging concern for a growing number of Kisangani's inhabitants. The local bourgeoisie had fled from the unrest and settled in Kinshasa or abroad, from where they could bargain with greater leverage for positions of authority.

The local inhabitants therefore had to rely on the middle class to keep their businesses afloat. The current situation has disrupted social relations. For some years now, it has been virtually impossible to leave the outlying neighbourhoods of Mangobo (from where diamond diggers had left in droves), Kabondo or Lubunga hoping to get help from a relative living in Makiso, a central neighbourhood. As a result, people now look to the diamond diggers returning home from the mines to sell their diamonds to dealers. But once home, these diggers often prefer to take up rooms in the many small hotels in town, where they can indulge in sex, and spend lavishly on clothes and alcohol – pleasures usually denied them due to the poverty of their families.[11] They see Kisangani as a place where they can get entertainment using their small fortunes earned from diamonds and forget the hardship of working in the mines. Once the money is spent, they return to the forest.

A Belgian Jesuit priest Reverend Fa Guy Verhaegen, parish priest of the teeming Matete neighbourhood in the Mangobo *commune*, indicates that, in his parish, diamond diggers very often return from the mines with very little money (Misser and Vallée 1997: 156). 'Occasionally, they come home after making a good deal. But often, they come, stay for three to four months and leave again after spending all their money. Not that they make any extravagant spending; they simply help their families and pay their children's school fees and then leave. There are some tens of thousands of people like that, mostly youths.'

Kisangani can no longer hold back its inhabitants: money and jobs now flow from the forest and its newly discovered diamond mines. Traders are similarly affected and prefer the mines to the city because prices are more attractive and sales much quicker. A study on the quantity of small game (bush meat) sold at the Kisangani market, covering a standard five-month period per year, revealed that sales fell sharply, by 70 to 75 per cent, over a period of sixteen years, from 23,115 units in 1981 to 7,075 units in 1989, and stood at barely 5,662 units in 1997. The authors of this study conclude that supply to the city dropped due to 'the rural bush-meat markets that recently sprang up [...] thanks to mining activities'. They comment: 'the fact that consumers moved closer to the source of supply of bush meat helped in opening new centres in the forest for the consumption of the meat of wild mammal species and probably in increasing the rate of hunting' (Belembo et al. 2001).

Resourcefulness of the poor

Increasingly, Kisangani is entangled in menial jobs that blur prospects for the future. People get into these jobs more out of obligation than by choice. Their newfound stability is fragile, however; they tell themselves, 'such jobs won't take us anywhere'. But then, they get more entangled in this stifling situation, just to maintain a semblance of happiness. Compared to Kinshasa or Lumumbashi, the margin of resourcefulness in Kisangani is narrower and the choice of what to do harder. Allowing oneself to be fooled is part of the survival mechanism. This is also true elsewhere, but here, it is said: 'what one needs is God's grace to succeed in liking what one has' or better still 'a beggar has no choice'.

As there are very few cars in Kisangani nowadays, the principal means of transport are bicycles, carts, home-made canoes, and of course trekking. People generally use firewood and charcoal for fuel while the staple foods are *chikwange* (manioc paste cooked in leaves), vegetable, cassava, caterpillars, bananas, etc. In other words, they depend more on the wild forest products in their environment than on the capitalist economy for subsistence.

Compared with Kinshasa, Kisangani looks like a village – or *'mboka'* in Lingala, the language spoken in Kinshasa, which has imposed itself on the rest of the country and the Congolese identity worldwide. The Kinois (inhabitants of Kinshasa) look on other Congolese as *'mbokatier'*, *'mowuta'* (Lingala slang) or *'Kisimamba'* (Swahili) – words used to denote (mockingly) the new *'Kinois'* who still lacks the necessary *'mayele'* (street skills) to become an integral part of the Congolese capital. While these different words depict a manifestation of social mobility, they can also be used to denote the shrinking of real urban spaces, affecting even vital spaces. A *Kinois* could have told a resident of Kisangani: 'I cannot understand how people can be happy here.' What is more, many operators, doctors and traders tried very hard in the 1990s to leave the city, preferably for Kinshasa.

For example, close to half the teaching staff of the University of Kisangani left during this period. In 1991, when the already acute economic crisis had not yet attained its current magnitude, we conducted a study of what was then known as 'the petty trade economy'. The study revealed that petty trade was not really part of the capitalist economy, but was developing as a response to poverty and scarcity (Omasombo 1992: 30–1):

> Relations between the capitalist economy and the petty trade economy in Kisangani are characterized by the relative independence of the former from the latter. There are extremely few cases of sub-contracting in this sub-sector. Similarly, capitalist businesses depend very little on the petty trade economy for their raw materials. However, the activities of the petty trade economy are mostly concerned with the marketing (or recycling) of producer goods imported by capitalist firms; often, they also depend on these firms for their raw materials and equipment.

> Thus, a crisis in the capitalist economy will negatively affect the most 'modern' and most productive sectors of the petty trade economy.

> The nature of relations between the two economies should be ana-lysed from the point of view of the functioning of the economic system as a whole. Peripheral capitalism (characterized by dependence and an outward-looking orientation) is capitalism that operates within the purview of an economy of scarcity (see works by Verhaegen). The petty trade economy therefore develops as a response to this scarcity and/or as a means of capitalizing on it. Thus, unofficial fuel retailers, popularly known as 'Kadhafi', exploit (and help to cause) fuel shortages. Also, non-motorized means of transportation (carts, canoes, bicycles) profit from the decline in the use of automobiles and the deterioration of the roads infrastructure.

With neither force of arms nor money, the lower classes of Kisangani rely only on their physical strength to cut out a vital space for themselves. People 'cover long distances on foot with goods on their back or on hand-pushed carts. They come on foot with livestock from as far as Ikela, situated some 350 km from Kisangani' (Maindo 2001: 54).

In Kisangani, the phrases *'Kobeta libanga'* (breaking stones), *'kobeta coop'* (entering into co-operation), which reflect the Congolese people's daily ingenuities as they struggle for a livelihood, have been replaced by more appropriate words like *'choquer'*. The latter comes from the Swahili word *'shoka'* which means axe, a farmer's tool. *'Choquer'* (pronounced *shokay*) therefore means 'struggling for a livelihood', and the struggling person is referred to as *'choqueur'*. In terms of activity, it means 'to sell just anything in order to earn some money to buy food and clothes, to pay children's school fees and to pay for healthcare, etc.'. As can be seen, life is reduced to the bare minimum.

True, various petty trades are gaining a foothold in Kisangani: *'Kadhafi'* (unofficial retailing of fuel), *'Quado'* (patching of tyres), 'mobile cold water vendors', shoe shiners, bicycle or umbrella repairers, etc. Tyre repairers, however, most of whom are retired soldiers or children of soldiers living in barracks, have almost no automobile tyres to patch. They resort to patching bicycle tyres (which is less profitable) and the motorcycle tyres of diamond miners.

In the eyes of the inhabitants of Kisangani today, a motorcycle, especially a Japanese-made Yamaha 100, is a symbol of social success. But, let us look more closely at transport by bicycle, which is fast replacing the cart and becoming the popular means of transportation in the town.

The bicycle is the means of transport most used within the town and between the town and the hinterland. It is used for transporting both people and goods. From the mid-1990s, many people in Kisangani purchased bicycles for use as taxis, locally referred to as *'toleka'*. These include military officers, senior state employees, and ordinary as well as near-bankrupt traders. In short, people from all walks of life with some resources saw this as an avenue for supplementing their incomes or for survival. For example in 1994, the provincial governor owned close to 200 bicycles, managed by a member of his family.

As of 1993 the use of *tolekas* became widespread in Kisangani. But this in no way means that before this date bicycles were never used for transporting people and foodstuffs in the town. The novelty was that people sitting on bicycle carriages were transported for a fee, as in a bus or a taxi.

'Tolekists' were an indicator of economic crisis. A study conducted in 1996 on 111 carriers[12] revealed that a hundred of them were aged between eighteen and forty, while just one was less than eighteen years old. For fifty-seven of them, the *toleka* was their main activity. Thirty-three of them lived exclusively on this activity, while twenty-four combined the *toleka* with other minor activities. Those who operated the *toleka* as a secondary activity were students (twenty-seven), corporate workers, soldiers, state employees, farmers and sometimes, to a greater extent, teachers. Forty-five lived in the Kabondo locality, twenty-eight in Mangobo, sixteen in Tshopo, six in the Kisangani municipality and two in Lubunga. The entire administrative town of Kisangani was therefore covered. The reason why Makiso, called 'the colonial town', had a high representation was because it was inhabited by many youths from the families of soldiers quartered in the military barracks. This neighbourhood was inhabited not only by the children of the 'enlightened' families from the colonial period, but also

111

by those who in 1973 'had acquired the nationalized Zairian wealth' (and were residing in the now dilapidated houses left by the former colonialists), as well as by those who had built small houses on the green spaces and sewers of the old town. On the other hand, the low representation of the Kisangani and Lubunga municipalities, the poorest in the town, can be explained by the fact that they were made up mainly of people from the Wagenia and the Mbole tribes, who still lived on the fringes of urban life, as they survived mainly on agriculture and fishing (*Référence Plus* 1993). They thought buying a bicycle was a great luxury.

This means of transport became so successful and popular that whenever the provincial governor returned home from a visit outside Kisangani, he would rally '*toleka*' riders to escort him from the airport, situated some 17 kilometres from the city centre, right to his residence.

Another indicator of the crisis in Kisangani is the assembly of '*toleka*' bicycles, an exercise generally consisting of assembling bicycle parts of diverse origins. A number of open-air assembly workshops, usually built on family land, can be seen in the town. The part that is most sought-after is the frame, made of pieces of welded pipes or obtained from old rundown bicycles. Some operators believe that bicycles bought from shops are less durable, and cannot carry as much load because of their weak frames.

People scour the Kisangani region to buy old broken-down bicycles from villagers. Those with more means extend their operations to West Africa and even Asia (Dubai and Taiwan). Assembling bicycles locally involves 'chain' work. While some of the manufacturers straighten bent or recycled parts, others gather them in preparation for mounting, and yet others apply a splash of paint on the assembled lot. All the myriads of petty jobs in the town (shoe repairs, maintenance of household appliances, manufacture of aluminium pots, joinery, auto mechanics, etc.) have as raw materials recycled goods – 'ecumenical equipment' as they are called in Kisangani, an allusion to the current religious trend of ecumenism.

In 1999, Kisangani had close to 2000 '*tolekists*' (*toleka* riders), who had formed a trade union[13] and held real meetings. '*Tolekas*' have certain distinctive features: their carriages are fitted with a small rubber cushion and are dressed beautifully with a well-knit cover. They sport such nicknames as Albatros, Pajero serpent, Tout terrain, Chien merchant, Maffia boy, Maison gorille, etc., ornamentally painted on the cover stickers and mudguards. Some bikes are decorated with small bulbs and are equipped with hooters that sound like mobile phones.

Meanwhile, as the following account amply demonstrates, the general standard of living had fallen so low that even a university lecturer was forced to swallow his pride and in all humility board a *toleka*.

K.N. is a university lecturer in Kisangani. He is nearing retirement and his physical health is becoming increasingly fragile. He has been living in Kisangani since 1972. He did his studies at the University of Kinshasa and claims that he was better off at the time than now despite his current title of professor. He said, 'I was fooled by my country: I was told as a student that life will be better as I moved up the academic ladder.'

While he was assistant lecturer in 1974, K.N. bought a VW car on credit. 'I had become a full man, with a wife and three children at the time and we were living well. The children rode to school in a car.'

In 1976, K.N. obtained a scholarship to study in Belgium. On his return in 1981 five years later, he brought back a car and some household appliances. The university lodged him in a comfortable apartment, a vestige of the colonial period. But, a few years later, K.N. could no longer maintain the same standard of living. His salary had shrunk ridiculously and he could not cope with the many breakdowns of his car. So, K.N. sold it to a 'repairer'[14] who paid him an agreed little sum at regular intervals while using the car. He used the money thus collected to open a small shop (known as Ligablot) in front of his compound. University students were his main customers. Their favourite items were washing soap and foodstuffs (sugar, rice, corn), sold in a cup called masibu.[15] K.N's wife sold in the store in the day and, after school in the evening, his children took over from her. However, this very low-income activity could hardly supply the household needs it had become the sole supplier of. Thus, the shop wound up rapidly.

A new opportunity came K.N's way again.

In 1990, President Mobutu offered cars to university lecturers based on their grades. Since K.N. was a professor, he was offered a Mitsubishi Galant. However, the car could not be collected from Kinshasa because K.N. lacked money for his air ticket to Kinshasa. The opportunity was too good to miss. K.N. thus decided to take a loan, planning to immediately resell the car for a profit and repay his debt, while keeping the profit for himself.

In Kinshasa, he immediately found a Lebanese buyer. However, there were too many problems waiting to be solved. He bought a small house in the Masina municipality in Kinshasa and a few dresses for his family and himself. With the balance, he could now return to Kisangani, repay his debts and eat for a few days. His extended family (uncles, sisters) were also expecting their share. Although K.N. no longer had money for them, he accepted to lodge some family members in his house in Kinshasa. 'I was harassed by my sister and her children who were expecting some financial assistance from me. I succeeded in escaping to Kisangani by air, without their knowledge.'

K.N. lectures in many of the university's faculties spread across the city. At one time, he was to travel close to five km from his home. It will be recalled that, as part of a new general supplies service in 1988, the government had bought three mini-buses to transport lecturers. These however suffered frequent breakdowns due to lack of maintenance and were replaced two years later by a *fula-fula*[16] lorry. Lecturers nicknamed this vehicle 'the Hearse' because it looked like those lorries usually used in transporting corpses (the only difference: it is painted white and not black). The lecturers felt that boarding a vehicle that offered no comfort, actually robbed them of the last remnants of their dignity. In 1991, no more vehicles were available for the transportation of university staff, because the upheavals that followed the introduction of democracy had taken their toll on what was left of state property.

The times were still very hard for K.N. Not only had the purchasing power of salaries plummeted, but salaries were not paid regularly. The only way out for him was to give lectures in the new private and State institutions, run with funds collected from students. However, his age and manifold responsibilities weighed down on K.N.: he soon tired of trekking to these different places, to deliver his lectures.

'I finally accepted to take the *toleka*,' declared K.N. nodding. How did he feel the first time? Sighing, he replied, 'When taking the *toleka* became fashionable in 1993, I refused to follow the trend. I felt it was humiliating and managed to resist for two years. However, I saw my friends one after another (people with whom I shared ideas) being transported on them. One day, on leaving my house without food, and feeling very weak, I finally overcame my reticence. I hailed a passing *toleka* and jumped onto it. Initially, I felt hurt when students stared at me. I looked down to give the impression I saw nothing and asked the rider to go faster because I was late. On arrival at the science faculty, students who were waiting in front of the hall made loud noises which I took as encouragement. I raised my right hand and they seemed to have accepted the day's gesture. I then continued to use the *toleka*, which is easy to find and especially cheaper than the other means of transport.'

K.N. says that acceptance of the *toleka* as a means of transport is a true reflection of the real state of the university, the town and even the country. 'Several of my younger colleagues are scandalized to see me on a *toleka*. I find their position unfair, but I forgive and try to understand them. However, what saddens me is the fact that they do not understand me. I have nothing to look forward to in life and have the feeling that I am living my last days on earth. In my present frame of mind, to refuse to take the *toleka* without finding an alternative would amount to not going to teach and therefore no more food on the table.'

K.N. recalls two sad memories with the *toleka*: 'I came crashing to the ground one day after my negligent *toleka* rider skidded on a stone. Thank God I came out in one piece and we fell in an area where there were few people. Two elderly on-looking ladies came to my assistance and pulled me up. Another day, I was riding on a bike after it had rained. On my arrival, my clothes were covered in mud splashed from the rear wheel of the bike. It was unfortunate indeed ... '

A Belgian priest in Kisangani said he used the *toleka* each time his motorcycle broke down; but he also became a general laughing stock as people would point at him, saying: '*mundele na toleka*' (a white man on a *toleka*). He once invited his native Congolese priest colleagues to his parish, situated in a neighbourhood some distance away from the city centre, rapidly accessible by *toleka*, but they failed to show up because they held the *toleka* in disdain. They would sometimes go as far as skipping mass on account of this prejudice. The only priest who took it firmly believed it brought dishonour on him.

The *toleka* does not seem to guarantee the livelihood of the rider. Given the context of abject poverty, however, some respondents expressed satisfaction with their work, while a good number said they were working to enrich the bike owners. Since they feel exploited, they cheat at will or even become temperamental with their bikes. They therefore strain every sinew to own their own bike.

The *toleka* profession wears out the rider physically: 'I am aged 32,' declared one rider in 1994. 'My bike transports in one trip, two large bags of charcoal for sale, one small one for my household, *pondu* (cassava leaves), cassava and firewood, weighing in all 232.5kg. On some days, I do up to three trips. This explains why my friends nicknamed me Machine.' Another adds:

It is six years now that I have been transporting foodstuffs by bike every day. I have added some 'improvements' to the carriage, reinforcing it with metal rods and sticks to make it stronger for heavier loads. I easily take on board two bags of charcoal and roll downhill even though I have no brakes. To brake, all I do is to jam the sole of my bare foot on the rear wheel and the effect is the same as having good brakes. Thus, buying brakes is an unnecessary expenditure. And what is more, brakes wear out tyres.

A third adds:

My name is Mbole and I have been residing in the Lubunga municipality for close to thirty years. I began this profession in 1968 when I was aged 13 in primary 4. The bicycle I used at the time belonged to my uncle, a

115

gendarme who brought me up after the death of my parents. When he too passed on later, his four young children became my responsibility. I myself have a wife and three children. Everyday, I bring back home cassava leaves, bags of charcoal and cassava that my wife sells in neighbouring markets. I struggle to ensure that my family eats and the children attend schools with affordable tuition fees. On weekends and public holidays, I take my whole family to the farm. However, I must admit that I have succeeded so far thanks to a fetish. Despite the strain involved in this work, I am still healthy. Most of my neighbours envy me for all that I have and they don't have. They try to harm me, but up to now, they have not succeeded.

Many *toleka* riders suffer from hernia, tuberculosis, sexual impotence and even age prematurely. Ninety-eight out of 111 respondents hope to leave the profession once they succeed in saving enough money to help them start another line of business. Among the people interviewed three years after the first survey, the hope of branching out, albeit without any clear alternative, is still alive. Many believe that they have failed in life. Consequently, they curse society, especially public officials, who are blamed for poor public management and are thus held responsible for their misery.

Conclusion

When the Zairian state collapsed during the Mobutu era, Kisangani was transformed into a town without a well-structured and buoyant economy. Tucked well inland, the town that is both alluring and fragile (on several counts) has also been the scene of many wars. In 1997, Roland Pourtier (1997: 7–30) observed: 'From Zaire to Congo: this territory is clearly in search of a State. Since the State machinery had been seriously weakened, administrative and military services were available mostly in towns and economically viable regions.'

The subject matter of this study was inspired by the collapse and/or crisis in Congo, a very striking illustration of which is the case of Kisangani. It brought to mind the disappearance of many African cities that used to be capitals of famous empires and kingdoms (Coquery-Vidrovitch 1993: 24–46). Kisangani came into the limelight thanks to the rise of Patrice Lumumba, who became the symbol of Zairian nationalism, or for the beauty of its girls. Many of the symbols of its glorious past are in ruins, with the town's landmarks fast disappearing.[17] Traces of modernism in Kisangani are being obliterated by the plunder of political and military officials and the different wars fought on its soil.

Perhaps the only timeless symbols of resistance that have not gone the way of the other landmarks, because they were at the origin of the town, are the Wagenia fishermen and the falls, situated at the entrance to Kisangani.

After more than a century of history, Kisangani has come full circle. It is now back to square one.

Notes

1 The most devastating events of the last few years have been: March 1997 – fighting between the troops of Mobutu's army and those of the Rwanda–Uganda coalition loyal to Kabila; September 1999 and June 2000 – fighting between Rwandan and Ugandan troops; May 2002 – combat pitting Rwandan troops fighting in the name of DRC against Congolese 'mutineers' backed by civilian protests. The decision taken by the United Nations in 2000 to make Kisangani a demilitarized zone has had very little concrete effect to date.

2 Kisangani is currently the headquarters of the Oriental Province, which is the largest province in Congo (503,239km²).

3 Since the mid-1960s called 'Wagenia Falls', from the name of the main tribe that inhabits the area and fishes in the river.

4 After Kinshasa (formerly called Leopoldville) and Lubumbashi (formerly called Elisabethville) in 1941, then Likasi (formerly called Jadothville) in 1943.

5 Figures given by the Kisangani municipal authorities.

6 Two-thirds are workers hired daily, and the bulk of these work as guards.

7 The brewery Bralima and soap-making company Sorgerie produce only intermittently, i.e. when they manufacture a stock of goods, they interrupt the production process pending sale of what has been produced.

8 In addition to new refugees, there was a body of Muslim Arabs who had not joined the conflict between Europeans and Arab leaders at the end of the nineteenth century. They had withdrawn in isolation into the Kisangani peninsula, where they have lived and remain to this day.

9 During the new war which began in August 1998, the new Rwandan occupying power rolled a few tractors into Kisangani to dig, sift the gravel and quickly mine certain fields reputedly rich in such diamonds seized from Pikoro. But production turned out to be nil and the local people attributed it to witchcraft.

10 Prior to the new war in 1998, the Minister of Mines, F. Kibassa, led a political/military delegation to Kisangani. He ordered the confiscation of all quarries from their owners, accusing them of spying for the enemy.

11 These diggers seem to have been conditioned to behave like the legendary Don Juan, in Camus (1942: 97). The digger, urged on by his 'insatiable appetite', is always looking for new conquests, with as much variety as possible. 'If he leaves a woman, it is not so much because he no longer wants her (for a beautiful woman will always remain desirable), but because his eye has caught another ...' Moreover, Josué de Castro believes that poor nutrition leads to increased sex drive and a net increase in fertility, pointing out that this could be explained by a complex mechanism in which psychological factors vie with physiological factors (De Castro 1952: 112–13).

12 Carried out by Nzeku Makhaba, a sociology student at the University of Kisangani.

13 'The Kisangani Bicycle Transporters' Association', otherwise known by the acronym ACT Kis.

14 A makeshift repairer with no formal training. They are referred to here as '*bricoleurs*'.

15 This is a plastic cup which Masibu, a Kisangani mayor, imposed as a unit of measurement on all rice and beans sellers. In Kinshasa, Dominique Sakombi, the then mayor, also imposed on sellers the same type of plastic cup (known later as *sakombi*).

16 This *Kinois* word means a type of public transport (usually in lorries) where passengers are often standing cramped in the vehicle. Unlike buses, *fula-fulas* carry bulky luggage, as well as packages of foodstuffs.

17 The spread of AIDS has jeopardized the business of 'prostitutes'; since 1992, there has been a significant rise in xenophobic sentiments among the indigenous population against the non-native population.

References

Belembo, M. et al. (2001) 'Évolution de l'exploitation du gibier mammalien à Kisangani (R.D. Congo) de 1976 à 1997', Kisangani: Laboratoire d'écologie et gestion des ressources animales, University of Kisangani (unpublished).

Braeckman, C. (2003) *Les nouveaux prédateurs. Politiques des puissances en Afrique centrale*, Paris: Fayard.

Camus, A. (1942) *Le mythe de Sisyphe*, Paris: Gallimard.

Conrad, J. (1899) *Heart of Darkness*.

Conseil régional de planification (1989) 'Diagnostic régional, Division régionale du Plan', October.

Coquery-Vidrovitch, C. (1993) 'Villes bantoues anciennes en Afrique Centrale', in T. J. Omasombo (ed.), *Le Zaïre à l'épreuve de l'histoire immédiate. Hommage à Benoît Verhaegen*, Paris: Karthala.

De Castro, J. (1952) *Géopolitique de la faim*, Paris: Les éditions Ouvrières.

Dossiers de l'ADIE (2003) *Organisation de l'espace et infrastructure urbaine en République Démocratique du Congo*.

Ilunga K. A. (1999) 'Le marécage ou le Zaïre des années 1990', *Revue Candienne des Études Africaines*, 33, 2–3.

Jewsiewicki, B. (1978) 'Histoire d'une ville coloniale: Kisangani 1877–1960', *Les Cahiers du Cédaf*, 5.

Maindo, A. M. N. (2001) *Voter en temps de guerre. Kisangani (R.D. Congo) 1997*, Paris: l'Harmattan.

Misser, F. and O. Vallée (1997) *Les gemmocraties – L'économie politique du diamant africain*, Paris: éd. Desclée de Brouwer.

Morinot, F. (2001) 'Les villes coloniales belges à travers l'illustration congolaise', in J. L. Vellut (ed.), *Itinéraires croisés de la modernité au Congo belge: 1920–1950*, Tervuren: Institut Africain-Cédaf and Paris: l'Harmattan.

Naipaul, V. S. (1982) *À la courbe du fleuve*, Paris: Albin Michel.

Omasombo, T. J. (1992) 'État, capitalisme et petite économie marchande', in G. Villers (ed.), *Économie populaire et phénomènes informels au Zaïre et en Afrique*, 2–3, Bruxelles: Institut Africain-Cedaf.

— (2001) 'Les diamants de Kisangani: De nouveaux seigneurs se taillent des fiefs sur le modèle de l'Etat zaïrois de Mobutu', in L. Monnier, B. Jewsiewicki and G. Villiers (eds), *Chasse au diamant au Congo/Zaïre*, Tervuren: Institut Africain-Cedaf and Paris: l'Harmattan.

Pourtier, R. (1997) 'Du Zaïre au Congo: un territoire en quête d'État', *Afrique contemporaine*, 183.

Référence Plus, La (1993) 'Les vélos font concurrence aux bus Sotraz et aux voitures-taxis', 6 November.

Solidaire, Le (1999) weekly published in Kisangani by the Provincial President of the Fédération des Entreprises du Congo, M. Mokeni, 27 November.

Verhaegen, B. (1990) 'Femmes Zaïroises de Kisangani. Combats pour la survie', *Enquêtes et documents d'histoire africaine*, 8.

— (1992) 'La petite économie marchande à Kisangani', *Économie populaire et phénomènes informels au Zaïre et en Afrique*, Les Cahiers du Cédaf, 3–4.

5 | The city centre: a shifting concept in the history of Addis Ababa

BAHRU ZEWDE

Historically, towns have grown around political, religious or commercial centres. The palace or castle, the church/cathedral or mosque, and the market have generally served as the nucleus for urban settlements that have ultimately produced some of the major cities known today. In more recent times, railway terminals have had the effect of serving as centres of bustling urban life. Yet as towns evolve into cities, they tend to assume a polycentric character. It is difficult to think of only one centre for a metropolis. Old centres diminish in importance and new ones emerge. Commercial and cultural centres tend to overshadow political and religious ones. Thus, the West End has come to overshadow the City in London and Times Square and Broadway likewise outshine Wall Street and its environs in New York.

Most cities of sub-Saharan Africa trace their origin to the colonial period. As such, they were influenced by the segregationist character of colonial urban policy. In effect, two towns have grown, one for the Europeans and another for the Africans. This pattern has become even more accentuated in situations where there is a sizeable white settler community. Ethiopia differs from this pattern in some significant ways. Urban development has been by and large autochthonous. Two exceptions in Ethiopia are the railway town of Dire Dawa in the east and the inland port of Gambella in the west. The former served for a long time as a sanatorium for the French community in Djibouti, who migrated in large numbers during summer to avoid the torrid climate of their colony. Eventually, they came to acquire a quarter of the town distinct from the area of Ethiopian settlement. In the case of Gambella, the British rulers of the Sudan converted the enclave they had acquired into a distinctive settlement opposite the Ethiopian village. In both cases, the two quarters were conveniently divided by a stream.

Addis Ababa falls into the pattern of autochthonous development referred to above. With the exception of the brief intervention of the Italians in the second half of the 1930s, its evolution had an internal dynamic. Brief though it was, however, the Italian occupation did leave behind some enduring features of the urban landscape. Nor is this to deny completely the pertinence of other external factors in the evolution of Addis Ababa.

As we will see in more detail below, railway and air transport have played an important role in shaping settlement patterns. The advent of the railway in 1917 was the single most important factor in the gradual and still perceptible southward shift of the city centre. This impact of the railway is consistent with its role in urban growth elsewhere in Africa. Indeed, cities like Nairobi owe their very genesis to the railway (Hanna and Hanna 1981: 20). Addis Ababa's two airports, constructed after the introduction of air transport into the country in 1946, have successively attracted settlement by the affluent classes of society. Ironic as it may sound, Ethiopians have invariably rushed to settle near airports, not run away from them.

Precursors

As an imperial capital, Addis Ababa has two illustrious predecessors: Aksum in ancient times (c. first to eighth century AD) and Gondar in the seventeenth and eighteenth centuries. Of the two, it is the latter that provides instructive parallels (and some important points of difference) with the evolution pattern of Addis Ababa. French travellers of the early nineteenth century were ecstatic about this once glorious city, dubbing it 'the Paris of Abyssinia' (Ferret and Gallinier 1847: 240). In his study of Gondar and other precursors of Addis Ababa, Donald Crummey made the following observation: 'Three major institutions shaped Ethiopian towns during our period: palace, market, and church. These institutions played three roles: political, economic and cultural. The institutions and roles intertwined' (Crummey 1987: 21). Indeed, one can say that Gondar had its genesis as a market town before it became a political and religious centre (Merid 1989: 61).

This fact constitutes the first major point of difference with the genesis of Addis Ababa. The site where Addis Ababa emerged had no commercial importance before the foundation of the town. The town of Rogge, an important staging point on the long-distance trade route from south-western Ethiopia to the Somali coast, lay some ten kilometres to the south east. On the other hand, like Gondar, Addis Ababa grew on the slopes of hills overlooking a panoramic expanse of plains leading to Lake Tana in the case of the former and the hills on the edge of the Rift Valley in the case of the latter. As two other French travellers observed: 'Gondar is built on a patchwork of isolated hills; it is a broken town. The town proper is located on the summit of a hill: on the slope and at the foot of the hill are found the different quarters' (Combes and Tamisier 1838: 341).

More importantly, Gondar, like Addis Ababa, grew around the political and religious centres, the famous castle complex and the renowned 'forty-four' churches respectively. Of the latter, the churches associated with the *abun*, the expatriate head of the Ethiopian Orthodox Church, and that of his Ethiopian subordinate (the *echage*) were of particular importance. The spontaneous and unplanned growth of Gondar is another feature it shares with Addis Ababa. To European eyes, Gondar presented a rather confused picture of 'an agglomeration of badly constructed houses, sprouting here and there without order and without plan. The routes of circulation were serpentine paths rather than roads in the strict sense of the word' (Ferret and Gallinier: 236).

Foundation and early years

Addis Ababa, which means 'New Flower' in Amharic, the lingua franca of Ethiopia, has had a life of just over a century. It was founded in 1886 by Empress Taytu, spouse of Emperor Menilek II (r. 1889–1913), who also gave the name to the new settlement. A major attraction of the site was the hot springs (Fel Weha) whose curative quality had invested them with special value to both royalty and nobility. The area was originally known by the onomatopoeic Oromo term, Finfine, expressive of the bubbling hot springs. Royalty and nobility had been shuttling there from their camps on the hills of Entotto to the north before they finally decided to move south for good. On the other hand, the move to the plains to the south was a natural outcome of the greater sense of security and confidence that Menilek and his entourage felt after they had subdued the surrounding population. Yet not all was plain ground in Addis Ababa. The hills that dotted the landscape became natural nuclei of settlement for the nobility, the highest hill being naturally appropriated by the emperor. It was on this latter hill, not very far from the hot springs, that the imperial palace, the *gebbi*, was constructed, forming the first major node of urban settlement.

But it took a while before the imperial couple and their entourage finally decided to settle on the new site. For some six years, they continued to shuttle between the hilly stronghold at Entotto and the new, more relaxed abode. Letters of Emperor Menilek continued to bear the name of Entotto as the place of writing. It was with the construction of a more permanent structure (a palace) that the shift to the new capital was sealed. That palace has endured up to the present time as the preferred seat of real power, despite attempts by Emperor Haile Selassie to shift it to two other, more sumptuous locations_– one to the north of Menilek's *gebbi* in 1934 and another to the south in 1955, the latter on the occasion of the Silver Jubilee of the emperor's coronation. Both the Darg and its strong man, Mangestu, and the current leader, Meles, have preferred to barricade themselves in the strategically commanding palace of Menilek rather than the more vulnerable palaces of Haile Selassie. Indeed, it is a clear illustration of the reality of power that the prime minister, who heads the government and exercises real power, prefers to reside in Menilek's palace whereas the president, who is essentially a mere figurehead, is considered sufficiently dispensable to be quartered in in Haile Selassie's Jubilee Palace, renamed the National Palace after the 1974 revolution that overthrew the emperor.

Although not to the same degree as in Gondar, the churches have served as foci of urban settlement, not to mention the fact that a number of neighbourhoods (*safar*) derive their names from them. Of the churches, the most important in the early years of Addis Ababa, though not the first to be established, was St George's Cathedral, located to the north west of the imperial *gebbi*. It arose on the site of a former Capuchin mission in an Oromo village called Birbirsa. The church attained particular prominence in the course of, and subsequent to, the Battle of Adwa (1 March 1896), when Ethiopian forces led by Emperor Menilek decisively defeated Italian troops and thereby guaranteed the independence of the country. The battle took place on the day of St George in the Ethiopian calendar and there was an apocryphal story that, at the height of the battle, St George was seen riding his famous white horse goading the Ethiopians on to final victory. The coronation of Emperor Haile Selassie in November 1930 in the same church and on the same day of the month enhanced even further the symbolic significance of the church. Appropriately enough, on the occasion of that coronation, an equestrian statue of Menilek came to be placed on the square facing the church.

The ultimate importance of the St George's area was not only as a religious centre, however. Soon, an important market grew up on the slope immediately to the south east of the church. It came to be known by the term Arada, so called according to a prevalent version because of the sloppy nature of the ground. The church is also commonly referred to as 'Arada Giyorgis' ('St George of Arada'). Foreign observers who visited the market in its early days were impressed by its vitality and diversity. A British traveller of the early twentieth century called it 'the commercial pulse of Abyssinia', adding: 'In the palpitating life and varied scenes of the market, one might see more of the people and their way of life in one morning than in a week's wandering about the capital' (Powel-Cotton 1902: 116, 168). This coupling of religious and commercial functions demonstrated by the St George neighbourhood was replicated only to a lesser degree in more recent times by the Qirqos church, located in the southern part of the city behind the railway station. Another church that came to have rival status with St George's as regards an important religious holiday is the Estifanos (St Stephen) church, located across the river from the Economic Commission for Africa (ECA). This church, characteristically built on top of a small hill, overlooks what in the pre-1974 period was known as Masqal ('Cross') Square, because it was there that the highly colourful ceremony commemorating the Finding of the True Cross by St Helena (mother of the Emperor Constantine) was held. In the revolutionary period (1974–91), the square was expanded and renamed Revolution Square and the Masqal ceremony was transferred back to St George's Square, where it was held in earlier years. But after the change of regime in 1991, the old Masqal Square has regained both its name and its functions. An additional factor for the growing importance of this square after the 1960s was that it became the entry point into the city of the main road from the international airport at Bole.

The *gebbi* and Arada were thus the two nodes around which Addis Ababa emerged in the early twentieth century. In the following pages, we shall examine how the centrality of these two points came to be challenged as the town expanded in all directions. For the sake of convenience, we shall divide our treatment of the subject into four distinct periods, more or less coinciding with the major chapters of the country's history in the twentieth century. These are: the period up to the fascist Italian invasion in 1935; the period of fascist occupation, 1936–41; the period from liberation to revolution, 1941–74; and the revolutionary period, 1974–91.

Developments up to 1935

The overall impression that the town gave to early visitors was one of 'a gigantic camp' (Gleichen 1898: 157). Over a half century, someone who had studied the evolution of the city from a more expert angle could also conclude with the following words: 'Addis Ababa was born around the royal tent of the Shawan king (i.e. Menilek, who hailed from the region by that name in south central Ethiopia), on a hill overlooking a thermal spring. The *gebbi* was created around the tent, and the camp around the *gebbi*' (Berlan 1963: 61). Yet a closer look would reveal that Addis Ababa in these early days was a collection of different camps rather than one camp. Much more apposite, therefore, is the summing up of another PhD study of the city: 'a settlement pattern clustered around a series of small nodes which are in turn clustered around larger main nodes; [...] a series of radiating paths and routes connecting these nodes as well as exterior areas; [...] the entire settlement [...] scattered in a series of clusters that were situated outward to a radius of well over one mile in every direction from the Palace' (Johnson 1974: 85).

Addis, in short, was in these early years a conglomeration of interspersed *safar*s. The term *safar*, meaning camp, has particular appositeness. For what were visible at the outset were a series of more or less self-contained camps. At the centre of them all was the royal camp, immediately surrounded not by settlements of the nobility but by the various servants and attendants of the palace. This gave rise to a situation that has not substantially changed to this day, namely that the imperial *gebbi* came to be surrounded by veritable slums, as the palace servants could not afford to erect imposing structures and their descendants have continued to live in those hovels. Yet these plebeian settlements were sufficiently important to give their names to a genre of *safar*, what we may call the occupational *safar*, each *safar* reflecting the specific function of the inhabitants in the imperial palace (workers, saddlers, guards, etc.).

This pattern was duplicated around the other hills or elevated areas of the city, as various members of the nobility erected their dwellings on top of them and these in turn came to be surrounded by the much more modest habitations of their dependants. Understandably, as we have seen in the case of the churches, these various 'camps' gave rise to another distinctive genre of *safar*, called after the name of the particular member of nobility whose dwelling served as nucleus (e.g. Ras Tasamma Safar, Ras Berru Safar, Fitawrari Habta-Giyorgis Safar, etc.). A third genre of *safar* – the community *safar* – evolved corresponding with groups who came and settled from different parts of the country, such as Gojjam Safar, Gondar Safar, Gejja Safar, Dorze Safar (Bahru 1987: 46–7).

It is possible to identify certain landmarks that gave this rather fluid original settlement a more permanent shape and character. The first, around 1902/1903, was the importation of eucalyptus trees from Australia. This development was of double significance. First, it gave the city its distinctive foliage. Early travellers commented on the scent of the tree that beckoned them as they approached the city. To this day, Addis Ababa remains a eucalyptus city. More importantly, the importation saved it from the fate of so many other capitals in the Ethiopian past that had to be abandoned as the perennial quest for wood forced a shift to another centre. A culture that was voraciously keen on deforestation but not particularly adept at reforestation could think only of moving on when forest resources were depleted. Indeed, Menilek had seriously considered moving his capital to Addis Alam, some 60 kilometres to the west, and had even built an alternative palace there. It was the protest of the legations, who had invested in more permanent structures in Addis Ababa, and the propitious arrival of the eucalyptus that persuaded the emperor to reverse his decision (Bahru 2001: 71). The legations were particularly fond of this saviour of Addis and their compounds are to this day adorned by old specimens of the exotic tree. Ethiopians also embraced it, as it greatly facilitated construction, initiating an important change of style from round to rectangular houses (Berlan 1963: 67ff).

The second major landmark was the beginning of the issuance of land charters in 1907. This gave property holders greater security and a stake in the fate of the city. Not only did the land charter become the most prized certificate of any urban household but it also contributed to activating the urban economy through sales and mortgages. It was on the whole a novel experience and the Amharic lexicon initially had no equivalent for it, preferring to describe it as 'the engineer's painting'. Later, presumably during the Italian occupation, the Italian term *'carta'* came to be used and is still in vogue. It is also of interest that the basic geographical frame of reference for the charters was the parish *(atbya)* rather than the *safar*, reinforcing the importance of the churches of Addis Ababa as settlement nodes. The measurement of land also gave a graphic image of the incredible feats of land-grabbing that some members of the nobility had performed. There were at least three known instances of aggregate possessions of over half a million square metres. The value of land also indicated the centrality or otherwise of a location, Arada land understandably fetching the highest price.

A third important landmark in this period was the arrival of the Djibouti–Addis Ababa railway in 1917. One serious analyst of the evolution of Addis Ababa has underscored the importance of modes of transportation in the city's evolution – first human and animal transport, followed successively by rail, motor and air transport (Johnson 1974: xvi). It had taken exactly twenty years to finish construction of the troubled line. But, once it reached its final destination, its impact on national life in general and that of the capital in particular was immediate and palpable. Although the imposing building that now graces the station was not erected until about a decade later, the terminal formed an important nucleus and point of reference. By accident or by design, the station was almost exactly due south of St George's Church and Arada, the commercial centre. What came to be known as the Station Road linked the two nodal points. As Martin Johnson has observed: 'the railroad focus was, and is, a different type of node than the two earlier nodes that had so much influence on city structure. Instead of being a focus of routes from many directions, it was a node that served the market by a single well-used road' (ibid.: 280).

Thus, the railway station gave the city a major artery that is still a dominant feature of its road network. Its primacy can be seen from the fact that, during the Italian occupation, it was baptized Viale Mussolini (Mussolini Avenue) after the fascist dictator who had launched the invasion. Subsequent to the end of fascist Italian rule in 1941, it was rechristened Churchill Road (a name it carries to this day), in gratitude to the British Second World War hero who helped launch the expeditionary force that terminated fascist rule in north-east Africa. The construction of the City Hall in the early 1960s gave this artery a faint resemblance to the Champs Élysées. The hall, 'with the symmetrical arrangement of its office wings, and the slender tower in the middle – looking out towards the monumental axis – seems to open up in a symbolic manner to embrace the city' (Dejene 1987: 207–8). A French master plan drawn in 1965 found the parallel and symbolism so irresistible that it envisaged a replication of the famed French avenue (Techeste 1987: 256). Unfortunately, like almost all master plans of the city to date, this one too came to naught.

The Station Road had an added significance for the future development of the city's road network. It gave rise to another important intersection, now known as Adwa Square, linking the Station Road with the Jimma Road, so called because it led to the coffee-rich town of that name in south-western Ethiopia. After the construction of the Haile Sellassie I Theatre (rebaptized the National Theatre after the 1974 revolution), Adwa Square became a major cultural and entertainment centre, competing with and eventually surpassing the old Arada (known as 'Piazza' after the Italian occupation). A southern branch of the Jimma Road came to pass directly in front of the station towards the Masqal-Revolution Square discussed above (Johnson 1974: 288). With the subsequent extension of this branch to what became Asmara Road, that square developed as the most important nodal point in south-west Addis Ababa.

The Jimma Road formed the southern lateral of a quadrangle, within which the pre-1935 city was primarily enclosed. The northern lateral was constituted by the road linking St George's Cathedral to the *gebbi* of Ras Makonnen (Menilek's cousin and right-hand man and father of Emperor Haile Selasse) at what came to be known as Seddest Kilo. It is worth noting that this *gebbi* formed the site of the first of the two palaces alluded to earlier to have been built by Haile Selasse, subsequently turned into the main campus of Haile Sellassie I University (now Addis Ababa University). The road linking Makonnen's *gebbi* to the imperial *gebbi* (Seddest Kilo to Arat Kilo) formed another major artery roughly parallel to Station Road. In the middle of the two (northern and southern) laterals was the most important thoroughfare linking Arada to Arat Kilo. Along this winding artery, later to be famous as Haile Sellassie I Avenue, were constructed the modern buildings housing the major expatriate firms. The architecture in this period was predominantly Indian-Arab in style (Dejene 1987: 202).

The coronation of Emperor Haile Selasse in 1930 forms another landmark of this period. As Johnson has aptly observed, it introduced the tradition of renovating the city on special occasions and erecting façades to cover the old and ugly (Johnson 1974: 290). In addition to Menilek's

127

equestrian statue cited above, the occasion gave rise to three other monuments. One of these was the statue of the Lion of Judah erected in the
square in front of the railway station. The Italians, who did not particularly like this symbol of Ethiopian invincibility, removed it during the
occupation. It has now been restored to its original place. The second
was a monument at Arat Kilo, a square that also reflected the shifting
fortunes of the country as the symbol of conquest and liberation (both
conveniently falling on 5 May, the first in 1936 and the second in 1941).
The third could be described as the epicentre of pre-1935 Addis, located
in the south-eastern corner of Arada. As was to be expected, it was called
Haile Sellassie I Square, until changed to De Gaulle on the occasion of
the French president's visit to Ethiopia in 1966. Such a dramatic act of
self-sacrifice was perhaps explicableby Ethiopian flirtation with France in
view of the imminent decolonization of its colony of Djibouti, an important
outlet for Ethiopia.

The Italian occupation, 1936–41

With the inauguration of the fascist Italian occupation in May 1936,
Addis Ababa was transformed from being the capital of Ethiopia to that of
the new colonial empire of Italian East Africa (Africa orientale italiana, in
its Italian rendering). This new entity was formed by the Italians through
the merger of their newly acquired prize with the old colonies of Eritrea and
Somaliland. The new colonial empire was divided into five ethno-linguistic
regions (Eritrea, Somalia, Amhara, Harar and Galla and Sidama) and a
sixth metropolitan region centred in and designated Addis Ababa. In due
course, however, Addis Ababa was changed to Scioa (Shawa). For some
time, the fascists had toyed with the idea of abandoning Addis Ababa as
the capital and moving it either to the west or east. Factors that militated
against the old capital were its altitude (which was found exhausting to the
new Mediterranean residents), the population concentration that hindered
new planning and the dense foliage that provided cover to insurgents
against fascist rule. In the end, however, considerations of prestige tipped
the balance and Mussolini decided to retain Addis Ababa as the capital
(Pankhurst 1987: 119–20).

A propos the issue of the city centre that is the theme of this chapter, the
fascists introduced to the capital the quintessentially Italian concept of the
piazza (square). In a small Italian town, the *piazza* is *the* centre where people
converge to relax and chat. It is also where the main shops are located.
But the bigger the town, the more *piazze* there are, giving Italian cities the
polycentric character that they have. Addis Ababa being a relatively big town
at the time of its conquest by the Italians, it also came to have more than one

piazza. The old city centre or Arada was christened Piazza Littorio. To the north, the square facing St George's Cathedral where the equestrian statue of Emperor Menilek had formerly stood was named Piazza Impero ('Empire Square'). The two nodes of the major eastern vertical route (the political axis – as it were – stretching from the new *gebbi* to the old one) were rechristened. Seddest Kilo became Piazza Roma ('Rome Square') and Arat Kilo Piazza 5 Maggio ('5 May Square'). The former was a tribute to the imperial capital, the latter commemorated the fall of Addis Ababa in 1936.

As already indicated, Littorio has endured to this day as *the* 'Piazza', the centre. Until it came to be challenged by other centres that grew up in subsequent decades, it was the centre of fashion and elegance. With its three cinema halls, it was also the major entertainment centre. All three were built during the Italian period. The names of the first two had been appropriately changed from Marconi to Adwa and from Italia to Ethiopia; the third was neutral enough to be merely translated from Impero to Empire. Piazza was where people went to wine and dine. The best Italian restaurant in the city, the Castelli, is still located there. It was where the young and trendy went to see and be seen, to show their new acquisitions, be it girlfriends (or boyfriends) and de luxe cars. In the 1960s, in particular, youngsters perambulating to and fro in the evening along the Haile Sellassie I Avenue (Corso Vittorio Emmanuele during the Italian occupation) were a common enough sight, in somewhat the same way that the thoroughfares leading to the *piazza* of small Italian towns attract evening crowds.

As a commercial centre, however, Piazza came to be challenged and ultimately overtaken by a new *entrepôt* in the western part of the town. This was another outcome of the fascist occupation period. In line with the colonial policy of segregation, all the more reinforced by the racist ethos that permeated the fascist order, the Italians embarked on an ambitious progamme of restructuring the capital. Using the Kurtume River as a natural divide, the eastern part – which constituted most of the old city – was reserved for the Italians, ironically designated 'nationals', while the eastern part was to develop as a separate town for the Ethiopians, '*gli indigeni*' ('the indigenous population'). To cater for the commercial needs of the Ethiopians, a new market was set up. Named *mercato indigeno* ('the indigenous market'), it later shed its ascriptive epithet and has come to be an enduring feature of Addis life as Mercato.

Mercato has two distinctive components: the open market and the shops, a number of the latter owing their origin to the Italian period. The former is reputed to be the largest open market in the continent. It is the scene of a dogged struggle for survival and of remarkable ingenuity and improvisation. The term Arada, initially associated with the pre-1935

129

market, was translocated to the new commercial centre. In its new context, it denoted not only commercial transactions but also inner-city smartness. The shops, expanded in the post-liberation period, offer a mixture of locally manufactured and imported goods. Both the open market and the shops have come to be dominated by the Gurage, reputed for their drive and enterprise. Mercato also became the centre around which a new urban settlement rose, inhabited mostly by the Gurage at the initial stage but eventually drawing other groups as well. Interestingly enough, the major settlement of the Gurage, located to the west of Mercato, came to be called Addis Katama (New Town).

Of the other settlements that emerged in the quarter reserved for the Italians, the most notable was probably Casanchis. The name arose from a corruption of the Italian term 'Case INCIS', the acronym standing for the Italian parastatal entrusted with constructing residential blocks for state officials (Istituto nazionale per le case degli impiegati dello stato). Relics of these buildings still house one of the city's police stations, the Ministry of Agriculture and the Ministry of Labour and Social Affairs. Otherwise, the quarter has come to distinguish itself – more than anything else – as one of the city's major night-life districts. The emergence and growth of Casanchis has had the effect of pulling the city south-eastwards and filling the gap, as it were, between the old *gebbi* and Urael, one of the city's earliest churches, now probably the most popular place of worship for the city's Orthodox laity.

A final important legacy of the Italian period was in the sphere of architecture. The Italians built a number of buildings that still form visible landmarks in the city, particularly in the Piazza area, along the Churchill Road (Viale Mussolini during the Italian period) and in the residential quarters of Casanchis and Case Popolare (the more plebeian counterpart of Case INCIS). With their solid and rectangular shape, these buildings brought a new style so different from the conical and largely wooden structures of the pre-1935 period. Not least of the value of these Italian-built edifices was their use for government offices and business enterprises as well as entertainment centres in the post-1941 period.

Liberation to revolution, 1941–74

If the railway station could be said to have played a decisive role in pulling the city southwards, the airports had an equally significant contribution in consolidating and deepening this process. In effect, they pulled the city first south-westwards and then south-eastwards. In the process, what Johnson (1974: 383) has dubbed 'the Modernizing South' was born. Two major nodes were created as points of entry into the city centre, Mexico

Square (formerly Maychaw Square) in the south west and Masqal/Revolution Square in the south east.

The first aeroplanes had made their appearance in 1929/30. But this was still the age of amateur rather than civil aviation. At the time, the race course at Seddest Kilo known as Janmeda (an ellipsis of Janhoy Meda or 'the Field of the Emperor') was deemed sufficient for landings and take-offs. With the inauguration of Ethiopian Airlines and the launching of the first international passenger service in 1946, it became necessary for a more open airfield and a terminal building. An airfield in the south-western outskirts of the city, yet another relic of the Italian period, was converted into the first international airport.

Contrary to experiences elsewhere in the world, where people equate airports with noise pollution, airports have exercised a strange magnetic pull on Addis Ababa residents. It is also true that, again unlike the situation in most countries, both airports in Addis Ababa's history have been located within a few minutes' drive from the city centre. The opening of the old airport resulted in a dramatic appreciation of the land in the neighbourhood, more specifically the area to the west and south of the airport. This became the site for the residential buildings of the affluent members of the society and the growing expatriate community. The road leading from the airport also gained prominence and stimulated construction. Of the buildings that came to line the road, the most important are the former Princess Tsehay Hospital (named after Emperor Haile Selassie's favourite daughter) and the Building College. Two other major buildings – the Soviet-sponsored Balcha Hospital and the Technical School – seem to be relics of the Italian period in their architectural style (Berlan 1963: 165; Johnson 1974: 381). The nodal point of the airport was designated Maychaw Square, after the major battle of the Italo-Ethiopian War of 1935–36. Later, presumably at the height of Ethio-Mexican friendship, it was changed to Mexico Square.

In 1963, as Ethiopian Air Lines entered the jet age, a new airport to accommodate the new aircraft was opened in the south-eastern outskirts of the city. At the time, this was deemed sufficiently far from the city centre. But it is now only ten to fifteen minutes' drive. Following the same curious logic that we have seen in the case of the old airport, the new airport also attracted large-scale settlement of the affluent and the expatriate. Bole, the name of the new district (and also of the airport), indeed remains to this day a symbol of affluence and class. There were two stages of this development. The first was marked by construction along the main road leading from the airport to Masqal Square – a process not yet completed, especially in the vicinity of the airport. The second involved construction in depth off the main road.

The Silver Jubilee of Emperor Hayla-Selasse's coronation in November 1955 was an event marked by considerable pomp and pageantry. It was as if the emperor wanted to show the world that Ethiopia had indeed finally joined the modern age. A grand exhibition showing the diversity of Ethiopian life and the notable achievements of the regime was staged, appropriately enough not far from the airport. More significantly for the theme of discussion here, some important buildings were constructed that contributed to accentuating two of the nodal points discussed above. The first building was the Haile Sellassie I Theatre (National Theatre after 1974), more grandiloquently dubbed the Opera. This building enhanced the nodal importance of Adwa Square by creating an entertainment centre rivalling and ultimately surpassing the triple cinema complex of Piazza. With the opening of the Ambassador Theatre less than a hundred metres to the north east, the cultural pre-eminence of Adwa Square was assured.

A second major building activity involved the Jubilee Palace and the adjacent Ghion Hotel. The former contributed to the southward pull of the politico-administrative axis that had thitherto stopped at Arat Kilo. This in turn ensured the nodal importance of Masqal Square. Ghion Hotel remained the luxury hotel until superseded by the Hilton in the second half of the 1960s. On the other hand, the building of the Hilton, the Ministry of Foreign Affairs opposite, and the headquarters of the ECA, opened in 1958 across the park from the Jubilee Palace, completed the process of building up the stretch of ground between the old *gebbi* and Masqal Square, the major south-eastern node of Addis Ababa (Johnson 1974: 381).

The 1963 summit of African heads of state that led to the founding of the OAU could only reinforce the above trends. The elevation of the status of Addis Ababa from a national capital to a continental metropolis enhanced the importance of the above quadrangle – marked by Africa Hall, the Hilton, the Foreign Ministry and the Jubilee Palace – and the importance of the Bole airport and Masqal Square. At the same time, it boosted the construction of upper-class residential buildings in the vicinity of both airports, old and new.

The period of the revolution, 1974–91

As is to be expected, the 1974 revolution in Ethiopia left a deep impact on Addis Ababa, as it did on the country as a whole. If anything, the impact on the capital was bound to be most pronounced, as it was the centre not only of national life but also of political contestation. The most decisive and bitter struggles for power were fought out not only in secret chambers of the palace but also on the streets of the capital. Addis Ababa also became the ultimate prized target of the guerrillas who in 1991 toppled the military regime known as the Darg that had appropriated the mantle of revolutionary leadership.

The first revolutionary measure that affected life in the city in a fundamental and enduring way was the nationalization of urban property and extra houses in July 1975. This was the second major blow that the ruling establishment suffered, the first being the nationalization of rural land that had been proclaimed in March of the same year. This measure had a number of ramifications. First and foremost, it stripped the rentier class of an important source of revenue. Second, the transfer of ownership of extra houses to neighbourhood associations (if their rent was below Eth Birr 100 or US$50 at the prevalent rate) or the parastatal set up for the purpose (if their rent was above that figure) contributed significantly to the atmosphere of drabness and dereliction that has marked the city's buildings. Unlike private owners, these extraneous organs were not keen on repair and maintenance. The continuation of the same administrative regime after the change of system in 1991 has meant that there has not been any appreciable amelioration of the situation. If anything, things have gone from bad to worse. The sterility of architectural style in the revolutionary period – as opposed to the dynamism and innovativeness of the pre-revolution period (Dejene 1987: 212–13) – has only tended to enhance the drabness.

Most importantly, the July 1975 proclamation was accompanied by the setting up of a new administrative structure. The lowest but most important unit of this new administration was the neighbourhood association (the *qabale*), followed in ascending order of hierarchy by the 'Higher' (*kaftañña*), the zone (*qatana*) and the city council (Clapham 1988: 130–6). The *qabale* became not only the administrator of the smaller houses (in many instances sheer hovels) but also became the battleground between the military regime and its civilian opponents, notably the members of the militant Ethiopian People's Revolutionary Party (EPRP). Many members of the former *qabale* administration, particularly members of the much-dreaded Revolutionary Defence Squad, are still in jail, undergoing trial for their role in the perpetration of the so-called Red Terror – the name given to legitimize the summary execution of suspected members of EPRP, as opposed to the 'White Terror' committed by armed squads of EPRP.

But once the bloody shoot-out was over and the regime had consolidated its seizure of absolute power, the *qabale*s began to have some of the attributes of neighbourhood associations, even if election of officials has always been strictly controlled by the government. This became the situation in the 1980s and has more or less continued to this day. Their shops supplied – albeit rationed – much-needed and scarce commodities at reasonable prices. The more affluent in the Bole area developed into entertainment and relaxation centres – some of them complete with tennis courts. In effect, some of these *qabale* have come to replace the old city centres as focal points of social interaction and entertainment.

As far as construction was concerned, the revolutionary period understandably resulted in what amounted to a freeze. This was particularly the case with regard to private construction. Few would be keen on building at a time when nationalization was the dominant ethos. This began to change only in the mid-1980s when, encouraged by the state, a number of housing co-operatives sprung up. This resulted in the growth of new residential quarters, almost entirely in the southern and south-eastern parts of the city. Because of the small plots of land allowed, these building were highly economical in nature (*qutaba*, denoting frugality, is the Amharic term for them) and tended to give the new quarters a crowded look.

But the further pull of the city south and south-eastwards accentuated the polycentrism that had come to be a perceptible feature of the city even before 1974. Shopping areas and refreshment centres sprang up to cater to the new constituencies. It is true that these new residential areas had no cinema halls. But, under the spartan regime that prevailed, the old cinema halls had ceased to attract their clientele because they could show only old and dated films. On the other hand, the phenomenal growth of video rentals had rendered even the old cinema halls irrelevant and fostered an in-house entertainment culture throughout the city as a whole.

The forced shift from command to mixed economy in the twilight hours of the military regime contributed to another boom in construction, this time in business enterprises (mostly hotels). But most of these hotels were not completed until after the fall of the Darg in 1991. Once they were completed, however, these hotels provided an alternative to the old established ones in the traditional centre in the provision not only of accommodation but also of refreshment and social intercourse. This in turn contributed to the accentuation of the city's polycentrism mentioned above.

The 1980s were also memorable for yet another effort to streamline the city's chaotic and spontaneous growth. This plan took for granted the polycentric character of the city and envisaged the development of 'a continuous urban system organized around six major sub-centres (*qatana* centres), and with limited and gradual expansion in the peripheral fringes and along the three main communication axes in the east, south, and west' (Techeste 1987: 263). The southern edge of the city was to serve as the main location for industry and transport infrastructure. The plan also provided for a green belt around the city with the twin purpose of peri-urban agriculture and recreation.

Like all earlier plans, this one too was not completed on the ground, partly for lack of the necessary legal mechanism (Tajebe 1968 Ethiopian Calendar: 112). It is currently undergoing revision. In a similar manner, a master plan drawn in 1956 by a British architect, Sir Patrick Abercombie, had been designed to 'foster a richer and more intimate community life' and provided for six satellite towns around the city (*Ethiopia Observer* 1957: 35). In a way, although it was sinister in its design and incomplete in its realization, the fascist Italian master plan was relatively more successful than all its successors. At the very least, it has given the city the permanent fixture of Mercato and foreshadowed the major artery (Viale Imperiale, as it was christened by the Italians) that extended the political axis to Masqal/Revolution Square.

Concluding remarks

Like many of its Ethiopian precursors, Addis Ababa owed its genesis to the twin pillars of church and state. These two institutions served as the nodes around which the city developed in its early years. The religious centre, St George, had the added significance of evolving as the commercial centre, Arada. For something like half a century, Arada was the social and cultural as well as the commercial centre of the city. The Italian occupation enhanced this role both by adding new buildings and by introducing the concept of Piazza. On the other hand, it contributed to the birth of a new commercial centre, Mercato, which eventually appropriated the name Arada.

But the expansion of the city depended more than anything else on the two universal indices of modern transport: the railway and the airline. Both developments, separated by something like three decades, were instrumental in drawing the city southwards and creating new centres of the city – going from west to east, Mexico Square, Lagahar (as the railway station area was known, through a corruption of the French term *la gare*) and Masqal/Revolution Square. These emerged in the second half of the twentieth century as the nodes from which the southern extension of the city radiated.

A distinctive feature of the city's evolution has been its spontaneous, not to say chaotic, growth. The city has consistently defied planning. The many master plans drawn from the 1930s to the 1980s have been confined to the shelves. In the 1950s, the idea of moving the capital to the young and still plannable town of Bahr Dar (on Lake Tana) was seriously considered. The idea was akin to the considerations that led to the birth of such new capitals as Brasilia (in Brazil) and Abudja (in Nigeria). Even then, it is doubtful if that would have meant the eclipse of Addis Ababa, just as Rio de Janeiro and Lagos have not lost their vitality despite the shift to new capitals. Moreover, as the eucalyptus saved Addis Ababa at the turn of the last century, its emergence as an African metropolis (as headquarters of ECA and OAU) ensured its permanence and centrality. As the century wore on, the city, chaotic and unmanageable, surged on, turning its back to the historic north and sprawling inexorably towards the resource-rich south.

References

[Ethiopian names, as is customary, are written with first name first]

Ahmed Zekaria, Bahru Zewde and Taddese Beyene (1987) *Proceedings of the International Symposium on the Centenary of Addis Ababa November 24–25, 1986*, Addis Ababa: Institute of Ethiopian Studies.

Amos, F. (1962) 'A Development Plan for Addis Ababa', *Ethiopia Observer*, Vol. VI, No. 1.

Bahru Zewde (1987) 'Early Safars of Addis Ababa: Patterns of Evolution', in Ahmed Zekaria et al.

— (2001) *A History of Modern Ethiopia 1855–1991*, London: James Currey.

Berlan, E. (1963) *Addis-Abeba la plus haute ville d'Afrique. Étude géographique*, Grenoble: Imprimerie Allier.

Bourne, L. (ed.) (1982) *Internal Structure of the City. Readings on Urban Form, Growth and Policy*, New York and Oxford: Oxford University Press.

Clapham, C. (1988) *Transormation and Continuity in Revolutionary Ethiopia*, Cambridge: Cambridge University Press.

Combes, E. and M. Tamisier (1838) *Voyage en Abyssinie*, Paris: Louis Desessar.

Crummey, D. (1987) 'Some Precursors of Addis Ababa: Towns in Christian Ethiopia in the Eighteenth and Nineteenth Centuries', in Ahmed Zekaria et al.

Dejene H. Mariam (1987) 'Architecture in Addis Ababa', in Ahmed Zekaria et al.

Ethiopia Observer (1957) 'Sir Patrick Abercombie's Town Plan', *Ethiopia Observer*, Vol. I, No. 2 (March).

Ferret, P. V. and J. Gallinier (1847) *Voyage en Abyssinie, II*, Paris: Paulin.

Gleichen, Count (1898) *With the Mission to Menelik 1897*, London: Edward Arnold.

Hanna, W. J. and J. L. Hanna (1981) *Urban Dynamics in Black Africa. An Interdisciplinary Approach*, New York: Aldine Publishing Co.

Johnson, M. E. (1962) 'Addis Ababa from the Air', *Ethiopia Observer*, Vol. VI, No. 1.

— (1974) 'The Evolution of the Morphology of Addis Ababa, Ethiopia', PhD thesis (UCLA).

Merid Wolde Aregay (1989) 'Gondar and Adwa: A Tale of Two Cities', *Proceedings of the Eighth International Conference of Ethiopian Studies*, Vol. II, Addis Ababa: Institute of Ethiopian Studies.

Municipality of Addis Ababa, Bolton, Hennessey & Partners (1961) 'Report on the Development Plan', Addis Ababa, mimeo.

Pankhurst, R. (1987) 'Developments in Addis Ababa During the Italian Fascist Occupation (1936–1941)', in Ahmed Zekaria et al.

Powel-Cotton, P.H.G. (1902) *A Sporting Trip through Abyssinia*, London: Rowland Ward.

Tajebe Beyene (1959 Ethiopian Calendar) *Addis Ababa ba-81 Amat west* ('Addis Ababa in 81 Years'), Addis Ababa: n.p.

— (1968 Ethiopian Calendar) *Addis Ababa Tenagar* ('Let Addis Ababa Speak'), Addis Ababa: n.p.

Techeste Ahderom (1987) 'Basic Planning Principles and Objectives Taken in the Preparation of the Addis Ababa Master Plan: Past and Present', in Ahmed Zekaria et al.

Virgin, General E. (1936) *The Abyssinia I Knew*, London: Macmillan.

6 | At the limits of possibility: working notes on a relational model of urban politics

EDGAR PIETERSE

Without transgression, without the red boundary, there is no danger, no risk, no *frisson*, no experiment, no discovery and no creativity. Without extending some hidden or visible frontier of the possible, without disturbing something of the incomplete order of things there is no challenge, no pleasure, and certainly no joy (Okri 1997: 32).

Limitations are ... conditions of possibility. However, to accept given limitations as that which determines all that is possible would make being unbearably heavy. Limits are truly enabling when, having given something its form, [...] the form engages with its own limits to fashion its own style. Foucault's notion of transgression signifies work on *enabling* limits (Simons 1995: 3).

Cities are slowly but surely rising to the surface of the South African political landscape. Yet scholarship and policy development on the city and new institutional initiatives seem disjointed and partial. As the opening quotations intimate, I am particularly interested in the prospects of a transgressive urban politics that can attend effectively to questions of inequality, distributive justice and cosmopolitanism. In a situation of rising inequality within and between urban areas in South Africa (and elsewhere), these are pivotal concerns to address as new political frameworks and identities are being assembled. At present, it seems difficult to conceptualize what a transgressive politics could look like in practical terms because analyses tend to be fragmented and partial.

Some scholars focus on institutional restructuring to give effect to the new local government dispensation ushered in by the *White Paper on Local Government* (March 1998) and associated legislation (Cameron 1999; Binns and Nel 2002). The institutional focus is often linked to analyses of new planning systems for local government: integrated development plans (IDPs), which are meant to inform the 'strategic direction' of institutional change (Harrison 2001a; Pieterse 2002a). Others focus on the new labour relations regimes that accompany some of these restructuring processes and on resistance from municipal trade unions and their alliances (McDonald and Pape 2003). Increasingly, there is also more research on urban social movements that organize against the privatization and corporatization of municipal services (McDonald 2002a). Studies of older social movements such as the South African National Civic Association are also in play (Heller and Ntlokonkulu 2001; Cherry et al. 2000), along with a focus on the mobilization capacity of ratepayer associations in (mainly white) middle-class areas (Beall et al. 2002; Saff 2001). In contradistinction, other studies point to the almost invisible and painstaking efforts of groups in poor communities to formulate, institutionalize, maintain and grow development projects that make a world's difference in terms of accessing scare resources to augment household livelihood strategies (Lyons et al. 2001, 2002). In betwixt such claim-making politics and collective survivalist strategies are the dangerous spaces of 'the everyday', where violent gangs seem to flourish as if on steroids and children negotiate the horrors of sexual predation (Segal et al. 2001; Soudien 2004). The twin spectres of violence and violation are also fuelling intense organization in middle-class areas leading, inexorably, to the 'brazilianization' of suburbs decked in the full regalia of gates, booms, surveillance cameras, privatized security and barbed wire (Bremner 1998; Jürgens and Gnad 2002). South African cities are being remade and reimagined at a ferocious pace and with worrying consequences from radical democratic and redistributive perspectives (Mabin 2000).

Despite the speed and intensity of urban change it is clear that agency is flourishing and much remains to be done to recast political practice in the city towards a more comprehensive understanding of what is going on, where things may be leading to and, crucially, how democratic politics can be tilted towards social justice and equity concerns.[1] Many intractable problems beset the current urban political landscape in South Africa. Ongoing reflection on these problems is a driving force for this chapter. I will mention a few salient issues as a lead into the main focus of the chapter. First, it seems as if the democracy-enhancing aspects of the new local government dispensation are being under-realized under the weight of technocratic rationality within municipal government (Harrison 2001b; Harrison and Todes 2001). Second, many metropolitan authorities seem determined to follow, somewhat uncritically, mainstream policy ideas about the importance of being 'world-class', 'competitive' and globally integrated at any cost (Robinson 2002). This seems to produce a neo-corporatist tendency that crowds out other equally legitimate forms of political engagement through direct action and symbolic contestation in the public sphere. The valorization of long-range strategic planning, such as *Joburg 2030* of the Johannesburg metropolitan authority, is but one

139

example. Unicity councils in Cape Town, Durban, Pretoria, among others, are following similar paths (Pieterse 2003; Todes et al. 2000).

Third, as intimated earlier, community-based militancy seems to be on the increase in the wake of toughening-up policies of municipal authorities. The resoluteness of municipalities is stoked by conditionalities of the national treasury, the ideological commitment of the ruling party to public/private service delivery 'solutions', and the non-collaborationist ideology that inform many of the organizations in this 'movement'. As a result, we can see a new landscape of conflict and contestation that is seemingly becoming mired in an oppositional iron cage logic that undermines co-operative or consensual outcomes. (My understanding of co-operation and consensus will be made clearer below.) Fourth, the interlocked conditions of pervasive inequality, impoverishment, institutionalized racism, poor health (caused in part by sweeping epidemics such as HIV/AIDS) and systemic violence are producing a growing class of people who are falling by the wayside of society as embodied reminders of our political impotence (Duiker 2000; Gotz 2004; Mpe 2001; see Biehl 2002 on equivalent processes in Brazil).

Urban politics and policies are more likely to address the complex and intractable conditions in our cities if these become more effective in animating social citizenship, drawing on the disciplining power of radical democracy, and fostering a culture of agonistic engagement that is institutionally mobilized and embedded. Such a project requires a more lucid conceptual framework of urban politics than is typically found in current scholarship on the city. By drawing on these diverse theoretical influences in the wake of the 'cultural turn', I am seeking to develop a conceptual model that can incite further research and critical debate as part of a larger process of animating the public sphere about the potentialities of vibrant politics – a politics of transgression, pleasure, joy and social justice (see Pieterse 2002b). In the next section, I summarize the conceptual scaffolding that underpins the relational model of urban politics, which comprises the bulk of the chapter.

Conceptual scaffolding

The conceptual model that is sketched in this chapter draws on a variety of recent theorizations in urban studies, political science, policy studies, urban planning and development studies. The common denominator is a concern with culture as constitutive of the social, alongside the economic and political. With the cultural turn comes an awareness that language, discourse and symbolic meanings are central to incessant processes of identity construction and the realm of agency in the spaces of the everyday

(Eade and Mele 2002). The conceptual challenge is to adopt an approach that recognizes the structuring effect of the economy, bureaucracy and discursive diagrams of power without relinquishing an understanding of the saliency of agency. In urban studies the actor-network approach of Ash Amin and Nigel Thrift (2002) stands out along with the post-Marxist formulation of Kian Tajbakhsh (2001). In development studies, Norman Long (2001) has gone a long way in formulating a sophisticated framework to capture the dynamic interplay between structure and agency and the space for political action beyond the restrictions of economic-deterministic epistemologies. These are consistent with deployments in post-colonial cultural studies (Ahluwalia 2001; Ashcroft 2001). I locate the following conceptual reference points squarely within this tradition of theorization. In the process I hope to alert the reader to the theoretical currents that flow through the conceptual model presented in the next section. The abbreviated discussion here will have to do since I do not have the space to develop my arguments in their theoretical fullness. This discussion is best treated as a form of prelude to summarize the theoretical anchors that bed down my conceptual model of urban politics.

1. Urban politics must be imagined, practised and institutionalized on an ethical basis. Ideally, this is a human rights-based framework that legally guarantees access to opportunities to flourish as a creative individual ensconced in multiple communities of affinity, which may or may not be in close proximity (Amin and Thrift 2002: Ch. 6). In South Africa, a strong basis for such an approach exists due to the constitutional entrenchment of all human rights: political, civil and socio-economic. It is vital to maximize this political potential in all spheres of citizenship and political practice.

2. Democracy is a necessary precondition for a vibrant political space that allows for regulated contestation of perspectives that are invariably imbued with particular interests. Formal liberal democratic norms and institutional procedures that rest on representative democratic institutions and the rule of law are wholly inadequate to address the structurally embedded relations and systems of inequality that characterize capitalist modernity (de Sousa Santos 1995; Unger 1998). More is needed. In this regard, the ideas of scholars who espouse the benefits of radical democracy are most convincing and promising (Gabardi 2001; Mouffe 2000; Squires 2002). More on the institutional expressions of radical democracy will be explored below.

3. The institutional design and functioning dimensions of urban politics are crucial for the effectiveness and democratic content of political

practices. Institutions are not merely containers of political intent, but rather mediate in a fundamental sense how interactions between diverse political actors (and agendas) are structured and channelled (Flood 1999). This awareness brings into view the importance of organizational dynamics and cultures of both state and non-state political actors, but also the importance of translating new political agreements into 'the routine practices of frontline officials [in government] if they are to make real differences to people's life chances and to give real respect to people's individual life circumstances' (Healey 2000: 918). In many ways, the conceptual model put forward in the chapter adds up to an attempt to illuminate the institutional interdependencies between various political domains in the city.

4. The conceptual distinctions between 'government', 'governmentality' and 'governance' are useful to understand and recast the potential and limitations of the local state, especially in an era of neoliberal dominance. In my usage here, government refers in practical terms to the structures, institutions and organizations of the state that regulate social practices.[2] Governmentality is a Foucauldian concept, which refers 'to the complex array of techniques – programs, procedures, strategies and tactics – employed by both non-state administrative agencies and state institutions to shape conduct of individuals and populations' (Gabardi 2001: 82). Governance denotes the relationality of power as it flows through networks between the state and institutional actors in the market and civil society. However, 'governance is not a homogenous agent, but a morass of complex networks and arenas within which power dynamics are expressed and deployed' (Healey 2000: 919). The purpose of my conceptual model is to bring these multiple networks and arenas of urban governance into view so that more fine-grained critical research can be conducted. I also hope to provoke investigations into practicable visions about radical politics that can produce more socially just and environmentally conscious outcomes, i.e. political discourses that emerge from practical struggles to test and transcend the discursive limits of governmentality efforts of the state.

5. The full measure of the urban political terrain can be apprehended only via an appreciation of spatiality. Cities can be understood spatially in terms of densities, proximities, intensities and their effects. Furthermore, the particular form of the spatial configuration that arises in a city shapes the horizons of possibility (Massey 1999). If the horizon is extremely limited, spatial configuration continues to produce segregation, fragmentation and exclusion. Alternatively, if the horizons are more open, we are more inclined to use the rich multiplicity of spatial

practices to unleash new ways of interaction and engagement. However, if the multiple spatialities of the city are repressed or erased (in official texts and regulations), it is virtually impossible to construct a radical democratic 'cosmopolis' (Sandercock 1998). In other words, recognition of the inherently heterogeneous time-spaces of the city feeds into political questions about how the city is imagined and represented. At its core, all urban struggles are in one sense or another about the politics of recognition and determination of identity.

6. This 'multiplex' perspective of the city rests firmly on a non-essentialist conception of identity and community. Kian Tajbakhsh explains that 'identities are not expressive of a deep "essentialist" core, but are best seen as contingent and articulated through interdependent and over-determined practices structured by both conscious intention and unconscious desire'. In other words, 'complexity is the *a priori* feature of social identity' (Tajbakhsh 2001: 6). Invariably the same applies to the notion of 'community', where urban theory meets critical perspectives from development studies. In development studies, Frances Cleaver (among many others) has successfully demonstrated how '"community" in participatory approaches to development is often seen as a "natural" social entity characterised by solidaristic relations' (2001: 44). She then goes on systematically to critique this approach, by pointing out the absence of 'coterminosity between natural (resource), social and administrative boundaries' (ibid.). Furthermore, she points out how processes of conflict, negotiation, inclusion and exclusion have been poorly analysed in the development literature with a tendency to romanticize community relations. This critical turn is vital for recasting development practice and reconnecting development strategy with questions of political power and especially distributional justice in all spheres of society: household, the street, neighbourhood, collections of neighbourhoods that coalesce as municipal areas and, of course, the city as a whole.

7. Finally, it is important to acknowledge that political contestation unfolds around specific, discursively constructed, points of crisis and imperatives to reproduce the political economic system. What is regarded as a *crisis* and finds its way into the public domain via the media is an important area of contestation. Representative democracy, collective and insurgent practices of subaltern classes, and quotidian practices to realize development projects rely on the (public) recognition of certain issues as valid political problems. Usually this is reflected in the discourses that circulate in (popular) media via newspapers, radio and television (and cyberspace?). Increasingly, successful political mobil-

ization of interests relies on capacity to set the agenda and frame the issues of the day. This point brings me back to my first assertion about the importance of an ethical horizon in political engagement. It seems clear that the potentiality of a rights-based discourse can be realized only through practical struggles that translate everyday violations into claims, demands, remedies and solutions that find recognition and expression in the public domain. In other words, politics is as much about content as it is about performance. The question is: how does one reimagine political agency at a subjective and collective level in ways that can transcend governmentality through performative practices in *all* domains of political action? It is hoped that the conceptual model elaborated in the next section will serve as a suitable starting point to answer this question.

Sketches of a conceptual model of urban politics

This section is the heart of the chapter. Here I aim to capture the multiple, interconnected and overlapping spaces of political practices in the city. In conceptual terms it is possible to delineate at least five domains of political engagement between the state, the private sector and civil society at various scales, ranging from the national to the local: (1) representative political forums; (2) neo-corporatist political forums that are comprised of representative organizations, typically the government, the private sector, trade unions and community-based organizations; (3) direct action or mobilization against state policies or to advance specific political demands; (4) the politics of development practice, especially at the grassroots; and (5) symbolic political contestation as expressed through discursive contestation in the public sphere. Figure 6.1 below depicts these five political domains in addition to distinctions between the political and public spheres that are continuously (re)constructed through engagement in each of these five spheres and their interfaces.

The value of this exercise is that it allows one to rethink political practice from multiple angles. Moreover, it opens up new ground for imagining more creative progressive political strategies to undermine and subvert the oppressive functioning of dominant interests in the city. The model rests heavily on Foucault's understanding of power and therefore locates discursive and symbolic dimensions of political practice as central to re-reading political institutions and agency (Flyvbjerg 2001: Ch. 8; Gabardi 2001: Ch. 4). I will briefly elaborate each domain in terms of key defining features, types of political practices, inter-connections with other domains and possible pitfalls. To animate the discussion, I will occasionally draw on examples, mainly from Cape Town, where my own research is ongoing,

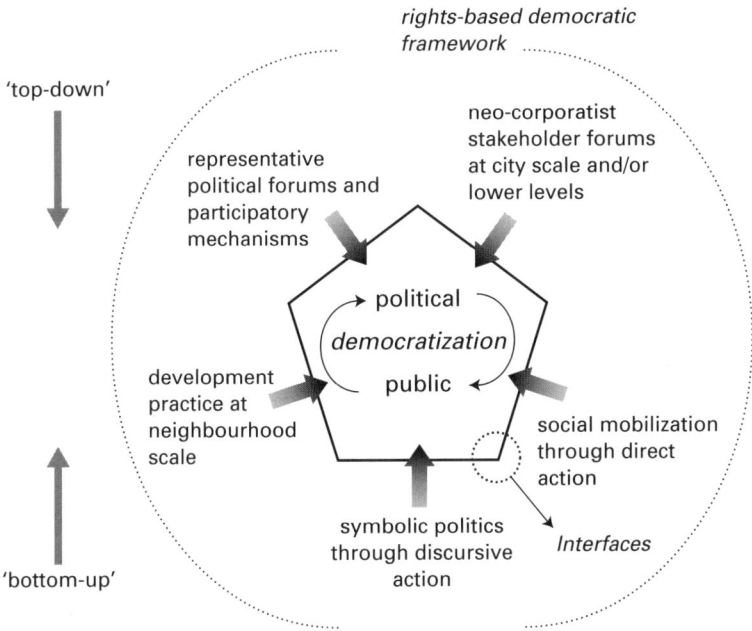

rights-based democratic framework

'top-down'

neo-corporatist stakeholder forums at city scale and/or lower levels

representative political forums and participatory mechanisms

political
democratization
public

development practice at neighbourhood scale

social mobilization through direct action

symbolic politics through discursive action

Interfaces

'bottom-up'

FIGURE 6.1 Dimensions of political engagement in the city

to illustrate certain points. Given the conceptual biases on which I base this model, the organizing thread that runs through this paper is a concern with progressive political practices and identities that will address urban inequality in a substantive manner.

Domain one: representative politics Political representation refers to the formal political system that characterizes national, provincial and municipal government. The parameters of formal politics are established in the South African Constitution (Act 108 of 1996), which makes provision for a proportional political system based on multi-party political contestation for electoral support. At all levels, the main avenue of political participation in this process is political parties elected on the basis of a proportional system, except at municipal level where a combination of proportional and ward-based systems are in effect. The democratic effectiveness of the system depends in large measure on the democratic nature of the respective political parties along with their rootedness in their constituencies (Goetz and Lister 2001; Heller 2001). It also depends on the quality and maturity of the institutional rules and systems that structure the functioning of political chambers, council and committee meetings and associated mechanisms for transparency, responsiveness and accountability (Blair 2000).

At the limits of possibility

145

The *White Paper on Local Government* laid a firm foundation for the establishment of developmental local government which is a normative approach to ensure that municipal government prioritizes the needs of the poor in fulfilling its governing functions. The framework further acknowledged that a developmental thrust is dependent on vigorous citizen participation to construct a participatory form of local governance (Pieterse 2002a). This policy framework, later encoded in various pieces of legislation, provides a solid foundation for participatory local governance where the full diversity and conflictual interests of the city can be expressed. Naturally this depends on 'political commitment' to formulate more practical policies to create various participatory governance mechanisms such as citizen juries, participatory budget councils, integrated development planning forums, area-based political committees, citizen opinion surveys, participatory action research studies to test policy preferences and options, transparency guidelines and support systems, and so forth (Borja and Castells 1997: 193–200; Hill 1994; Pieterse 2000).[3] Beyond political commitment, it also depends on the tangible accountability of the elected politicians.

The literatures on urban regimes, growth coalitions and elite pacts demonstrate the subtle and blatant ways in which (organized) business interests that rely on public investment frameworks and spending (for transport, land-use zoning and preparation, environmental guidelines, etc.) exert their influence over the decision-making and functioning of local government (Barkin 1997; Hiller 2000; Mossberger and Stoker 2001). If one approaches participatory instruments with a naïveté about these relations it easily becomes a form of camouflage for what is really going on in the city. The point about participatory local governance is to increase the democratic oversight of active citizens, especially those whose human rights are systematically denied due to inadequate services and lack of opportunities. However, this is unlikely to take root unless citizens are well organized and supported by municipal government actively to organize themselves into independent and articulate voices. A twelve-year programme on 'community management' in poor/informal areas in developing countries undertaken by Habitat underscores the importance of self-organization and appropriate state support (Lüdeking and Williams 1999). These qualifiers point to the importance of the political values and practices of the political parties that hold majority power in the council. Even though it is a neglected subject in the literature, it is clear that the democratic culture – open or closed – within political parties is a vital aspect in embedding meaningful participatory local governance.

There remains surprisingly little systematic research on the African National Congress (ANC), especially in terms of local dynamics within branches and spill-over effects into municipal councils. Nevertheless, most commentators seem to be in agreement that the ANC is struggling to redefine its ideological commitment to internal democracy as a political value and cultural practice (Marais 2001; Peet 2002). The nature of the list formulation process, which is an integral component of the proportional electoral system, seems to reinforce a hierarchical culture in the organization along with an upward-looking sense of accountability as opposed to the reverse. This is compounded by the determination of the organization's leadership to keep crucial national debates about the economy, political reform, developmental issues and foreign policy outside of the public domain to avoid the impression that there are divisions within the party. Unsurprisingly, it has the opposite effect (see Saul 2001; Cronin 2002). The ANC is losing credibility among the intelligentsia (black and white) as the torch-bearer for robust democratic contestation. With this said, it is important to emphasize that my own research in Cape Town suggests that there are many grassroots members of the party who are equally worried about this tendency and use their branches and other forums to challenge it. This contradictory drift towards less openness and a suspicion of direct opposition undermines the emergence of strong democratic leaders that can transcend the party machinery to become influential in the public sphere and with the citizenry.

Democratic and visionary leadership among the elected representatives in (municipal) government is a vital ingredient of this conceptual model. Such leaders need to set the tone in establishing governance networks that are robust, based on healthy agonistic contestation and broad-based so that societal programmes can be undertaken to shape the future of the city (Landry 2000). What all this means will become clearer as I proceed to other political domains. But first a few more comments on the inter-relationship between the representative domain of politics and others identified in the model. I started off with a discussion of the representative domain of political practice, because it is in this domain that an enabling climate can be constructed for the flourishing of political agency in other domains of social action. In particular, municipal government (and visionary leaders) is an important precursor for the establishment of 'neo-corporatist' forums to undertake strategic planning regarding the future trajectory of the city. In fact, close synergy between the IDP of the municipality and the broader city development strategy (CDS) that emerges from multi-stakeholder governance forums is essential (Pieterse 2003). Given the built-in bias, towards more organized, well resourced and articulate voices in multi-stakeholder forums, however, the elected politicians have a vital role to play in ensuring that marginal and poorly organized interests in the city, who should be the primary beneficiaries of the developmental local government mandate, can also find their issues infused in the deliberations. There are few guarantees that this is likely to happen, but this does not negate the conceptual assertion. When I elaborate on autonomous agency by subaltern classes and groups below it will become clearer that I locate this conceptual assertion within a larger theoretical diagram of agonistic, conflict-ridden contestation between various political agendas in the city. Seen from that position, it is legitimate to invoke the democratic expectation about the ideal role of elected politicians.

There are many other dangers when it comes to the functioning of representative politics. Ongoing research by scholars on the impact of the expansive policy edifice on the capacity of municipal politicians to exercise their roles is indicative of the danger of malfunctioning due to overload. Some of the evaluative studies of IDPs point in this direction (Harrison 2001a; Harrison and Todes 2001; Binns and Nel 2002). Other studies point to the debilitating effect of declining regional economies on the developmental aspirations of local government (Todes 2000). Some research also points out the persistent disjuncture between policy rhetoric and continuing business as usual at the expense of the urban poor (McDonald 2002b; Williams 2000). These research findings all underscore the danger of vesting all hope for radical democracy in the emergence of effective representative democratic institutions. Much more is required, as the remainder of the chapter will demonstrate.

Domain two: neo-corporatist stakeholder forums Stakeholder-based forums refer to formal deliberative institutions that provide a regulated and predictable space for negotiation and contestation between state, civil society and private sector representative organizations on urban issues of (mutual) concern, even if for different reasons. Commonly they are referred to as multi-stakeholder forums. In their book, *Local and Global*, Jorge Borja and Manuel Castells (1997) set out the case for the necessity of these kinds of deliberative spaces to co-create strategic plans for the city. They frame their argument against the backdrop of the impact of globalization processes on cities. Such impacts make it more important than ever that public infrastructure investments (especially transport and communication) are carefully made and in terms of a larger strategic vision of where the urban economy is headed. By definition, such a vision cannot be the fabrication of municipal planners but must arise from properly structured processes of participation and deliberation, because it must not only be viable but also politically embedded among the diverse stakeholders in the city. Without legitimacy, strategic plans are bound to run aground on the banks of political conflict and corruption. The perspective of Borja and Castells clearly operates on shifts away from master planning to strategic planning to accommodate the complexity of urban life. It also builds on the strong participatory thrust that propels discourses on greater decentralization and deliberative democracy (Fung and Wright 2001; Minogue 2002). Ideas about participatory local democracy are now thoroughly mainstream, even if poorly implemented (Nederveen Pieterse 2001). The World Bank and other multilateral development institutions are feverishly promoting CDSs across the globe. The CDS methodology is a more sophisticated rerun of the city consultation concept that UN-Habitat and the United Nations Environment Programme have been pioneering since the late 1980s (Pieterse 2000). This bouquet of policy thinking seeks to lock municipal government into multi-stakeholder processes of planning and monitoring to compensate for the limited resources and capacity of most Third World local authorities. It also aims for increased legitimacy, which has been eroded by decades of authoritarian and patronage-based political decision-making. Recent moves in most South African cities to initiate strategic planning processes or build ownership around visions such as *Joburg 2030* demonstrate the impact of this category of political action (City of Johannesburg 2002).

Despite the rapid spread of multi-stakeholder strategic planning and deliberation, a number of criticisms have been levelled against the theory and practice. In summary, four criticisms of stakeholder forums can be gleaned from the literature: (1) It legitimizes decisions that are taken by proxies of elite interests and consequently fulfils a function of co-optation through 'corporatist localism' (Ruppert 2000); (2) It potentially subverts the emergence of oppositional political discourses and practices by framing such actions as illegitimate and undemocratic, because these emanate from outside of the negotiation framework (Fainstein 2000); (3) It reinforces divisions within poor and marginalized communities because these forums tend to draw in relatively better-off community associations that crowd out less organized and articulate associations (Cooke and Kothari 2001); (4) It undermines informal and non-rational livelihood strategies of the poor through an insistence on working with formal planning frameworks and rationalities (Cleaver 2001). These are insightful points and my own research on urban political processes in metropolitan Cape Town confirms these dangers (Pieterse 2002c; Pieterse forthcoming).

Nevertheless, it is instructive to bear in mind that the stakeholder forum mechanism is now firmly entrenched in South African political life. At the dawn of the transition process (late 1980s), a number of negotiation forums started to emerge at a local level as white municipalities entered into negotiations to end or circumvent rates and service charge boycotts (Shubane 1995). These institutional forms became somewhat paradigmatic throughout the transition because they provided a model to allow oppositional political organizations to retain their relative autonomy while renegotiating the terms of their relationship as the process of democratization shifted power to the black majority and their representative organizations (former political liberation movements such as the ANC, PAC and the like). In other words, the forums provided a guarantee against unilateral decisions that would radically alter economic and political relations in society. It is for this reason that many regard them as reformist corporatist institutions that simply serve to entrench vested elite interests by diffusing militant social action by subjugated classes (Bond 2000).

Should these criticisms lead us to reject the role of multi-stakeholder forums in advancing radical democratic urban politics? I think not. It is crucial to remain aware of the depoliticizing dangers of such forums along with the built-in tendency to cater for well-organized, -resourced and articulate political groups. Yet, given the complexity of urban development challenges it is imperative to build broad-based agreement, even if provisional and continuously renewed, about the future direction of the city and how to get there. The constitutional obligations to use developmental local government progressively to realize everyone's socio-economic rights must be the touchstone for the institutional rules and agenda of such forums. In other words, in terms of institutional design and functioning, provision must be made for ensuring adequate representation of potentially marginalized groups and ensuring that the search for consensus does not rule out the necessity of agonistic engagement. The work of Michael Gunder and Jean Hillier, among others, points to a series of useful principles that can be used to ensure fair and critical deliberation (Edmunds and Wollenberg 2001; Gunder in press; Healey 2002; Hillier 2002).

The progressive potential of these mechanisms, however, can be secured only if civil society actors maintain their autonomy and actively pursue political strategies that unfold in spheres of engagement and communication outside of the chambers of stakeholder forums. The leverage power of groups representing the interests of the poor and future generations in forums will be dependent on the power of such constituencies in the public sphere, in particular the power that comes from direct action to shape agendas and lay claims to constitutionally defined rights and entitlements. Furthermore, strong social organization at the grassroots potentially strengthens the accountability of elected politicians. This relational dynamic can be harnessed to ensure that conservative agendas that will further exploit the poor become inconceivable for the political class.

The multi-stakeholder forums can then become discursive spaces where a more redistributive 'consensus' can be constructed and consolidated. The fact is, unless business interests and the middle classes are publicly and incessantly compelled to subscribe to the importance of redistribution, it is virtually impossible to use local government service provision and taxation as effective tools to achieve greater equity in the city. Multi-stakeholder forums can be important sites of contestation and engagement socially to construct such political agreements. This is dependent on the social power of the poor and other marginal groups established through effective organization and mobilization around everyday struggles. It also depends on effective facilitation of such processes, which is often lacking. It is furthermore dependent on the circulation of alternative discourses and substantiating knowledge that demonstrates how distributive justice can work to the benefit of all citizens in the city. As stressed earlier, it is crucial to appreciate the *relational* inter-dependency between various domains of political practice.

Domain three: direct action Direct action involves various forms of collective action by (disadvantaged) groups aimed at stretching the liberal democratic constitutional framework to its limit.[4] This assertion implies that social movements and looser, issue-specific, social groups must claim their rights and entitlements through non-violent social action focused on concrete issues that shape the quality of life of their constituencies. In South Africa's recent history, there are a number of examples where such action resulted in favourable constitutional judgments on the rights to shelter for children, protection from forced evictions (see Liebenberg 2002) and access to essential drugs and medicines (*Sunday Independent*, 7 April 2002).

In recent years, there has been a noteworthy increase in social mobilization *against* state policies, premised on an anti-neoliberal and anti-globalization platform. At a national level, examples would include public protests against debt, the arms deal and privatization. (These tend to be based in urban areas and are becoming a feature of political cultures in the cities.) At a local level, there has been a noticeable increase in community-level protests against the privatization and/or commercialization of some municipal services and the related disconnection of services and/or eviction of defaulters (Desai 2000; McDonald and Pape 2003). The common thread in these protests is a radical political economy analysis that ascribes the root cause of increasing poverty and inequality to the Growth, Employment and Redistribution (GEAR) macro-economic policy of the government. In terms of this perspective, GEAR is a natural reflection of an elite pact (comprised of the new political and – black – economic elite) that is determined to slot into the unequal system of globalization, even if it is at the expense of the working classes and the unemployed (Bond 2000). As a result, a new brand of highly politicized social formations has taken root at the grassroots and sections of the NGO community. This group seeks to deconstruct and replace the mainstream development programme of the state. This is highly significant, because it signals the emergence of a series of much more pronounced political fault lines that cut through the ruling tripartite alliance, the NGO sector and organized grassroots organizations.

In a sense, the primary function of progressive direct action is to maintain political momentum for redistribution and realization of human rights, especially socio-economic rights. Of all the political practices in the city, this type pushes most blatantly at the boundaries of the possible (in discursive, political and juridical terms). Direct action seeks to disturb the tranquillity of 'business as usual', whereby local governance unfolds at an arm's length from the citizenry and politicians nestle snugly in the bosom of elites. It potentially shakes up the middle-class lack of interest in life beyond the suburb; that is, livelihood challenges in the township, shanty town and other spaces of marginalization. Street conflicts, clashes and destabilizations that spark off direct action are prerequisites for political agreements to address urban inequalities. Such agreements will invariably involve attitudinal and behavioural change among the middle classes, because they will have to fund more aggressive redistribution and more effective government. (Not that their financial contributions are proportionately more significant than what the poor are already contributing simply to survive despite inadequate support from the state.)

To be sure, direct action is not about consensus. Invariably, it raises political temperatures and solicits conflict from those who stand to lose if demands are acceded to. From an agonistic political perspective such conflict is necessary to combust crisis, which in turn can produce political engagement and provisional agreements between opponents to allow governance and management to carry on. The challenge is to foster a political culture that is embracing of social mobilization politics along with institutionally defined pressure valves to absorb and channel the energy unleashed by direct action. Participatory mechanisms associated with representative political domains can be useful mediating channels to ensure that the demands of claimants are articulated to actual plans, agendas and budgets of local government as requisite in terms of the IDP process. Similarly, task teams that undertake the work of multi-stakeholder forums can expand their deliberations to address the claims and issues of those on the streets. The oft forgotten relational dynamic of urban politics comes to the fore yet again.

Such a conception of course rejects social mobilization for the sake of it; that is, militancy without a purpose, without a potentially winnable demand. It remains unclear whether the recent social mobilization in many South African cities is merely reactive or premised on a clear strategy to articulate the diverse domains of political practice in the city. Hard, ideologically pure rhetoric tends to militate against reflexive and adaptive political strategy. Such rhetoric is impervious to strategic, contingent political praxis. Much of the rhetoric that seems to travel along with new formations such as the Anti-Privatization Forum seems to fall into this category.[5] It is unlikely to produce radical incremental political solutions that can be institutionalized to achieve lasting redistributive effects. It runs the risk of creating a lot of symbolic attention without translation into practicable reforms that may not fulfil the entire demand, but represent a step in the right direction. (Of course I recognize that in some strands of Marxist social theory the point of social mobilization is merely to demonstrate the impossibility of solutions in a capitalist framework. Therefore, militant political action for the sake of inducing conflict is the *raison d'être*.) The Treatment Action Campaign (TAC) and Homeless People's Federation seem to be more adept at understanding the use value of direct action to shape agendas and make room for provisional solutions that will in future become the focus of further mobilization, renegotiation and even incorporation by the state (Pieterse and van Donk 2002).

There is one more dimension of direct action that is relevant for my purposes here before I move on to discuss development practice as a domain of politics. Collective action through embodied public displays of protest, celebration, defiance or whatever is not inherently progressive or conservative. In my view, progressive direct action is marked by the political philosophy and agenda of the movement and more importantly, the values of the actors who constitute the movement. Participation by the poor and marginalized citizens in social movements or processes can have a profoundly empowering psychic effect, as we know from the works and examples of Paulo Freire, Mahatma Gandhi, Commandante Marcos and Frantz Fanon. However, this is contingent on the democratic culture of such organizations and the space for self-realization through experimentation and performative play. Ostensibly progressive agendas do not automatically translate into progressive inter-personal relations between activists, nor do they translate into an emphasis on self-realization as part and parcel of the larger social change desired by the movement. What I have in mind here is a form of politics sensitive to issues of interiority as well as exteriority (Alvarez et al. 1998; Orbach 1996; Pieterse 2002b). This culturally attuned understanding of political agency is a vital part of redefining progressive political agency in our times. Surely our research of these movements needs to be attuned to the political strategies and ideas as well as the politics of self-realization. This is particularly important in the next domain of political practice.

Domain four: grassroots development practice

So long as we confine our conception of the political to activity that is openly declared we are driven to conclude that subordinate groups essentially lack a political life, or that what political life they do have is restricted to those exceptional moments of popular explosion. To do so is to miss the immense political terrain that lies between quiescence and revolt, and that, for better or worse, is the political environment of the subject classes. It is to focus on the visible coastline of politics and miss the continent that lies beyond. (Scott 1997: 323)

The public heroics of social movements are usually what grab our attention when we think about political agency in the city. As the work of James Scott suggests, however, the political terrain is much broader and more variegated than this. I am particularly interested to draw attention to the quotidian spaces and practices of grassroots development projects and their institutional frameworks. In my reading, the politics of development practice unfolds at the neighbourhood scale (and beyond), where autonomous and state-dependent projects are undertaken to improve the quality of life and livelihoods, to protect against the vicissitudes of crime, violence and other shocks, and to deliberate future trajectories for the community in relation to other communities and the larger regional economic-ecological system.

Elsewhere I have elaborated the content and institutional dimensions of community-based development processes, with particular reference to anti-poverty programmes that are most urgent for the urban poor (Pieterse 2001). In a similar sense, one could categorize shopfloor struggles to improve the quality of work and establish workplace democracy in this category (Mackay and Mathoho 2001). Both types of social practice involve the establishment of practical rules and norms that can regularize interactions between powerful interests (e.g. government departments with bundles of resources for specific programmes) and the subaltern in terms of effective ways of meeting the minimum standards of 'human dignity' as espoused in the Constitution. In addition to clarifying norms and standards, grassroots development practice also involves the active construction of systematic projects to address a variety of consumption, productive, information and political needs. Here I have in mind savings clubs (*stokvels*), community gardens, neighbourhood watches, public art clubs, soup kitchens, shelters for the abused, community crèches, drama societies, religious clubs, sports organizations, primary health care circles, and so on (Andersson 1999; Swilling and Russell 2002).

The recent study, *The Size and Scope of the Non-profit Sector in South Africa*, confirms that community life is teeming with associational practices aimed at developmental processes to create and augment livelihood strategies (Swilling and Russell 2002). There are many ways of categorizing and analysing these practices. With my eye on urban politics, I want to foreground territorial considerations without underestimating the importance of sectoral logics for organization (i.e. thematic clubs that can cut across neighbourhoods). Territorially defined development organizations have received particular attention in the post-apartheid era as government legislation often promoted the establishment of community forums – essentially clusters of development organizations at the grassroots – to serve as interfaces with government programmes. The health committees, water committees and policing forums immediately spring to mind. Furthermore, the reorganization of development finance institutional routes has also been undertaken with a view to providing more funding to such organizations. These initiatives build on a long legacy in South Africa of community-based mobilizations around welfare, self-defence and educational initiatives (Patel 1992). However, what do all these observations mean for radical democracy and the horizon of distributive justice in the city in times marked by neoliberal ideology?

In the first instance, it is vital to appreciate the *experiential* importance of participation in community-based associations aimed at improving the quality of life of oneself and fellow residents. The recent work of Arjun Appadurai on slum dweller associations in Mumbai argues for the importance of taking seriously 'the capacity to aspire' in thinking about this issue. Appadurai (forthcoming) develops a layered argument that development, and especially its imagining, is deeply embedded in local cultures that people draw on to function in a day-to-day sense. Some of these cultural resources will be consistent with dominant societal values and norms that reproduce the acceptability of perverse inequalities. Other cultural resources may hold the germ of critique, of thinking about alternative social configurations that can lead to an improvement in quality of life and sense of self. The challenge is to use the future-shaping essence of development practice to expand 'the cultural map of aspirations' and in the process expand social citizenship and especially voice (Appadurai forthcoming: 5).

It is inconceivable that such political faculties can be cultivated outside an associational context. The argument can be extended. Social learning that arises from development projects can socialize uninformed and unrecognized citizens into democratic values such as accountability, transparency, (agonistic) deliberation, inclusivity, review and majority decision-making. In this sense, it prefigures the democratic rules of the larger political game that unfold in representative arenas. In other words, the experience of organizational democracy in development projects can concretize the meanings of democratic citizenship.

In the second instance, participation in development projects often also enables people to see the bits and pieces of the state and how they function in contradictory ways at different scales. For example, those projects which benefit from the government's Poverty Alleviation Fund administered by the Independent Development Trust for the Department of Social Development learn that the social development objectives of a national department may be very different from the social development initiatives of municipal government. In the larger political game, strategic political positioning and action depend on a differentiated understanding of the state and the contingent opportunities for alliances when appropriate (Evans 2002). As long as organizations of the poor fail to capitalize on the, always contingent, contradictions between various arms of the state, they are unlikely to move their agendas forward, let alone recalibrate the priorities of the government.

In the third instance, grassroots projects can be invaluable sites of experimentation with alternative ways of doing development. State bureaucracies tend to be rigid, hierarchical and conformist institutions. Little room is left for creativity, learning and innovation despite incessant change management efforts.[6] In part, this is attributable to the organizational logic of large rules-bound and -driven institutions. In part, it is a function of the need for political control and oversight over the functioning of government. The literature on organizational change and learning in the public sector suggests that these tendencies can be mitigated only by powerful external pressures that either show up the failures of government or provide compelling alternatives that allow new discourses to come into play (Barnard and Armstrong 1998). On rare but very important occasions, grassroots initiatives can demonstrate alternative approaches to development that can be absorbed by the state and in theory lead to more equitable outcomes. A case in point is the influence of the Homeless People's Federation on the Department of Housing and their adoption of the 'people's housing process' policy (see Bauman and Mitlin 2002).

These three instances make it clearer why grassroots development associations are such an important aspect of the larger political canvas in the city. It would be misleading to suggest, however, that it is easy to achieve these impacts because of the dangers associated with this category of organization. Many of these grassroots organizations operate in an apolitical fashion and tend to reproduce welfarist models of social change. Such an approach deflects attention away from the structural underpinning of maldistribution of public resources. These organizations are also prone to co-option because of financial dependency issues. This is less likely to be a problem in cases where development projects also incorporate membership fees/savings into the organizational methodology, but that is rare. An even more insidious problem is the potential of development projects to dissipate pent-up anger and militancy – the fuel of 'spontaneous' combustion that is so essential for direct action. The highly regulated and routinized political frameworks in South Africa, which construct sharp insider/outsider boundaries, undermine the rise of social movements willing to occupy political arenas of public direct action. For reasons argued earlier, this is a problem for advancing radical democracy and distributive justice.

In terms of the conceptual model, it is important to review grassroots development practice in relation to neo-corporatist forums and the departmental programmes carried out by municipal government. Due to the inherently tame and consensual style of politics that one finds in this sphere, it can be anticipated that umbrella organizations of these grassroots types are likely to participate in multi-stakeholder deliberative forums, ostensibly to represent 'the community' voice. This makes such organizations of strategic importance to social movements that may prefer to stand outside the discursive ambit of deliberative forums. On many issues, informal alliances with these organizations will complement public actions with good effect. On other issues, social movements may wish to back their positions and agendas in these forums through the media and other forms of projection and agitation in the public domain. On every single issue of note in the city, symbolic politics will be key, and symbolism thrives on waves of compelling and widely shared messages. With this point it is appropriate to move on to a discussion of domain five of political practice: symbolic politics through discursive action.

Domain five: symbolic politics

power is both embedded in and effectuated through a crucial combination of knowledge and language, or what is called discourse. Discourse in this sense is the complex mixture of ideas and expressions through which individuals both perceive and in turn try to explain social reality. Discourse therefore also defines the parameters and criteria people use to ascertain and calculate the *potential courses of action* and to choose particular cours-es of action in specific circumstances. It is thus the primary [...] medium of both understanding and action. (Goverde et al. 2000: 14)

Paradoxically, the symbolic or discursive domain is the most under-studied and under-theorized compared to the previous four domains of practice. Paradoxically, because Foucault suggests that we are surrounded and enrolled by discursive power all the time. It is the ground we move on, the air we breathe, because we cannot step outside of it if we are to make a (conscious or unconscious) decision about our next move. Discourses pro-vide a lens on the world, our everyday spaces and ourselves. They constitute the everyday and specialist knowledge we draw on to make sense of larger systems of power that shape thought and behaviour through regulation of bodily practices. Put differently, we internalize discourses about what is appropriate to think about, what to think (or believe) about the issues we should think about, and how to act in consistent ways with what we believe. All of this comes to us as unquestionable truths and that is the core of the power of discourse. It renders certain historically and politically constructed assumptions as self-evident and obvious, beyond the remit of questioning or reversal. For discursive power to work its magic, it must insinuate itself culturally; that is, be embedded in our daily sensibilities and practices which are culturally specific and contingent. Here I am ap-plying a notion of culture as

the historical transmission of a learned repertory of embodied human practices expressed in symbolic codes through which individuals and social groups develop and perpetuate a way of life. It is a set of signifying activities shaped by and infused with relations of power. Culture implies not only language, values, beliefs, and mores, but material objects and processes organized in time-space locations. Culture is therefore a complex social ecology of object, subject, and intersubjective relations. (Gabardi 2001: 89)

For my purposes in this chapter, I want to draw attention to the political potency of discourses about the *identity of the city* and the policy impera-tives that flow from it. In a recent article, Jenny Robinson highlights the problematic obsession of many local government managers with becom-ing 'world-class' and 'globally competitive' (2002). The work of Jo Beall and colleagues on Johannesburg, Alison Todes on Durban and my own research on Cape Town confirms the observation of Robinson (Beall et al. 2002; Pieterse 2003; Todes 2000). The discourse on the imperative of becoming world-class or globally competitive inexorably leads to policy commitments to maintain levels of infrastructure that are deemed world-class and favourable to attracting foreign investors. If such high-cost and high-maintanance infrastructures are not sufficiently *in place*, literally, then of course investment strategies need to be devised to ensure that sufficient resources are mobilized to make such 'essential' investments possible (see Graham and Marvin 2001). If this means that fewer resources are available for investing in infrastructure-poor areas, especially in times of economic slowdown, then this is a rational sacrifice for the longer-term good of the city. In this context, neo-corporatist forums then become important sites of reproducing and legitimating such discourses to the point of expunging oppositional ones, or at least casting such perspectives as 'out of touch with reality'. Crucially, municipal discourses such as these are reinforced by national discourses as expressed through the macro-economic commitments of the government and the industrial strategy that prioritizes investment in high-tech sectors that will enable South Africa to 'compete' globally, irrespective of whether the educational base exists for the realization of such an economic trajectory.

To understand the discursive parameters of urban politics, it is important to pay attention to the following kinds of municipal discourses about:

- the size and sources of the municipal finance envelope;
- the options for service delivery and the differential consequences for various categories of citizens;
- the degree and quality of citizen participation – are residents in the city defined as customers, clients, citizens, or defaulters?;
- the identity of the city and especially its future as defined in planning frameworks, IDPs and city visions that emanate from stakeholder forums and are popularized in the public sphere through print media and the airwaves.

Since most of the functioning of discursive power is abstract and fluid, I will draw on one example from Cape Town during the recent period (post-1996) when the African National Congress (ANC) came into power to govern the City of Cape Town municipality. At the outset of their tenure, ANC councillors quickly set themselves up to institute policies that will unravel and remake the apartheid city – tackle head-on racialized segregation and unequal access to urban resources. For the politicians this meant addressing institutionalized racism that structured the allocation of the budget between white and black areas and providing housing for black communities alongside traditionally white areas to ensure access to economic opportunities and other urban resources. They achieved reasonable results on the first aspect but hardly any progress on the second. Discursively this was legitimated through a shift in policy objective from 'equitable outcomes' to 'equitable opportunities'. At the start of their tenure, the criterion for success was whether the city was becoming more socially just by ensuring that all citizens experienced a relatively equal standard of living through a rigorous application of distributive justice. At the end of their tenure, senior officials defined as their primary criterion of success whether they were able to ensure that everyone had equal access to opportunities in the city, with no comment on their responsibility with regard to the overall quality of life and social justice in the city. For the current argument, the point is that the politicians and officials got away with this discursive redefinition with very little opposition or protest from the affected communities or collective associations representing the urban poor. In one sense, it points to the serious weakness of progressive civil society organizations in the city. In another sense, it illustrates the subtle play of power that underpins discursive strategy. Furthermore, it is certain that wider circuits of power came into play.

If South African cities are to become spaces of greater possibility for radical democracy and distributive justice, this domain of political practice will have to be taken much more seriously. Symbolic contestation through the deconstruction and reconstruction of dominant discourses is a prerequisite for achieving impact in terms of political strategies in all four of the other domains discussed before. Symbolic politics functions through cultural resignification and therefore implies more creative practices which target the media, especially radio and popular newspapers; public spaces in the city, especially streetscapes and squares invested with symbolic meaning; and spaces of collective consumption, such as schools, clinics, libraries. Symbolic contestation clears the ground to ask fundamental questions about given discourses such as: what are the underlying rationalities of this discourse? What conditions make it possible for this discourse to pass as given and valid? What are the goals of the discourse? How can the elements of the discourse be challenged and rearranged to turn the discourse on itself and make new meanings and imaginings possible which can be pursued through direct action or development practice or municipal policy? More presciently, to return to my earlier concern about the identity of the city, a discursive sensitivity makes it possible to recast questions such as these: who is the city for? Whose identities and cultures are embodied by representations of the city? How can the futures of the city be reimagined to reflect a radical openness as opposed to the conventional approach whereby there is only one alternative?[7]

Interfaces The drawback of any conceptual model is that it superimposes a false sense of structure on complex, fluid social realities. The conceptual model of urban politics developed here is no exception. There is much that leaks from the model to smudge the artificial boundaries between urban spaces and associated political practices. Cultural identities and practices are constitutively porous, relational and marked by dissensus within some aspiration for consensus (Appadurai forthcoming). For these reasons, I want to foreground the numerous spaces of interface between different types of political practice. Because of space constraints, I will refer to one striking example which is theorized in the evocative work of Asef Bayat on what he categorizes as 'the encroachment of the ordinary'.

Asef Bayat, in the tradition of James Scott, seeks to capture political agency in a zone in between what I would label direct action and development practice (Bayat 1997, 2000; Scott 1997). Bayat studies the everyday practices of survival and circumvention, undertaken at the expense of the elite, that the ultra poor engage in to carve out spaces to dwell, move around and earn an income in the city where their very presence is deemed illegitimate and illegal. It is a nuanced and layered argument which is best summarized by the author:

> The notion of 'quiet encroachment' describes the silent, protracted and pervasive advancement of ordinary people on those who are propertied and powerful in a quest for survival and improvement of their lives. It is characterized by quiet, largely atomized and prolonged mobilization with episodic collective action – open and fleeting struggles without clear leadership, ideology or structured organization. While quiet encroachment is basically a 'non-movement', it is distinct from survival strategies or 'everyday resistance'. First, the struggles and gains of people at the grassroots are not made at the expense of fellow poor or themselves, but of the state, the rich and the general public. For example, in order to light their shelters, the urban poor tap electricity not from their neighbours, but from the municipality power poles; to raise their living standard they do not prevent their children from attending school and send them to work, but rather they squeeze the hours of their own formal job in order to work a second job in the informal sector. In addition, these struggles should not be seen as necessarily defensive, merely in the realm of 'resistance', but as cumulatively encroaching, meaning that the actors tend to expand their space by winning new positions to move on to. This kind of quiet activism challenges fundamental aspects of state prerogatives, including the meaning of 'order' and control of public space. But the most immediate consequence is the redistribution of social goods via the (unlawful and direct) acquisition of:

collective consumption (land, shelter, piped water, electricity); public space (streets, intersections, parking areas); and opportunities (favourable business conditions, locations and labels). (Bayat 2000: 24–5)

This provocative conception clearly has resonance and relevance in the South African context. Yet it would be incorrect to locate it as either direct action or politics of development practice. It occupies a zone in between but is also highly amenable for deployment in creative politics of discursive contestation about who the city is for, even if not by the protagonists of quiet encroachment themselves. This example should suffice to stress the point that the model can be seen as a heuristic to explore discrete domains of political practice and their hybrid interfaces. Now, for some comments on the final elements of the model: political and public spheres.

Public sphere + political sphere = vibrant democracy? In terms of the conceptual model, elected politicians carry out their function primarily in two domains of political practice: the representative sphere and neo-corporatist forums. And together, these two constitute the formal 'political sphere' in the city, anchored in the deliberations of the municipal council chamber. In the political sphere the governmental priorities of the city are defined, contested and reviewed through highly structured, procedural mechanisms of deliberation. Both the content and systems of deliberation have a structuring effect on what is defined as legitimately part of the political sphere and what is not. As I have already argued before, discursive power and its underlying knowledges are the grids that define the horizon of political imagination and intervention. This political horizon is mediated via the media and legitimating knowledge institutions such as universities, technikons, think-tanks and opinion-poll survey companies that reflect back to society curves of opinion and attitudes with a gloss of scientificity. In the absence of dissent and conflict, the political sphere can easily dominate and structure the broader public sphere where state and civil society engagements are mediated. In other words, top-down political practices can eclipse bottom-up processes that emanate from civil society, effectively asphyxiating democratic citizenship.

For this reason, it is vital to stimulate and animate a vibrant public sphere. In the traditional Habermasian sense, the public sphere 'is a space which mediates between society and the state where the public organizes itself and in which "public opinion" is formed' (Barker 2000: 151). In this sphere, citizens engage discursively and rationally in public reasoning to arrive at the greatest public interest on a given issue. My theoretical starting points lead me away from the rational deliberative model of Habermas in order to promote a conception of the public sphere more favourable to the possibility and hegemony of radical democracy. This refers to 'a radical pluralistic public sphere of contestive identities, moralities, and discourses. It endorses a politics of diverse social, cultural and political movements organized around the values of cultural recognition, direct democracy, and performative resistance' (Gabardi 2001: 109). This conception is premised on the insight of Chantal Mouffe that we can never fully reconcile the tensions between equality (maximization of egalitarian spaces of differences) and liberty (maximization of democratic rights), but instead deploy the tension to animate agonistic contestation within the ambit of universal human rights (Amin and Thrift 2002). The tension produces agonistic pluralism in the polity.

Ongoing research and obsessing about the political economy of urban development in Cape Town in the post-apartheid era leave me surprised at how much is not surfaced and voiced in the city (see Abbot 2000; Pieterse 2002b; Turok 2001; Watson 2002; Wilkinson 2000). So much of the latent conflicts between groups and representations continues to be repressed or dissipated by discourses that seek to construct the city as a place of harmonious co-operation towards a shared future. Political contestations are mostly ritualized around banal conflicts pertaining to intra- and inter-party personality clashes as opposed to substantive ideological differences articulated around everyday concerns for viable employment, shelter, community services, and so on. Occasionally, questions about structural racism and its impact on the ability of certain groups to access basic services are foregrounded through momentary interventions such as a three-day cultural festival on 'one city, many cultures'. Yet even then the representations are mainly organized in terms of a depoliticized model of multiculturalism that celebrates diversity without paying attention to how inequality is tied to structural difference. Opportunities to use such public moments to saturate the media, educational institutions, public spaces, community facilities with unsettling questions about the persistence of prejudice, racism and discrimination are simply not taken up. But the real political tragedy unfolds in the quotidian spaces of everyday consumption of public services and spaces in the city. What we do not have is a political interest to foster a grounded politics of difference that challenges the ascribed and assumed identities of people and communities. Without such destabilization it is impossible to stimulate the experiential framework amenable to a larger project of radical democracy across the city, including its pasts and futures. In a moment I shall say more about pasts and futures, but first more on the need for acts of transgression and social learning in spaces of the everyday.

On the everyday, much can be learnt from the recent work of Ash Amin (2002) on the crises of racism and inequality in British cities. In the wake of ethnic riots in 2001, Amin explores the conventional approaches to deal with difference and inequality in the city. He observes that much faith has been stored in the promotion of public spaces for greater mixing, the development of mixed housing estates and the increasing mixture in public schools. Despite these conscious attempts to promote multicultural mixing, however, they often make little difference in terms of shifting racist and discriminatory attitudes and behaviour. Amin argues that '[h]abitual contact in itself, is no guarantor of cultural exchange. It can entrench group animosities and identities, through repetitions of gender, class, race, and ethnic codes, and paradoxically, through interventions working the grain of everyday interaction. Cultural change in these circumstances is likely to be encouraged if people can step out of their daily environments into other spaces acting as sites of "banal transgression"' (ibid.: 13). Amin continues to detail what such sites of banal transgression may look like and how they can be maintained. Suffice to say for my purposes here that this conception of everyday spaces provides an immensely fertile ground to reconceptualize the technologies and rationalities of service delivery as its unfolds at street level, in public libraries, public squares, transport interchanges, public parks, sports fields, and so on. Surely notions such as partnership can be radically recast through this lens whereby citizens from different bases of subjectivity are socialized to undertake joint problem-solving and maintenance of public resources. However, the politics of banal transgression must be simultaneously anchored in the past and the future, which also need to saturate the public sphere.

Reconstructing the past through symbolic political gestures of memor-ialization is indispensable to demonstrate the interdependencies of groups and the historically constructed nature of boundaries and identities in the city. Heroic narratives of key moments and key leaders are replaced by modest narratives about everyday resistance against totalization projects in particular sites and spaces in the city. With the colonial apartheid history we are endowed with, there is an infinite well of memories and stories to draw on to reconstitute the historical premise of the city. Similarly, the future provides a rich resource for imagining a plurality of trajectories of the city, infused by the diverse spatialities of the city. In such a public sphere it becomes very difficult for exclusivist discourses to find a foothold and exert dominance over deliberations about the use and allocation of public resources.

In summary, the argument here is simply for a recognition that at the nexus of the present (everyday transgressions in combination with an agonistic public-political sphere), the past (memory) and the future (open-ended), we are perched on the edge of a politics of potentiality; i.e. a transgressive politics of radical democracy and distributive justice.

Conclusion

By crossing the limits of possibility one encounters transgression. The perverse persistence of brutal inequality in the post-apartheid city requires a politics of transgression that valorizes agonistic engagement in a radical democratic public sphere. An ethic of transgression is a prerequisite for political action that will shift the 'frontier of the possible', following the injunction of Ben Okri. In this chapter, I have attempted to clarify a conceptual model of urban politics that can serve two functions. On the one hand, it can stimulate a stronger *relational* perspective of urban political practices across a plurality of action spaces: formal and informal, symbolic and concrete, collaborative and contestationary, with a sensibility of agonistic pluralism. Too much of the current scholarship on the post-apartheid city is fragmented and partial, undermining our ability to get a handle on what is going on and how the status quo is maintained and bolted in place. This aspect of the model is about incitement for more comprehensive analytical accounts of political practices in the city, that is the fullness of political identities in variegated time-spaces of the city.

On the other hand, I have also sought to demonstrate that a radical democratic practice in the city is multi-dimensional and constitutively open-ended. If one considers the multiplicity of domains of political practice alongside the subjective imperative of identity politics, it is clear that progressive politics cannot be imagined *a priori* nor in simple good/bad terms. A progressive agenda is by definition a complex latticework of numerous transgressive practices that range from psychic interiors to the monumental spaces that symbolically 'embody' the city for its citizens and the world at large. In between there is an infinite series of strategic and tactical manoeuvres that can be deployed to remake political identities, boundaries and horizons. It is only at the coalface of practice and resistance that the tactical co-ordinates can be defined and used as a resource to construct focused political communities in difference and solidarity. Such an appreciation allows for the natural coming together of an unflinching critique of the workings of dominating power, especially during our neoliberal times, and reverence for the complexity and indeterminacy of political practice. For me, echoing James Holston (1998), this constitutes the challenge, pleasure and joy of insurgent citizenship for the city yet to come.

Notes

This chapter is informed by research under way as part of completing a PhD on urban integration and urban development policy in South Africa post-1994. The research is part funded by: a Chevening Fellowship grant, an Ernest Oppenheimer Memorial Trust grant, and a grant from the Social Policy Department at the London School of Economics. I am further indebted to Mirjam van Donk, Jenny Robinson, Katherine McKenzie, Alan Mabin and Jo Beall for their comments and encouragement. The useful comments of the anonymous reviewers have also been beneficial. The usual disclaimer applies.

1 The dramatic levels of income inequality and seriously high levels of service deficiency are sufficient to underscore the importance of normative politics. A comprehensive overview analysis of urban poverty and its inter-relationship with inequality in South Africa can be consulted in: PDG and Isandla Institute (2002).

2 In other words, it is related to, but more narrow than, the Foucauldian conception, whereby: 'Government is any more or less calculated and rational activity, undertaken by a multiplicity of authorities and agencies, employing a variety of techniques and forms of knowledge, that seeks to shape conduct by working through our desires, aspirations, interests and beliefs, for definite but shifting ends and with a diverse set of relatively unpredictable consequences, effects and outcomes' (Dean 1999: 11).

3 In an earlier study I provide a full discussion on the gamut of participatory governance policies and tools with due regard for contextual specificity and dangers associated with this relatively recent trend (Pieterse 2000).

4 There are obviously many instances where (relatively) privileged and conservative groups also embark on direct action to get their political grievances across. By focusing on disadvantaged groups I am merely signalling an analytical preference to highlight the actions of this category of social actors but not to create an impression that other groups do not engage in this political arena.

5 There is as yet limited published material on the Anti-Privatization Forum. I base my observations on statements taken from their website and contributions to the 'Debate: SA discussion list' list serve during 2002 <debate@lists.kabissa.org>.

6 This is not to denigrate the important and complex work of effective institutional change in large public sector organizations. Studies on 'synergy' between the state and civil society organizations demonstrate just how crucial it is to pursue organizational transformation to enhance the developmental capability of government departments, especially where they act in concert with civil society organizations (see Evans 1996; Tendler 1997; Abers 2000). Nevertheless, drawing on participant observations I am also certain that much of what passes as change management quickly becomes ritualized practices of adaptation with little interest in fulfilling the developmental mandate of the government.

7 The theoretical basis of such an approach is elaborated in: Eade and Mele (2002), Massey (1999), Robinson (2002) and Tajbakhsh (2001). Strategic actions that flow from such an approach are deftly argued in: Amin (2002),

Amin and Thrift (2002), Graham and Marvin (2001: Postscript) and Sorkin (2001).

References

Abbott, J. (2000) 'Cape Town: Seeking Social Sustainability in a Fast-Growing City', in M. Polèse and R. Stren (eds), *The Social Sustainability of Cities. Diversity and the Management of Change*, Toronto and London: University of Toronto Press.

Abers, R. (2000) *Inventing Local Democracy. Grassroots Politics in Brazil*, Boulder, CO and London: Lynne Reiner Publishers.

Ahluwalia, P. (2001) *Politics and Post-Colonial Theory. African Inflections*, London: Routledge.

Alvarez, S., E. Dagnino and A. Escobar (1998) 'Introduction: The Cultural and the Political in Latin American Social Movements', in S. Alvarez, E. Dagnino and A. Escobar (eds), *Cultures of Politics. Politics of Cultures. Re-visioning Latin American Social Movements*, Boulder, CO and Oxford: Westview Press.

Amin, A. (2002) 'Ethnicity and the Multicultural City. Living with Diversity', Durham: University of Durham.

Amin, A. and S. Graham (1997) 'The Ordinary City', *Transactions of the Royal British Geographic Society*, 22, pp. 411–29.

Amin, A. and N. Thrift (2002) *Cities. Reimagining the Urban*, Cambridge: Polity.

Andersson, G. (1999) 'Partnerships between CBOs, NGOs and Government in South Africa. Insights Derived from Experience', Pretoria: US-AID South Africa.

Appadurai, A. (forthcoming) 'The Capacity to Aspire: Culture and the Terms of Recognition', in V. Rao and M. Walton (eds), *Culture and Public Action*.

Ashcroft, B. (2001) *Post-Colonial Transformations*, London: Routledge.

Barker, C. (2000) *Cultural Studies. Theory and Practice*, London: Sage Publications.

Barkin, D. (1997) 'Will Higher Productivity Improve Living Standards?', in R. Burgess, M. Carmona and T. Kolstee (eds), *The Challenge of Sustainable Cities. Neoliberalism and Urban Strategies in Developing Countries*, London: Zed Books.

Barnard, A. and G. Armstrong (1998) 'Learning and Policy Integration', in J. Schnurr and S. Holtz (eds), *The Cornerstone of Development. Integrating Environmental, Social and Economic Policies*, Boca Raton: Lewis Publishers and IDRC.

Bauman, T. and D. Mitlin (2002) 'The South African Homeless Federation: Investing in the Poor', Paper presented at Rural and Urban Development Conference, Rietvleidam: History Workshop and National Land Committee.

Bayat, A. (1997) 'Un-Civil Society: On the Politics of the "Informal People"', *Third World Quarterly*, vol. 18, No. 1, pp. 53–72.

— (2000) 'Social Movements, Activism and Social Development in the Middle East', *Civil Society and Social Movements Programme Paper*, Geneva: UNRISD.

Beall, J., S. Parnell and O. Crankshaw (2002) *Uniting a Divided City. Governance and Social Exclusion in Johannesburg*, London: Earthscan.

Biehl, J. (2002) 'Vita: Life in a Zone of Social Abandonment', *Social Text*, Vol. 19, No. 3, pp. 131–49.

Binns, T. and E. Nel (2002) 'Devolving Development: Integrated Development Planning and Developmental Local Government in Post-apartheid South Africa', *Regional Studies*, Vol. 36, No. 8, pp. 921–45.

Blair, H. (2000) 'Participation and Accountability at the Periphery: Democratic Local Governance in Six Countries', *World Development*, Vol. 28, No. 1, pp. 21–39.

Bond, P. (2000) *Elite Transition. From Apartheid to Neoliberalism in South Africa*, London and Pietermaritzburg: Pluto and University of Natal Press.

Borja, J. and M. Castells (1997) *Local and Global. The Management of Cities in the Information Age*, London: Earthscan.

Bremner, L. (1998) 'Crime and the Emerging Landscape of Post-Apartheid Johannesburg', in H. Judin and I. Vladislavic (eds), *Blank____ Architecture, Apartheid and After*, Rotterdam: NAI.

Brenner, N. and N. Theodore (2002) 'Cities and the Geographies of "Actually Existing Neoliberalism"', *Antipode*, Vol. 34, No. 3, pp. 349–79.

Cameron, R. (1999) *The Democratization of South African Local Government: A Tale of Three Cities*, Pretoria: J. L. van Schaik Academic.

Cherry, J., K. Jones and J. Seekings (2000) 'Democratization and Politics in South Africa Townships', *International Journal of Urban and Regional Research*, Vol. 24, No. 4, pp. 889–905.

City of Johannesburg (2002) *Joburg 2030*, Johannesburg: City of Johannesburg.

Cleaver, F. (2001) 'Institutions, Agency and the Limitations of Participatory Approaches to Development', in B. Cooke and U. Kothari (eds), *Participation: The New Tyranny?*, London: Zed Books.

Cooke, B. and U. Kothari (eds) (2001), *Participation: The New Tyranny?*, London: Zed Books.

Cronin, J. (2002) 'Post-Apartheid South Africa: A Reply to John Saul', *Monthly Review*, Vol. 54, No. 7, pp. 28–42.

Dean, M. (1999) *Governmentality: Power and Rule in Modern Society*, London: Sage.

Desai, A. (2000) *The Poors of Chatsworth. Race, Class and Social Movements in Post-Apartheid South Africa*, Durban: Madiba Publishers.

Duiker, S. (2000) *Thirteen Cents*, Cape Town: David Philip.

Eade, J. and C. Mele (2002) 'Introduction: Understanding the City', in J. Eade and C. Mele (eds), *Understanding the City. Contemporary and Future Perspectives*, Oxford: Blackwell.

Edmunds, D. and E. Wollenberg (2001) 'A Strategic Approach to Multistakeholder Negotiations', *Development and Change*, Vol. 32, No. 2, pp. 231–53.

Evans, P. (1996) 'Introduction. Development Strategies across the Public–Private Divide', *World Development*, Vol. 24, No.6, pp. 1,033–7.

— (2002) 'Introduction: Looking for Agents of Urban Liveability in a Globalized Political Economy', in P. Evans (ed.), *Livable Cities? Urban Struggles for Livelihood and Sustainability*, Berkeley: University of California Press.

Fainstein, S. (2000) 'New Directions in Planning Theory', *Urban Affairs Review*, Vol. 35, No. 4, pp. 451–78.

Flood, R. L. (1999) *Rethinking the Fifth Discipline. Learning within the Unknowable*, London: Routledge.

Flyvbjerg, B. (2001) *Making Social Science Matter: Why Social Inquiry Fails and How It Can Count Again*, London: Sage.

Fung, A. and E. O. Wright (2001) 'Deepening Democracy: Innovations in Empowered Participatory Governance', *Politics and Society*, Vol. 29, No. 1, pp. 5–41.

Gabardi, W. (2001) *Negotiating Postmodernism*, Minneapolis: University of Minnesota Press.

Gardiner, M. E. (2000) *Critiques of Everyday Life*, London: Routledge.

Goetz, A. M. and S. Lister (2001) 'The Politics of Civil Society Engagement with the State: A Comparative Analysis of South Africa and Uganda', Brighton: Institute of Development Studies.

Gotz, G. (2004) 'Velaphi's Dreams', in E. Pieterse and F. Meintjies (eds), *Voices of the Transition: The Politics, Poetics and Practices of Social Change in South Africa*, Johannesburg: Heinemann Publishers.

Goverde, H., P. G. Cerny, M. Haugaard and H. Lentner (2000) 'General Introduction: Power in Contemporary Politics', in H. Goverde, P. G. Cerny, M. Haugaard and H. Lentner (eds), *Power in Contemporary Politics. Theories, Practices, Globalizations*, London: Sage.

Graham, S. and S. Marvin (2001) *Splintering Urbanism. Networked Infrastructures, Technological Mobilities and the Urban Condition*, London: Routledge.

Gunder, M. (in press) 'Passionate Planning for the Other's Desire: An Agonistic Response to the Dark Side of Planning', *Progress in Planning*, Vol. 60, 85 pages (downloaded on 15 May 2003 from <www.sciencedirect.com/science/journal/03059006>.

Harrison, P. (2001a) 'The Genealogy of South Africa's Integrated Development Plan', *Third World Planning Review*, Vol. 23, No. 2, pp. 175–93.

— (2001b) 'Romance and Tragedy in (Post) Modern Planning: A Pragmatist's Perspective', *International Planning Studies*, Vol. 6, No. 1, pp. 69–88.

Harrison, P. and A. Todes (2001) 'The Use of Spatial Frameworks in Regional Development in South Africa', *Regional Studies*, Vol. 35, No. 1, pp. 65–72.

Healey, P. (1997) *Collaborative Planning: Shaping Places in Fragmented Societies*, London: Macmillan.

— (2000) 'Planning Theory and Urban and Regional Dynamics: A Comment on Yiftachel and Huxley', *International Journal of Urban and Regional Research*, Vol. 24, No. 4, pp. 917–21.

— (2002) 'On Creating the "City" as a Collective Resource', *Urban Studies*, Vol. 39, No. 10, pp. 1,777–92.

Heller, P. (2001) 'Moving the State: The Politics of Democratic Decentralization in Kerala, South Africa, and Porto Alegre', *Politics and Society*, Vol. 29, No. 1, pp. 131–63.

Heller, P. and L. Ntlokonkulu (2001) 'A Civic Movement, or Movement of Civics? The South African National Civic Organization in the Post-Apartheid Period', *CPS Research Report*, Johannesburg: Centre for Policy Studies.

Hill, D. (1994) *Citizens and Cities. Urban Policy in the 1990s*, New York: Harvester Wheatleaf.

Hiller, H. (2000) 'Mega-Events, Urban Boosterism and Growth Strategies: An Analysis of the Objectives and Legitimations of the Cape Town 2004 Olympic Bid', *International Journal of Urban and Regional Research*, Vol. 24, No. 2, pp. 439–58.

Hillier, J. (2002) 'Direct Action and Agonism in Democratic Planning Processes', in P. Allmendinger and M. Twedwr-Jones (eds), *Planning Futures. New Directions for Planning Theory*, London: Routledge.

Holston, J. (1998) 'Spaces of Insurgent Citizenship', in L. Sandercock (ed.), *Making the Invisible Visible. A Multicultural Planning History*, Berkeley: University of California Press.

Jürgens, U. and M. Gnad (2002) 'Gated Communities in South Africa – Experiences from Johannesburg', *Environment and Planning B: Planning and Design*, Vol. 29, No. 3, pp. 337–53.

Landry, C. (2000) *The Creative City. A Toolkit for Urban Innovators*, London: Comedia and Earthscan.

Liebenberg, S. (2002) 'South Africa's Evolving Jurisprudence on Socio-economic Rights: An Effective Tool in Challenging Poverty?', *Law, Democracy and Development*, Vol. 6, No. 2, pp. 159–91.

Long, N. (2001) *Development Sociology. Actor Perspectives*, London: Routledge.

Lüdeking, G. and C. Williams (1999) 'Poverty, Participation and Government Enablement. A Summary of Findings, Lessons Learned and Recommendations of Habitat/ISS Evaluation Research (1996–1998)', Nairobi: Habitat.

Lyons, M., C. Smuts and A. Stephens (2001) 'Participation, Empowerment and Sustainability: (How) Do the Links Work?', *Urban Studies*, Vol. 38, No. 8, pp. 1,233–51.

— (2002) 'The Impact of a Changing Policy Framework on Isolated Communities: A South African Experience', *Habitat International*, Vol. 26, No. 2, pp. 191–212.

Mackay, S. and M. Mathoho (2001) 'Worker Power: The Congress of South Africa Trade Unions and Its Impact on Governance and Democracy', *CPS Research Report*, No. 79, Johannesburg: Centre for Policy Studies.

McDonald, D. A. (ed.) (2002a) *Environmental Justice in South Africa*, Athens and Cape Town: Ohio University Press and UCT Press.

— (2002b) 'Up Against the (Crumbling) Wall: The Privatization of Urban Services and Environmental Justice', in D. A. McDonald (ed.), *Environmen-*

tal Justice in South Africa, Athens/Cape Town: Ohio University Press/UCT Press.

McDonald, D. A. and J. Pape (eds) (2003) *Cost Recovery and the Crisis of Service Delivery*, Pretoria and London: Human Science Research Council and Zed Books.

Mabin, A. (2000) 'Urban Policy – Presences and Absences', background paper prepared for Urban Policy Lekgotla publication, Johannesburg: Graduate School of Public and Development Management, Wits University.

Marais, H. (2001) *South Africa. Limits to Change. The Political Economy of Transition*, 2nd edn, London and Cape Town: Zed Books and UCT Press.

Massey, D. (1999) 'Cities in the World', in D. Massey, J. Allen and S. Pile (eds), *City Worlds*, New York: Routledge.

Minogue, M. (2002) 'Power to the People? Good Governance and the Reshaping of the State', in U. Kothari and M. Minogue (eds), *Development Theory and Practice. Critical Perspectives*, Basingstoke: Palgrave.

Mossberger, K. and G. Stoker (2001) 'The Evolution of Urban Regime Theory. The Challenge of Conceptualization', *Urban Affairs Review*, Vol. 36, No. 6, pp. 810–35.

Mouffe, C. (2000) *The Democratic Paradox*, London: Verso.

Mpe, P. (2001) *Welcome to Our Hillbrow*, Pietermaritzburg: University of Natal Press.

Nederveen Pieterse, J. (2001) 'Participatory Democracy Reconceived', *Futures*, Vol. 33, No. 5, pp. 407–22.

Okri, B. (1997) *A Way of Being Free*, London: Phoenix House.

Orbach, S. (1996) 'Couching Anxieties', in S. Dunant and R. Porter (eds), *The Age of Anxiety*, London: Virago Press.

Patel, L. (1992) *Restructuring Social Welfare. Options for South Africa*, Johannesburg: Raven Press.

PDG [Palmer Development Group] and Isandla Institute (2002) 'The Role of Cities in Poverty Alleviation', CD Rom, Pretoria: South African Cities Network and Department of Provincial and Local Government.

Peet, R. (2002) 'Ideology, Discourse, and the Geography of Hegemony: From Socialist to Neoliberal Development in Postapartheid South Africa', *Antipode*, Vol. 34, No. 1, pp. 58–90.

Pieterse, E. (2000) *Participatory Urban Governance. Practical Approaches, Regional Trends and UMP Experiences*, Vol. 25, Nairobi: Urban Management Programme.

— (2001) 'In Praise of Transgression. Notes on Institutional Synergy and Poverty Reduction', *Development Update*, Vol. 3, No. 4, pp. 39–69.

— (2002a) 'Participatory Local Governance in the Making. Opportunities, Constraints and Prospects', in S. Parnell, E. Pieterse, M. Swilling and D. Wooldridge (eds), *Democratising Local Government. The South African Experiment*, Cape Town: UCT Press.

— (2002b) 'Fragile Certainties: Reflections and Provocations on the Soft Subversions that are Human Flourishing', Cape Town: Isandla Institute.

— (2002c) 'From Divided to Integrated City? Critical Overview of the Emerging Governance System in Cape Town', *Urban Forum*, Vol. 13, No. 1, pp. 3–37.

— (2003) 'Problematising and Recasting Vision-driven Politics in Cape Town', in C. Haferburg and J. Oßenbrügge (eds), *Ambiguous Restructurings of Post-Apartheid Cape Town: The Spatial Form*, Hamburg and London: LIT Verlag, Munster.

— (forthcoming) 'Critical Invention and Interventions. Opportunities and Pitfalls of the New Politics Emerging in Cape Town', in S. Robins (ed.), *Limits to Liberation. Citizenship and Governance after Apartheid*, London: James Currey.

Pieterse, E. and M. van Donk (2002) 'Incomplete Ruptures. The Political Economy of Realising Socio-Economic Rights in South Africa', *Law, Democracy and Development*, Vol. 6, No. 2, pp. 193–229.

Robinson, J. (2002) 'Global and World Cities: A View from Off the Map', *International Journal of Urban and Regional Research*, Vol. 26, No. 3, pp. 531–54.

Ruppert, E. (2000) 'Who Governs the Global City?', in E. F. Isin (ed.), *Democracy, Citizenship and the Global City*, London: Routledge.

Saff, G. (2001) 'Exclusionary Discourse Towards Squatters in Suburban Cape Town', *Ecumene*, Vol. 8, No. 1, pp. 87–107.

Sandercock, L. (1998) 'The Death of Modernist Planning: Radical Praxis for a Postmodern Age', in M. Douglas and J. Friedmann (eds), *Cities for Citizens. Planning and the Rise of Civil Society in a Global Age*, Chichester: John Wiley and Sons.

Santos, B. de Sousa (1995) *Towards a New Common Sense: Law, Science and Politics in the Pragmatic Transition*, London: Routledge.

Saul, J. (2001) 'Cry for the Beloved Country: The Postapartheid Denouement', *Monthly Review*, Vol. 52, No. 8, pp. 1–51.

Scott, J. C. (1997 [1990]) 'The Infrapolitics of Subordinate Groups', in M. Rahnema and V. Bawtree (eds), *The Post-Development Reader*, London: Zed Books.

Segal, L., J. Pelo and P. Rampa (2001) 'Into the Heart of Darkness: Journeys of the Amagents in Crime, Violence and Death', in J. Steinberg (ed.), *Crime Wave. The South African Underworld and its Foes*, Johannesburg: Witwatersrand University Press.

Shubane, K. (1995) 'Revisiting South African Conceptions of Civil Society', in R. Humpries and M. Reitzes (eds), *Civil Society after Apartheid*, Johannesburg: CPS and FES.

Simons, J. (1995) *Foucault and the Political*, London: Routledge.

Sorkin, M. (2001) *Some Assembly Required*, Minneapolis: University of Minnesota Press.

Soudien, C. (2004) '"Fighting for a normal life": Becoming a Young Adult in the New South Africa', in E. Pieterse and F. Meintjies (eds), *Voices of the Transition: The Politics, Poetics and Practices of Social Change in South Africa*, Johannesburg: Heinemann Publishers.

Squires, J. (2002) 'Democracy as Flawed Hegemon', *Economy and Society*, Vol. 31, No. 1, pp. 132–51.

Swilling, M. and B. Russell (2002) *The Size and Scope of the Non-profit Sector in South Africa*, Durban/Johannesburg: Centre for Civil Society/Graduate School of Public and Development Management.

Tajbakhsh, K. (2001) *The Promise of the City. Space, Identity, and Politics in Contemporary Social Thought*, Berkeley: University of California Press.

Tendler, J. (1997) *Good Government in the Tropics*, Baltimore, MD and London: Johns Hopkins University Press.

Todes, A. (2000) 'Reintegrating the Apartheid City? Urban Policy and Urban Restructuring in Durban', in G. Bridge and S. Watson (eds), *A Companion to the City*, Oxford: Blackwell.

Todes, A., T. Dominik and D. Hindson (2000) 'From Fragmentation to Compaction? The Case of Durban South Africa', in M. Jenks and R. Burgess (eds), *Compact Cities. Sustainable Urban Forms for Developing Countries*, London: Spon Press.

Turok, I. (2001) 'Persistent Polarization Post-Apartheid? Progress Towards Urban Integration in Cape Town', *Urban Studies*, Vol. 38, No. 13, pp. 2,349–77.

Unger, R. M. (1998) *Democracy Realised. The Progressive Alternative*, London: Verso.

Watson, V. (2002) *Change and Continuity in Spatial Planning. Metropolitan Planning in Cape Town under Political Transition*, London: Routledge.

Wilkinson, P. (2000) 'City Profile: Cape Town', *Cities*, Vol.17, No. 3, pp. 195–205.

Williams, J. J. (2000) 'South Africa: Urban Transformation', *Cities*, Vol. 17, No. 3, pp. 167–83.

TWO | **Urban practices**

7 | Life in a high-density urban area: Anguwar Mai Gwado in Zaria

MOHAMMED-BELLO YUNUSA

The resolution of problems of environmental degradation, everyday life and poverty requires an in-depth understanding of the socio-economic milieu of various social categories in urban residential sectors. Most common residential sectors are the high-density areas inhabited by the poor. This chapter focuses on two aspects of life in high-density areas to demonstrate the daily life and coping strategies of the people in densely developed and populated sectors of urban areas. These two aspects are lifestyle (housing condition, diet, wear, social network, environmental maintenance etc.) and income-generating activities (employment, amount of income, use and control of incomes etc.). How a city is lived, i.e. the daily life of the people, is all-encompassing. This chapter focuses on the socio-economic characteristics of respondents, housing types and facilities, welfare, social networks and support systems in the Anguwar Mai Gwado area of Zaria. The discussion narrows down to daily life activities of respondents in the analysis of income and time expenditure. The chapter highlights differences in time expenditure among social categories, as the patterns are not the same for all social strata.

The study is located in the Zaria urban area, and more specifically, the Anguwar Mai Gwado ward of the Sabon-Gari district. Zaria, like most African towns, has low-density land use devoted to administration and the residential requirements of colonial and post-colonial elites and high-density land use devoted to the indigenous population (Pacione 2001: 449).

Urban high-density area – what is it?

Urban formation follows specific codes and guidelines inherent in zoning laws and building codes derived from urban development plans. Using zoning laws, city planners specify types of building permitted in sectors of the town. Thus, planners regulate plot sizes, building heights and quality of building materials. On the other hand, building codes regulate the number of persons per dwelling unit, quality of electric wiring, planning, among others. Both zoning laws and building codes, as in the urban development plans, prescribe the location of various urban land uses and the quantity of land devoted to each. Overall, the 'building codes regulate how a city is constructed and spatially arranged' (Witzling 1994: 809).

Urban density is the designed population capacity of urban land (Chapin 1965: 43). In other words, the number of persons in an area at a given time expresses the density on the urban land. In residential areas, density is number of persons per hectare (pph). Any approved density per land area constitutes what is 'considered desirable in public interest from the standpoint of public health and safety' (ibid.: 44).

To enforce residential density, which is divided into low, medium and high, building types are broken down into density types. The Bichi Urban Development Plan (Kano State Government 1978: 88) specifies gross figures for residential density as low (75 pph), medium (125 pph) and high (175 pph). The upper and middle class often inhabit the low- and medium-density residential areas in Nigeria. The high-density areas are left for the poor. The use and control of urban densities is central to the protection of public interest in the sense of preventing 'conditions injurious or hazardous to the physical well being of the people of the community' (Chapin 1965: 41).

The processes and rate of urban growth are major factors in the development of a controlled urban area as an ideal urban development practice. The processes and rates of growth are overwhelming and inestimable. The United Nations International Children's Fund has found 'uncontrolled urbanization in less developed countries [responsible] for the widespread creation of danger zones [and] that too many people are being squeezed into cities that have neither jobs, shelter, nor schools to accommodate them' (Knox and Marston 2001: 400). The danger zones are the high-density areas where the substantial majority of those trooping to towns and cities live.

The processes of creating the danger zones are also not amenable to control by physical planners and urban development managers. Rapid urban expansion has enabled towns and cities to exceed planned boundaries and engulf nearby villages that are hardly prepared for urban functions. The urbanization of villages that suddenly become the abode of the poor, unemployed and unskilled migrants due to cheap land only creates areas injurious to urban inhabitants. Conditions injurious to the physical wellbeing of the people develop when obtainable density exceeds planned densities. It is from this perspective that this study examines the character of an urban high-density area in relation to the everyday life of the people. This chapter examines the formation, spatial characteristics and livelihoods of a high-density area to demonstrate how the uncontrolled process of urbanization and urban expansion creates a spatial formation that conforms to but differs from a conceptual and planned urban high density and produces discernible life patterns.

Urbanization is a challenge to an ill-equipped migrant in towns and cities as to the choice of where to live and what to do to make a living. In confronting the challenge, the poor seek shelter in high-density areas characterized by lack of planning, poor street networks and barely inhabitable structures. Building types and the total environment make these areas prone to disasters such as flooding and fire. In terms of urban management, the high-density areas are places with serious problems of unemployment, serviceability, liveability and management. Combining these with poverty, the danger under which people live is unimaginable. It is in this context that the assertion that '10 million people are dying annually in densely populated urban areas from conditions produced by substandard housing and poor sanitation' (Knox and Marston 2001: 400) becomes worrisome.

In high-density housing areas, the living style and coping strategies vary across socio-economic strata and gender, as even the poor are not homogeneous. The import of this study is in the unveiling of the varieties of the living conditions of individuals and groups in urban high-density housing areas. In the context of the spatial formation and characteristics of a high-density area, this study examines the activities of inhabitants of high-density areas with the purpose of bringing out the implications for the ability of individuals to generate income, improve welfare and even manage the living environment.

The study problem

The problem is to examine the socio-spatial characteristics of high-density areas and to demonstrate the extent to which such areas conform to the plan for high-density areas of towns and cities. Thus, this study raises certain salient questions about the people and environment of high-density areas. What urban development policies and programmes shape the character of high-density areas? What is the physical state of slum environments? What is the history of such slums, how do people come to live in them and from where do they come? How do men and women organize their lives in high-density areas? This inevitably leads the study to look at the social networks and associations of the study group *vis-à-vis* the institutions of urban administration. How have all these affected the socio-economic lifestyle of the people in high-density areas? Resolution of these issues enriches the understanding of the complexities of life in high-density areas of urban systems. The major thrust is to examine the relationships between the spatial formation of peripheral growth and engulfment *vis-à-vis* the daily life of its inhabitants and to demonstrate how this conforms to universal urban growth and expansion processes.

Aims and objectives

Given the concept of a high-density area, its development and infrastructural needs, this study sets out to examine Anguwar Mai Gwado as a high-density area to highlight processes of formation, administration, spatial characteristics and lifestyle of the people who live in it. The main task is to document the conditions of habitation, the environmental characteristics of squalid housing and the livelihood strategies of households. The objectives of this study therefore are:

i) to document the housing, environmental and living characteristics of households in a high-density area of the Zaria urban area;

ii) to study how individuals live in such an environment in relation to urban management and macro-economic policies;

iii) to examine the structure and organization of the income-generation activities of households and identify the roles of members in household maintenance and sustenance; and

iv) based on a critical analysis of the situation, to conclude by highlighting the implications of the findings for policies and suggest how to improve high-density housing conditions and socio-economically empower the inhabitants of urban areas.

Methodology, sampling and data collection

The research documented the migratory history of Anguwar Mai Gwado dwellers and analysed household environmental management techniques as part of the efforts of poor people to mobilize resources to complement efforts of the state in urban administration. The ability of the urban poor to mobilize resources and improve conditions of living in high-density areas in relation to livelihood strategies and income-generation activities is dependent on daily life demands. Thus, the methodology unveils the livelihood strategies and income-generation activities of households.

The data collected covered livelihoods of families (types of employment, sources and quantity of incomes) and relationships within and between households and the agencies of urban administration. Hence, the variables measured include housing conditions (which embraces facilities, services and utilities, occupancy ratio, rent, ownership etc.), types of income-generating activities, income levels and sources. In relation to livelihood techniques, a research recorded daily activities of thirty individuals (as a sub-sample of the main sample of one hundred) to establish daily life patterns in the high-density area of Zaria. Data collected also covered the social network and support systems (unions, associations and involvement with urban administration) of respondents. The study also documented individual and household efforts to maintain the environment to establish environmental management strategies in the community.

Research instruments The research also involved intensive interviews combining the use of structured and unstructured questionnaires. The structured questionnaires generated data to establish statistical aggregates and patterns while the unstructured questionnaire and interviews documented historical and qualitative data that bring out the main issues in this study. The data determine points of convergence and divergence in the experiences of individuals and groups.

To establish the daily life of the people, it was pertinent to know how individuals, groups and households spend their time daily. To establish this, thirty persons in ten households as a subsample of the hundred household heads had their hourly activities recorded. An hourly activity diary, prepared in the form of an interview schedule, collected the data. This aspect of data collection took the form of recording individual activities from 7 a.m. to 11 p.m. for a week. It is in this context that data collected reflect livelihoods of families, paying particular attention to time spent on economic, social network and other activities. Discussions were held across various households, with groups, around the theme of the research, to get an impression of opinions.

Sample and sampling To discern the gender and generation issues involved in high-density life and survival, the study focused on sampled households. Using systematic sampling procedure, we drew a sample of a hundred households from housing clusters in the area. Thus, a hundred household heads were initially interviewed. We also drew a sample of ten households as a sub-sample from the sampled hundred households for the administration of the hourly record of activities questionnaire. In each of the ten households, three other members of the households had their hourly activities recorded for a week. By implication, those interviewed in the ten households that formed the sub-sample are four including the head.

Data collection on the environmental management efforts of the state covered urban administration agencies such as local councils and urban development boards. This was with particular reference to how urban administrative agencies, in conjunction with high-density area residents, work together to improve life in high-density areas of urban centres. This further brings out the character of relationships between urban administrators and high-density area residents.

Location of study area The study is located in the Anguwar Mai Gwado ward within the Sabon-Gari urban district of the Zaria metropolis. Anguwar Mai Gwado is located on marshy land. Originally, it was a small village in the peri-urban area of Zaria. It therefore has the characteristics of a rural village, lacking all socio-economic facilities, services and utilities. Urban expansion and the need of low-income earners for housing enhanced the development of Anguwar Mai Gwado and its absorption into Zaria Township. The issue is that Anguwar Mai Gwado is the zone of a peripheral squatter settlement that 'accommodates the impoverished migrants to the city and is the worst section of the city in terms of housing quality and public service provision' (Pacione 2001: 449). After its incorporation into Zaria, Anguwar Mai Gwado became another focal point, with its centre and a market. Thus, Anguwar Mai Gwado provides shopping, residential and drinking-joint services to nearby neighbourhoods such as the military depot and Juchi Waje.

Currently, Anguwar Mai Gwado occupies a land area of about 5.71 hectares, containing about 540 compounds. This gives a density of approximately 94.6 compounds per hectare. The compounds provide housing for multiples of families. According to the 1991 population census, Mai Gwado has 6,689 males and 5,654 females, i.e. 12,343 persons. The projected population in 1996 is 14,426.[1] This population gives a density of 2,161.6 persons per hectare. This is about twelve times the recommended density in the Bichi Master Plan and about fourteen times the proposed high density in the Zaria Master Plan.

The Zaria Master Plan is specific on density requirements. The plan proposed that 50 per cent of Zaria urban land use should be devoted to residential land use (Kaduna State Government 1979: 170). In its proposed densities, the plan indicated three types of gross densities for all residential areas. These are 'High density, medium density and low density with 150 pph, 110 pph and 90 pph respectively as gross densities. The university district comes under the medium density (110 pph) area, the city centre and Sabon Gari districts come under the high density (150 pph) area' (ibid.: 201). From this it is obvious that Anguwar Mai Gwado is within the proposed high-density area of Zaria, being located in the Sabon-Gari district. Already, the Sabon-Gari area has 225 pph, exceeding the proposed standard of 150 pph as in the Zaria development plan.

Housing and spatial characteristics of Anguwar Mai Gwado Buildings are usually made of mud and rendered with cement, although there are buildings that are completely mud and others that are completely composed of cement materials. We also saw a few tin houses during the survey. In the same vein, most buildings' floors are mud and cement. About a fifth of the room floors are concrete. All houses have corrugated-iron roofs. About 45 per cent of mud houses are not rendered with cement. Tenants pay 250 naira per month in mud houses and 350 naira per month in concrete houses. Given these building materials, the houses are prone to the vagaries of rainstorms and erosion.

From physical observation of the ward, most houses could be reached on foot, bicycle or motorcycle. The access ways or paths are irregular, very rough and serve as drainage for storm water and household waste water. There is no drainage system in the ward. The houses become waterlogged and some are washed away by heavy rains. According to the inhabitants, houses in the area often collapse during the rainy season. Overall, since domestic waste water drains into access ways or paths and causes nuisance to neighbours and others, the houses are generally dirty.

A brief on Anguwar Mai Gwado

Anguwar Mai Gwado started in 1918 as an informal settlement on marshy land. It was then a village in a rural setting. The initial settlers were farmers who had migrated from Kofar Doko in old Zaria City to the current site of the military depot and finally to its current site, behind the walls of the military depot. The available agricultural land adjacent to the ward further attracted more settlers as farmlands were converted to residential uses by newcomers. The return of First World War veterans in 1932 exacerbated the development and growth problems of the settlement. From about 1960 onwards, the ward swelled with squatter settlers (*yan shara guri zoana*). At that time government or planning agencies had not taken control of the growth and development of the ward. It is therefore without facilities, services and utilities.

It was not until the end of the 1970s and early 1980s that facilities and services were extended to the area by urban government and management agencies. Water supplies were extended to the ward between 1979 and 1980 by the water board of the state government. In the same vein, the Local Government Council (LGC) started construction of culverts and a health centre in 1991 while a primary school was established for the community in 1981.

Since the area had been engulfed by urban expansion, the need to control its development and make it conform to urban structures became imperative. Development control, in the sense of approval of development plans by relevant agencies, started between 1990 and 1992. Since 1991 no buildings were erected without a certificate of occupancy and an approved development plan. This standardized housing production in the area. However, the ward is still characterized by taps without water, lack of a drainage system, poor electricity supply and heaps of garbage and human waste. The entire environment is filthy, with human waste littering the place, especially between buildings. Furthermore, the ward is prone to run-off erosion, which the people, particularly the rich, try to control using small sandbags.

Water is drawn from streams and shallow wells. Some households go to the city centre to fetch drinking water. From a group discussion it was gathered from the residents that local government health inspectors in the area formerly focused on drainage, toilets and bathrooms. The development control officials from planning authorities are not interested in these. These officials now focus on buildings and demand sweeteners from developers. During the time the state planning agency, Kaduna State Urban Planning and Development Authority, was not active in the area, the traditional rulers were the sole authority regarding land allocation. The community bought electricity poles, which were then appropriated by National Electric Power Authority, but no electricity was supplied.

Putting all this together, it is apparent that the environment of Anguwar Mai Gwado lacks virtually all the necessary infrastructure, even as a segment of an urban area with a high number of inhabitants.

The Sabon-Gari Local Government Council and traditional administrative structures administer Anguwar Mai Gwado. There is a Sarkin Juchi and Mai Gwado (i.e. the Hakimi) who operates under the Zaria Emirate Council. The Hakimi has the Mai Anguwar (ward head) under him to administer the Anguwar Mai Gwado ward. The Mai Anguwar sees to the day-to-day affairs of the Anguwar Mai Gwado. The Mai Anguwar reports issues beyond his resolution to the Hakimi, who monitors issues of peace and development. The Hakimi takes reports to the Local Government Council for attention. As the Mai Anguwar is the direct link between the people and the Hakimi, so is the Hakimi the link between the community and the Local Government Council. Further to this, youth organizations and community leaders have direct links with the Emirate and the local government councils.

Urban policies and Anguwar Mai Gwado In the pre-colonial period there were no uniform rules and standards to guide urban layout and development. This is not to say that no norms and values produced specific spatial forms and patterns from one community to another. The current urban development and management standards and structures are products of the 'modern state' produced by colonialism. Initial urban development policies were formulated in 1861 in Lagos colony. Between 1861 and 1927 policies focused on health and hygiene matters, control of hazards (spread of fire and diseases), protection of parts of cities occupied by colonial administrators, housing and road regulations, definition of hierarchies and classes of towns and cities and land acquisition procedures. In 1946, the Nigerian Town and Country Planning Ordinance was enacted.

The 1946 ordinance aimed at replanning, improving and developing towns and cities in Nigeria. Though the northern region adopted the ordinance in 1963, it did not guide the growth and development of the study area. At the time of the study, the area was not on the map of the Zaria metropolis. This was so because the study area was not part of the Zaria urban area until it was engulfed. The adopted planning law of 1963 is still operational and provides a framework for the establishment of the Kaduna State Urban Planning and Development Authority (KASUPDA). Agencies that are currently responsible for the management of Anguwar Mai Gwado include KASUPDA, which controls development, the Sabon-Gari Local Government Council, the Kaduna State Government and various non-governmental agencies. The KASUPDA is responsible for the enforcement and monitoring of development control measures, maintaining roads, open spaces and drains, and the upgrading of blighted areas such as Anguwar Mai Gwado to ensure availability of services, facilities and utilities to the citizens.

Currently, a major agency responsible for the development of Anguwar Mai Gwado is the Local Government Council, which has statutory responsibilities to provide all services, utilities and facilities except water, electricity and telephone to citizens. Furthermore, the council, according to the 1992 Urban and Regional Planning Law, has the duty to prepare and adopt local and town plans in its area of jurisdiction. Discussions with council officials reveal that they are not aware of these statutory provisions, let alone building up capacity towards executing their responsibilities.[2]

Despite the inability of the local council to manage and develop urban areas, the Federal Government of Nigeria articulated an Urban Development Policy in 1997. The policy noted the need to improve the economic base of towns and cities, to enhance their employment and income-generating capacity. Nowhere is this more needed than in the high-density areas of the towns and cities where the socio-economic and spatial base is weak.

Demography characteristics of respondents The character of a given area makes it attractive to specific social groups, just as social groups create their own spatial structure and forms; spatial forms and characteristics are thus expressions of social (and economic) values in society (Smith 1999: 13–14). This is perceived through a study of the socio-demographic and economic characteristics of residents in Anguwar Mai Gwado.

The demographic characteristics discussed include sex, age, educational attainment, acquired skills, employment and income as well as respondents' places of origin. These characteristics give the background of the residents and provide a basis for understanding the dynamics of life in urban high-density areas.

SEX OF RESPONDENTS The household heads interviewed were eighty-five males and fifteen females. The sex distribution of the sub-sample indicates that sixteen (53.3) were females and fourteen (46.7 per cent) were males. This indicates higher female presence among the sub-sample than males, attributable to the fact that the females were more available, at home, for the hourly record keeping than males were. Though not estimated in absolute terms, from discussions there are indications that there is a prevalence of female-headed households in the area. Wives and families of deceased or transferred military personnel, whose barracks are next to the area of study, tend to settle in the area with their children.

AGE OF RESPONDENTS The household heads are all aged above thirty years. In the sample, 40 per cent are within 30–49 years, 20 per cent are aged between 50–60 years. All others (40 per cent) are above sixty years of age. The mean age for the thirty respondents (other members of households) is 30.2 years. Those aged below twenty years are ten (33.3 per cent), 21–30 years are fifteen (50 per cent) and those above thirty-one years constitute only 16.7 per cent, that is five persons. It is obvious that the other members of households studied are younger than the household heads. This is understandable and expected, since other members are dependants, under the care and authority of household heads.

EDUCATION OF RESPONDENTS Among the household heads, only ten persons did not have any form of education. Taking into account Islamic, primary and secondary and post-secondary education, 30 per cent have low education, 60 per cent have medium education and 10 per cent have a high level of education.

In the sample of thirty respondents, a third had no schooling (either formal or informal) at all, 23.4 per cent had up to ten years of schooling and the remaining respondents, that is 42.4 per cent, had up to thirteen years of schooling.

A further analysis of levels of education of heads of households showed that 50 per cent have Islamic or Qur'anic education. In addition, 10 per cent have primary education, 30 per cent have post-primary (secondary school, craft school, technical or teachers' college) and 10 per cent have a post-secondary education. This is commensurate with years spent in school. Those with post-secondary education spent about fourteen years in school while those with primary education spent about three years. By implication, some of the respondents dropped out of primary school before completing the seven or six years' primary education programme.[3]

SKILLS OF RESPONDENTS Respondents have various skills, that is an ability to use their own hands to do something and earn income or make a living. Among household heads, skills listed include driving a vehicle (taxi or bus operation), farming, photography, tailoring and trading, among others. These skills only enable them to participate in the urban informal sector and agriculture. Among the sample of thirty, while seven (23.4 per cent) have no skills, twenty-two (76.6 per cent) have several skills in tailoring, carpentry, masonry, baking and trading and oil extraction from peanuts. In any case, only 66.7 per cent practise their skills for income earning.

EMPLOYMENT OF RESPONDENTS One of the conditions for meeting the housing rights of citizens is access to employment and other means of livelihood (Eze 1996: 15–21). The issue of employment is more critical under the Structural Adjustment Programme (SAP), which started in 1986. The economic situation created by SAP imposes the need for income generation, by all possible means, on the poor. As the naira became valueless through devaluation, large sums of money were required for daily family needs. The decline in the value of the naira is revealing. According to the Central Bank of Nigeria (1998: 186), in 1986, 2.0206 naira exchanged for one US dollar. By 1995, it was 81.0228 naira to a dollar. The naira had declined by 4,009.8 per cent against the dollar in ten years! By mid-1998, it was 393.5 per cent over the 1995 exchange rate as 82.7114 exchanged for one US dollar. This massive devaluation was harsh for the people, particularly the poor, and they were forced to derive income from various sources.

In the effort to generate income from all possible sources, members of households tend to pursue multiple economic activities. In short, the inhabitants adopted multiple modes of existence (Mustapha 1991: 9–14) in a situation that lacked multiple opportunities due to the declining power of patrons on the demand side. In any case, this expanded the range of the urban informal or marginal economy.

The activities in which respondents engaged in include farm work, formal employment (full-time and part-time) in public and private sectors and employment in non-formal sectors. Among the thirty respondents, 23.3 per cent have formal employment and 76.7 per cent are engaged in non-formal employment. Those in formal employment spend a mean of 5.6

187

hours a week at the workplace. Those in non-formal employment spend a mean of 19.6 hours a week working at various places of economic activity. Those in non-formal employment spend more time at work than those in formal employment. The time requirement of formal employment makes it desirable as a source of 'cheap money'.

In the sample of the household heads some are either working or have worked in government establishments. Indeed, 10 per cent worked for private individuals as security guards or domestic help and 40 per cent said they do not need to work, possibly due to factors of age and other disabilities. About 20 per cent indicated their inability to secure employment and 10 per cent are either in the organized public or in private sectors. Generally, the elders tend to depend on the younger ones for survival.

INCOME OF RESPONDENTS Respondents indicated their sources of income and how much they get from each source in a month. The mean monthly income from the economic activities of household heads is relatively high and is N27,710.00 a month (about $US235). This falls within the 1997 earnings range (18,739–36,965 naira) of junior staff in the public sector and it is four times the minimum wage (5,996 naira) in the public sector in 1998. Among other members of households, earnings from employment are not too impressive. The mean net income per month from economic activity for this group is 19,000 naira. This is about three times the minimum wage in the public sector in 1998. Considering the inflation rate in the national economy, these incomes are low for a household of about 6.5 persons. That is to say that these wages appear high 'but low when aspirations, needs, and urban prices are taken into account' (Hanna and Hanna 1971: 81). This is compounded by the wide gap that exists in the income of the household heads, as indicated by a standard deviation of N43,947.40 in the income distribution of the respondents.

In addition to income earned by the respondents, about 20 per cent receive cash gifts from friends and parents. Those who receive gifts get amounts generally under 3,000 naira a month, except in a case of a respondent who had a gift of 20,000 naira to set up an economic activity. As for the sub-sample of thirty, respondents indicated that they receive cash gifts from parents (50 per cent), brothers (46.7 per cent) and friends (10 per cent). The cash gifts range between 60 naira and 5,000 naira per month. While household heads live on personal income, other members live on both their own income and on gifts. The support received by other members of households is small, but it may help in dealing with the financial demands inherent in urban life.

The socio-economic character of respondents in Anguwar Mai Gwado echoes the general characteristics of such areas. Processes of rapid urbanization propel people with this profile to an urbanizing village in the peri-urban area where sub-standard housing and poor sanitation are major features of their environment. The general character of this area may not have changed over time, as the current environment resembles the characterization of slums by Hanna and Hanna (1971: 75–103), which touched on employment, income, education, housing and the general environment.

PLACES OF ORIGIN AND HOUSEHOLD SIZE Regarding the places of origin of respondents, a majority came from Kaduna State, within which the settlement is located. Others are drawn from various parts of Nigeria, particularly Benue, Taraba, Adamawa, Borno, Katsina, Kwara and Rivers, among many others. This widespread catchment area is attributable to the retirees and other workers who have found a place to settle in the ward.

The households surveyed have an average of 2.9 adult males, 3.1 adult females and an average of 3.8 male and female children. Between 1999 and 2000, an average of 0.7 males and 0.5 females migrated from elsewhere to the various households. In any case, within the same period 1.3 males and 3.0 females migrated out of the households. The rate of female migration is higher, possibly due to marriage. The majority of household heads interviewed settled in Anguwar Mai Gwado from about the late 1970s onwards. The migrants to the ward came in search of livelihood opportunities or through the mere chance of public service transfer. Some of those who came to Zaria on transfer have retired and settled in the ward with their families.

Time and money expenditure of respondents

Time and money expenditure represent the pursuit of the needs and aspirations of individuals and households. The pattern of expenditure indicated how individuals and households meet commitments and needs using time and money. In line with this, respondents indicated the proportion of time and income spent on some listed activities[4] that represent a range of household demands and networks or associational life.

Time expenditure Respondents were asked to indicate the proportions of their own time spent on earning income for themselves, earning income for the household, participating in household activities or chores, visiting friends and relatives and attending activities of associations and clubs. In the sample, it was found that 40 per cent spent 30–40 per cent of their time seeking income for themselves, with only 10 per cent of the respondents spending 60 per cent of their own time for the same purpose. Regarding money for household needs, 40 per cent of the respondents spend between 20 per cent and 40 per cent of their time on this, but it was also observed that 30 per cent virtually spend the whole of their time for the same purpose. From these data it can be said that major proportions of individual time are spent seeking income for self and household.

Some of the respondents are involved in household activities; it was found that 40 per cent of the respondents spend 100 per cent of their time on these. Some may be women saddled with household chores. The remaining 60 per cent spend 10 per cent to 30 per cent of their time on household activities or chores. Socializing and social networking are not too popular among the respondents, particularly the household heads. Generally, they spend less than 10 per cent of their time either visiting friends or attending to organizational (societies, clubs, associations etc.) activities. This contradicts data from other members of households on daily activities to be discussed later.

Income expenditure On proportions of income spent on food, self, school fees, health bills, house maintenance, electricity and water, the responses indicate that food excepted, household head respondents generally spend less than 30 per cent of their income on all others. In fact, 40 per cent to 60 per cent spend less than 10 per cent of their incomes on self, health, electricity and water respectively. In the sample, 80 per cent of the household heads spend 50 per cent to 80 per cent of their incomes on food for their households: a high proportion of the heads' income goes into household feeding.

Among the other members of the household, 13.3 per cent spend 60 per cent of their incomes on food, another 6.7 per cent of the respondents spend 70 per cent of their income on self-maintenance. Further to this, 23.3 per cent of the respondents spend 10 per cent of their own money on health, while another 20 per cent spend about 10 per cent of their income on building maintenance. Among other household members, as among household heads, income expenditure on food and self is outstanding. However, the other members spend more of their incomes on themselves rather than household upkeep.

PROPERTIES OWNED BY RESPONDENTS To establish the stock of wealth of household heads, they indicated their moveable and unmoveable properties. The data showed that 80 per cent own houses, which they either built or inherited from parents. Noteworthy is that 40 per cent of those who own houses have them at their 'home'[5] places. Despite this, 60 per cent of the household heads rent houses and 40 per cent are owner-occupiers. In addition to houses, 70 per cent of the sample have farmlands which were inherited, bought, borrowed or gifts. There are indications that the farmlands are fragmented, as 40 per cent have two plots, 14 per cent have three plots, with another 14 per cent holding up to five plots of farmland.

Furthermore, among household heads, except for television sets, not many moveable properties are common. Thirty of the respondents have cars, but a third of them use theirs as taxis. Further to this, sixty others have television sets, forty have videotape players and thirty have motorcycles. Ten respondents use the motorcycles as taxis for income generation. Other members of sampled households interviewed own various properties, which include houses (10 per cent), farmland (33.3 per cent), cars (10 per cent) and motorcycles (6.7 per cent). While farmlands are used for agricultural production to support families, motorcycles and cars are used as taxis to generate income.

Housing types, facilities and maintenance

Ownership of housing affects general life patterns and income bases. House ownership is thus significant for understanding gender problems among urban households. Indeed, ownership of housing is significant as regards the social, economic and political wellbeing of individuals and social groups. Thus, housing is seen as an embodiment of facilities, services and utilities that condition healthy living and participation in socio-economic activities.

Further to this, the availability and affordability of good housing is important for poverty reduction in urban areas, especially when housing is perceived as a major factor in the socio-economic production and welfare of individuals and groups in society. Low-income, high-density areas of Nigerian towns and cities are a negation of good housing, as such houses lack or have inadequate basic household facilities, services and utilities (Makinwa-Adebusoye 1992: 137). This type of housing imposes inconveniences and the risk of disease on poor urban households.

All households surveyed live in the compound type of houses that have many rooms to accommodate extended-family members. In the compounds where many families live together, each family has a specific room allocation, but shares facilities in the compounds. Migrants inhabit such compounds. Sharing of compounds by many families, particularly by migrants, is prevalent in Anguwar Mai Gwado. The indigenous population of the area tends to have very large compounds that accommodate multiple wives and wives of children and other dependants. Most of the compounds have between four and sixteen rooms and between four and fourteen sleeping rooms or bedrooms.

191

Household infrastructure is specified at the point of house-development plan approval by the planning agencies. Most of the houses in Anguwar Mai Gwado have no approved development plans. Therefore, whatever facilities are available in the houses are mere reflections of what is perceived as part of a house or what can be afforded by housing developers. Not all compounds have kitchens, though over half of the households (60 per cent) have a kitchen while others cook in the open or in bedrooms. Nearly all (90 per cent) of the compounds have bathrooms, bath places or constructions of corrugated-iron sheets. Most compounds tend to have two to three bathrooms or places to cater for males, females and visitors. Ninety per cent of the compounds have toilet facilities. The toilets are mainly of the pit type.[6]

Domestic water supply in about eighty of the compounds comes from wells dug between 1973 and 1990. The wells are ageing and maintained twice a year to improve their quality and quantity of water. In addition to well water, sixty of the households are connected to the municipal pipe-borne water supply, though the taps are dry most of the time, particularly in the dry seasons. The people are not too keen to connect tap water supply lines for fear of the cost and bureaucracy, coupled with the perceived inefficiency of the water board. Part of the problem is the cost because the water board increased its water rates for high-density areas by 19 per cent (from 600 naira to 714 naira) a month in 2001.

In addition to wood and kerosene as sources of domestic energy, sixty of the households have electricity supplied by the National Electric Power Authority. Electricity was installed in the study area between 1976 and 1987. The health centre that was started in 1991 is not yet fully operational. A notable health facility is a traditional 'orthopaedic hospital', run by a traditional bonesetter from Borno State who settled in Mai Gwado in 1989.

Most compounds and their drainage systems are cleaned or maintained frequently. However, 10 per cent of the sampled households claimed that they do not clean the drainage very often. All respondents insisted that they need the help of all household members to clear drainage lines as often as possible. Other members of households clean the house environment very often or often. Yet a majority clear gutters very often (23.4 per cent) or often (50 per cent). The Sabon-Gari Local Government Council is active in environmental maintenance of the area. According to the data, 80 per cent of household head respondents said that the council repairs roads and streets, 40 per cent said the council clears gutters and another 40 per cent also said it clears refuse and garbage.

Further to the individual, household and government efforts to maintain the environment, the Mai Gwado Youth Development Association is involved in paths and pavement maintenance, clearance and development of drainage lines. The Mai Anguwa, the Hakimi and the local council authorities are informed of any development activity within the association. According to this information, these authorities mobilize resources (other members of the community, hoes, wheelbarrows and brooms etc.) and other support necessary for the activities. To this end, these institutions constitute a framework for environmental maintenance in the area.

Welfare of respondents

The issue of welfare was probed from the point of view of what the respondents eat, their ability to add to clothing and an account of the most frequent health complaint in the household. At the level of other members of households' survey, the focus was on acquisition of new clothing and shoes. Given these, respondents were presented with a list of some food items and were asked to indicate the ones they currently obtain for household consumption. Over 60 per cent, and in some cases 90 to 100 per cent, of the households buy rice, beans, bread, cassava, fish, guinea corn, maize, onions, millet and tomatoes for household consumption in addition to the 50 per cent of the sample that buy vegetables, 30 per cent that buy milk, 20 per cent that buy meat and the 20 per cent that buy yams for their households. Overall, no respondents buy eggs for their households. This is not conclusive, as malnutrition has been an agelong problem in urban areas (Hanna and Hanna 1971: 97).

In respect of clothing, half of the household head respondents (50 per cent) bought new clothes between 1995 and 2000. At the time of the survey it was found that 40 per cent had bought new clothes in the year 2001. In the same way, 60 per cent bought new shoes between 1995 and 1999, and 30 per cent of the respondents bought new shoes in the year 2001. The data revealed that most other members of household respondents acquired new clothing in 2001. Indeed, among other members of households surveyed, 80 per cent of the respondents bought new shoes and 83.3 per cent bought new clothes in various months of the year 2001.

From observations and discussions, together with the data collected, major health problems in the households surveyed are headaches and stomach pain. Other common problems such as diarrhoea and body itching etc. were not indicated as problems by the respondents. In addition, from the data, households are supplied with an adequate range of food types, but the quantity supplied is examined in this study.

Social networks and support systems Associations of various types and purposes such as trade unions, religious associations, women's organ-

A high-density urban area

izations, youth groups, ethnic associations and professional associations pervade African towns and cities. These institutions, together with inter-personal relationships, are crucial to individuals, groups and household production, survival strategies and general livelihood patterns. From this perspective, the study raised issues on civil society values and institutions that exist in the study area and how they relate to the urban life of people in Anguwar Mai Gwado. Only civil society institutions such as ethnic, religious, trade and thrift associations were focused on.

Issues raised with respondents included their social networks as they re-late to membership of various associations and what these associations help with at individual and household levels. Membership of social organizations is not prevalent among heads of households. It was found that ten respond-ents hold membership of a rotating credit institution (*adashi*) from 1998, thirty others are members of or joined various ethnic unions (between 1985 and 1991), another thirty are members of religious organizations, twenty are members of co-operative societies and ten belong to a sports club. None holds membership of a trade union or a social club. The respondents are neither members of craft guilds, formal trade unions nor social or drinking clubs.

As for other members of households, 36.7 per cent belong to various associations, including credit, religious, ethnic unions and social clubs. According to household heads who belong to these associations, the as-sociations help them with organizing naming (50 per cent) and marriage (30 per cent) ceremonies in the households. No associations help with household supplies and maintenance. The nature of assistance the heads get from relatives follows the same pattern. According to them, relations help with naming (90 per cent) and marriage (50 per cent) ceremonies whenever they come up in the households. Friends also help, as do rela-tions.

As for the household heads, civil society is significant only in organizing ceremonies that are rather expensive. Among other members of house-holds, the pattern of gains of membership is slightly different. Rather than receive assistance from the various clubs and associations, other members of households pointed to diverse assistance they get from parents and rela-tives on one hand and friends on the other. It was indicated that parents and relatives assist them in the areas of naming ceremony (60 per cent), own marriage (46.7 per cent), feeding (20 per cent), payment of health bills (53.3 per cent), electricity bills (10 per cent) and household cleaning (16.7 per cent). Friends' assistance to the respondents is mainly in the area of naming ceremony (40 per cent) and own marriage activity (30 per cent). By implication, although the respondents are involved in various union activities, family and inter-personal networks are more beneficial to the survival of other members of households.

The data revealed that, except for minor road maintenance, the government does nothing to improve the physical state of the area. The household heads were unanimous on this. However, some community-based organizations and non-governmental organizations (particularly the Mai Gwado Youth Development Association) help the community with the construction of culverts to control erosion. Further to these community benefits, it was gathered from discussions with residents that although the members of the associations gain financial assistance and support from the associations, respondents are not willing to admit it, as they find it embarrassing. Still, members of ethnic, religious and area development associations derive psychological satisfaction from associating with their fellows and this gives them a great sense of accomplishment.

Weekly activity pattern of respondents

The urbanization process brought people of diverse backgrounds together. People of diverse socio-cultural identities and backgrounds often have diverse interests, worries, fears and aspirations. Individuals in urban areas face diverse political, social and economic problems. Time is expended on resolving these problems and fears. Time is used for a wide variety of activities, its expenditure a measure of areas in which individuals and groups are productive. Therefore time, being a productive resource, requires prudent management for maximum achievement of livelihood and welfare ideals. Time expenditure thus provides a framework for understanding the dynamics of poverty management among the urban poor.

First, facing the issues of everyday life and poverty requires an understanding of how individuals in community spend their time. An important angle to this understanding is inherent in establishing the pattern of time expenditure, particularly of the group in question. In this context, understanding how people live in and cope with their socio-economic environment, from the point of view of time expenditure, is significant to the understanding of the urbanization process and implications for dwellers in high-density areas.

Second, the empowerment of high-density area inhabitants requires the knowledge of how individuals, groups and households spend their time daily. This enables planners to work out ways of mobilizing the people's time for a range of urban activities, including income generation. To facilitate a meaningful analysis and discussion of the data, the activities were grouped thus:

A high-density urban area

a) farm work: livestock and agricultural production;
b) education: formal schools and Islamic learning centres;
c) formal employment: working in government and organized private sectors;
d) other employment: trading, artisanship, production and sale of certain items;
e) recreation: sports, sitting around, sleeping;
f) social networks: sitting with friends, attending club meetings, visiting and receiving friends;
g) household chores: sweeping, cooking, childcare, etc; and
h) worship: offering prayers and attending preaching sessions.

The allocation of time to production, devotion, recreation and social networking, among other things, is a complex decision-making process that is informed by needs and priorities. The allocation of time to any activity indicates demand for time and the apportionment of time to meet personal, family and even community needs.

The categorization of income-earning activity into farm work, formal and other employment reflects the forms of employment in the area. Urban agriculture is a significant economic activity of the urban poor, particularly of those in a peri-urban area such as Anguwar Mai Gwado. Due to the widespread activity pattern of the people, it was found that except for recreation and social networking, in which all respondents were involved, not all the respondents were involved in all the activities (Table 7.1).

From Table 7.1 it is indisputable that activities like seeking education and devotion take up little of the respondents' time. Much of the respondents' time is spent on recreation and social networking. Social networks

TABLE 7.1 Proportions of respondents involved in various categories of activities

Activity	No. of respondents	%	Mean hours
Devotion	12	40	3.6
Farm work	7	23.4	4.0
Education	9	30	2.8
Other employments	23	76.6	22.2
Formal employment	7	23.4	7.1
Recreation	30	100	38.2
Social networking	30	100	31.4
Household chores	26	60.0	21.9

Source: Survey, 2001.

are 'reciprocal links' which individuals and families sustain as a means of 'getting by' in urban areas. The mean hours spent in these two activities by respondents are much higher than time spent on income-earning activities like farm work, formal and other employment. From this general pattern of time expenditure among the people, it can be noted that the most productive activity critical to the people is social networking. Social networking brings people and resources to households in times of need. Activities that improved income are viewed as individual activities and therefore hours spent on them are dependent on types of employment. Given this general pattern, are there any variations across gender and socio-economic categories?

Gender and hours spent on activities by respondents Traditionally, certain roles in society are allocated on gender bases. This can be noted in the socio-economic responsibilities of men and women in the society. In Nigeria, much of the housework is allocated to women. Also, due to Islamic creeds, which limit the circulation of women, women are not too noticeable in economic activities outside the home. To generate income, therefore, women devote their time to petty trade and petty commodity production in the non-formal sector of the urban economy. Their children, mostly less than ten years old, hawk the commodities, once produced. On the other hand, the men take positions in the formal, informal and agricultural sectors of the economy to earn incomes.

As shown in Table 7.2, many of the household chores are apportioned to women. The household chores include cooking, sweeping and caring for children and other family members. Under paid labour these activities

TABLE 7.2 Mean hours spent by respondents on various activities per day by sex

Activity	Mean hours per week	
	Male	Female
Formal employment	10.9	3.8
Recreation	37.4	38.9
Social networking	34.3	28.9
Farm work	8.0	0.6
Other employments	23.1	21.4
Household chores	14.3	28.6
Devotion	5.9	1.7
Attending school	2.6	2.9

Source: Survey, 2001.

save the family some money, which would have been spent on the employment of a cleaner, cook and nanny. The use of women for these activities at household level represents one of the ways of circumventing the cost of living in urban areas. In any case, these roles are culturally assigned to women and therefore most males do not pay for these services, at least in Nigeria. Also, females spend far less time in farm work, devotion and – to some extent – formal employment. This is indicated by the mean hours spent on these activities by females per week.

In all cases, the males spend more hours per week on all activities except for seeking education than the females. It is not incidental that males even spend more time on social networking than the females, since the females have limited circulation due to Islamic values, which subject the movement of females to the approval of males. Though both sexes appear to be equally unproductive economically, the males generally spend more time on economic and income-earning activities than do the females. This is understandable, since the males are expected to fend for the households.

Age and hours spent on activities Age is a major factor that influences the kinds of activities individuals can embark upon. For instance, as shown in Table 7.3, hours spent by individuals on household chores, recreation and possibly social networking appear to decline as age increases. On the other hand, hours spent on devotion appear to increase with age. The older ones also tend to spend more time on formal employment than on farm work, on which the younger ones and middle-aged respondents tend to spend less time.

TABLE 7.3 Mean hours spent by respondents on various activities per week by age

Activity	Mean hours per week		
	10–20 yrs	21–30 yrs	31 yrs and above
Formal employment	3.0	8.1	12.2
Recreation	40.0	37.4	36.2
Social networking	32.1	32.1	28.0
Household chores	26.3	21.0	16.0
Other employments	20.0	22.9	24.4
Attending school	2.8	3.1	1.8
Farm work	2.0	6.7	0.0
Devotion	1.8	4.8	3.8

Source: Survey, 2001.

The younger respondents spend more time on recreation, social networking and household chores than the elder group. This was re-echoed at one of the discussion sessions with the residents. The discussion group asserted that: 'Teenagers and the elderly members of Anguwar Mai Gwado practically do nothing all day. While teenagers roam the streets, play games and hold parties, the elder ones merely stay at home. The middle-aged members of this area who are petty traders stay in their shops, kiosks and sheds all day.'

Although the pattern of variations across age groups is not clear-cut, there are indications that activities in which individuals may spend time correlate with age.

Level of education and hours spent in activities The higher the level of educational attainment, the higher the tendency not to excessively engage in one activity or another. Observations in the study confirm this. The highly educated in the sample recorded higher mean hours in formal employment, social networking, devotion and farm work than all educational groups in the sample. At the other extreme, respondents with no form of education at all did not spend any proportion of their time on farm work, formal employment and devotion. The lack of participation in farm work and formal employment is attributed to old age or other disabilities, as earlier noted.

It can be observed, however, that respondents with no form of education tend to spend more hours per week on seeking education and attending to household chores. Given that those with no education are implicitly not involved in farm work and formal employment, but spend up to a mean

TABLE 7.4 Mean hours spent by respondents on various activities per week by levels of education

Activity	Mean hours per week			
	None	Primary	Secondary	Post-secondary
Formal employment	0.0	7.5	6.8	10.0
Recreation	40.0	40.1	36.8	40.7
Social networking	20.0	32.8	31.1	33.3
Household chores	31.0	21.5	21.4	23.3
Other employments	20.0	22.8	22.4	20.0
Attending school	9.0	3.5	1.6	6.0
Farm work	0.0	3.8	2.7	14.0
Devotion	0.0	2.3	4.1	6.0

Source: Survey, 2001.

TABLE 7.5 Mean hours spent on various activities by respondents by households per week

Households	1[a]	2[b]	3[c]	4[d]	5[e]	6[f]	7[g]	8[h]
1	0.0	33.3	33.7	13.3	20.3	3	10.0	6.0
2	0.0	40.3	33.3	27.0	26.7	9.3	6.7	3.0
3	20.0	40.0	40.3	23.7	13.3	0.0	7.0	3.0
4	0.0	40.0	33.3	27.0	27.0	3.0	0.0	0.0
5	0.0	40.0.	26.7	17.0	27.3	3.3	0.0	9.0
6	10.0	40.0	26.7	30.7	26.7	0.0	3.0	0.0
7	0.0	40.3	33.3	23.7	20.0	3.3	0.0	3.0
8	20.3	40.0	26.7	17.0	6.7	0.0	0.0	6.3
9	10.3	26.7	26.7	16.7	27.3	0.0	0.0	3.0
10	10.0	41.0	33.3	23.3	26.7	6.0	13.7	3.0

Notes: a) Formal employment; b) Recreation; c) Social networking; d) Household chores; e) Other employments; f) Attending school; g) Farm work; h) Devotion
Source: Field survey, 2001.

of twenty hours per week in other employment, they are also not likely to be the aged population in the sample. However, it is suspected that those with no education also have low income.

Across the households, a pattern of time expenditure across gender, age groups and levels of education was also observed. The data showed that only forty households have members in formal employment. The forty spend between ten and twenty hours a week at work. Except for households numbers one and nine in the table, all other household members spend about forty hours a week in recreation. On the whole, it can be observed that in virtually all the households, members spend little or no time in formal employment, schooling, doing farm work and devotion.

It should be noted that some household members are not even involved in certain activities. This is particularly so with formal employment, farm work, schooling and devotion.

A sketch of individual life patterns To illustrate life further (spatial characteristics, demographic profile and multiple modes of household economy) in Anguwar Mai Gwado, individuals were interviewed on their lives in the ward. Sketches of individual lives are thus presented in this section. Names of respondents have been replaced with fictitious ones for reasons of anonymity.

ELIZABETH She has lived in the ward for seven years with a husband and now with a one-year-old child. They are tenants renting two rooms for 200 naira a month. In the compound, a well supplies them with water. The house is not connected to electricity or the municipal water system. The kitchen is too small for all tenants in the compound, therefore she cooks with a stove in their room. There is a roofless bath place and a toilet with a falling wall.

The husband, from Plateau State, was in the military but is now retired. He sells vegetables in the main market of Zaria at Sabon-Gari. His trade is the major source of income for the household. Elizabeth used to knit to augment household income, but she has had to stop, as there was no market for her products.

HANNATU A thirty-five-year-old who came to Nigeria from Ghana, she has lived in Anguwar Mai Gwado for fifteen years. She came to Nigeria with a husband but now lives alone. She was a hawker taking her wares round the neighbouring villages of Zaria for sale. Now she owns a shop, where she stays all day.

As a secondary school leaver, she describes living in the ward as fair except for problems of water supply, which have been persistent for three years. Ordinarily, the place is peaceful and her trade is progressing. She spends her time keeping her shop and taking care of her children.

SULEIMAN He is twenty-two years old and was born in Zaria. As a secondary school leaver, he is not working but depends on his parents for everything. He says he is comfortable except for the lack of electricity (which prevents him from viewing television) and water supply (he is sometimes asked to fetch it). Household water is collected from the taps in the military depot or from a well. Further to this, he complained that the ward has no roads, though it is peaceful and sociable. Suleiman lives in Anguwar Mai Gwado simply because his parents still live in it, otherwise he would have migrated to Borno State. He spends his time playing games and hanging out with friends.

SALISU Born sixty years ago in Wase, in Plateau State, he came to Zaria in 1983 for military reasons. He retired in 1986 and settled in Anguwar Mai Gwado to enable him to train his children in neighbouring schools. He has a primary school leaving certificate. Currently a pensioner, his wife is a trader.

The household occupies its own compound-type house, part of which is rented out to others. Salisu describes the tenants as careless and dirty. According to him, the youth of the ward are uncontrollable and stubborn. As a retired person, he is not engaged in any economic activity, thus he spends his time visiting friends, resting and playing games all day. His entire family depends on his pension and rents for survival.

From these sketches it is clear what the problems of the area are; they include unemployment, underemployment and poor sanitary conditions. It is also apparent that the households diversify income as members engage in various economic activities. The characters generally fit into the statistical categories discussed earlier. People engage in petty trade and commodity production while spending more time on recreation and social networks.

Conclusion

The endeavour of this paper has been to establish the nature of daily life, livelihood and spatial structure in a high-density area. Anguwar Mai Gwado is largely made up of youth and middle-aged people who are from various parts of the country. The kind of economic skills the people have enable them to be self-employed, producing and selling goods and services in the urban informal sector.

The incomes are relatively high compared with the national public-sector minimum wage for junior workers, but low relative to the needs and aspirations of the people and to price levels. In addition to their income, the people have a stock of wealth given the proportion who own houses, farm lands, motor cars, motorcycles and television sets. Some of these properties are used for income generation, particularly the cars and motorcycles. Ownership of housing is significant to individuals and households as 'a cultural good, a source of self expression – a means – to determining access to wider social, cultural and environmental services' (Jarvis et al. 2001: 122). What is apparently important to the respondents is housing as a cultural good and a source of self-expression. Thus, it was found that their houses do not necessarily constitute part of the urban housing supply, since the houses are located at 'home places' outside the Zaria urban centre.

Much of the income earned, particularly by household heads, is expended on food. The food expenditure is further supplemented by income earned by other members of the households. From the types of food items bought for household consumption it is realistic to note that the people feed well. However, this has to be taken with caution, as the quantity of calorie intake *per capita* was not measured.

The community and household infrastructure is rather poor. The ward lacks roads, drainage and efficient water and electricity supply. It was also observed that households, the LGC and some community-based organizations are involved in drainage, road and environmental management in the ward. At household level, it was noted that facilities are either inadequate to cater for all in the compound or are completely non-existent.

It was expected that certain civil society organizations would form part of the support systems of the urban poor. It was found that the people are members of co-operative, ethnic and religious associations as well as social clubs and credit societies. It was not clear how much these associations and societies benefit their members, but the psychological effects of being a member and the reciprocal gift and support system inherent in the relations are beneficial to the people. It was, however, obvious that people generally rely on family members and inter-personal social networks for certain activities, particularly marriage, naming ceremonies, health bills and suchlike. It is no wonder, therefore, that social networking and recreation take up a good proportion of the daily time of people in Anguwar Mai Gwado. It should also be noted that, this support aside, even the inter-personal networks are not geared towards improving the income-earning abilities of households, except for the mobilization of resources to support members when the need arises.

It was, however, observed that females spend much of the day on recreation and household chores while the males spend the day on social networking, other employment and devotion. It is interesting to note that devotion increases with age, as the youth spend more time on recreation and helping with household chores. It is noteworthy that payment of females for household services would increase their individual incomes and the non-payment enables the entire household to cope with urban living.

This study has attempted to make a link between spatial structure and characteristics of high-density areas on one hand and the lifestyle, livelihood and social fabric on the other. These connections have been pursued from the perspectives of gender relations and practices, civil society interconnections, i.e. in the words of Jarvis et al. (2001: 121), 'practical concerns of everyday life', and housing density development standards as contained in master plans.

Anguwar Mai Gwado illustrates a case of village urbanization due to the uncontrolled growth and expansion of towns and cities. Overwhelmed villages like Anguwar Mai Gwado in the peri-urban area started with substandard housing and poor sanitation in the first place. This process was exacerbated by the influx of people into Anguwar Mai Gwado. The crisis of housing and environmental problems in the study area is compounded by inadequate attention to the management and expansion of such developments. The Zaria urban development plan did not establish any framework for density control, so the situation was worsened for Anguwar Mai Gwado when it was swallowed up by urbanization and settled by migrants. As it is, Anguwar Mai Gwado has neither the urban design features of the indigenous Zaria City nor those of Sabon-Gari (a commercial-cum-residential area adjacent to Anguwar Mai Gwado), which is laid out in a grid-iron pattern. Thus, the study area does not replicate either the Western or the indigenous models of urbanization. The spatial structure and character discussed are an expression of aspects of social differences in Zaria. This social difference is inherent in the profile of the respondents.

The process of engulfment is continuous and unavoidable given that urbanization in Africa is an ever-growing phenomenon. Thus urban governments and planners should work together to attain two main objectives, preventive and curative. In the first instance efforts should be made to upgrade and redevelop already engulfed villages in peri-urban areas of towns and cities based on basic planning principles and standards. This will serve to improve the infrastructural base, housing stock and quality in such areas and reduce, if not remove, the 'danger zones' that form part of town and cities in Nigeria.

Further to the curative measures, preventive policies are needed to manage urban expansion and the swallowing of suburban villages. Central to the policy is the preparation of the villages to take on both urban functions and landscape and make them hospitable to healthy human habitation and activity systems. The need to outline development preconditions in addition to building codes that must be met by developers in the peri-urban settlements provides a basis for a healthy engulfment of peri-urban settlements. For instance, in Stockholm 'one vital precondition for new housing developments outside of the city boundaries was a tramway system' (Pardon 1996: 86). Urban development managers have the responsibility to insist on the extention of facilities, services and utilities to peri-urban villages before developments are permitted in such places. Urban development plans and preconditions remain crucial to the control of urbanization and the urban expansion process, so that negative socio-economic and spatial consequences of engulfment can be avoided.

Notes

1 National Population Commission: results of 1991 national population census of Nigeria with projections to 1996.

2 It takes international institutions such as the World Bank and the United Nations Development Programme to sensitize the local councils to their responsibility for uplifting the standard of living of the urban poor in high-density areas. This is similar to the experience of Ma'aruf Sani working with the UNCHS in Kauru, a high-density area around Abuja, Nigeria's capital city.

3 The primary school programme used to be for seven years. With the adoption of the 6–3–3–4 educational policy (six years of primary education, three of junior secondary school, three of senior secondary school, and four of university) it became six years.

4 Proportions were expressed as one part out of ten maximum parts of either income or time. A part therefore represents 10 per cent.

5 A home place is where the respondents actually come from in the sense of where the ancestors and parents live or lived.

6 The pit toilets are either not accessible to some categories of the inhabitants or the toilets have low capacity to cope with needs as human faeces litter open spaces in Anguwar Mai Gwado.

References

Central Bank of Nigeria (1998) *Statistical Bulletin*, Vol. 9, No. 1, Abuja.

Chapin, S. (1965) *Urban Land Use Planning*, 2nd edn, Chicago, IL: University of Illinois Press.

Eze, O. (1996) *The Right to Adequate Housing in Nigeria,* Lagos: Shelter Initiative.

Federal Government of Nigeria (1992) *Urban and Regional Planning Law*, Abuja.

— (1997) *National Urban Development Policy*, Abuja.

Hanna, W. J. and J. Hanna (1971) *Urban Dynamics in Black Africa: An Interdisciplinary Approach*, Aldine: Atherton Inc.

Jarvis, H., A. Pratt and Cheng-Chong Wu (2001) *The Secret Life of Cities: The Social Reproduction of Everyday Life*, New Jersey: Prentice Hall.

Kaduna State Government (1979) *Zaria Master Plan – 2000*, Ministry of Lands and Survey, Kaduna State, Kaduna.

Kano State Government (1978) *Bichi Master Plan*, Kano State Urban Development Board, Kano, Nigeria.

Knox, P. L. and S. A. Marston (2001) *Places and Regions in Global Context – Human Geography*, New Jersey: Prentice Hall.

Makinwa-Adebusoye, P. K. (1992) 'Housing: A Critical Health Need of Women', in M. N. Kisekka (ed.), *Women's Health Issues In Nigeria,* Zaria: Tamaza Publishing Company.

Mustapha, A. R. (1991) *Structural Adjustment and Multiple Modes of Social Livelihood in Nigeria*, Geneva: UNRISD, DP. 26.

Pacione, M. (2001) *Urban Geography: A Global Perspective*, London and New York: Routledge.

Pardon, W. M. (1998) *Stockholm's Annual Rings – a Glimpse into the Development of the City*, Uppsala: Almqrist and Wiksell Tryckeri.

Smith, S. J. (1999) 'Society – Space', in P. Cloke, P. Crang and M. Goodwin (eds), *Introducing Human Geographies*, London, New York, Sydney and Auckland: Arnold.

Witzling, L. P. (1994) 'Urban Planning', *Encyclopaedia Americana* International Edition, Vol. 27, Grolier Incorporated.

8 | Ethnicity and the dynamics of city politics: the case of Jos

VICTOR A. O. ADETULA

Urban ethnic-based organizations in Africa are generally known for supporting their members in adjusting to life in the cities. It has long been realized that members of the ethnic, clan and village unions that dot African cities are significantly better adjusted to the urban environment than non-members. The various ethnic and cultural associations they belong to provide members with critical information on opportunities available in the cities, and also on how to access them. They serve as a platform for bringing various actors together and also facilitate the consolidation of resources, which in turn maximize the value of individual activities and earnings in the urban centres. In doing all these, urban-based ethnic associations functionally replaced the extended family units within whose tradition of socio-co-operation the new entrants into the cities were brought up. As members of the same clan, village, ethnic or language group came together to provide their kinsmen and kinswomen with a sense of socio-economic and psychological security, either through guardianship or the actual provision of materials, associational forms developed around group interests. The concept that adequately captures this is 'associational ethnicity', which Eghosa Osaghae describes as 'organization-based ethnicity', which 'derives from the ethnic group or category, but does not have to be located in the ethnic territory' (1994: 7).

Associational ethnicity is mostly associated with urban areas, but questions about how these associational forms have evolved, and how they work, important as they are for conducting the mapping and assessment of the capacities of contemporary African cities, have not received adequate scholarly attention. Also of importance is an understanding of the operational dynamics of these associations. Thus the following questions guide the study of associational ethnicity in urban Nigeria: what practices are entailed? What is the glue that cements real collaboration beyond ethnic ties or regional origins? While we know, for instance, that ethnic and cultural associations shape urban politics, provide platforms for competition and struggle for space, opportunities and resources, limited knowledge exists on the conduct of the relationships between associations, and also with public institutions.[1] The present effort attempts to provide answers to some of the questions highlighted above, using selected cases of urban ethnic and cultural associations from Jos, Nigeria.

Nigerian cities, like other urban centres in Africa, have a very rich associational life. In many Nigerian cities the associational forms date back to the period of colonial rule, when urban welfare associations generally provided the springboards for nationalist agitation against European rule (see Arifalo 2001). In post-colonial Nigeria some of these urban associations (in addition to new ones) have continued to thrive, as a recent national survey on 'Changes in Attitudes Toward Democracy and Markets' in Nigeria shows. According to the survey, a substantial number of Nigerians belong to associations that operate outside state control; nine out of ten respondents claim membership in various associational forms that include religious groups, community development associations, trade/farmers' unions and professional/business associations. While a little more than half of those interviewed described themselves as playing an active role in their associations, 52 per cent said that they had attended a community meeting within the past year (Lewis et al. 2001: 25). Nigeria associational life exists in varied forms, as observed by Björn Beckman:

> The country bristles with organized interests at all levels of society, from village and community associations to specialized professional groups, including the associations of old-boys (and girls) from the most prestigious professional schools of the world, numerous and prosperous enough to rent luxury hotels for their annual conventions. Trade unions and employers' associations, lawyers, doctors, teachers and students keep intervening dramatically in the public arena, contesting government regulations and policies and pursuing the demands of their members. An average marketplace is criss-crossed by associations of traders, craftsmen, transporters and labourers enforcing prices and rules of competition, negotiating with police, the tax collectors and other agents of the state, occasionally engaging in violent battles. (1997: 25)

Ethnic and cultural associations are the most common form of association found in urban Nigeria. Some of these operate as 'tribal unions', 'hometown associations', 'development unions' or 'progressive associations', which, in addition to helping their members adjust to urban life, serve as a link between the urban and the rural, for the benefits of the home communities (usually the home town).[2] In some cases the so-called 'cultural associations' or 'development unions' are in practice 'regional' or 'state' associations made up of communities of people from the same region or province. Usually these are local populations of people who belong to different social classes, but are bound together by common cultural, ethnic or language identity, which they emphasize and exaggerate. This they do through 'retribalization', which, according to Abner Cohen, is the process through which a cultural or ethnic group reorganizes its own traditional customs, or develops new customs under traditional symbols, 'often using traditional norms and ideologies to enhance its distinctiveness within the contemporary situation' (1969: 1). This form of group dynamics in the urban arena is the basis of urban ethnicity.

In many Nigerian cities the struggle for public space is a defining feature of inter-ethnic relations. This is the situation in many African countries, where ethnic and cultural associations have been elevated to project group identity, which has increasingly become crucial for the political behaviour of the individual (Nnoli 1994: 18). The 1980s economic crisis aggravated the trend through economic policies and programmes that further estranged the state from the people, leaving few (in some cases none) authentic connections to the people. In Nigeria, for example, the Structural Adjustment Programme to which Nigerians were subjected intensified urban ethnicity and gave urban ethnic associations a new prominence (Osaghae 1995). What ends do urban ethnic and cultural associations seek to advance, and what means and resources are employed in their operations? What are the material and social resources available to the associations, and how have these – especially social resources such as social networks – been deployed to promote the general wellbeing of members? How have these associational forms evolved, and what political spaces do they occupy or seek to occupy?

Peter Ekeh provides a useful insight on the public realm in Africa, which he maintains is not a single consolidated public realm, 'which effectively offer[s] common platforms for the activities of the state and the public behaviours of individuals'. In contrast, the public realm in Africa is segmented into 'civic public realms' over which the state presides and enjoys some monopoly, and also the 'primordial public realms' which offer platforms for individuals' public behaviours (1992: 200). In many African cities ethnicity has become the key instrument for fostering social cohesion. Associational life is dominated by identity solidarities (ethnicity or kinship), operating within the confines of their particularistic concerns and ethnic/clannish orientations. In Western political thought, this would be considered a limitation. In Africa, however, ethnic associations unite individuals on the basis of ascribed identity (such as ethnicity, kinship, and culture) rather than shared professional or political interests. This pattern of associational life is prominent in regions of the world where the development of commodity relations is still at a rudimentary stage. In such societies, Claude Ake says, 'the elements of civil society are a mixture of secondary and primary groups'. He explains further that those primary groups, 'especially ethnicities, nationalities, kinship groups, communal groups, language groups and religious sects, tend to be very influential in such societies' (1997: 6). The extent of 'pressures and anxieties' in developing societies, which are largely the consequence of 'state building and the push of development', creates a strong tendency among the people to focus on holistic identities, which provide 'the requisite solidarity for dealing with threats that are cultural, ubiquitous, and multifaceted' (ibid.).

In Africa, 'individuals are not perceived as being meaningfully and instrumentally separate from the [various] communities to which they belong', but rather are 'placed within the family, kin and community networks from which [they] issued' (Chabal and Daloz 1999: 52). Thus, whenever (s)he is confronted with the challenges of urban life, 'the ordinary individual' has always 'sought to attain his [*sic*] security and welfare needs' from 'kinship organizations which have accordingly grown bigger and bolder in African history, experiencing a path of development directly opposed to that in European history' (Ekeh 1992: 191). This is the context in which ethnic associations in the cities replace the principle and practice of the extended family – the tradition of social co-operation under which urban residents were raised in the rural areas (the home towns) – and are now expressed in the association's function of ensuring the socio-economic and psychological wellbeing of fellow kinsmen. Thus, a new entrant into the extra-tribal community of the urban environment through the kinship associations is provided with traditional social support to facilitate his or her adjustment. In this regard, the association creates a new solidarity with which the entrant can identify.

Thus ethnic associations, generally taking the form of kinship organizations, reinforce traditional social values, and also legitimize community social structures. These different ethnic-cultural groups in Nigerian cities, as in many other African countries, are in competition over scarce resources. In the face of this competition, the associations function as adaptive mechanisms for individuals who have migrated from the 'home town' communities in rural localities to the unfamiliar urban centres. The function of these associations transcends the social, economic, religious and cultural realms to include the 'political' in a 'more inclusive and more extensive' sense to that obtaining in the West:

It is more *inclusive* in that it contains the multiple aspects of the relationship between individual and the community [...] so that, for example, the fact that a person belongs to a particular village or age group may have significance for some political activities. It is more *extensive* in that it projects with varying degrees of intensity into the other realms of human existence; social, economic, religious, cultural, etc. ... (Chabal and Daloz 1999: 52)

On the evidence of Nigeria, ethnic and cultural associations in the urban centres emerged during the colonial period in reaction and response to the logic of colonialism. During this period public spheres were constructed to serve the public interests of different ethnic and cultural groups. In post-colonial Nigeria not much has changed in the nature and character of the state as well as its relationship with society. Thus the role perception of these associations has remained largely unchanged. Peter Ekeh remarks that although these associational forms are associated with ancient structures of kinship, they are essentially 'modern social formations whose goals are to enhance the collective welfare of unique primordial groupings in the modern circumstances of multiethnic and polyglot nation-states in Africa' (1992: 205).

Some examples are needed here. During the colonial period there was Egbe Omo Oduduwa, a Yoruba pan-ethnic tribal union, formed to increase the Yoruba share of resources in Nigeria. It later metamorphosed into the Action Group, which exerted greater influence on the political directions and affairs in the old Western Region of Nigeria. Similarly, the Ibo State Union wielded significant influence on the Igbo-dominated National Council of Nigeria Citizens (NCNC). Supporting kinsmen through a host of welfare activities is usually the trademark of ethnic associations in urban Nigeria. In contemporary Nigeria we have Afenifere for the Yoruba, Ohaneze for the Igbo and the Arewa Consultative Forum for the Hausa-Fulani, all playing roles similar to those of the ethnic and region-based associations of the colonial era. Not only do these forms of associations pervade urban life in Nigeria – the city historically has remained the breeding ground for them – but they also influence individuals' political preference and behaviour, a function facilitated by the porosity of the boundaries between the individual and the communal. In the next section we seek to verify some of these conceptual and theoretical assumptions about the activities of urban ethnic and cultural associations in a Nigerian city.

The case study: Jos metropolis

The city of Jos in north central Nigeria is taken as a case study. It is the capital of Plateau State. This essay draws data first from my participation in a community action project under the auspices of the African Centre for Democratic Governance, Jos, in 1997. This project involved 120 urban-based voluntary associations. Between 2000 and 2001, with the support of CODESRIA through its Multinational Working Group on 'Urban Social

Process and Change in Africa', I was able to undertake a follow-up study of a selected few ethnic and cultural associations. During this stage, I focused on the evolution as well as the nature and character of these associations' engagement in the public realm. I closely observed the associations, and had informal interviews to collect qualitative data on their modes of operation. Key association officials (such as presidents and secretaries) were contacted specially for informal interviews. A field team made up of four field workers with previous experience in data collection and interviewing were appointed and trained. The actual fieldwork lasted for about six months. The few selected associations whose activities and operations were studied in full included the Berom Educational and Cultural Organization, the Jassawa Development Community, the Afizere Cultural and Community Development Association, the Igbo Cultural Association, the Tiv Women's Association and the Yoruba Community.

What are the political dynamics by which these associations mobilize to occupy political spaces in Jos? What ends do they seek, and by what means do they pursue these ends? With these broad questions in mind I discuss the context from which some selected urban ethnic associations in Jos metropolis operate. What are the ends they seek to advance? That is, what are the key issues on which particular associations focus? What are the operational dynamics of these associations? What are the various normative organizational practices established and deployed by these associations in order to accomplish the task they set themselves? What are the resources and means they apply in their operations?

One key underlying assumption that guides the study reported here is that ethnic and cultural associations are regarded as important political institutions in the urban polities, capable of generating ways to engage the political process. That is, they are capable of functioning as part of broader institutional networks, which mobilize people into public life through the provision of political information and participatory resources. This assumption, if expanded, shows urban ethnic associations as capable of connecting people to the political process. In this context, urban ethnic associations are seen as helping to build 'social capital', or the features of social life – networks, norms and trust – that enable participants to act together more effectively to pursue shared objectives (Putnam 1993: 167). The dynamics through which urban-based ethnic and cultural associations enter and consolidate their influence in the public sphere (either in the cities or their 'home' communities) is examined. I argue that urban ethnic associations have the potential to serve as agents of political mobilization and as intermediaries between the individual and the state, fostering political connection and engagement. However, the operations and activities of selected urban ethnic and cultural associations in Jos metropolis reveal many constraints on their capacities as political actors.

Jos: brief history and social setting

Jos, originally occupied by the Berom, Jarawa and Anaguta, was founded officially in 1915. Jos metropolis today encompasses three local government areas – Jos north, Jos south and Jos east. The 1990 provisional census puts its population at 496,409.[3] It is a microcosm of Nigeria with respect to the composition of its population, which is made up of people of diverse ethnic and cultural backgrounds. In 1926, when the Plateau Province was created as part of the Northern Region, Jos became its headquarters until May 1967, when the regions were dissolved and replaced with the twelve-state structure. By 1930, however, Jos was on course to become a rapidly growing urban centre, courtesy of the growing tin mining economy and increased commercial activity.

Since that period Jos has always had a substantial population of people from virtually all the major ethnic groups in Nigeria. Very early in the life of Jos, Leonard Plotnicov neatly captured this when he wrote: 'Geographically and culturally, almost everyone is a stranger to Jos' (1967: 4). He took notice of the settlement patterns in Jos, and noted, in particular, the residential segregation. For example, that 'there were residents to warrant the designation "Hausa Settlement, Jos", courtesy of the colonial administration policy which kept culturally dissimilar ethnic groups separate' (ibid.: 41).

The economy of Jos during this period was associated mainly with the colonial tin mining. The quest for labour power for the colonial tin mining economy spurred an influx of migrants from Chad, Niger Republic, Borno, Kano, western Nigeria, Benue Province, Bauchi Provinces and other areas of southern Nigeria. Over time, this led to the concentration of people of diverse ethnic and cultural backgrounds that eventually culminated in the growth and development of migrant communities in Jos. In response to the difficulties of urban life, the migrant communities formed welfare associations along ethnic and cultural lines. Thus the early ethnic associations that sprang up in Jos were those of the Igbo and Yoruba and to some extent the Hausa-Fulani communities. The Berom, Afizere and Anaguta, who claim to be the original 'owners' of Jos, were later to form their associations in reaction to the perceived threat of marginalization and 'internal colonization' by the Hausa-Fulani.

The Berom, Afizere and Anaguta are mainly subsistence farmers, with some involvement in activities such as blacksmithing and pottery making. Few of those employed in local or state government agencies come from the lower cadre. Only very few from among the groups of the 'owners' are in federal government establishments, with the exception of the military and police services. A significant proportion of the population that cut across almost all the ethnic groups is engaged in the public sector alongside a strong representation in the informal sector. The bulk of the former is employed in the state bureaucracies – federal, state and local government – including such parastatals as the University of Jos and the Steel Rolling Mill, to cite just two. The organized private sector remains relatively weak, except for small-scale commercial activities in the hospitality industry such as hotels, restaurants, etc. and the sale of spare parts and building materials. Commercial activities, ranging from the traditional vending of items such as chickens, vegetables and yams, to used clothes, electrical appliances and the most sophisticated trade forms, dot the city's economic landscape. The majority of residents in Jos live in sub-standard housing in densely populated areas such as Angwan Rukuba, Nasarawa Gwong, Angwan Rogo and Dilimi. The rich are concentrated in high-income areas such as Ray Field, Liberty Dam ('millionaire quarter'), Government Reservation Areas (GRA), and other sparsely populated zones.

The provision of services and infrastructure in the city of Jos is the responsibility of the Jos Metropolitan Development Board (JMDB). While the sparsely populated, high-income settlements such as the GRA and Ray Field are well served with social amenities, provision of social services in relatively older settlements such as Nasarawa Gwong, Dilimi and Angwan Rogo, which harbour close to 80 per cent of the population, is anything but efficient. Social services such as pipe-borne water, public conveniences or navigable roads hardly exist, and where they do, are barely functional or at most more expensive than efficient. A visit to public parks, where close to 75 per cent of traffic into and out of the city converges, exposes one to a chaotic scene of epic proportions. Yet the people – individually and collectively – pay taxes and other levies. They know the purpose for which these taxes and levies are paid, that is, to provide social services. They know that local governments are obligated to provide these services.

The glaring evidence of urban deterioration has not provoked responses from the many ethnic and cultural associations, either in the form of civic action or otherwise, geared towards putting pressure on the local administration to improve the provision of social services and infrastructure. Yet the Jos metropolis enjoys a flourishing associational life, much of which is either ethnic based or composed of communities of people from the same region or sharing the same language and culture. The primary focus of the activities of these associations is helping members cope with the difficulties of urban life, and their activities range from mutual self-help and assistance during burials, weddings and other ceremonies, to development of 'home' communities. There is another category of urban cultural associations to which the Jassawa Development Association[4] and the Berom Educational and Cultural Association belong. These associations, in addition to empowering members of their various nationalities, have also sought increased accommodation in the public space within the city and even in Nigerian society at large.

Overview of selected ethnic and cultural associations

'Indigenes' and 'landowners' associations The Berom generally believe that they are the 'real indigenes' of Jos, and they boldly make this claim in their accounts of the history of Jos (see Gwon 1992: xxxi). While they do this, they regard the Anaguta and sometimes the Afizere as 'their nephews' (ibid.: 17), and by implication joint owners of Jos. Since colonial times the quest for security has made the Berom and the other ethnic groups in Jos pursue specific frameworks of identity formation. This has been mostly expressed through the formation of ethnic solidarity groups such as the Berom Progressive Union, the Yergam Union, the Middle Zone League and the Non-Muslim League, which entered into various alliances as part of early political movements in the Middle Belt.

Ethnic solidarity groups were very important during colonial rule, especially in Jos Township. They constituted earlier forms of nationalism 'expressed by the formation of ethnic organisations couched in development associations' (Mangvwat 1995: 294). The Berom Progressive Union was one of the early ethnic associations in Jos through which the 'indigenes' made appropriate representations to government. It was organized in 1945 by Patrick M. Dokotri and other Berom elites, 'to foster pan-Birom unity and partly to agitate for the payment of fair compensation to the Birom people in return for the use of their lands by British tin-mining companies on the Jos Plateau' (Sklar 1963: 345). Sen Luka Gwom, a leading chronicler of Berom history, lends credence to the above. He claims the purpose of the Berom Progressive Union was 'to bring Berom together to protect their land, which they found was being threatened by massive destruction, to create a better degree of public awareness and public enlightenment among the Berom for identity and recognition' (1992: 209).

Christianity is a dominant religion among the 'indigenes' groups. From its inception, the Berom Progressive Union had a very strong Christian background. Five out of the six original founders of the union were Christians; there was initial suspicion that the union was set up to promote Christian principles and values. But it was in the case of the Northern Nigerian Non-Muslim League, formed in 1949, that the influence of Christian religion in the identity formation of the indigenous groups was most evident.

The Berom Progressive Union was one of the ethnic solidarity groups that joined with other similar ethnic associational groups that came together and formed the United Middle Belt Congress (UMBC). For example, the closeness of the two organizations was demonstrated in their having to share a common secretary: Patrick Dokotri was the secretary to both the Berom Progressive Union and UMBC. The latter was dominated essentially by the non-Hausa-speaking people from northern Nigeria, notably the people from the present Plateau, Benue and Kogi States. The 'big regional parties', especially the Nigeria People's Congress (NPC), tried to make inroads into Jos. But the Berom, who associated the party with the Hausa-Fulani with whom they had issues to contest, resisted these efforts. Thus, the Berom and other groups that were referred to as 'indigenes' joined the UMBC *'en masse'* 'for self-determination, defence of their land and self-identity and recognition' (Gwon 1992: 212). As Monday Mangvwat observed: 'Information concerning party ideology is somewhat irrelevant to the UMBC because this was not an issue. Its membership therefore did not reflect any particular ideological orientation. The binding sentiment within the UMBC was simply a strong anti-Muslim and anti-Hausa-Fulani feeling.' Thus the UMBC was no more than 'an amalgam of ethnic associations united in their association to Hausa-Fulani' (1995: 303).

The Berom Progressive Union played its role as one of the political movements that championed ethnic particularism. The Jos Tribal Party, under the leadership of Patrick Dokotri, later succeeded the union. In the post-colonial era, the Berom Educational and Cultural Organization (BECO) emerged as the umbrella organization for all the Berom cultural groups, which include the Berom Youth Movement (BYM), the Berom Intellectual Revival Organizational Movement Club (BIROMC), the Berom Elders Council, and the Berom Women's Association (BWA). The leaders of the Berom and indeed BECO have remained very active in the Middle Belt Forum, which provides the platform for political elites from the Middle Belt. During the Second Republic, it would seem that the Berom maintained one political camp in their massive membership of the Nigerian People Party, probably to challenge the Hausa/Fulani-dominated National Party of Nigeria.

Long years of military rule affected the operations of ethnic and cultural organizations. During military rule these associations came under serious scrutiny from successive military regimes that were generally intolerant of social movements that might advocate alternative style of governance. The paradox, however, was that the military governors who were appointed for the various regions (later states) always had as part of their initial briefings directives from the 'centre' to consult with local groups before making political appointments. It is worth noting that during this period many of these associations collapsed into mere praise singers or appendages of military rulers, whom they often lobbied to advance parochial and sectional interests. For example, each time a new military administrator was appointed for Plateau State, it created tension in inter-ethnic relations, especially between the 'indigenes' and the Hausa-Fulani, both lobbying to secure commensurate numbers of political appointees. The situation became so tense in the late 1980s that civil servants in Plateau State Government were banned from holding offices in ethnic and cultural organizations. During this period, the activities of BECO were drastically scaled down. With the return to civilian rule, however, it has bounced back to life along with other ethnic associations in Jos.

'Settlers' and migrant groups The word 'settlers' is used routinely, especially by the 'indigenes' of Jos (notably the Berom, Afizere and Anaguta) to describe the descendants of early Hausa-Fulani immigrants to Jos. The latter have also been derogatorily labelled 'non-indigenes', 'strangers' and 'invaders'. The Hausa-Fulani were part of the migrant labour that came into the tin mines of Jos in the 1940s, mainly from Bauchi, Benue, Borno, Kano, Katsina, Niger, Sokoto and Zaria. Apart from the 'pull factor' of the colonial tin mining industry, the growth of commerce in Jos also facilitated the growth of the Hausa-Fulani community in the city.

It is worth mentioning here that the Hausa-Fulani generally are one of the best-known ethnic groups in trading activities in Nigeria. In Jos they are engaged mostly in commercial activities, especially wholesale and retail trades, which they, for a very long period, dominated along with the Yoruba until the coming of the Igbo people from eastern Nigeria. A small percentage of peasants of the Hausa group are involved in small-scale year-round farming and cattle grazing. The Hausa middle class is largely engaged in retail trading, while the wealthy are involved mostly in speculative businesses, transport, estate ownership and petroleum distribution. The activities of the Hausa-Fulani peasants, especially as they relate to land use, such as dry-season farming (*fadama*), have always brought them into conflict with the Berom, Anaguta and Afizere, whose livelihood also depends essentially on accessibility to land and its natural resources. For example, on 10 April 1997, communal clashes erupted between the Berom and the Hausa-Fulani in Gero in the Jos south local government area of Plateau State. The panel set up by the Plateau State Government established that the immediate cause of the fracas could be traced to what happened at the farm of one Alhaji Ibrahim Umaru, a dry-season farmer resident in Gero. It was noted, however, that the fighting was deeply rooted in the history of socio-economic and cultural experiences of the area. Such conflicts over resources have often served to bring up accumulated grievances and rivalry over political and economic power.

Although there are no accurate official statistics of population distribution by ethnic and cultural groups in Jos, the population of the Hausa-Fulani in Jos is significant enough to provoke concerns and attention from 'indigenes' groups that feel threatened by the former. Apart from their number, a probable source of threat is the influence of the Hausa-Fulani on the economy of Jos in relation to other ethnic and cultural groups. Compared with the 'indigenes', the Hausa-Fulani are well ahead in the control of the economic life of Jos. As mentioned above, the question of land has historically drawn the 'owners' into constant conflicts with the Hausa-Fulani. The rivalry between the 'owners' and the 'settlers' has remained at the base of inter-ethnic relations in Jos, which have frequently flared up into conflict. Although there were attempts during the Second Republic to get the Hausa-Fulani to 'adjust positively to the natives', these efforts at reconciliation were not very successful. Worthy of mention is the personal intervention of the then civilian Governor of Kano, Alhaji Abubarkar Rimi. But the challenges were too much for the Hausa-Fulani in Jos.

The youths subsequently responded with the formation of the Jassawa Development Association, which has since continued to provide the Hausa-Fulani community with a forum from which to articulate its positions *vis-à-vis* the other groups, as well as to mobilize its members for political action.

The Jassawa Development Association is composed mostly of Hausa-Fulani youths, most of whom were born and raised in Jos, and who therefore are emotionally attached to Jos as their birthright. This conviction has found expression in the demand of the Jassawa youths for 'certificate of origin' and 'indigeneship' from the authorities of the Jos North Local Government Council.[5] This generation of Hausa-Fulani in its agitation often claims that it has no other place to call home than Jos. While the older generation of Hausa-Fulani in Jos identifies with the agitation and protest of its youth, its support for Jassawa Development Association has surprisingly remained tacit. Denied the overt support of the Hausa-Fulani elders, the Jassawa Development Association has not been able to evolve developed structures that parallel those of other groups. Besides, the Jassawa Development Association has had a series of leadership crises that have almost left it moribund and of limited relevance, particularly when there are no contests with other ethnic groups in Jos.

The Jassawa Development Association remains a loose association of Hausa-Fulani youths. The Jassawa community, however, is still fundamentally committed to its traditional approaches to mobilization, which revolve around the use of the Islamic religion and Hausa culture and customs, but more importantly to the former.[6] On the evidence of the cultural orientations and displays of the Jassawa community, there is hardly any element of the Hausa culture that is completely free of the influence of Islam. Also, symbolic social institutions that are usually built around heroic accomplishments of cultural groups to memorialize their illustrious past are now readily available for image-boosting purposes. Some Hausa-Fulani people interviewed claimed that their community had at one time had its own traditional ruling institution. But the reality today is that the Hausa-Fulani have no traditional ruling institution compared with those of other migrant communities in Jos.

For example, the Yoruba has the Oba of Yoruba, and the Igbo has the Eze-Igbo. In the absence of a traditional ruling institution capable of symbolic representation of the group, the Jassawa community has consolidated its use of Islam as an instrument of mobilization for political and social activism among the Hausa-Fulani. Islam has provided the Hausa-Fulani political elites in Jos with an opportunity to strengthen and consolidate its support among Hausa-Fulani Muslims. This mode of politics is not limited to the Jassawa community. The use of religion for social mobilization has found its way into some Christian churches in Jos, especially those with a high concentration of Berom, Anaguta and Afizere. Since the violent riots of September 2001, many Christian organizations in Jos have become more vocal and active in city politics in the tradition of the 'liberation theology' of some Latin American societies.

The Igbo Cultural Association (ICA), formerly known as the Ibo State Union, is the umbrella association for all the Igbo tribal and clan groups in Jos. The Igbo Cultural Association has long-established structures and patterns of operations that are more developed compared with those of other migrant communities in Jos. This can be explained in terms of the Igbo's early experimentation with associational ethnicity in other places in northern Nigeria, which provided the Igbo community in Jos with precedence and also a model to look up to.

The Igbo were also part of the influx of early immigrants who came to Jos as part of the labour force for the colonial mining economy. Up to the Second World War, the Igbo were mainly in mining, government and related activities. But with the war came the opportunity for the diversification of the economy, and the Igbo found themselves in such activities as transportation, lorry repairs and trade in consumer goods. The Igbo population in Jos today is engaged primarily in commerce, including the importation of consumer and intermediate goods, estate ownership, transport (small- and large-scale), the service sector, spare-part dealing and retail trading. The Igbo's increased involvement in commerce exacerbated competition with the Hausa and the Yoruba who, prior to the coming of the Igbo, were indisputably the 'African entrepreneurs' in Jos. It was not long before the ethnic groups clashed, as was witnessed in the 1945 Hausa–Igbo riot (Plotnicov 1971: 301). Whatever the immediate cause of the riot, it is plausible to argue that competition, frustration and perceived status insecurity were responsible for the clash (ibid.: 305).

The Igbo Cultural Association enjoyed relative stability compared with other groups, partly as the result of its established institutions and the social structures set up to pursue its objectives. For example, the Igbo community established the office of the Eze-Igbo. The Eze-Igbo functions as the traditional head of the Igbo, and also acts as the custodian of Igbo culture, customs and traditions in Jos. He also mediates and settles disputes between the individuals and organizations (mostly home town associations) that comprise the ICA. The office of the Eze-Igbo is fully integrated into the organizational structure of the ICA.

The Yoruba have the greatest number of 'home town associations' and 'development unions' in Jos. These exist at both town and village levels. There are development associations for all the Yoruba-speaking states – Lagos, Ogun, Ondo Oyo, Osun and Kwara. Town-based organizations include associations such as the Owo Progressive Union (OPU), Iseyin Progressive Association and Ekiti Parapo. The Yoruba Community in Jos serves as the umbrella for all these associations. Besides helping to provide their kinsmen and kinswomen with the necessary coping and survival strategies, the town associations and unions function as well-established links with the home towns, usually in the rural areas of origin. Serving as the intermediary between the communal and stable system of the home town and the individualistic and crisis-ridden city, these town associations provide succour for their kinsmen in Jos. Through them development is channelled back to the rural home towns in the form of development assistance, scholarships and special projects.

Women's associational groups In many of the urban ethnic and cultural associations in Jos, women are largely excluded from the mainstream activities of the various associations. In the Jassawa Development Association, for instance, women are not members and are hardly objects of consideration during deliberations and meetings except by default. This may be explained in terms of the pervasiveness of Muslim religious and social values, which relegate women to the private sphere, and do not accommodate public association of male and female. Although women are allowed to form their own organizations, these groups are expected to limit their activities to domestic, familial and community issues. This is an essential element of the Muslim culture found in northern Nigeria, which accords respect and honour to Muslim women who do not operate in the public context, but are secluded and veiled.

Within this Muslim culture for women, a new awareness has emerged, which has culminated in the establishment of the Federation of Muslim Women's Associations in Nigeria (FOMWAN). Although originally conceived as a religious organization, FOMWAN has now transcended its initial mandate to include active involvement in discourse on broader social issues. Noticeably, women's groups in northern Nigeria are beginning to carve out new roles for themselves in the public sphere, and FOMWAN is to a large extent an expression of this phenomenon. FOMWAN has spread all over the Nigerian cities, and it is operating largely within the framework of Islamic rites and values. There is a viable FOMWAN chapter in Jos through which the Jassawa community relates with the Hausa-Fulani women as a group. This is done only when it becomes necessary for women to be involved in carrying out the agreed decision of the Hausa-Fulani community in Jos. A period of electoral politics and competition has seen the use of this link for the purpose of supporting mobilization for the preferred candidates of the Hausa-Fulani community. There may be other smaller Muslim women groups in Jos, but FOMWAN has remained the main channel through which the Hausa-Fulani are co-opted into inter-ethnic competition.

Exclusion of women from the public realm is not limited to the Hausa-Fulani community in Jos. Other communities also have in place some variety of partial exclusion. The Tiv Women's Association (TWA) was formed 'to protect the interests of Tiv women in Jos'. But more importantly, TWA was established in response to the social exclusion of women by the male-dominated Tiv Development and Cultural Association (TDCA). The irony, however, is that the TWA still operates under the umbrella of the TDCA, as one of its 'women's sections' spread all over urban centres in Nigeria (Ityavyar 1997).

Concern for the material survival of kinsmen and -women is a major consideration for urban associations in the city, and women's associations like the Tiv Women's Association and Berom Women's Association are no exception. In effect, these women's associations undertake apparently limited activities to garner material and psychological support for their members. Women's associations in Jos, although engaged in collective activities, have rarely shown much interest in pursuing more generalized goals. Their activities are centred on savings and credit, which essentially support members' involvement in the urban informal sector. The Tiv

Women's Association in Jos has a relatively developed savings and loan scheme called 'Bam'. This entails a monthly 'contribution' by all members to a common fund that is made available to any member in need, usually as a loan to address such common but serious needs as payment of children's school fees, settlement of hospital bills, or initial capital for a small-scale business. A similar system of saving is found among members of the (BWA), made up largely of Berom women. They meet regularly and contribute money, which is made available to 'fellow sisters' as loans to help the latter start small businesses. This practice is an adaptation of the rural tradition of communal work parties among the Berom, whereby 'wives of the same clan' move from one farm to another on a rotational basis to provide labour.[7]

The Tiv Women's Association, like most women's associational groups in urban Nigeria, is deeply involved in religious ceremonies, burial rituals and rites, wedding ceremonies, cultural festivals, recreational activities and sports events, which in effect prove the essence of non-material coping strategies against urban vulnerability. These welfare activities are better developed among female urban groups in Jos than their male counterparts. For example, part of the welfare activities of the TWA consists of assisting the sick and bereaved. During illness, members of the association are expected to stand by their ailing member to provide psychological comfort and relief: 'Visits are usually paid to the sick member whether in the hospitals or at home. They [members of TWA] go in groups and individually. Many people confess their appreciation [...] A good number say it is a thing of pride to them when many people came to see them, especially in the hospital before the watching eyes of other patients' (Ityavyar 1997).

Also, the solidarity of TWA members becomes stronger during bereavement, exemplified in the following testimony of a TWA member on the association's policy on 'burying its members':

> The policy is that whether the deceased member is employed or not, the association should make available a coffin and transport [for] both members of the association and the bereaved family to the burial ground – usually to Tivland. The extent of the association's involvement in the funeral arrangements depends on the financial strength of the bereaved family; sometimes, where the group stops, individual members take over as the situation demands. At such times of bereavement, every Tiv person can be contacted to contribute towards this need. For some members, this is equal to life insurance. (ibid.)

Because low-income women in urban centres are generally more vulnerable than their male counterparts, women's associational forms have revolved around activities that are close to women in terms of their gendered character. Thus savings schemes are found in almost all the women's associations in Jos, and are particularly well developed among members of the BWA and also among Igbo women traders from the same clan or village. In the case of the latter, an element of an age grade system is introduced. These women's associations meet regularly, usually during weekends, celebrate with one another and contribute money, which is made available to 'fellow sisters' as loans to help the latter start a small business or avert impending bankruptcy. For the Berom women, this practice is an adaptation of the rural tradition of communal work parties among the Berom, whereby 'wives of the same clan' move from one farm to another on a rotational basis to provide labour.

Operational dynamics: economic, social and cultural strategies How have the ethnic and cultural associations in Jos organized themselves, and through what means, for political functions in the Jos metropolitan city? Typically, ethnic and cultural associations in urban areas strive to maintain their distinctiveness and exclusiveness, promote and consolidate identity formation, as well as address the welfare and material needs of their people.

Ethnic and cultural associations in Jos have adopted specific identity formation strategies. The Berom Educational and Cultural Organization, for example, inaugurated a series of cultural and social activities such as the annual festival of Nzem Berom. These annual celebrations provide platforms for the flamboyant display of the richness of Berom culture. On this occasion, as recorded by Sen Luka Gwom, 'the whole of the traditional past is recalled, and images of one's passed relations and events are recollected. It is then one would not know when his head would begin to nod like a lizard in appreciation and thanksgiving to almighty DAGWI (Almighty God).' The celebration of Nzem Berom among the Berom community in Jos is more than cultural entertainment. Recently, it has become a political tool in the hands of Berom political elites, who have introduced political communications into what initially started as a cultural festival. While the robust and extravagant celebration of Nzem Berom provides the right forum for the whole social order of the Berom as a cultural group to be collectively acted out, the occasion also provides opportunities and licence for Berom elites to manipulate cultural resources such as oral literature (songs, praise poems, proverbs and slogans) and humour in the political sphere.

The use of myths of origin by the 'indigenous' communities such as the Berom, Anaguta and Jarawa to boost their claims has become more regular in Jos. The Berom Educational and Cultural Organization takes the lead in this area. Notably, Berom Historical Publications (BHP), with the support of a crop of Berom intellectuals through the BIROMC, is focusing on the preservation and projection of Berom identity.[8] The Hausa-Fulani elites have also been similarly engaged in a reconstruction of the history of Jos to authenticate their claims as 'the founders' of Jos.[9] Aside from the myths of origin projected by the 'indigenes' and 'settlers', other cultural strategies have been devised by virtually all the various cultural communities in Jos – the purpose of which is to project their exclusiveness. Traditional political institutions have served to promote cultural consciousness among the various people in Jos. The Hausa-Fulani 'settlers' sought anchorage in the Sarkin Hausa. Between 1902 and 1947, the Hausa-Fulani ruled Jos with the title of Sarkin Jos. The Berom negotiated and got the title of 'Gwong Gwom' in 1947, which they have jealously guarded as the symbol of their uniqueness as a group. The office of the Oba of Yoruba, which is relatively recent in Jos, is less visible in the organizational structure of the Yoruba community.

The various communities have institutionalized a number of cultural events and activities, with their respective ethnic associations playing the lead, to encourage interaction among kinsmen and -women, and to promote shared cultural values and identities. All the cultural communities in Jos now sponsor 'Cultural Day' – a celebration that takes the form of socio-religious festivals and rituals. There are numerous such festivals and rituals held by migrant communities in Jos. With the expanded proselytization of Jos city, these festivals and rituals have now been 'modernized' to fit into the monotheistic belief systems that pervade the city.

In this regard it is possible to find Christians in Jos celebrating 'Annual Harvest Thanksgiving' or 'Service of Songs', seasoned with the cultural flavours of the ethnic or cultural groups that are dominant in the various Christian sects.[10] Also, the proselytizing efforts and methods of some of the Christian churches and missions have consciously or unconsciously promoted and strengthened ethno-cultural identity, as observed in the activities of the Berom Bible Translation Group and the Berom Rural Mission.[11] If the Christian faith is serving the interest of the communities of 'indigenes', and to some extent the Igbo and Yoruba communities, the Hausa-Fulani people have parallels in their interaction with the Islamic faith to which most Hausa-Fulani belong. As with the Christians, major Muslim festivals are celebrated among the Hausa-Fulani as cultural events that serve to reproduce the Hausa-Fulani identity in the city.

Two religious networks – Jama'atu Nasri Islam (JNI) and the Izala groups – are associated with the Hausa-Fulani community in Jos. These associations operate primarily as umbrella Muslim religious bodies. However, beyond that they tacitly provide the platform for the Hausa-Fulani to articulate their position on several issues, from religion to politics. The Jama'atu Nasri Islam Hall in Jos is located close to the central mosque in Jos, and it is the usual place for the meeting of the Hausa-Fulani, rather than – as is often wrongly assumed – in the mosques themselves. At such meetings of Jama'atu Nasri Islam, discussions are frank and blunt among the people, who usually seek justification for actions and positions within the context of the Islamic faith. The fact that key members of the Jassawa Development Association are also leading members in the Jama'atu Nasri Islam makes the task of social mobilization among the Hausa-Fulani considerably easier. Also, regular Muslim programmes in the city have provided an opportunity for the Hausa-Fulani to come together as a family of Muslim worshippers, but with the underlying purpose of promoting a form of cultural identity that is contiguous with the Islamic religious identity.

The involvement of ethnic and cultural associations in specific benefit-yielding activities, such as the founding of schools, the building of halls and shops, as well as other forms of investment, is well established, and has enhanced identity formation and contributed significantly to the welfare of members. The welfare contents of the activities of the ethnic associations in Jos have served further to consolidate group consciousness and identity among members. In times of crisis the Hausa-Fulani usually find comfort in the intervention of both the Jassawa Development Association and the Jama'atu Nasri Islam. Both usually serve as a link to the larger Muslim family outside Jos, especially for the purpose of support and assistance to Muslim 'brothers and sisters'. Some concern, however, has been expressed over the prospect of using such links to 'externalize' local conflicts, as alleged in the recent Jos crisis, when 'friends' of parties in conflicts were said to have facilitated the importation of arms into Jos along with other relief meant for the victims of violent conflicts.

At a broader level, the welfare content of the activities of the various ethnic and cultural associations has been deepened to include the establishment of educational institutions for the benefit of their members. Also, this strategy has been extended to the economic sphere with the establishment of ethnic-based financial institutions. For example, the Hausa-Fulani established the Jassawa Community Bank, while the Berom elites founded the Renuyel Community Bank and Bukuru Community Bank with a view to facilitate the accumulation of capital by members of their ethnic groups.

With the active support of their respective ethnic associations, ethnic-based trading networks have been developed to consolidate a hold over particular economic sectors. Over the years, the Igbo have dominated the trade in motor parts, electrical supplies, clothing and shoes, and long-distance transportation services. Random interviews were conducted among traders of different ethnic origin in Jos's main market between 1999 and 2001. The purpose was to investigate the sources of initial capital for the trading activities of the interviewees. Few Igbo traders depend on co-operative thrift societies as a source of capital for their trading activities. The very few who belonged to any co-operative societies were members of thrift societies exclusively for the Igbo. Many Igbo traders in Jos are in business, courtesy of their *'oga'* (usually of the same ethnic or clan origin), who usually brought them up as 'an apprentice'. The key element in this arrangement is trust, which membership in the Igbo Cultural Association builds through its rules, regulations and other norms that cover virtually all aspects of life, from politics to business. Accordingly, the ICA promotes informal networks among members to help in such areas as raising capital to start or expand business ventures. This type of informal network of mutual support comes in handy for Igbo traders who may have recorded losses during conflicts. Similarly, the ICA's paternalistic influence is fast penetrating the public sector, such as the University of Jos and other public agencies, where Igbo elites have also taken to using the ICA to negotiate or renegotiate space *vis-à-vis* other ethnic groups in the university.[12]

The organization of a particular ethnic or tribal monopoly around particular trading activities and services does not leave out other ethnic and cultural groups. For example, the Yoruba enjoy a monopoly in the sales of plastic products, and the Igbo have organized monopolies in the sales of automobile spare parts, 'ready-made' dresses, long-distance commuters' transportation, and also a near monopoly in the sales of used clothes (*'okrika'*), which they share with the Hausa. The Hausa have for long enjoyed a monopoly of trade in petroleum products, long-distance trade in food items, kola nuts and livestock as well as dry season farming (*fadama*). Although there are no clearly discernible patterns yet, it appears that distinct and ethnically marked occupational groups are evolving around trade and other informal activities dominated by other ethnic groups.

Jos has witnessed 'industrial action' by different ethnic occupational groups, either in protest or in solidarity with their parent ethnic or tribal unions. In 1994 Hausa/Fulani butchers slaughtered cows on the streets to protest about the suspension of Mallam Aminu's appointment as chairman of Jos north Local Government Council. Following the 7 September 2001 civil disturbance, during which the Igbo communities lost kinsmen and millions of nairas' worth of property, Igbo traders 'closed down' their shops for some days, partly in solidarity but more in protest.[13] The May 2002 civil disturbance in Jos also brought out the Yoruba traders on 18 July 2002 to declare 'a day of fasting and prayers' for peace in Jos. The Hausa-Fulani 'closed' down their market stalls on 30 October 2002 and also went to town to protest about what they called the 'indiscriminate arrests' of their people in connection with a series of violent conflicts around Jos. This form of political engagement by urban associations has become more regular in the city since the return to civil rule in Nigeria.

Struggle for power and resources Politics as the struggle for power and resources among constituents within a political system exists in Jos metropolis, with ethnic and cultural associations the main players. At different times, the struggle has involved land access and use, the creation and control of local government administration, and political appointments. Other migrant communities in Jos, notably the Yoruba and Igbo, have become involved in the struggle for power, although on a considerably lower scale, to ensure the security of economic spaces they either already occupy or seek to occupy. Thus, at different times these migrant communities, using their various ethnic and cultural associations, have been involved in the struggle for space within the city.

One instance of competition for economic space was the 1945 Hausa–Igbo riot, which was essentially a struggle over control of commerce. Apart from open conflicts, as experienced in this riot, migrant communities have had to negotiate space with the 'indigenes' communities and in some cases the 'settlers' communities. The results of the 1999 local government elections reflect compromise among all the dominant ethnic and cultural communities. The local government that was inaugurated 'took care' of all the migrant communities whose votes 'could change things'. Beyond the election victory of the People's Democratic Party, the newly inaugurated local government administration has had to appoint non-elected supervisory councillors from both the Igbo and Yoruba communities so as to 'carry along' a majority of the voters from the two communities of migrants. As the stage was set for the local government polls in 2003, the various communities resumed negotiations among themselves.[14]

In the struggle for power in Jos, associational groups such as the Berom Educational and Cultural Organization, Jassawa Development Association and the Afizere Youth Movement have provided rallying points for the articulation of their members' demands and protests. For example, the mandate of the BECO is to cultivate 'unity, love, progress and understanding among Berom people'. Among other things, however, this mandate has been interpreted to include addressing the land question and, by implication, the ownership of Jos. Land questions and a perception of the lack of representation featured prominently in the early political conflicts in Jos, especially during colonial rule. While the land questions still are at the base of many conflicts in rural areas around Jos, conflicts in urban Jos are now more centred on control of the political apparatus of the city. These conflicts have pitched the Hausa-Fulani against the Berom, Anaguta and Afizere, especially during electoral competition.

The Hausa-Fulani enjoyed dominance of Jos local administration during the colonial period. They also represented Jos in the regional government and to some extent the central government. For example, Alhaji Garba Baka-zuwa-Jere of the Jassawa community was the first elected representative of Jos in the Northern Regional Assembly, and Alhaji Isa Haruna, a Hausa, represented Jos in the Pre-Independence Conference of Nigeria. During the Second Republic, three prominent members of the Jassawa Development Association represented Jos in the Plateau State House of Assembly, while the Federal House of Representatives had Alhaji Inuwa and Baba Akawu, both members of the Jassawa. Moreover, the Jassawa provided the leadership of the old Jos Local Government. In 1991, in the Jos north local government elections, a member of the Jassawa group emerged as executive chairman, while eight out of the fourteen elected councillors were also members of the Jassawa.

The 'indigenes', or 'owners', were late starters. It was not until 1950, for instance, that an 'indigene' Berom man, D. B. Zangs, was nominated to the Northern Regional Assembly. This trend in power and resource distribution in Jos metropolis provoked responses from the various associations of the 'indigenes' groups, notably the Berom, Anaguta and Afizere who, with some support from the Yoruba and Igbo groups, mobilized support around the issues of marginalization and imbalance in the allocation of resources and power to challenge the domination by the Hausa-Fulani. Since the 1990s, resistance has intensified, and on some occasions has escalated into violent confrontation, as in the disturbances of 12 April 1994. There were tensions over other public appointments in 1996 and in 1998, and also on 7 September 2001 following the appointment of Mukhtar Muhammad, a Hausa, to the post of Poverty Alleviation Co-ordinator for Plateau State, which was resisted by some who claimed to be 'indigenes'. The roles of ethnic associations in all this have ranged from mobilizing members for active political participation to the outright use of violence. This dimension of political interaction among the ethnic groups in Jos is worth exploring further with reference to some cases of actual involvement of ethnic associational groups.

The appointment of Mallam Aminu Mato, a Hausa-Fulani, as chairman of the Caretaker Management Committee of Jos north Local Government Council in April 1994 provoked a chain of reactions from the various ethnic groups, which precipitated the 12 April 1994 riot. The Berom, Anaguta and Afizere groups demonstrated their outright rejection of Mato's appointment in a peaceful protest on 5 April 1994. Tension mounted when the new chairman could not immediately take over the management of local government affairs after he was sworn in. The government intervened by suspending his appointment. While this action placated the Berom, Afizere and Anaguta, for the Hausa-Fulani group it was an affront to their collective pride. On 11 April Hausa-Fulani butchers slaughtered cows and other animals on the highway near the abattoir to protest against the government's suspension of Mato's appointment. On 12 April, the Hausa-Fulani community, led by youths of the Jassawa Development Association, embarked on a demonstration that culminated in a large-scale riot that spread through the city.

On 7 September 2001, Jos witnessed one of the most violent ethno-religious clashes in the history of modern Nigeria. Violent conflict erupted in the city when the federal government appointed a member of the Jassawa community as the Poverty Alleviation Co-ordinator. Before the appointment, there had been tensions in the relationship between the 'owners' and 'settlers' aided by allegations and counter-allegations of social and political exclusion. Thus when the appointment of Mukhtar Muhammad was announced, the various groups of 'indigenes' and 'non-indigenes' launched into a war of words against one another. The Jassawa community received such messages as 'Trace your roots before it is too late' and 'This office is not meant for Hausa-Fulani or any non-indigene' from the 'indigenes'. They, in turn, responded through an organization in the name of Hausa-Fulani Youths (Under 25), issuing and circulating leaflets bearing messages such as: 'Yes, the loss of a few families wouldn't bother us. After all for every single Anaguta's life and their allies, there are thousands of other Hausa-Fulani. Let's see who blinks first' and 'The seat is dearer to us than our lives. In that case, do you have the monopoly of violence? Blood for blood. We are ready.'

Conclusions and policy issues

The aim of the study reported in this chapter was to analyse how the associational ethnicity that has emerged in Jos since the colonial period has developed, essentially through formal and informal social networks that unite people around ethnic, cultural and religious identities. The analysis included, among other things, the underlying factors that motivated and induced people to participate actively in ethnic and cultural associations, and attempted to analyse how these associations perform a number of survival tasks in the face of urban hardship. Lastly, it analysed the strategies through which the various associations promote identity formation and also engage in urban politics. In conclusion, policy issues are discussed and recommendations given.

The mandates of ethnic and cultural associations in Jos reveal marked similarities in their goals and objectives, centring on such claims as 'promoting the welfare of members' and 'developing the home towns'.[15] While these ethnic and cultural associations wield significant influence over the political behaviour of individuals, very few of the ethnic associations in Jos have the capacity for serious political engagement, beyond the primordial public space, to contest the civic public space with the state. Whereas there is discontent with central and local government performance, especially in the provision of amenities, ethnic and cultural associations in Jos have not seriously engaged the state in either advocacy or campaigns for improvement in the provision and maintenance of public amenities. In contrast, the associations have largely sought accommodation within the structures and institutions of the state to advance narrow group interests. The ensuing competition for space in the public realm through access to state resources has generated more conflicts than co-operation among different ethnic and cultural groups.

Jos has continued to experience its share of inter-ethnic conflicts. The colonial authorities and to some extent successive military regimes were able to curb the wave of urban conflicts. Since the inauguration of civilian rule in May 1999, however, the rate of urban conflict in the country has generally accelerated. Jos is indisputably one of the hot spots for violent ethno-religious conflicts in recent times. In a period of twelve months, Jos has experienced two bloody ethnic-religious conflicts.[16] The outskirts of Jos have not been left out of the fray, as the conflicts have redefined relationships among the various ethnic and cultural groups in the villages around the city. Sympathizers with their respective kinsmen in Jos have replayed and reproduced the Jos experience in the outskirts. Such was the case in Vom (near Kuru), when the Berom and the Hausa-Fulani clashed just a few weeks away from the 7 September 2001 violence in Jos.

The city has in recent times experienced increased pressure, consequent on the upsurge in population with the influx of people from neighbouring states. Some of these are either displaced persons fleeing from the conflict areas of Kaduna, Bauchi, Taraba, Nasarawa and Benue states or Christians relocating from the northern states that have adopted the Sharia criminal code. With this trend, goods and services have become increasingly scarce and competition for them has increased. For example, competition for market stalls and spaces in Jos's main market (before it was burned in January 2002) was already generating tension among various ethnic groups. All this has serious implications for associational ethnicity in Jos. Officials of some ethnic associations reported a significant increase in membership registration and also the additional burden on the welfare system helping their kinsmen and women to adjust to the realities of urban life.

While these pressures mount, ethnic and cultural associations like the BECO, the various youth leagues of the 'indigene' organizations and the Jassawa Development Association appear ill-prepared for the greater task of forming organizations that might transcend narrow ethnic, cultural and regional boundaries. Ethnic patronage is evidently on the increase, and there is no doubt concerning the desirability of ethnic and cultural distinctiveness on the part of the various ethnic and cultural identity groups, especially in the face of fierce electoral competition. It should be mentioned that, in the past, ethnic and cultural unions served to make the Jos urban setting welcoming to new entrants by facilitating adjustment and increasing their involvement in urban life, usually culminating in the new entrants' membership of recreational clubs (such as the Plateau Club and Yelwa Club) and other 'specialized' unions (e.g. trade unions). This period witnessed the emergence of detribalized social networks of non-parochial associations of educated elements in the Middle Belt such as the UMBC, which forged links with political parties to actualize its mandate. Reminders of such inter-cultural co-operation still exist in the activities of a few gender-based organizations, such as the Country Women's Association of Nigeria (COWAN) and the National Council of Women's Societies (NCWS).[17]

The efforts of the few broad-based multi-ethnic social networks in Jos, however, have recorded limited success. Looking at the recent peace-building initiatives championed by the women in Jos, one can argue, on the one hand, that the prospects for inter-ethnic co-operation in Jos are very bright. This scenario requires, however, a new social order: a responsive state with adequate capacity to mediate in social conflicts and mitigate the level of social contradictions in the society so as to create an enabling environment for the efforts of detribalized groups like the COWAN, NCWS and other recreational clubs and 'specialized' unions that will continue the process of detribalization in Jos into the future. Central and local governments should be able systematically to respond to urban associational ethnicity and other forms of collective action, possibly through some form of regulatory framework for their activities and operations.

The resurgence of interest in broad-based multi-ethnic social networking by target groups in the urban centres of Nigeria has been encouraged largely by international development agencies, increasingly concerned about the deterioration in public security in many urban centres, which is occasioned by ethno-religious conflicts. This enlightened support of the international community is likely to continue. Also, the general state of insecurity in Jos is already forcing the federal government in particular to show interest in the affairs of Jos, and indeed in the activities of urban associations.

On the other hand, however, dominant interest groups within Jos city have continued to demonstrate a lack of interest in inter-ethnic co-operation. Their continued adherence to 'retribalization' for the projection of ethnic and cultural exclusiveness, the paucity of initiatives and readiness to support broad-based initiatives for national integration and peaceful coexistence, and the gross abuse and misuse of power through ethnic patronage have the tendency to aggravate ethnic rivalries. It is obvious from the above that if urban ethnic associations are to serve as agents of social change, a new social order has to be in place that will reverse the social and economic deprivation and inequalities in the city that aggravate inter-ethnic competition. In this regard, a change is conceivable in the realm of urban governance. The urban administrative process of the Jos metropolis needs to be sensitive to the dynamism and sophistication of its environment. It is expected to provide essential services and, at the same time, to mobilize human and material resources in the city for development.

Notes

1 I am grateful to members of CODESRIA's Multinational Working Group on 'Urban Processes and Change in Africa', and especially to Professor Abdou-Maliq Simone, who made his comments and review available to me through a good deal of on-line correspondence.

2 The rural–urban linkage that these associations facilitate provides the urban dwellers with opportunities to engage in the political process of their various local communities that benefits from resources remitted back to the localities from the urban centres to aid development programmes, usually in the forms of scholarships and sponsorship for young pupils, construction of public utilities and provision of social amenities.

3 Since the move of the federal capital to Abuja, and the recent introduction of the Sharia legal code in most parts of northern Nigeria, Jos has continued to experience an influx of people. This has implications for available land space as well as available public infrastructure and services.

4 'Jassawa' is a term used to describe the Hausa-Fulani community in Jos, and the Jassawa Development Association is the main ethnic and cultural association of the Hausa-Fulani.

5 Jos north local government area has the largest concentration of Hausa-Fulani in Jos, and is also the hottest spot for Berom–Hausa–Fulani conflict. The control of Jos north is constantly an issue of contestation between the two communities.

6 It is common knowledge that Islam successfully penetrated Hausaland and replaced its 'original' Hausa culture with the Muslim culture.

7 Insights from the author's previous research on impacts of tin mining on livelihoods among the Berom women of the tin mining areas of Du, Foron and Gyel that was carried out between 1995 and 1998 with the Fund for Leadership Development of the Population Program of the Macarthur Foundation, Chicago.

8 Berom Historical Publications has published two volumes on Berom history and culture.

9 Mohammed Gambo of the Department of Religious Studies, University of Jos, provided useful insights in this regard.

10 The author observed this trend in the St Luke's Anglican Cathedral Church, Jos, and also St Paul's Anglican Church, Jos, where the Yoruba and Igbo are respectively in the majority. In the two churches mentioned 'church associations' have assumed ethnic dimensions. However, in Ecwa and Cocin, with their high concentrations of the indigenous groups (Berom, Jarawa and Afizere), church groupings are devoid of overt ethnic coloration.

11 Interviews with Samuel Godongs and Garus Logams, both active members of the Berom Educational and Cultural Association.

12 Author observed that staff members of the University of Jos have become increasingly prominent in ethnic and cultural associations. The Igbo Cultural Union and Egbe Izokar Omo Yaruba for the Igbo and Yoruba communities respectively have covertly advocated adequate representation of their ethnic/cultural groups at all levels of governance in the university.

13 Also, between 10 and 12 September 2002, Igbo traders, acting on the directives of the authorities of the Igbo Cultural Associations, closed down their shops. This time it was to enable the Igbo community to participate in the voter registration exercise conducted by the Independent National Electoral Commission (INEC).

14 None of the prospective Igbo candidates for the local government in Nigeria was willing to confess to any political alliance with the 'indigenes', but rumours circulating in the premises of the Secretariat of the Igbo Cultural Association at 22 Zik Avenue, Jos, had it that negotiations were already at very high levels in this regard.

15 Apart from ethnic and cultural associations, there are other associational forms based on common economic/commercial interests, including the traditional vending of items such as chickens, vegetables, yams, potatoes, used clothes, electrical appliances etc.

16 On 7 September 2001 there was a civil disturbance in Jos. Also, in May 2002 Jos experienced another violent conflict. Two violent conflicts within a year have drastically affected Jos, as residents now live in fear and suspicion of neighbours, and new settlement patterns are emerging. Agwan Rogo quarters that used to harbour hundreds of University of Jos staff and students who could not be accommodated on the university campus have been renamed 'Zamfara' by some over-zealous Muslim youths. It is possible that their Christian counterparts in some Christian-dominated areas are acting in a similar manner.

17 On 28 August 2002, women in Jos metropolis, drawn from all women's organizations including COWAN, NCWS, FOMWAN and Zumata Mata

(Women Christian Fellowship), undertook a 'peace walk' to protest against the incessant violent conflicts in Jos.

References

Aina, A. (1994) 'The State and Civil Society: Politics, Government and Social Organisation in African Cities', Paper for the United Nations University Project on 'Urban Challenges in Africa', Conference held in London, UK, December.

Ake, C. (1997) *Why Humanitarian Emergencies Occur: Insight from the Interface of State, Democracy and Civil Society*, United Nations University/ World Institute for Development and Economic Research, Research for Action, 31.

Arifalo, S. O. (2001) *The Egbe Omo Oduduwa: A Study in Ethnic and Cultural Nationalism (1945-1965)*, Akure: Stebak Books.

Beckman, B. (1997) 'Interest Groups and the Construction of Democratic Space', in J. Ibrahim (ed.), *Expanding Democratic Space in Nigeria*, Dakar: CODESRIA National Studies Series, pp. 23-35.

Chabal, P. and J. Daloz (1999) *Africa Works: Disorder as a Political Instrument*, London and Bloomington: International Institute/James Currey and Indiana University Press.

Cohen, A. (1969) *Custom and Politics in Urban Africa: A Study of Hausa Migrants in Yoruba Towns*, London: Routledge and Kegan Paul.

Ekeh, P. (1975) 'Colonialism and Two Republics in Africa: A Theoretical Statement', *Comparative Studies in Society and History*, Vol. 32, No. 4, pp. 660-700.

— (1992) 'The Constitution of Civil Society in Africa History and Politics', in B. Baron et al. (eds), *Democratic Transition in Africa*, Ibadan: Centre de Recherche de Documentation Universitaire, Institute of African Studies, University of Ibadan, pp. 187-213.

Freund, B. (1981) *Capital and Labour in Nigerian Tin Mines*, London: Longman.

Gwon, S. (1992) *The Berom Tribe of Plateau State of Nigeria*, Jos: Fab Educational Books.

Ityavyar, N. (1997) 'The Welfare Content of Ethnic Associations in the Jos Metropolis: The Case of the Tiv Development and Cultural Association in Jos', Paper for the National Workshop on Community Based Organizations in Jos Metropolis organized by the African Centre for Democratic Governance, Jos, 9-11 June.

Jacobs, C. C. (1997) *Studies in Berom History and Culture*, Jos: Berom Historical Publications.

Lewis, P. et al. (2001) *Down to Earth: Changes in Attitude Toward Democracy and Markets in Nigeria*, USAID–Nigeria: Afrobarometer.

Little, K. (1972) 'Voluntary Associations and Social Mobility Among West African Women', *Canadian Journal of African Studies*, Vol. 6, No. 2, pp. 278-88.

Mabogunje, A. (1995) 'Institutional Radicalisation, Local Governance and the Democratisation Process in Nigeria', in D. Olowu, K. Soremekun and

A. Williams (eds), *Governance and Democratisation in Nigeria*, Ibadan: Spectrum Books, pp. 1–15.

Mangvwat, M. (1995) 'Oral Sources and the Reconstruction of Party Politics on Jos Plateau, 1950–1966', in U. Y. Bala and K. George (eds), *Inside Nigerian History: 1950–1970*, Ibadan: Presidential Panel on Nigeria Since Independence.

Nnoli, O. (1994) *Ethnicity and Democracy in Africa: Intervening Variables*, Centre for Advanced Social Science, CASS Occasional Monographs No. 4.

Olukoshi, A. (1997) 'Associational Life', in L. Diamond, A. Kirk-Greene and O. Oyediran (eds), *Transition without End: Nigerian Politics and Civil Society Under Babangida*, Ibadan: Vantage Publishers, pp. 450–76.

Osaghae, E. (1994) *Trends in Migrant Political Organizations in Nigeria: The Igbo in Kano*, Ibadan: French Institute for Research in Africa, University of Ibadan.

— (1995) *Structural Adjustment and Ethnicity in Nigeria*, Uppsala: Nordiska Afrikainstitutet.

Plateau State Government (1998) *Government Views and Decisions on the Report of the Administrative Committee on Gero Communal Clash in Jos South Local Government Area.*

Plotnicov, L. (1967) 'An Early Nigerian Civil Disturbance: The 1945 Hausa–Ibo Riot in Jos', *Journal of Modern African Studies*, Vol. 9, No. 2, pp. 297–305.

— (1971) *Strangers in the City: Urban Man in Jos, Nigeria*, Pittsburgh, PA: University of Pittsburgh Press.

Putnam, R. (1993) *Making Democracy Work*, Princeton, NJ: Princeton University Press.

Rakodi, C. (ed.) (1997) *The Urban Challenge in Africa: Growth and Management of Its Large Cities*, Tokyo, New York and Paris: United Nations University Press.

Robinson, M. and G. White (1997) *The Role of Civic Organisations in the Provision of Social Services: Towards Synergy*, Research for Action 37, World Institute for Development Economics Research (WIDER), and Helsinki.

Sklar, L. R. (1963) *Nigerian Political Parties: Power in an Emergent African Nation*, New York, London and Lagos: Nok.

Stren, R. E. and R. White (1989) *African Cities in Crisis*, Boulder, CO: Westview Press.

Tostensen, A., I. Tvedten and M. Vaa (2000) 'The Urban Crisis, Governance and Associational Life', in A. Tostensen, I. Tvedten and M. Vaa (eds), *Associational Life in African Cities: Popular Responses to Urban Crisis*, Uppsala: Nordiska Afrikainstitutet.

9 | Urban development and urban informalities: Pikine, Senegal

MOHAMADOU ABDOUL

'The city is disintegrating. Does this mean that the disease that afflicts the reason which founded it (city concept), and its professionals is the same that is affecting urban dwellers? Perhaps the cities are deteriorating at the same time as the procedures, which organized them.' Michel de Certeau, *The Invention of the Daily Newspaper*

This study explores some of the dynamics of the urban changes currently taking place in African cities. It is based on empirical observation of a local public space (a district council) in which current changes are perceptible in the political order, i.e. in a process of reconfiguration of the power relationships between the various city stakeholders.

These processes are analysed through the concept of informality, i.e. a coexistence of various types of reference frames and of political regulation on a space, where agreements and power sharing between public and traditional authorities, and actors of the associative movement, are negotiated.

The study sets out to investigate how, around certain problems (land, urban sprawl, informal income generation), local authorities and associations and networks can provide sensible regulatory solutions to the urban crisis.

Urban development and informality

In many publications on the African city, ever-expanding urbanization, ever-worsening poverty are generally blown out of all proportion to the point of presenting themselves as the sole causes of urban crisis.

Incontestably, one of the most notable developments of the past few years in Africa is so-called 'uncontrolled or disorderly' urbanization which, when added to demographic growth, is regarded as an essential aggravating factor in the urban crisis. The latter manifests itself as unemployment, housing problems, abject poverty, environmental problems, lack of or poor social services and the inadequacy, negligence or incompetence of the state and its administrative units.

Faithful to this reading of African urban contexts, a considerable number of studies are today devoted to the problems of sustainable development and poverty alleviation.[1] From this point of view, analyses are made with regard to problems related to urban management (citizenship, decentralization, participation, good governance); urban infrastructure and services (water, electricity, road networks, drainage systems, education, health, transport, housing, etc.); the exclusion of minorities and other social ills (insecurity, violence, prostitution, drug abuse). On the basis of the combined effects of these problems, all point to the fact that there is, indeed, an urban crisis, which has to be addressed urgently. Recommendations, when they exist, generally tend to focus on the development of programmes or projects with strong technical orientation, which, themselves, are underlain by an epistemology of normative action (governments, municipalities) or by alternative programmes (non-governmental organizations, basic community associations, economic interest groups, etc.). Some actors (the state, administrative technical services, associative structures, NGOs), either separately or collectively, have to manage the conception, development and realization of the project or programme in question.

On the basis of such an epistemology, clarifying the reality of processes and real dynamics is reduced or evaded. The analyses suggested do not take into account either the complexity or historical depth of the changes currently taking place in African urban contexts. Indeed, an analysis based on 'urban crisis' or 'structural poverty' or the 'situational' approach, as René de Maximy (2000: 47) rightly pointed out, proceeds from the adoption of a theoretical posture founded on an eminently normative and curative approach. He also wrote, with much relevance, that: 'to talk of urban crises is not innocent. It is understood that this phenomenon is temporary and the decisions required shall be taken according to this ill or malaise.' Although this crisis is real and profound, it is also a problem concerning a method of thinking or acting, based on the problem of regulation and/or regularization of aspects of urban life, which fall within the informal, spontaneous, irregular and illegal sectors. This terminology, on which this type of speech is based, is the work of economists, political analysts, civil engineers and urban development experts, who find in it an explanation of the urban crisis and a justification of the restrictive or repressive intervention of the so-called informal activities.

Yet if there is an approach that reduces this informality, it is certainly one that takes into consideration only the dynamics, which it expresses solely by its dimensions of income generation, the search for the improvement of standards of living and of the living environment, or the relationship between this sector and the formal sector or the state. Hence the need to widen the scope of understanding of this concept, which entails going beyond the prescriptive, legalistic and economic vision, so as to take into consideration a number of social, political and cultural phenomena, which all combine their effects to act as catalysts of change that intervene in the African urban context. A description of these phenomena alone cannot explain the dynamics under way. Their consequences for the people and especially the population's reaction to their impact constitute an essential aspect, not yet sufficiently analysed, which should be taken into account by anyone who wishes to account for the process of change in African urban development.

Evidently, these changes refer to the notion of confluence between state regulation and control, and social dynamics, be they political, economic, real estate or any other. What we refer to as informality emerges from the tension between the two poles in their coexistence and concomitance. Understood as such, the notion is consubstantial with the urbanization process and is the catalyst for urban development. It is at the dawn of the evolution of this dual nature and the combined meaning of both areas of urban development in their inter-relationship that changes in urban development are envisaged here.

Informality is a category, recorded in the political, economic and social history of Africa. Its origins and characteristics can be traced from pre-colonial African cities, their perpetuation and consolidation in the colonial period as well as their development and explosion after the colonial period, especially from the residential, social and professional perspectives (Coquery-Vidrovitch 1991: 171–96). From this historical perspective, urban development processes can be analysed politically, that is, in the forms of socio-cultural organization. So, the informal nature of urban development is an age-old issue and is expressed by the tension of the phenomena arising from what a state organ controls and what is beyond its control.

Therefore, the concept of informality covers a much wider reality, for it falls both within the social framework and even within the scope of nation building, and changes in the structure and nature of authority (Gallissot 1991: 21). As such, this concept is a permanent instrument for observing changes in urban development. It takes into account the complex nature of the process of evolution within a given space, a series of interactions not only between the stakeholders, the nature and objective of their actions, but equally between the stakes and strategies the stakeholders map out for the development of a type of urban area, which is planned by the formal and informal sectors. This concept also presupposes the analysis of the various aspects of this space at much higher levels, which may influence it in one way or the other. When all is said and done, the informal sector plays an important political role. It is a power relationship which, depending on the actors and structures, is given media coverage by focusing on specific domains and resources, offered to the people through individual or collective possibilities to give meaning to their lives. This document sets out to study these interactions and informalities. It is through these aspects that urban development takes place in all its different forms. The problem here lies in analysing the methods of (re)shaping spaces, social relationships and networks of relationships, which in the final analysis regulate the political and economic processes as well as land appropriation and utilization. It presupposes the consideration of a diversity and variety of initiatives and actions taken within the migratory flows that impact upon and shape urban development. Social and institutional organs and corporations of complementary or conflicting interests constitute the basis of these flows, depending on constructions, which are sometimes planned, organized and well thought out, but which are also often haphazard or fortuitous.

This study focuses on the observation of the changes in urban development from the spatial and economic dimensions in their relationship with politics. This perspective is perfectly illustrated by the Thiaroye-sur-mer council and the Santhiaba neighbourhood, where urban development is being undertaken in conjunction with space construction, which shows how a situation of informality is linked to the process of urbanization, and to the power relationship between the various decision-making bodies and the various forms of legitimacy.

Space and development: real estate and power stakes

In an article in the journal *Courrier-Afrique-Caraïbes-Pacifique-Union Européenne*, devoted to 'urban development', Catherine Coquery-Vidrovitch (1995: 50) defines urbanization in the following terms: 'Urbanization is, first of all, a process that has to do with space [...] However, it is also a social process that generates contradictions [...] It is not only a pole of attraction, but also a pole for spreading ideas; it is, therefore, a place for blending memories.' Looking at urbanization from the spatial and social perspective enables us to grasp real estate and political dynamics, which have to do with city construction and changes that are taking place.

Santhiaba is a neighbourhood in the Thiaroye-sur-mer District Council, which is part of Pikine. Pikine, which emerged in 1952 as the great expansion zone of Dakar,[2] the capital of Senegal, was transformed into an autonomous town from September 1996, and today comprises sixteen district councils. Although it is still strongly linked to the entire Dakar agglomeration, it is also characterized by specific problems and dynamics. The city's high population growth rate, overpopulation in the neighbourhoods, a high unemployment rate, peculiar environmental problems (coastal pollution, periodic flooding in some areas, an inadequate drainage system), increased insecurity and violence, and also the multiplicity of people's reactions to the management of public services, jobs, environment, etc., constitute a priority observatory for the phenomenon of current urban changes.[3]

The surface area of the Thiaroye-sur-mer District Council is estimated by council authorities to be made up of some three square kilometres. It is a small area hemmed in by the sea and the national road number one, linking the capital of Senegal to the rest of the country. It shares boundaries in the north with Tivaouane Diacksao and Guinaw Rail District Councils, in the east with Diamaguene-SICAP Mbao District Council, in the west with Daliford, and in the south with the Atlantic coast.

Initially, this council was a traditional village inhabited by the Lebou fishermen and farmers,[4] who occupied the periphery of Dakar situated on the south coast of the Cape Verde peninsula. Like the other villages of the same category, Thiaroye-sur-mer was gradually integrated into the urbanization process.

This land, which is already quite limited, symbolizes the expansion of the Cape Verde urban area in general, and Pikine city in particular. It is a good example of the human concentration process on the peripheries of Pikine city. As a result of natural growth and the gradual exodus of the population from rural areas or other neighbourhoods of Dakar and Pikine, habitable land became increasingly limited in a zone whose average density in 1988 was 14,538 persons per square kilometre. This gives an exact idea of the enormous population pressures on the land. According to statistics from the 1988 population census, Thiaroye-sur-mer had 30,290 inhabitants distributed in 1,934 homes[5] and 3,181 families. Division according to gender showed that there were 15,194 males and 15,096 females. A forecast undertaken in November 1998, based on the above-mentioned census, resulted in a total of 40,700 inhabitants. This population growth led to a rapid expansion of built-up land, which took over land meant for market gardening. This led to an exacerbation of problems linked to the issue of access, the mastery of the land, real estate and informal practices, which constitute the basis of more general problems.

In this council area, the creation of space is at the centre of the processes of urban change. The gradual occupation of land results in a neighbourhood characterized by several utilizations of land, which presents a picture with characteristics of complementary and antagonistic interactions between the various stakeholders. The modalities and logic of the picture, notably the strategies for the accumulation of land and real estate business revenue, the stakes of controlling an area, shed light on the types of informality that form the basis and, in some way, govern the management of real estate property.

From its initial village and rural configuration, Thiaroye-sur-mer increasingly took on popular urban features. The initial nucleus of homes located on a sandy stretch of maritime coast still maintains the characteristics of a village although, today, it is built totally of concrete. In this initial nucleus, however, the built-up area still has a high density, without habitable land, with narrow and winding lanes, housing constructed according to the type of homes in which families live in close proximity to each other: the area moved from a situation whereby a home was made up of a single family to one comprising ten families, some of which are cohabiting in the same precinct despite their lack of kinship. It is in this way that the incorporation of Thiaroye-sur-mer in the urbanization process changed the manner of occupation of the inhabitable area, and upset family and social structures.

As the years went by, however, the population density of the settlement area grew at an increasingly significant rate. This necessitated the acceleration of the plan for the extension of space in the north, in the Santhiaba neighbourhood, where there is still some space left. Actually, the space extension process started after the colonial period, because of the need for homes, industries and social and administrative services.

Space extension The first encroachment of homes built on farm land dates back to 1939, following the need for residential land. Since this date, the expansion has continued at regular intervals, in 1953, 1955 and subsequent years, with the parcelling out of land in order to, on the one hand, enable family members to settle in cramped conditions in homes or, on the other, to sell these homes to third parties referred to as 'foreigners'. However, it was actually from the 1980s onwards that the expanded area of Thiaroye-sur-mer started playing host to inhabitants from areas outside Thiaroye-sur-mer. It was at that time that an ever-growing number of areas, not often suitable for habitation, were reclaimed through the filling of depressions, on dried swamps and on farm land. This creation of space that results in urbanization is a genuine form of real estate and property informality in Thiaroye-sur-mer.

In addition to land for settlement, sites were ceded for the setting up of industry. These transfers were brought about through sales or tacit contracts, giving priority to the employment of Thiaroye-sur-mer inhabitants. Consequently, that is how the land, on which a shoe factory (Sofac) was constructed, was sold to Lebanese businessmen, in addition to the industrial units for textiles (Icotaf and Sotiba), the storage and processing of fishery products (Cape Verde), which later on became Cotonnière, and match production (Cafal) in which a good number of persons – who today are retired – worked. The setting up of industries constituted an occasion for intense negotiations. Thiaroye-sur-mer inhabitants asked to be given priority in the recruitment of human labour. They were granted this in most cases. In these industrial units, Thiaroye-sur-mer men, who abandoned market gardening as soon as the space for it dwindled away, largely provided the labour. Just like the mushrooming of undeveloped sites in the area, salaried work, therefore, constitutes a mechanism of urban integration of a community, which adopts a rhythm of life necessitated by the type of organization of modern business enterprise characterized by fixed hours and pay vouchers at the end of the month.

Space production also has to do with relations with the state, which installed, from the colonial era, equipment and social services on traditional family land. The gradual acquisition of equipment and social services in Thiaroye-sur-mer, installed essentially in Santhiaba but serving the entire district council area, is also a factor in bringing about the integration of this area into an irreversible process of urbanization.

The national road, the main and only terrestrial road entering and leaving the Cape Verde peninsula, reached Thiaroye-sur-mer in 1924. The road strengthened the link with the rest of the town. The first school was opened in 1927 near fields belonging to the Mbayene family. The first dispensary in Thiaroye-sur-mer was established in the premises of this school. It was later transferred, after opposittion, to the land of one of the families: the Diobenes. The electricity network and public water taps reached houses in the area in 1953/54.

This effort to provide the area with the social services that characterize urbanization did not come free of conflicts with the colonial administration, which relied on traditional authorities to reduce the social problems and to facilitate negotiations between the authorities and traditional landlords. During the colonial period, there were, however, violent conflicts relating to land ownership coupled with political rivalry, which fanned the hatred between some families.[6]

Generally speaking, however, when it had to do with providing some amenities for the Thiaroye-sur-mer inhabitants, opposition to traditional landlords was resolved by the authorities and politicians, who had some influence on the inhabitants. This process of dialogue and negotiation with traditional landlords stemmed from the tacit acknowledgement by the colonial authorities of the rights of the Lebou people over the land in the Cape Verde peninsula.[7] This tradition was maintained after independence. Hence, for instance, the 350 hectares of land ceded to the state at the beginning of the 1970s by the Lebou traditional rulers for the expansion of Dakar city.[8] In return, the state was committed to setting up infrastructure for the opening up and rehabilitation of the area granted to it (Gaye 2002: 2). There were still landlords at this time who had reserved land, but the need for settlement land and basic social services continued to grow as the population increased.

Threats of population pressures on the area following massive rural exodus towards Pikine city, owing to the severe drought of the 1970s, created a double movement for the appropriation of land. The government was pursuing its efforts to provide equipment while traditional landowners were selling and/or constructing on farm land.

A health post was set up in 1995 with funds from the World Bank. A maternity centre was set up in 1989, but it started functioning only four years later, due to the absence of staff and health equipment. In addition to health infrastructure, Santhiaba had structures for public, private and professional education during this period: two government primary schools, a French and Arabic school, a private school and a centre for vocational and technical education for girls. A youth and cultural centre was built on land belonging to the Demene family in 1981. We can equally talk of the existence of a big mosque, a Muslim cemetery and some developed public areas in Santhiaba,[9] although the areas were not maintained and consequently fell into serious disrepair.

The development of urban market gardening in built-up areas This zone is also a piece of land where urban market gardening developed and played an important economic role, although it is made up of a few hectares today. It supplied vegetables to most of the inhabitants of Thiaroye-sur-mer and neighbouring councils. It enabled whole families to live. Describing the limits of Guinaw Rail, an 'irregular' neighbourhood in Pikine to the north of Santhiaba neighbourhood, which is separated by the national road, Roger Navarro (1991: 216) wrote:

> On the southern coast of the Cape Verde isthmus, Genaw-Rails [*sic*] (behind the railway line in Wolof language) is opposite Thiaroye-Guej village (Thiaroye-sur-mer). At this height, right from the Rufisque road (the national road), we can easily see the southern border of the neighbourhood. This sector has a double space. First of all, it is that of market gardening called the Niayes of Cape Verde. The Lebou people of Thiaroye-sur-mer, a tribe of fishermen and traditional landlords of Cape Verde, cultivated these gardens, which had small palm groves. The area, which is nearer this farming zone, looks like a vast construction field. Several

houses are being constructed (in permanent structures). Builders are busy here and there; heaps of 'bricks' (meaning: sun-baked rubble sand mixed with cement) clearly signify ownership of parcels of land to anybody who wants to see their owners' projects.

With built-up land generating more revenue than agriculture, market gardeners gradually lost their principal source of income and their means of subsistence because of the construction of houses on the area reserved for it. In about ten years, the area left for market gardening was reduced by half. With the pace of current progress in construction, urban market gardening will disappear from this zone in the years to come. In the face of this danger, market gardeners have, as a collective start, formed an Economic Interest Group (GIE)[10] to preserve their activity, and mutually to strengthen themselves against the advancement of construction.

The rate at which this space is occupied shows the enormous land stakes and a hidden struggle between traditional landowners, council authorities, state workers, market gardeners, real estate promoters, etc., in the entire area of the depression called the Niayes. All these stakeholders map out, on this space, strategies for the ownership or conservation of property on this land, strategies that stem, according to the stakeholders, from legal or informal procedures or from a combination of the two. Mamadou Diouf (1998: 19–20) aptly summarized this situation when he wrote:

> In most cases, urban morphology seems to be produced by an architecture, whose dynamic factor is the identity and ethnic re-composition aimed at owning land. These re-compositions often lead to the use of several approaches, which result in the demand for various types of land. This superimposition of highly heterogeneous systems and forms of ownership has consequences not only on the urban morphology, but also on social relations and solidarity networks.

The superimposition of rights (law number 64/46 of 17 June 1964 on national state land[11] and customary real estate rights of first occupants) and the aims of the authorities, in general, and the council authorities, in particular, on land, pushed traditional landowners to build there and/or to sell plots to persons from other zones of the Dakar built-up areas, who were in search of affordable rented or real estate property. Thiaroye-sur-mer, which is 12 kilometres from downtown Dakar, is part of these nearest peripheral zones, where, according to Navarro (1991: 216), 'construction is increasing gradually everyday on farmland. This situation of very rapid urbanization is typical of the entire irregular zone of Pikine. Elsewhere, in other irregular neighbourhoods, "building" land is already saturated.'

Thus, in the extension zone, situated in the Santhiaba neighbourhood, construction of houses for rents generates revenue for traditional land-owners and the increasing number of 'foreign' new landlords. Here, we are in a situation that is quite new. The land issue is coupled with a formidable construction economy.[12] The traditional landowners, the landlords, who used to distribute land for agricultural activities, activities on which families depended, transformed themselves into land promoters by selling portions of land in order to have money (Coquery 1991: 197–213). We are far from the 1950s, when traditional authorities used to offer gifts of land taken by the authority from family real estate property in Thiaroye-sur-mer.

This situation triggered off a latent and, occasionally, open conflict between traditional landowners and council authorities. Beyond the access to land resources and control over land, it had to do with a confronta-tion between two types of legitimacy and legality. The ambition of the council is financially to develop part of this land (servicing) with a view to selling the plots for a substantial amount and to carrying out a social and educational project on another part: a government high school, and a complex municipal stadium. Traditional landowners, market gardeners and new foreign residents in this zone rather saw this project as a loss of their land and property rights. Numerous meetings with the various stakeholders came to a sudden end. The stiff resistance put up by the Thiaroye-sur-mer inhabitants forced the council to look for a different site for the construction of its government high school.

Traditional landowners and traditional authorities, who are often the same persons, adopted various strategies, depending on the circumstances. There was even a general mobilization all over Thiaroye-sur-mer for the maintenance of traditional rights over land situated in the Niayes zone of Pikine, outside the council area, through means such as signing a petition and requesting the services of a lawyer (from the Lebou tribe). The most common strategy, however, was that of a *fait accompli*: the construction of a building on the land. Construction sites are increasing steadily. Some of these sites, which began several years ago, are yet to be completed. What has made a good number of houses in this zone unfit for living is the fact that there are recurrent floods during every rainy season and ground water, which is almost flowing on the surface of the land. Houses are flooded by stagnant water every year. Beyond using these houses as dwelling places, what traditional landowners want is a strategy to mark their land: in addi-tion to a land title, a building permit is the surest way of owning a piece of land here. Despite these guarantees, have houses illegally constructed on urban land in Cape Verde been preserved from the recent demolition operations carried out by administrative authorities?

Space development and the phenomenon of urban expansion are, from all indications, a normal situation in the evolution of a city. A clear approach to spatial geography, that is, the material configuration of land, is, today, less productive and veils the complexity of the phenomenon of urbanization. In fact, an analysis of this complexity presupposes the putting into perspective of the threefold classification that includes perceived space, conceived space and experienced space (Oatley 2001: 19); in a nutshell, going beyond materialism by adding to it the various cultural, religious and political imaginations, which are everybody's concern.[13] This perspective enables light to be shed on the stakeholders and on the competition in urban areas, where conflicting interests constitute a factor of enormous potential. However, it also fundamentally illustrates the relationship of force between legal procedures and informal procedures, which draw their legitimacy from historical and cultural references that still have a strong response in the context of African cities, though, from the socio-cultural and economic point of view, they have undergone great changes. The situation in Thiaroye-sur-mer is, in several ways, similar to that of the two district councils of north and south Yeumbeul. In this zone, de Sorbier (2002: 17) says:

> most of the residential areas are linked to a maze of small and entangled
> streets. Part of the urbanized council area was supposed to be unfit for
> construction (floodable areas, constantly flooded areas, swampy areas
> and slippery soil, because they are situated on old dunes near the coast).
> Three-quarters of the houses in the area are constructed without land titles.
> According to customary law, the council area belongs to the traditional
> area of the Lebou council. Consequently, with regard to the Senegalese law,
> transactions were tacitly carried out, and the Lebou people took advantage
> of the occasion to speculate on this great territory (between 16 and 20 km²).

Beyond the access to and control over land, what is at stake here is the confrontation between two different political philosophies, that is, two types of representation and claims on legitimate authority. This fundamental aspect in the life of relations in Thiaroye-sur-mer is noticed more in the exercise of local authority.

Local authority: duality of territorial legitimacies

The heritage of the old traditional village is expressed in Thiaroye-sur-mer by the survival of forms of organization and traditional decision-making specific to the Lebou group. They are characterized by a socio-political organization of the gerontocratic type: close social, parental and family ties, that are quite solid; and community identity that is strongly felt and lived.

This structuring of the social and political organization is the basis of a very long-lived imaginary policy, which cohabits with the council authority.

Although completely integrated in the city of Pikine and having lost almost all the characteristics of rural nature, the inhabitants of Thiaroye-sur-mer continue to consider and to call their locality a village. This attitude concerns what Achille Mbembe (2000a: 15) calls 'the re-enchantment of tradition', i.e. the invention of a collective imagination, constructed from referents based on a community speech from two angles: 'the rehabilitation of origins and of belonging' and the claim-appropriation of a territory, on which the construction of an identity is based and legitimized. This phenomenon of reinventing tradition is reflected in Thiaroye-sur-mer by the establishment of a local political authority and by an 'administrative' networking of the territory.

Indeed, Thiaroye-sur-mer has a council of notables chaired by the village head. Each of its members has a council membership card. This authority was set up in 1991, following the example of Lebou de Yoff, a twenty-four-member executive body known as the Association of Freys in replacement of another structure called 'Até Togne' (judicial body). In each of the twenty neighbourhoods of the council area, five representatives were appointed, including a head of the neighbourhood. The Association of Imams and two dignitaries, the President of Diambour, a sort of local assembly, and the representative of general Khalife of Mourides, support the council of notables.

The role of the council of notables is to manage 'all the customary and religious problems of the village in close collaboration with the district council'.[14] The administrative units of the council are the bodies that execute all its decisions. It takes decisions on the regulation of family ceremonies, the prohibition of the tam-tam or playing of music during winter, the security of the neighbourhoods, the enforcement of decisions concerning city planning and drainage systems, etc. The council is empowered to bring matters before the 'competent authorities' in the event of non-compliance with its decisions.

In reality, the traditional authorities of Thiaroye-sur-mer regulate the entire social life of its inhabitants. The remarks of the president of Freys amply illustrate this fact, when he says 'all that enters Thiaroye-sur-mer passes through Freys, as well as all that leaves it'. It is impossible to circumvent the traditional authorities in all decisions, initiatives and actions. Such a situation is attested by this written request addressed to the Thiaroye-sur-mer village head by the Cultural and Sports Associations (ASC) for the placement at their disposal of space where the village head would construct a football field.

The consideration of the village concept as concrete reality is an eminently political category. It subsumes a space and its human and material components under the iron rule of a legitimate authority. The custodians of this authority 'naturally' assume the management of the destinies of the community. Thus, a territorial identity, which legitimizes a local specificity, is built on an urban space, even though its configuration shows a strong presence of 'non-native population' and a very visible cosmopolitanism – a situation that leads to practices and/or exclusivist attitudes with obvious political and cultural bases.

Traditional and religious authorities, the heritage of a political organization of the village type, though no longer what they used to be, nevertheless continue to have a great impact on the decision-making machinery. The traditional political stakeholders have managed to maintain their primary role by continuously equipping themselves with well-structured decision-making authorities and with quite effective information flow and communication channels. This situation is made possible by the maintenance of a symbolic system of the origins and membership, and by an identity construction, made concrete territorial control. But it should be noted that such authority simultaneously adopts a vocabulary of modernity and positions itself theoretically as a support structure to the municipal and administrative authorities. The council of notables meets, indeed, in a 'General Assembly'; keeps 'minutes of its meetings'; establishes an 'association'; and provides its members with 'cards'. The Association of Freys, the executive body of the council of notables, organizes meetings by sending individual convening notices of meetings in which the agenda is specified. The deliberations take place in the 'public square, at the village head's residence'. Topics discussed may relate to land matters, for example the meeting at which issues such as the Pikine land, the football field, among other issues, were expected to be discussed.

From another perspective, it declares its collaboration with the municipality and acts as the people's police on behalf of the 'competent authorities'. This is where the ambiguity of its position and that of the local administration *vis-à-vis* the latter actually lies. For instance, the decision to place a ban on public events in winter is taken by the council of notables, but it is the administrative authority, the senior divisional officer, who signs the prohibition order. This example shows not only the control that traditional authorities have over the people, but also their ability to influence decisions taken by the local administrative authorities. Control over the territory is real.[15] This is the case with the current urban process in the cities of Tiraouane and Gueoul (Sow n.d.: 3), where the Thiaroye-sur-mer municipality demonstrates the will of traditional authorities to influence decisions on local governance. In this connection, the spatial development constitutes a political tool, based on the mobilization of symbolic resources such as history, which legitimizes and concretizes the development of land.

Although a country with a long tradition in decentralization, Senegal introduced a major reform in 1996 on regionalization. This new reform set up, *inter alia*, the district council. The smallest administrative unit was thus transformed into a local authority with its own financial, human and technical resources. By transferring part of its prerogatives to this local authority, the central state authority is trying to strengthen its capacity to intervene, especially with regard to the satisfaction of local needs in terms of public service delivery and efficient and optimum regulation of the area. Therefore, the municipal council and its various structures also exercise control over the area. Its legitimacy derives from the transfer of authority at the central level (the state), and the local level (local authorities). Its political base is an area within which the agents of this authority – who are elected – exercise public authority. The Thiaroye-sur-mer District Council is an outcome of the reform of the law on the 1996 decentralization. Its municipal council comprises thirty-six members from three different political parties: AND Jef PADS (two members), PS (six members) and PDS (twenty-eight members). There are six women in the municipal council. The mayor and his two assistants make up the executive staff. In addition to the council secretariat work, the municipal secretariat manages four other services (halls and markets; general administration and finance; landed property and civil status; and youth, sports and leisure). The district council set up ten technical commissions including finance; culture; youth, sports and leisure; halls and markets; planning; environment and fisheries resources; administrative and legal affairs; education; health; population, social action, regional development, and housing.

The adoption of this method of organization aims at good administrative and operational management of the council area. By streamlining the areas of competence of the municipality into so many sectors of activity, the district council seeks to provide itself with the organizational means necessary for the effectiveness and efficiency of its local development mission. However, it is still necessary for financial resources and powers to be commensurate with these ambitions.

The mayor proposes the council budget, voted by the municipal council and approved by the sub-divisional officer, who represents the state. In 1997, the district council budget was estimated at FCFA59,100,000 but only FCFA16,166,511 was effectively collected, representing 15.73 per cent of the projection, which stood at FCFA63,145,538, although the sub-divisional officer approved it at FCFA57,531,289. Yet only FCFA27 million was collected by 31 December 1998. The experience of the district councils is new. For this reason, the new council team lacks adequate experience and its human, material and financial resources are very limited, compared with its local development prerogatives as well as the diversity and complexity of problems to be solved.

The institution of district councils, therefore, creates a new centre of power opposed to the one established by traditional and religious authorities. A clash is thus observed in two land management approaches which, nevertheless, consult each other, assist each other with regard to certain aspects of local management, and disagree on some other issues. What is more, political divergences and competition between political parties affect the relations between local decision-making bodies. However, areas and channels of dialogue exist and are being developed. The last local elections of May 2002 allowed for the change of mayors and municipal councillors. The outgoing mayor of the Thiaroye-sur-mer District Council was elected mayor of Pikine city. His outgoing first assistant was, on his part, elected mayor of Thiaroye-sur-mer. The first action of the two mayors, after their installation in their respective duties, was to meet with the customary and religious authorities of Thiaroye-sur-mer.[16] Both mayors, who are sons of the soil, came to see the customary and religious authorities to ask for their prayers and blessings for the successful exercise of their new duties.

The mayor of the Thiaroye-sur-mer Council 'also called for the involvement of traditional authorities in municipal management for a concerted council development'.[17] In the course of their discussions, the traditional authorities disclosed, to the mayors and the rest of the participants, their will to tackle the issue of the allocation of land for the construction of the district council head office and a football field. Furthermore, they suggested that the mayors should collaborate with all the political parties represented in Thiaroye-sur-mer with a view to working for a concerted council development. There are power stakes that derive from this political duality. These stakes are expressed through the social, economic, political and cultural life of Thiaroye-sur-mer. As a matter of fact, the various coexisting authorities can each exercise a certain legitimacy, which derives from completely different directions. These sources of legitimacy are the basis of the recognition and support of the people for whom and on whose behalf decisions are taken and with whom the activities are carried out.

The various authorities inevitably fall within the logic of tolerance, complementary action, exploitation and mutual competition. Consequently, out of their dynamism, they consciously or unconsciously impact upon the construction of the living environment, given that the basic stake here is effective presence in public areas in which the game of the stakeholders appears to break new grounds for urban government and estabilish new horizons for the exercise of authority (Appadurai 2001: 23–43). It has to do with nothing other than the jerky process of the redefinition of frameworks for the regulation of the local public space, which was well described by Kombe and Kreibich (2000: 232) when they wrote: 'The widening gap between the need for governance and available administrative services cannot be bridged in the foreseeable future by continuing the conventional practice of highly centralized, top-down urban management with unrealistic legal norms and unachievable standards.' Within this framework of the game of stakeholders, associations and networks play a key role.

Associations and networks: catalysts of urban development

Decentralization demonstrates the failure of the centralized and Jacobinic state model. Lat Soucabe Mbow (1992: 205) sums up this failure in these terms:

> Practices of the past three decades have led to a break in the relations between the state and the city, owing to the political and economic changes that took place beginning 1981. After dominating the urban sphere thanks to a suffocating legal arsenal and massive use of capital in development programmes conceived and carried out through its instruments of action, the central government is faced with the challenges of the field. While doing this, it gives back to local authorities and the people their own share of responsibility in urban management in order to better guarantee its duty of guiding, coordinating and supervising.

As a matter of fact, state disengagement imposed by international finance institutions and bilateral donors laid the public space open to a formidable development of associations, which are increasingly becoming professional in local development actions. This demonstrates the great capacity for change in form and adaptation to the social and institutional constraints and requirements of their environment, which is also undergoing constant change (Niang 2000: 99–159). The activities of these associations provide for the individual and collective needs of their members. They also increasingly provide for the municipality in its functions dealing with the management of the living environment and the delivery of social services. On the basis of legitimacy, which they have gained through their ability to mobilize, 'they put up resistance and impose dialogue on establishments and authorities, for the occupation of space' (Diouf 1998: 23).

These developments reveal a process of empowerment through economic initiatives, on the one hand, and the methods of regulating public space, on the other. Such empowerment is illustrated by the phenomenal development of self-organization and investment practices on public space carried out by people who negotiate and work with the authorities. By doing this, the people construct a 'new universe and new arenas of authority'. They forge new forms of solidarity and a citizenship through which they readapt, in their own way, to their land (Wade et al. 2002: 26). This citizens' commitment is quite often expressed through the support of NGOs, which are spurred on by the conduct and follow-up of social projects, the organization of forums, open information days, the creation of frameworks for dialogue, the drawing up of local development master plans, etc. This liberation of popular initiatives was still more evident in the economic domain, especially from the 1980s onwards.

Indeed, neo-liberal reforms greatly characterized African economies and did not (far from it) check the economic crisis. The main consequence of this persistent crisis was the fact that methods and mechanisms for generating revenue were gradually made more informal. This is an urban phenomenon that has become generalized and is undergoing constant change. For this reason, it is the expression of a more and more obvious type of restructuring of economic activity in African urban areas.

Thiaroye-sur-mer is an area where informal economic activities abound. These include activities relating to fisheries products (traditional fishing for men, processing and marketing of fish for women), urban market gardening, trading, handicrafts, woodwork, motor mechanics, private telephone service (telecentres), trading in vehicles and hardware, garages for the parking of heavy trucks and embryonic industrialization with small-scale manufacture of slabs etc. A series of local activities located in all parts of the council adds to this other set of activities. The local activities include so-called public but paid water points, several Moorish shops and small-scale trading for local sales and retail etc.

Through the various activities of this economy, most of the youths, men and, above all, women in Thiaroye-sur-mer actively contribute not only to the survival of households but also to the social development of the district council. Women in this council are particularly dynamic: they run the water points, market gardening produce; invest in the catering sector; and, of course, there are more women than men who register and make savings (*tontines*, savings and loan institutions). However, above all, they also process and sell local products in various settings and organizations. These settings have become genuine structuring elements of urban life, particularly on the basis of their size, and economic, social and even economic weight. As the authors of the synthesis of French Cooperation on Urbanization in Africa (ISTED 1995: 78) wrote:

The informal economy was not only a way of producing and marketing, which could absorb a few elements of modernity to the traditional structures. It was also, and above all, the key factor of a way of efficient socio-political regulation, largely determining urban forms and ways of intervening in the latter.

These activities allow for a wide circulation of money through non-commercial systems of relationship such as *tontines* and family ceremonies. Through these networks, cash, which is invested in social activities, constitutes the basic element. Indeed, it is in this social domain, which is essentially feminine, that the sense of belonging, duty, solidarity, compassion, empathy and obligation is cultivated. This relationship strengthens the dynamics of the establishment of the community, family, lineage, neighbourhood, brotherhood, etc. The success and survival of women and their families depend mostly on these solidarity networks.

Among the various forms of income-generating sources, GIE (Economic Interest Groups) and larger groupings such as unions or networks are increasingly adopted. This phenomenon has undergone significant development since the mid-1980s. This is a perfect example of an informal sector, because this phenomenon has witnessed a significant growth such that its function and role are important in the social development of the territory and the construction of African urban life.

So, the new organization into large groupings of networks is a powerful instrument of capital accumulation from informal activities. Indeed, neighbourhood *tontines* are gradually being transformed into savings and loan co-operatives, thus shifting towards a situation where the funds accumulated are spent not only on provisions, social amenities and for prestige (family and religious ceremonies, as well as feasts), but equally on productive investments. This emerging phenomenon, however, is accompanied by the evolution of individual riches through the broadening of the scope of intervention or the nature of the activity. In fact, we are witnessing the birth of a new entrepreneurship, where women occupy important positions (Sarr 1998: 218).

In the Thiaroye-sur-mer Council area, groups such as 'Pencum Senegal' and 'Pencum Demba' are involved in the purchase, processing and marketing of fishery products, which they sell in Senegal and other African countries. 'Pencum Demba' is made up of five GIE groups and has a membership of 290 men and women. For its part, the 'Lebou Gui' network is creating a good impression. This network is made up of sixteen women's groups with a membership of 416. These groups are involved in various processing and marketing activities of sea and local products (fruit juice etc.), sewing, embroidery, and suchlike. According to its leader, the network's turnover stands at FCFA10 million per half-year.

The various groups working in the domain of fishery product processing in Thiaroye-sur-mer are grouped under the GIE fishing local union of Thiaroye-sur-mer, which is a forum for discussions and the control of processing and marketing activities of fishery products. It is affiliated to the national organizing structure of this sector. This structure plays a very significant political role, and particular attention is paid to it in the mapping out of strategies for political parties and local political stakeholders.

As can be observed, economic associations, groupings, networks and unions in Thiaroye-sur-mer are structures established locally, but which, at the same time, are open to the rest of the country. Their source of supply includes various wholesale fish merchants, who are also middlemen between the local fishermen and businesspersons in the exportation network. Their customers include traders from various markets in the capital, the regions and even from some countries in the West African sub-region.

The internal (locally based) and external (distributing their products out of Thiaroye-sur-mer) strategy of income-generating activities of this new crop of business people addresses the requirements imposed by the economic changes that have taken place in the past decade. These changes include weak state regulation due to the free market economy, unemployment and unchecked competition. Setting up groupings and pooling resources are means of getting access to information about markets and opportunities for knowledge and expertise, without any accompanying obligation to share this information with other members of the group. This way, operators multiply and increase their business opportunities. This network is also a forum for tough and keen competition, a forum for the race for economic resources.

These unstable groupings and regroupings of social relationship are responsible for developing the town and organizing the urban area according to the same family, relationship, religious, political, economic and professional parameters.

Indeed, the economic network is multi-functional. The logic for setting it up is based on two factors: while other segments are converging towards the work, others are breaking away from it. The image presented is that of a fishing net, the mesh of which is knitted by the close relationship in residence, friendship, profession, politics, etc. According to relationships of interest, some ties are consolidated, while others are either strained or drift apart. Consequently, the network is an occasion for crystallizing heterogeneous urban identities through the setting up of interest groups and diversifying the nature of their use (social, economic, political). There-fore, the existence of these structures is revealing concerning the impressive psycho-sociological capital resources of the stakeholders and animators in the urban sector (de Certeau : 1990). Businesspeople are getting into vari-ous relationships – family, religious, political, etc. – and are operating in groups, whose conditions for setting them up have greatly changed because the mobilization and/or access opportunities to economic, financial and other resources are very haphazardly used.

The example of Pencum Senegal is a good illustration of how the net-work functions. It was set up by combining two women's GIEs involved in the purchase, processing and marketing of fishery products. Initiated by an individual in 1962, Pencum Senegal became a GIE in 1990 and was structured according to the form agreed upon by two GIEs: Bok Jom and Feek Beeg Jamm. The Pencum Senegal Entente has a membership of 117 women. These women have employed fifty-six other women and forty-three men. Their annual turnover is about FCFA220 million, if we are to go by the official statistics from the fishery service department. These women have customers in Senegal, in some other African countries and in the United States. The importance of this combined structure was immediately felt as well as the need for its continuous development. Furthermore, it en-tered into a partnership and exchanged information with other structures, both at the national and international levels. For this reason, its members have been able to receive training in the domains of the smoking, salting and drying of fish; increase the financial value of the by-products of raw materials (swim bladders, fins); conserve manufactured products, and im-prove hygiene as well as quality. Moreover, Pencum Senegal manufacturers received literacy courses and initiation in management. Their members developed a skill, so that today, they are considered the foremost experts in their domain of activity.[18] Their fame enabled them to participate in the Dakar international trade fair and in many other national forums. Pencum Senegal has also obtained financial assistance to organize exchange visits and studies in some countries in the sub-region such as Gambia and Ghana and to attend a meeting organized by an NGO in Paris.

The Pencum Senegal Entente is a typical example of an informal activity geared towards greater professionalization and expansion of its scope of activity, notably through a locally based strategy with a global connection. The importance of this processing and marketing unit was such that its leader was compelled to accept a political post. She was convinced by the people to accept a replacement in the Thiaroye-sur-mer municipal council. Her members worked hard to influence the public authorities in order to obtain an unloading quay for the fishermen's catch close to the site of their organization, which, similarly, obtained significant financial assistance for its rehabilitation.

The analysis of the informal economy in an underprivileged urban area, as described above, illustrates the great adaptation capacity of the stakeholders of this type of economy in an urban setting, which is constantly disintegrating and being rebuilt. The ease and fluidity of this economy can be explained by the close connection of the informal economy to the process of social and political dynamics, notably by making use of alliances. This economy is closely interwoven with the social and political environments within which its operators set up associations and networks, which are based on various relationships (family, religious, political allies, etc.), and operate in groups whose conditions for setting them up have greatly changed because the said conditions are made very haphazardly, according to opportunities for the mobilization of and/or access to economic, financial or political resources.

Conclusion

Finally, informality is an inclusively spatial, political, professional and economic category that acts in a given political situation. It has a profound historical dimension. It is a way of interaction between two methods, a mode of organization and policy management, of space occupation and of economic activity. Based on their similarities, differences and strategies in controlling the two levels, specificities are established in the African urban context. Their relationships constitute the base of urban development and the spur for change.

The methods of informal control in the Thiaroye-sur-mer urban space constitute a basis and driving force behind the ongoing urban changes. They are already part of the urbanization process through, especially, space development strategies. These changes have given rise to the organization of economic activity and have also ensured social redevelopment. In fact, they have encroached on the areas of competence of public authorities and have taken over areas the public authorities failed to regulate. The state control of the use, access, registration and allocation of real estate resources, institution of taxes on real estate and on economic activities is hit by the culture of evasion and refusal to negotiate and to tolerate. The relationship between the various stakeholders is based on posture, attitude and the practice of accommodation.

From the economic standpoint, the Thiaroye-sur-mer GIEs have developed significantly, at the levels of membership and volume of activity, financial accumulation as well as the variety and diversity of their relationship with other partners. Beyond the multiplicity of individual or collective income-generating strategies, informal activity is a mechanism to connect the local to the global world. The setting up of associations and the integration through the increasing networks facilitate the development of economic activities through various sources, although capital accumulation does not always follow capitalist logic. Income and benefits are very often invested in the economic reproduction system, and the alienation of clients and political support. Rather, its objective is social, although individual wealth is created. However, these incomes and benefits are reinvested in reproduction or distribution.

Finally, today, informality is a means of regulating the living relationship and the urban framework in Thiaroye-sur-mer. It provides structure to the ongoing changes. In this capacity, it is, *de facto*, the only method by which Thiaroye-sur-mer is being constructed. As such, informality should be seen as objectivizing the ongoing urban changes in underprivileged urban contexts.

Notes

1 Among the more impressive literature written on the issue, we can cite some publications as an illustration. See Stren et al. (1993); A. Osmont, *The World Bank and Towns, from Development to Adjustment* (Paris: Karthala, 1995); French Ministry of Cooperation, 'Dynamics of African Urban Development South of the Sahara, in the Countries within the Domain of French Cooperation', Document issued in compliance with order No. 900373 of the Ministry of Cooperation, and forwarded to ISTED on 27 March 1995; the 'Urban Mechanisms and Logic' Working Group, specifically for Senegal, a trend reflected in the following works: A. Sane, 'Pikine City Monographic Study' (interim document), Social and Urban Development Program and North–South Cooperation, ARDIS, Dakar, September 1996; S. Wade, 'Association Dynamics in the West African Urban Area, Regional Thesis' (interim document), Dakar, ENDA ECOPOP/PREFAL (Regional Training and Assistance Program to Local and Basic Initiative Associations in the West African Urban Area), 1989; M. C. Diop, *The Fight Against Poverty, Towards Council Policy Definition, and Urban Management Programme*, African Regional Office, 1995.

2 For more details on Dakar, see Roger Navarro's descriptive thesis (1991: 215–37). The author focuses on the various phases of urbanization, in line with the encroachment of the Lebou villages and their cultivation land on Cape Verde's urban territory. Today, Dakar, the capital of Senegal, covers less than 1 per cent of the 196,722km^2 total land surface of the country. Dakar is the highest point in West Africa, which gives it a very strategic position from the geopolitical point of view. At the administrative level, the capital has been divided into four municipalities since September 1996. In order to encourage proximity management, these municipalities are further divided into district councils: nineteen in Dakar, sixteen in Pikine, five in Guediawaye, and three in Rufisque. At the demographic level, according to the 1995 estimates, the population of Senegal stands at 7,884,257; the Dakar urban community, which

is made up of four villages, represents a total of 21 per cent, that is 1,655,514 inhabitants, of which 795,969 are men (48 per cent) and 863,545 are women (52 per cent).

3 Since the 1970s, Pikine has witnessed two population influxes: the first occurred when people were chased out of the thickly populated shanty neighbourhoods in Dakar, while the second, which occurred as a result of rural exodus in the 1970s and 1980s, significantly increased urban population. Today, Pikine city is said to have close to one million inhabitants, who occupy an area of about 80km^2.

4 The Lebous were the first habitants in the Cape Verde peninsula, where they are settled in four villages that make up the 'Lebou Republic'.

5 Homes are settlement units whose main characteristic is to bring together all the family (in the general sense of the word) members, according to a disposition that is centred on the home of the family head. The family head controls all the social and economic life of the family: he distributes roles and duties, authorizes as well as allocates resources.

6 The inhabitants are not very forthcoming about the intricacies of these land conflicts due to political sentiments resulting from the struggle between Senghor and Lamine Gueye for representation in the National Assembly.

7 The colonizer asked for compensation for the displacement of villages situated on the land, which featured on his urbanization plan. This led to the development of what is today the central town (Dakar Plateau). The implementation of the first urbanization plan, referred to as Pinet-Laprade Plan, caused the displacement of the Kaye, Tamn, N'Garaf, Therigne and Hock villages between 1858 and 1914. However, the Lebous did not hesitate to take advantage of their status as citizens, conferred on them by their settlement in council areas with full powers, to preserve their traditional rights on the land.

8 The project known as the 'Land Rehabilitation Operation', which was funded by the World Bank, was carried out within the framework of the programme to construct houses to reduce the population pressure on the town.

9 Santhiaba is one out of twenty neighbourhoods in the Thiaroye-sur-mer council district. It has a population of about 3,000 inhabitants, made up of many ethnic groups with a predominant Wolof/Lebou group (66.46 per cent). Some 50.54 per cent of the population are men, while 49.46 per cent are women. About 99.99 per cent of the population are Muslims, while 27.34 per cent of family heads are women.

10 In effect, GIE groups, which are regulated by law number 85/40 of 29 July 1985, offer a good legal framework for the exercise of economic activities under the form of associations, which, however, is one of the main requirements. This concerns the setting up of a group of two or more legal entities or natural persons with the view to creating opportunities capable of ensuring or developing the economic activity of its members, or even improving or increasing the outcome of this activity.

11 This law, adopted in 1964, stipulates, in substance, that any unregistered land and any land that is not cultivated belongs to the state.

12 For further comparison with other situations, see Canel et al. (1990), Ch. III, 'Appropriation of Urban Land in Conflict', Paris, pp. 27–60.

13 In this light, see Cheik Guèye's well-documented thesis (1999) about the Touba healthy town, in which he describes at length how the land used by 'urban development *marabouts*' can lead to urban development based on symbolic representations and allegiance, including state and religious representatives.

14 Report of the Thiaroye-sur-mer council of notables, 13 September 1998.

15 A great many research works largely illustrate centralizing land control as an instrument of policy influence at the local level. For instance, in Sale, Morocco (a place near Rabat), Abdeleghani Abouhani (n.d.) illustrates this issue in his (French) book entitled: 'Power, Town and Local Notables, When Notables Develop Towns', which is not the case with Thiaroye-sur-mer and Lebou territories in the Cape Verde peninsula, in general. It is not up to Sale to show the confrontation between the local and municipal notables, but rather to show how the notables manage the municipal councils themselves. These notables use their positions to manipulate the law in order to preserve and consolidate, especially, their own landed interests, and also use this opportunity to conquer power.

16 This meeting was held on 3 July 2002 in the residence of the village head. Present at the meeting were the following: the village head and members of his family, the mayor of Pikine city and Thiaroye-sur-mer District Council, as well as municipal councillors, the leaders of Njambour and Frey, notables, imams, and – remarkably enough the first of its kind – officials of basic community associations and women.

17 See the report of the meeting held on 3 July 2002 between the mayors of the Thiaroye-sur-mer District Council and Pikine city, as well as the traditional and religious authorities of Thiaroye-sur-mer.

18 The Pencum Senegal Entente participated in the eighth edition of the competition for the president's award for the promotion of the women. This group won the second prize, which was marked by a certificate, a FCFA1 million cheque, and a mill worth FCFA4 million.

References

Abdoul, M. (2001) 'Les rapports sociaux hommes et femmes à travers les activités économiques féminines et la gestion du cadre de vie', in F. Hainard and C. Verschuur (eds), *Femmes dans les crises urbaines, Relations de genre et environnement précaires*, Paris: Karthala / MOST, pp. 168–201.

Abouhani, A. (n.d.) *Pouvoirs, villes et notabilités locales, quand les notables font la ville*, Paris: URBAMA.

Akindes, F. (1998) 'L'échec des sciences sociales dans l'accompagnement du rapport de l'Afrique à la modernité. Une lecture à partir de l'expérience de l'Afrique subsaharienne', 9th General Assembly of CODESRIA, ' Epistemologies', Dakar, 14–18 December.

Antoine, Ph., Ph. Bocquier, A. S. Fall, Y. M. Guissé and J. Nanitelamio (1995) *Les familles dakaroises face à la crise*, Dakar and Paris: IFAN, ORSTOM, CEPED.

Appadurai, A. (2001) 'Deep Democracy: Urban Governmentality and the Horizon of Politics', *Environment and Urbanisation*, Vol. 13, No. 2, pp. 23–43.

Canel, P., Ph. Delis and Ch. Girard (1990) *Construire la ville africaine, chronique du citadin promoteur*, Paris: Karthala and ACCT.

Certeau, M. de (1990) *L'invention du quotidien, 1. arts de faire*, Paris: Gallimard.

Coquery, M. (1991) 'Secteur informel et production de l'espace urbanisé en Afrique', in C. Coquery-Vidrovitch and S. Nedelec (1991).

Coquery-Vidrivitch, C. (1991) 'L'informel dans les villes africaines: essai d'analyse historique et sociale', in Coquery-Vidrovitch and S. Nedelec (1991).

— (1995) 'Villes d'Afrique noire: les héritages de l'histoire', *Le Courrier*, bimonthly, No. 149, January–February, pp. 50–1.

Coquery-Vidrovitch, C. and S. Nedelec (eds) (1991) *Tiers-mondes: l'informel en question?*, Paris: l'Harmattan.

Diouf, M. (1998) 'La société civile en Afrique: Histoire et actualité, Notes provisoires', Ninth General Assembly of CODESRIA, transcontinental working group, 'Social Actors and Public Space', Dakar, 14–18 December.

Ela, J.-M. (1998) 'Les sciences sociales à l'épreuve de l'Afrique: les enjeux épistémologiques de la mondialisation', Ninth General Assembly of CODESRIA, 'Epistemologies', Dakar, 14–18 December.

Gallissot, R. (1991) 'Société formelle ou organique et société informelle', in C. Coquery-Vidrovitch and S. Nedelec (1991).

Gaye, I. D. (2002) 'Développement local et formation des acteurs. Une articulation par le diagnostic environnemental: Cas de Yoff', International Conference on Decentralization and Local Government, Dakar, Senegal, 25–26 April, University of Cheikh Anta Diop (Ecole Nationale d'Economie Appliquée), University of Toulouse-le Mirail and University of Konakry.

Guèye, Ch. (1999) 'L'organisation de l'espace dans une ville religieuse: Touba (Sénégal)', unpublished doctoral thesis, Louis Pasteur University, Strasburg, geography faculty, two volumes.

ISTED (1995) 'Dynamiques de l'urbanisation de l'Afrique au sud du Sahara: dans les pays du champ de la Coopération française', working group 'Mécanismes et logiques de l'urbanisation', document produced for the Ministry of Cooperation, 27 March 1995.

Kombe, W. J. and V. Kreibich (2000) 'Reconciling Informal and Formal Land Management: An Agenda for Improving Tenure Security and Urban Governance in Poor Countries', *Habitat International*, 24, pp. 231–40.

Maximy, R. de (2000) *Le commun des lieux*, Mardaga: Architecture + Recherches.

Mbembe, A. (2000a) 'À propos des écritures africaines de soi', *Bulletin du CODESRIA*, no. 1, pp. 6–22.

— (2000b) 'Essai sur l'imaginaire politique en temps de guerre', *Bulletin du CODESRIA*, nos 2, 3 and 4, pp. 6–22.

Mbow, L. S. (1992) 'Les politiques urbaines: gestion et aménagement', in M. C. Diop (ed.), *Sénégal, trajectoires d'un Etat*, Dakar: CODESRIA, pp. 205–31.

Navarro, R. (1991) ' "Irrégularité urbaine" et genèse de l'africanité urbaine au Cap Vert (Sénégal)', in C. Coquery-Vidrovitch and S. Nedelec (1991).

Ndione, E. S. (1994) *L'économie urbaine en Afrique, le don et le recours*, Paris and Dakar: Karthala, Enda graf Sahel.

Niang, A. (2000) 'Les associations en milieu urbain dakarois: classification et capacités développantes', *Afrique et Développement*, Vol. XXV, Nos 1 and 2, pp. 99–159.

Oatley, N. (2001) 'L'apparition de l'Edge (of) City: Quels mots pour les "nouveaux espaces urbains?" ', in H. Rivière d'Arc (ed.), *Nommer les nouveaux territoires urbains*, Paris: Editions Most UNESCO, Editions de la Maison de l'homme, pp. 17–38.

Penouil, M. (1992) 'Secteur informel et crise africaine', *Afrique contemporaine*, special edition, fourth quarter.

Sarr, F. (1998) *L'entrepreneuriat féminin au Sénégal, la transformation des rapports de pouvoirs*, Paris: l'Harmattan.

Simone, A. (1998) *Mutations urbaines en Afrique*, Dakar: CODESRIA.

— (2001) 'Between Ghetto and Globe, Remaking Urban Life in Africa', in A. Tostensen et al. (2001), pp. 46–63.

Sorbier, P. de (2002) 'Le programme des Comités de Développement Locaux au Sénégal, l'exemple de Yeumbeul, Commune d'arrondissement de la périphérie dakaroise, où les habitants fabriquent leur développement', unpublished paper, University of Toulouse-le Mirail, geography department.

Sow, O. (n.d.) 'Territorialités concurrentes et gouvernance des villes: Les enseignements des petites et moyennes villes du Vieux Bassin arachidier au Sénégal', unpublished paper.

Stren, R. E., R. R. White and M. Coquery (1993) *Villes africaines en crise, gérer la croissance urbaine au sud du Sahara*, Paris: l'Harmattan.

Tostensen, A., I. Tvedten and M. Vaa (eds) (2001) 'The Urban Crisis, Governance and Associational Life', *Associational Life in African Cities, Popular Responses to Urban Crises*, Nordiska Afrikainstitutet.

Wade, S., M. Soumaré and E. H. Ly (2002) *Organisations communautaires et associations de quartier*, Dakar: UNESCO.

10 | Formal and decentralized financing of housing: Operation 200,000 Houses, Marrakesh

MOHAMED GHERIS

Moroccan urban structures are being subjected to a lot of pressure as a result of demographic growth and rural exodus. Between 1960 and 1994, the overall population of the kingdom grew at a rate of 3.5 per cent, while the urban demographic growth rate stood at 5.9 per cent. This pressure translated into a shortage of housing, officially estimated at 700,000 units. Even though this shortage is not uniform across all the urban areas of the kingdom, its accumulation and rapid increase are the result of an inextricable combination of factors (land tenure, speculation in real estate, high cost of building materials, low purchasing power of households, insufficient tax incentives, ill-adapted methods of financing). The city of Marrakesh, with its heterogeneous landscape and chaotic planning, is a perfect crystallization of all these problems. Measures taken by public authorities to provide low-cost housing have always been inadequate and poorly conceived, a situation that has forced the population to resort to other, mostly illegal alternatives and practices, such as clandestine housing or officially unrecognized informal systems of financing. We will focus on the latter, that is, the informal or decentralized systems of financing of housing, and examine their theoretical basis. This will enable us to understand the magnitude of the present housing crisis in Morocco.

As was the case with developed countries between the 1980s and 1990s, developing countries gradually abandoned the economics of indebtedness for the economics of financial markets (Hicks 1974). Developing countries were made to develop their financial institutions, that is, strengthen their undeveloped and poorly diversified financial systems. This process has two distinct components: first, the increase in savings made through intermediaries and second, the increase in investments driven by the former as a result of the increase in lendable funds from financial intermediaries (Assidon 1996).In countries going through transition, however, financing seems to be determined by other considerations, that is, by determinants independent of savings made through intermediaries. This has led us to the hypothesis of systems of financing which do not directly link the availability of financing by banks to the prior collection of lendable funds.

According to traditional theories, the inefficiency of financial systems in developing countries is caused by structural deficiencies. This theory holds that the cultural, economic and social development of financial systems is at variance with civil society and the needs of the people. It is an elitist system since it excludes most agents. Formal financial institutions, most of them transplanted, since they are often branches of foreign banks, are facing a legitimacy crisis. Banks are often managed in an inefficient and costly manner (the CIH, Crédit Immobilier et Hôtelier, Banque Populaire au Morocco) because they are controlled by the state and do not have any obligation to produce results, a situation that has led to the accumulation of bad debts resulting from budget deficits and poor management of public enterprises. This has had a negative impact on investment financing. However, classical analyses have ended at such findings.

Studies on the shortage of housing or on urban problems in Marrakesh are rare and the few that do exist are outdated. There is practically none on the construction and financing of houses in this town under the 200,000 houses programme. However, some general studies have been carried out on the financial reforms carried out in Morocco in the 1990s. For example, the new banking law of 1993, a reproduction of reforms carried out in other countries, notably France, is having an impact on the financing of housing, even though its enforcement has just started. This very liberal banking law has the following objectives: deregulation, elimination of middlemen, opening up of the banking sector, reduction of credit controls and the liberalization of interest rates.

The law, however, does not set any limits to the extension of the amount of bank loans (credit controls were abolished in 1991). The liberalization of rates started in July 1990 with the liberalization of credit interest rates and continued in October 1990 with that of interest rates on medium- and long-term loans. This reform was also intended to revitalize monetary and financial markets. Indeed, the existence of a dynamic inter-bank market and secondary financial markets makes it possible for the Central Bank to play its role as liquidity regulator. In this respect, preferential financing schemes were gradually abandoned in all sectors except in areas such as the housing sector. For their part, the redeemable stock portfolio of banks was gradually reduced to barely 15 per cent in 1998 as against 40 per cent a few years earlier.

Similarly, the concept of the universal bank came into being with the opening up of the banking sector. Normally, this should have made it possible for the other commercial banks to finance housing, but the CIH is still enjoying what amounts to a monopoly in the financing of low-cost housing in Marrakesh, even though all commercial banks have been granted the authorization to engage in such activity. Consequently, many people who do not meet the eligibility criteria laid down by the CIH cannot have access to loans and are thus forced to turn to other sources. This explains why there are many informal systems of financing that need to be officially recognized. There are a few studies, however, that examine such issues.

One of these is the World Bank report that deals with the financing of housing in Morocco. It touches on general issues only, however, although it points out the lack of transparency and the low level of competition in the finance sector. It also pointed out that 'rigid control mechanisms resulted in the omnipresence of the State in the financing system, a situation that immediately led to results such as poorly developed financing system, lack of competitiveness and lack of incentives to encourage savings'. It also pointed out the existence of an eviction effect in the finance system at the expense of private investment in housing and the stranglehold by the Caisse de Dépôt et de Gestion (CDG) on institutional savings. The report also insisted that reforms on the financing of housing in Morocco should not be limited to the 'financial' acquisition of housing, but should also be aimed at improving the efficiency of the financing system. In this respect, the report recommended the putting in place, 'as a matter of priority, of measures to facilitate the participation of the private sector in the development of housing so as not to stifle a potential supply reaction'. Reforms on the financing of housing should come only after obstacles to the supply of housing have been removed.

In 1994, Najab Laraichi Bedoui observed in the *Al Maouil* review of the Agence Nationale de Lutte Contre l'Habitat Insalubre (National Agency for the Fight Against Unhealthy Housing) (ANHI)

> that there is a persistent gap between the ever increasing demand for housing and the financing possibilities that real estate developers and low income households can have in order to afford housing. The situation would have been worse had the dynamic of private construction that mobilised informal savings not stepped in to reduce the current shortage, especially as the gap between the cost of housing and the purchasing power of households is forever widening.

Unfortunately, this review failed to carry out an in-depth and theoretical or empirical analysis of the way the decentralized system of financing functions.

Later in 1997, the study on the financial and fiscal aspects of housing in Morocco (*Aspects financiers et fiscaux du logement au Maroc*), commissioned by the Ministry of Housing, examined three specific areas, including the system of housing finance, low-cost housing and land taxes.

The study revealed that the housing sector in Morocco is one of the few production sectors in which the state still plays a dominant role. The role of the state can be seen in the vast array of institutional mechanisms, all controlled by the Ministries of Housing and Finance. Specifically, the study highlighted the low involvement of the formal system of financing and the predominance of informal financing and the private construction of houses and the low participation of banks in spite of the availability of large liquidity reserves. Additionally, the study outlined the lack of diversity in loan instruments (loans on mortgage at fixed rates) and the lack of a secondary mortgage market. It recommended increased competition among financial institutions, promotion of greater access to institutional savings and liquidity, and a system of direct assistance.

This study also failed to carry out a detailed analysis of the decentralized or informal financing of the economy in general and of housing in particular. The authors of this report did not see the substantial amounts of hoarded liquidity and contingency savings as a financial opportunity that should be channelled into the formal system, a move that would increase the volume of liquidity in banks and lead to a drop in interest rates, a determining factor in the financing of housing. But four years after the publication of this report, no concrete action has so far been initiated to remove the obstacles to financing! Even though the strength of this report lies in its practical and operational nature, it does not make any recommendations for the promotion of the role of the banking sector in the economy (embryonic in Morocco) or for the 'modernization' of the informal channels (largely predominant) used in financing both the economy and housing. In Marrakesh, there is an acute shortage of housing: demand far outstrips supply.

Marrakesh is the capital of the Tensift El Haouz region.[1] Founded in 1070 by the Almoravid, Abou Bakr Ibn Omar, it soon became 'the centre to which all major caravan routes or most roads converged and the most important stop after the High Atlas for those moving from the South to the North'.[2] It replaced Aghmat as the capital of a great empire that stretched from Andalusia to Mauritania. Beginning as 'a veritable parade ground and rear base especially against the Berroutas of Tamesna',[3] it later attracted people from the south and other regions because of its politics, strategic position and cultural and religious influence.

In this city, religious (Ben Youssef mosque) and military (Dour El Hajour) monuments as well as 10km of battlements (built at the beginning of the twelfth century by Ali Ben Youssef) were constructed. The Almoravids chose the site where Marrakesh is presently located for strategic, political and economic reasons. According to Deverdun,[4] there was the political need not only to move as far away from Aghmat as possible, but also to have a site from which the entire Atlas could be monitored and which could attract people, wealth and also drain water.

Between 1147 and 1269, the Almohads turned Marrakesh into the greatest capital of the western Muslim empire. Impressive monuments such as the Koutoubia, the El Mansour Mosque, the Agdal and the Menara Gardens were built during the rule of this dynasty. This prosperity gave a cultural (many scholars such as Ibn Rochd, Ibn Tofail, etc. lived there) and demographic boost to the city (the town had almost 150,000 inhabitants).[5]

Later on, the Merinids abandoned it for Fez, which they made their capital. At the beginning of the sixteenth century, its population dropped to 20,000 inhabitants[6] as a result of frequent epidemics (the black plague) and attacks it suffered at the hands of the Masmoudas mountain dwellers. Between 1547 and 1668, Marrakesh became the capital of the Saadians and regained all its former splendour. This could be seen in the construction, by King Al Mansour, of the matchless El Badii Palace, with inspiration from Grenada.

Under the Alaouites, Marrakesh was once again relegated to second place and became mostly the capital of the south. This role was maintained by the protectorate, which built an industrial zone in it and a railway line for the transportation of its mineral and agricultural riches to the Atlantic. The decline of the caravan trade and the development of trade relations with Europe stimulated the growth of the Atlantic region of the country at the expense of inland towns.

As concerns town planning, Yacoub Al Mansour (1106–43) was the main architect of the town and its structure remained unchanged right up to the twentieth century: functional intra-mural neighbourhoods that made up the medina, surrounded by extra-mural orchards.

From 1912, under the protectorate, the urban structure of Marrakesh underwent extensive changes. These changes can be summarized as follows:

• Splitting of the city. The city was split into two with the establishment of the European town, which later on became the main business centre of the city. This segregation stemmed from the desire of General Lyautey to separate the Medina from the modern town to preserve the identity of the 'natives', but also to show the superiority of the European and Christian civilization over the Muslim society.[7] As has rightly been pointed out by A. Rachik, the urban planning advocated by Lyautey was based on a relatively specific social plan, which sometimes resembled a utopian ideological system. Ostensibly, this system of urban planning was advocated by Lyautey as a way of respecting the customs of the 'natives', but in reality, it was motivated by hygienic considerations, fear of, and contempt for, the 'natives', and consequently by a strong desire to gather this 'dangerous' (in the hygienic sense) population and keep it as far away as possible from the European part of the town so as to be able to control it more easily.[8] Later on, the officials of the Protectorate set up an industrial zone for agro-food processing factories.[9]

- Lack of industrialization of an urban economy dominated by crafts, trade and a handful of agro-food industries. The economic fabric remained much as it had been in the past (except, maybe, for the tourism and leisure industries), with the rapid expansion of the 'informal' sector[10] and a high unemployment rate.

- Increase in the levels of poverty[11] and marginalization, easily seen in the more segregated areas: an increasing number of slums in the Medina and the spread of unhygienic *douars* existing side by side with luxurious estates and villas, both of them encroaching several hectares into the urban area. Consequently, the Tensift region (Marrakesh alone accounts for 70 per cent of its urban population) has become the second poorest region out of the seven regions of the kingdom.[12] The following are some indicators that confirm this situation: the number of school-age children attending school in Marrakesh is lower than the national average; higher incidence of child labour and more single women; the gross rate of employment is higher (the poor are often obliged to have two jobs to make ends meet); relatively lower population growth than in the other coastal towns, because of the horizontal extension of the town (development of new state lands by ERAC-Tensift in Massira I, II, III, Douar Laskar).

Between the 1960 to 1971 and 1971 to 1982 periods, the annual growth rate of the town moved from 2.9 per cent to 3.3 per cent; meanwhile, that of other similar towns averaged 4 per cent and 3.3 per cent respectively. Between 1982 and 1994, the town had 232,778 additional inhabitants, representing an average of 19,398 inhabitants per year, the equivalent of 3,966 households.[13]

Even though the programme to construct 200,000 houses was intended as a solution to the shortage of housing in Marrakesh (about 4,700 houses for Marrakesh), it did not question the chaotic planning of the town. Since the housing problem in Morocco is a structural one, the solution proposed by state authorities only helped to accentuate imbalances and anomalies. In Marrakesh, the official supply of housing is mainly in the hands of one operator, ERAC-Tensift, a public real estate company. But, due to lack of co-ordination, public action in this area did not take several aspects of the problem into consideration, especially the financing of housing. Creative solutions (not often recognized) were proposed by the population. The analysis of these solutions will not only enable us to take a critical look at conventional theories but also to propose new avenues for research.

Chaotic town planning and shortage of housing in Marrakesh

As the town had no industrial fabric that could generate wealth through the creation of added value and thus generate greater incomes for the urban population, the latter were exposed to the vicissitudes of the back country in crisis (the pastoral and farming systems suffering seasonally from drought and structurally from poor productivity). The result was the chaotic and unplanned expansion of the town. The main characteristics included the heterogeneous nature of types of urban houses, lack of planning and urban management, and the shortage of housing in general and of low-cost housing in particular.

Since the independence of the country,

> The operations carried out up till now, often at great cost, have never been comprehensive enough to provide solutions to all the problems faced. Spot actions carried out up to now have not worked, both socially and politically, and all the money invested has not stopped overcrowding in *medinas*, the proliferation of slums and clandestine villages and the rapid increase in the shortage of low-cost housing.[14]

The heterogeneous nature of types of urban housing As previous studies have shown,[15] one of the characteristics of Marrakesh is the heterogeneous and diversified nature of its urban landscape. Bellaoui notes:

> Marrakech is a perfect example of a town whose general development has been far from linear and whose glorious past, as symbolized by the coherent and uniform *medina*, is in complete contrast with its present situation, characterized, among other things, by the excessively heterogeneous nature of its urban landscape. Far from being a font of splendour and hence a motivating factor, the *medina*, with its surrounding *douars*, has become the source of almost all the problems that the biggest and one of the most prestigious towns of Morocco is facing today.[16]

The town features four types of housing:

- the age-old *medina*, consisting of houses with patios and no apparent social segregation;[17]
- the new town or Gueliz, made up of sub-divisions with different

functions (commercial and services areas, industrial zones, residential and hotel areas);

- land developed by the private and public property developers: due to high population densities and the rural exodus to the *medinas*, public authorities initiated projects to develop land and build low-cost housing with improved sanitation and resettlement areas (unit III), for new neighbourhoods for construction by private individuals (Massira I, II, III, Azli) and recently to construct high-rise buildings as part of the 200,000 houses programme; and

- unauthorized urban *douars*:[18] according to the 1998 census of unauthorized houses, urban Marrakesh had 156 *douars* as against only sixty-one in 1991, representing about 150,000 persons, that is 22 per cent of the total urban population of the agglomeration.[19]

Lack of town planning and urban management The proliferation of unhealthy housing alone adequately illustrates the failure of the town planning policy in Marrakesh. This failure is all the more incomprehensible when we consider that a large portion of the land (35 per cent) is state-owned.

Unfortunately the availability of state land has not had a significant impact on town planning in Marrakesh. According to the public authorities, this is due to the existence of many undeveloped state lands (*non aedificandi* and *non altius-tollendi* zones) and a shortage of areas suitable for habitation (Mechouar, El Kabash).

In the absence of town planning, one can say that there is only urban extension;[20] in fact, an urban policy has to:[21]

- set objectives and provide the necessary means;
- resolve the internal conflicts faced by the central state, which is the main actor that formulates policy. However, the central state has not one but several policies, which vary depending on the political, geographical and historical situation ...
- harmonize the activities of the state, which is the main actor. However, 'the State, no matter the degree of its cohesion, the extent of its power and the transparency of its urban policies, is not the only actor involved in urban management. Complicity among actors, convergence of interests and even collusion among some of them can weaken or even annihilate the impact of actions by public authorities';[22]
- ensure convergence between global planning (allocation of resources) and town planning (allocation of land);[23]
- ensure convergence between the state and the region (decentralization); and

- ensure convergence between the state and the private sector: implementation schedules.

Very often, inconsistencies in urban policies stem from the fact that 'provisions are made separately for the needs of the various areas and it is only afterwards that an effort is made towards harmonization, a situation that most often results in waste, both of land and other resources'.[24]

In this respect, the SDAU of Marrakesh notes: 'the voluntary action of big public land developers, whose choice of sites is often dictated more by the availability of land than by the desire to occupy the land in a rational manner, can, in the short term, interfere with the natural expansion of the urban area. Already the rapid expansion of the Massira neighbourhood to the west is a disruptive force.'[25]

Shortage of housing in general and of low-cost housing in particular On the basis of the sizes of households, which stood at 5.5 persons from 1982 to 1990, at 5.2 from 1990 to 2000 and at 5.1 from then onwards, the SDAU

TABLE 10.1 Size of households by 2010

	Population	Households	Persons per household
1990	590,000	114,000	5.2
2000	750,000	147,000	5.1
2010	950,000	186,000	5.1

Source: SDAU of Marrakesh 1991.

TABLE 10.2 Trend in number of authorized houses in Marrakesh

Year	Number of building permits	Number of authorized houses
1982	1,075	1,1,699
1984	1,292	2,135
1986	1,551	2,668
1988	1,425	2,089
1990	1,251	1,867
1992	1,204	1,741
1994	613	987*
1996	–	–
1997	1,240	2,187*

* Department of Statistics
Source: regional statistics reports.

of Marrakesh[26] was able tò make the following projections concerning the number of households by 2010:

Considering a hypothetical situation where there would not be any shortage of housing, 3,800 houses per year would have to be built by 2010. In terms of achievements,[27] Table 10.2 indicates the trend in the number of authorized houses in Marrakesh.

A comparison between the demand for housing and authorized constructions shows a serious shortage, amounting to about 50 per cent (even during the years of greatest production, such as in 1997).[28] How did the authorities respond to this huge demand?

Shortage of housing in Morocco and solutions by the state

The state reacted by:

- enacting laws, rules and regulations governing town planning;
- developing land in urban areas;
- rehabilitating unhygienic housing;
- constructing low-cost houses under Operation 200,000 Houses. This was done mainly by bodies under the supervisory authority of the Ministry of Housing (ERAC, ANI, SNEC);
- granting tax benefits to real estate developers and interest bonuses to home buyers, especially buyers of low-cost houses; and
- financing real estate development and home buying by banks in which the state owns majority shares.

It was therefore a multidimensional reaction since it was regulatory, financial. In this study, we shall focus on two types of actions carried out by the state to provide a solution to the housing problem in Marrakesh: the 200,000 Houses Project and the modalities to finance it (especially the post-financing period).

Operation 200,000 Houses 1994 was a turning point in the housing policy of the kingdom, because prior to this date, the state, through the bodies under its supervisory authority, was concerned mainly with curbing the proliferation of unsanitary housing (slums, clandestine housing) through the rehabilitation of poorly equipped neighbourhoods and the provision of developed plots for the construction of houses. This policy was generally formulated and implemented by bodies under the supervisory authority of the state. The developed plots were intended for the poorest category of the urban population, although some of the plots were sold to the more affluent (for the construction of villas or high-rise buildings). This policy thus excluded those in the middle-income bracket who could not afford a plot, and whose only alternative was renting a house, often in slum areas. The demand for housing by this category (lower middle class with a monthly income of less than 36,000Dhs) was substantial and had to be satisfied. In his speech of 3 March 1994, the king recommended, as part of an initial programme, the construction of 200,000 houses for this social category,[29] with state assistance and on very favourable conditions.

Many financial, fiscal, land tenure and town planning measures were taken to ensure the success of this operation:

- the low-cost house was defined as a house that cost below 200,000Dhs and had a surface area of less than 100m²;
- loans were granted for a period of twenty-five years at a state-subsidized interest rate of less than 6 per cent;[30]
- taxes and duties on low-cost houses were abolished;
- taxes and duties on land, land development and building permits and fees to various land administrations, the Office National d'Electricité (National Electricity Corporation) and the Office National de l'Eau Potable (National Water Corporation) were reduced;
- a mortgage market was set up in May 2000;[31]
- state-owned land was sold to various land developers at a symbolic price and measures were taken to preserve state land earmarked for the implementation of the low-cost housing programme;
- central and local standing committees were set up to identify appropriate sites for the implementation of this programme; and
- procedures for the use of state, communal and collectively owned lands for urban development purposes were streamlined and accelerated.

By 1999, only a first instalment of 48,000 houses had been constructed and most of them were unsold.[32]

Shortcomings of Operation 200,000 Houses In addition to the wide gap between the number of houses planned and the huge demand, the project had many other shortcomings.[33] It targeted mostly employees of the public or semi-public sectors and offered very few choices or alternatives in terms of residential areas. Financially, it maintained the existing system of bonuses, very costly for the state and which did not effectively act as an incentive to ownership and failed to improve the system of financing of housing. Instead, the programme strengthened the institutional mobilization of resources[34] by the CIH and hence strengthened the monopoly it enjoyed. In so doing, it prevented the emergence of competition that would have helped to bring down the cost of loans and make them more accessible. With respect to production, the operation strengthened the role of public real estate developers, but failed to provide the housing sector with an appropriate solution.[35]

Operation 200,000 Houses brought all the inconsistencies in the system of financing of housing in Morocco to light.[36] This system was characterized by the near monopoly enjoyed by one lending institution, the CIH, which granted almost 75 per cent of all housing loans.[37] This was made possible by the existence of a discriminatory legal and regulatory environment, established privileges enjoyed by the CIH[38] and practices whereby loans were granted from rationed resources (differentiated interest rates). Because of this, conditions of eligibility for loans were often very stiff and discriminatory and interest rates unreasonably high (except in recent years).[39] In Marrakesh, the state reacted directly by constructing about 4,000 houses under the 200,000 Houses Programme.

Action of the state in Marrakesh and its impact Real estate development in Marrakesh is mostly in the hands of bodies under the supervisory authority of the state such as ERAC-Tensift, which is the main developer. It is very difficult accurately to assess the work done by these public bodies in overall real estate development. Still poorly organized, private real estate developers play a rather minor role, although some of them (Chaabi and Chkili) are beginning to emerge as serious players. Moreover, low-cost housing projects that, in the past, were of no interest to private developers have started attracting them, mostly because of the tax benefits granted under the 200,000 Houses Programme.

Here, a distinction should be made between two types of real estate

TABLE 10.3 Total number of units built by ERAC-Tensift

Year	Number	Percentage
Total as of 31.12.1989	25,953	41
1990	4,448	7
1991	3,441	5
1992	4,787	8
1993	5,638	9
1994	6,016	10
1995	4,578	7
1996	415	1
1997	2,381	4
1998	5,470	9
Total	63,127	100

Source: Progress report of ERAC-Tensift, 1998.

development, both dominated by pubic actors. There is the development of land, in which the private sector has for long been participating through the development of plots for the construction of low-cost and luxury housing. This was mostly on small surface areas and involved little mobilization of funds. Even in this area, state-controlled bodies were the major actors. Additionally, there is real estate development proper (construction and sale of houses), which is largely in the hands of state-controlled bodies in general, and of ERAC-Tensift[40] in particular. These bodies have the means necessary for the implementation of major projects. Private real estate developers are more involved in the development of small-scale operations (a dozen or so houses).

It should be pointed out that the construction of houses by private individuals is very common and helps to satisfy three-quarters of the demand for housing in the town. This construction by private persons constitutes the non-industrial component in the production of houses in Marrakesh. We can see therefore that state-controlled bodies, in general, and ERAC-Tensift in particular, dominated real estate development.

ERAC-Tensift – the leading real estate developer in Marrakesh A breakdown of the work done by ERAC-Tensift shows that by the end of 1998, it had constructed 16,042 houses, developed 43,029 plots, provided 3,638 commercial facilities, seventy-six offices and 5,937 relocations, all amounting to a total of 130,000 houses that could house some 720,000 people, that is about half the size of the urban population of the region.[41] Table 10.3 shows the total number of structures put up by the end of 1998.[42]

Given its diversified, indeed assorted, activities, ERAC-Tensift helps to curb unhygienic housing, develops industrial zones, builds roads, etc. These activities weigh heavily on its already overstretched budget, a situation faced by the other ERACs of the kingdom.[43] By reason of its legal status (public establishment), the general context of the economy of the country (the dominant role of the state, even though economic liberalization is proclaimed as the strategic choice), the nature of the demand it endeavours to satisfy (a fundamental need) and the position it occupies in the housing market (leading actor, especially in Operation 200,000 Houses), ERAC is a budget-consuming enterprise (disproportionate operating budget). It has little regard for customer preferences, as evidenced by the fact that the financing arrangement and the products (especially low-cost houses) offered to customers do not often meet their requirements. In 1997, the operating budget of this body stood at 25.65 million dirhams for a turnover of 86 million dirhams, that is, about 29 per cent. In 1999, this budget went up to about 27.35 million dirhams for a total workforce of 174 employees.

273

TABLE 10.4 Work done by each developer (Operation 200,000 Houses)

Developer	Units (houses)	Percentage
ERAC/Tensift	4,764	77
ANHI	164	2.6
SNEC	520	8.3
Private	720	12.1
Total	6,168	100

Source: Délégation Régionale de l'Habitat de Marrakech.

Again, returns on investments were low as a result of the following factors:

• shortage of state-owned lands: ERAC is increasingly buying land at market prices;
• lack of a dynamic marketing policy: unsold stocks at the end of 1998 were evaluated at 1,730 million dirhams;
• wasteful financial management: ERAC-Tensift is highly indebted, particularly towards the CIH. As of the end of 1998, it owed 510 million dirhams to the CIH, 150 million of which were due; and
• negative profitability: in 1997, the company had a negative balance of about 190,000 dirhams.

Out of forty-five loan repayments, amounting to 683 million dirhams, ERAC paid 199 million dirhams as financial costs, a clear indication of very poor financial management. The said financial costs were then passed on to the buyers. According to the director of the institution, 'this situation is due, in part, to the high interest rates charged by CIH and to the non-repayment of loans relating to operations that have been completely marketed'.[44]

It was, however, the 200,000 Houses Programme that really brought to light the structural shortcomings of the institution.

ERAC-Tensift, principal body in the implementation of the 200,000 Houses Programme Projections concerning the provision of low-cost housing in Marrakesh are ambitious; they show that the Ministry of Housing is planning to develop about 1,000 additional hectares in the following areas especially:

• Bab Marrakesh: surface area of 150ha, with 12,000 units, 5,000 of them low-cost;
• Harbil: surface area of 600ha, with 48,000 units, 23,000 of them low-cost; and

Name	Number of units		VIT	VIT	Start
	Houses	Commercial	LCH	MDH	period

Marrakesh – Menara Préfecture:

Name	Houses	Commercial	LCH	MDH	Start period
Souss 2	240	72	40,958		Aug '95
Tensift 2	233	87	41,325		Dec '95
Ibn Khaldoun 1	84	32	13,960		Jan '95
Ibn Khaldoun 3	70	24	11,983		Dec '95
Gharb 2	193	28	31,180		Nov '95
Gharb 3	99	10	13,270		Nov '95
Tafilalet 2	186	54	29,803		Nov '95
Oum Errabia	300	104	64,781		Feb '96
Tafilalet 4	71	27	11,881		Nov '95
Haouz	261	23	37,676		Nov '95
El Harti 1° T & 2° T	388	116	61,533		Jan '96
Anbar 1° T	181	142 + 13 B	38,470		Oct '95
Sebou 1° T	149	25	22,780		Dec '95
Ibn Toooumert	164	105	50,962		Aug '95
Total	2,619	849 + 13 B	470,562		

D'El Kelâa, Sraghna Province:

Name	Houses	Commercial	LCH	MDH	Start period
Allaymoune Ext	–	46		3,700	Dec '97
Aouatif 1° T	–	495		26,000	Nov '94
Total	–	541		29,700	

Essaouira Province:

Name	Houses	Commercial	LCH	MDH	Start period
La Lagune 4° T	–	685	42,976		Aug '92
Azlef	–	763	49,189		Aug '92
Total	–	1,448	92,165		

Total General

Houses	Plots	COM	VIT/MDH
2,619	1,889	849 + 13 B	592,427
	5,470 Products		

Source: ERAC–Tensift.

- M'Hamid: surface area of 200ha, with 20,000 units, 10,000 of them low-cost.

This will amount to a total of 60,000 housing units over the next few years.[45] A total of 6,168 housing units have effectively been constructed in the Tensift region (mostly in Marrakesh) over a surface area of 29ha at a cost of almost 1,000 million dirhams. The first part of the national programme to construct 200,000 houses is divided among the various developers as shown in Table 10.4. This table shows that 82 per cent of the 200,000 Houses Programme was implemented in Marrakesh by public establishments. Out of this figure, 77 per cent was handled by ERAC-Tensift alone. Table 10.5 gives us a complete breakdown of the share handled by ERAC-Tensift.

Products that do not meet customers' requirements An analysis of the three components of low-cost housing, that is, the neighbourhood, the house and the method of financing, shows that the products supplied did not meet the requirements of buyers. Most of the houses built in Marrakesh under Operation 200,000 Houses were in Ham. This neighbourhood is subdivided into three smaller neighbourhoods over a surface area of 294ha:

- Ham 1: 107ha, with 3,060 plots: 1985
- Ham 2: 92ha, with 3,044 plots: 1986
- Ham 3: 95ha with 2,241 plots: 1991

The houses constructed in Ham were divided into three zones: blocks of flats; low-cost and individual housing; and residential area (villas).

Table 10.6 gives us an idea of projections. The sizes of the areas earmarked for these utilities were determined using national standards, even though all the utilities were not provided. However, the portion of Operation 200,000 Houses realized in Marrakesh, almost all of it in Ham, on a surface area of 41ha, not including works (4,764 houses), was incorporated,

TABLE 10.6 Distribution of surface area of utilities by activity and sector (surface area in m²)

Activity	HAM I	HAM II	HAM III	Total
Schools	42,876	33,396	45,451	121,723
Youth and sports	32,717	1,005	742	34,464
Health	8,259	5,128	699	14,086
Administration	9,327	12,166	106,339	127,932
National promotion	984	1,375	848	3,207
Culture	4,886	–	1,117	6,003
Equipment of neighbourhood and Habous				
Total	122,700	58,076	163,728	344,504

Source: ERAC-Tensift, 1999.

one might say, 'by force' into this area, in violation of the town planning norms in force.[46] Again, the number of utilities did not increase at the same pace as the growth of the population of the neighbourhood.[47] The survey of seventy-five households benefiting from this programme that we conducted confirmed this situation.

TABLE 10.7 Level of satisfaction in the neighbourhood

Degree of satisfaction	Number of households	Percentage
High	27	36
Average	41	54
Low	5	7
No answer	2	3
Total	75	100

Source: Personal survey, March–April 2000.

Table 10.7 shows that the degree of satisfaction in Ham is average (54 per cent) mainly because of lack of utilities and a high level of nuisance. Again, there are major disparities in Ham itself. In Ham I (1985), for instance, the shortage of utilities is not as serious as in Ham III (under construction).

TABLE 10.8 Nuisances in the neighbourhood

Nuisances	Number	Percentage
Great	23	31
Average	13	17
Low	37	49
No answer	2	3
Total	75	100

Source: Personal survey, March–April 2000.

Table 10.8 shows that 31 per cent of the households surveyed suffered from serious nuisances in their neighbourhoods as a result of pollution (proximity to a hammam), insecurity (frequent assaults) and construction work that lasts too long.

As with the environment of the product, the housing itself did not meet the requirements of the customers. All the surveys came out with the same findings, that co-ownership is not adapted to the living habits of Moroccans, a situation made worse by the small sizes of the houses, and the high cost of the product.

TABLE 10.9 Surface areas of houses

	Houses	Surface area
50m² ==> 59m²	14	18.5
60m² ==> 69m²	31	41
70m² ==> 79m²	25	33
80m² and above	4	5
Undetermined	1	2.5
Total	75	100

Source: Personal survey, March–April 2000.

Table 10.9 shows that about 60 per cent of the buyers own houses with a surface area of less than 70m².

In addition to the small size of the houses, the houses were obviously not tailored to the needs of the customers. As we can see in the following table, more than 77 per cent of the houses bought were subsequently modified by their owners.[48]

TABLE 10.10 Modifications made

	Number	Percentage
None	24	33
<3,000 Dhs	12	16
3,001–10,000 Dhs	11	15
10,001–20,000 Dhs	14	18
20,001–30,000 Dhs	7	9
>30,000 Dhs	7	9

Source: Personal survey, March–April 2000.

The survey shows that home owners who did not carry out modifications on or redo parts of their newly bought houses failed to do so for lack of means and not because they were satisfied with the product. Again, they complained of other problems such as poor insulation and poor lighting. As concerns prices, most of those surveyed unanimously confirmed that the products sold by ERAC-Tensift were too expensive. The survey showed that most home buyers viewed the company as a speculator that took advantage of the shortage in housing and of Operation 200,000 Houses to construct low-quality houses and sell them at exorbitant prices.

It should first be pointed out here that finance is of capital importance, considering that a house is a product that cannot (or only very rarely) be bought for cash. Financing thus often requires long-term loans. All those who acquired houses under the 200,000 Houses Programme financed the purchase with loans granted by the CIH.[49]

According to respondents, problems of financing can be summarized (Table 10.11) as concerning the inability of households to have access to bank loans and the high cost of loans.

TABLE 10.11 Home buyers' opinion of bank loans

	Number	Percentage
Adapted	26	38
Fairly adapted	3	6
Not adapted	38	56
Total	67	100

Source: Personal survey, March–April 2000.

Table 10.11 shows that 56 per cent of respondents were of the opinion that bank financing is not adapted (duration of loans too short, high interest rates, bureaucratic bottlenecks in CIH).

An interesting aspect here is the 'financial' itinerary of home buyers: many of them were forced to turn to *tontines* or to pseudo-mortgages to build up savings, which were later used as first instalments to ERAC-Tensift (30,000 Dhs) (41 per cent turned to *tontines* and 34 per cent resorted to pseudo-mortgages).

TABLE 10.12 Went to the *tontine*

	Number	Percentage
Yes	31	41
No	44	59
Total	75	100

Source: Personal survey, March–April 2000.

Also Table 10.13 shows us another informal method of financing (since it is not officially recognized) in Marrakesh, the pseudo-mortgage. Its mechanism is simple: the owner of a house borrows money from a person to whom he gives his house as collateral for the duration of the loan. A relatively low rent, which does not appear in the loan agreement, is paid to the owner of the house.

TABLE 10.13 Status of occupation before the purchase of the house

	Number	Percentage
Tenant	24	32
Proprietor	4	5
Pseudo-mortgage	26	34
With a family	18	24
No door	1	2
Others	2	3
Total	75	100

Source: Personal survey, March–April 2000.

This enables the temporary occupant of the house to build up 'compulsory' savings, which will then be used as initial payment for the purchase of a house.[50] This method makes it possible to ease some of the pressures in the market for urban housing in the towns of the kingdom. Since most urban households in Marrakesh cannot afford the rent for a decent house, they are obliged to resort to the pseudo-mortgage as the first step towards buying a house. In fact, most respondents (60 per cent) are of the opinion that pseudo-mortgage rates (generally between 30,000 and 60,000 Dhs) are affordable (Table 10.14).

TABLE 10.14 Evaluation of pseudo-mortgage rates

	Number	Percentage
High	29	39
Average	30	40
Low	14	18
N.A.	2	3
Total	75	100

Source: Personal survey, March–April 2000.

The table below shows that almost 72 per cent of the respondents think that the rates are within reach (Table 10.15).

This description of informal financing practices shows that several financing methods or systems exist side by side. Paradoxically, it is the practices that are not officially recognized that predominate.[51] The description of the trio, neighbourhood-housing-financing, has highlighted the inconsistencies in the Moroccan low-cost housing policy. The solutions provided by public authorities were not often satisfactory, for several reasons.

TABLE 10.15 Appreciation of the accessibility of pseudo-mortgage

	Number	Percentage
Accessible	54	72
Averagely accessible	7	9
Not accessible	11	15
N.A.	3	4
Total	75	100

Source: Personal survey, March–April 2000.

Most of the houses under the 200,000 Houses Programme were built in Ham I, II and III, resulting in high population densities in these neighbourhoods without the attendant increase in the number of utilities. This, coupled with insecurity, has created a feeling of frustration in the population. As concerns housing per se, the solution proposed under the 200,000 Houses Programme was not very satisfactory: small size of the houses, poor quality–price ratio, co-ownership, non-respect of commitments with respect to green spaces, VAT exemptions, etc. by ERAC. Additionally, the conditions put in place by the duo ERAC-CIH are very stiff (initial payment of 30,000 Dhs too much for households, interest rates considered too high by low-income households) and too rigid (financing at fixed rates and fixed annual instalments).

The official housing policy in Morocco is designed as if the country's economy depends on the banking system, with well-lubricated mechanisms. But this is not the case, as the economy relies little on banks – a situation that has an obvious impact on the mobilization of savings – and the banking system contributes only 14 per cent of the financing for all the houses built.[52]

The official system of financing is thus marginal and exclusive (Picory and Geffroy 1995). It does not recognize the existence of other 'decentralized' or informal systems of financing.[53] These informal systems can coexist perfectly with the official system and even help strengthen it. Efficient economic policies (macro- and micro-) thus have to establish a connection between the various informal and formal channels.

Informal or unofficial financing may be defined as 'financial activities or operations that are legal but not officially registered or regulated, and which are not carried out by official finance institutions'.[54]

How can we theoretically explain the relationship that may exist between these various systems of financing?

Attempts at interpretation

The orthodox theory operates in terms of financial dichotomy. According to this theory, informal financial markets are most often the outcome of discriminatory price measures, eviction effects resulting from the indebtedness of the public treasury towards the Central Bank and of high transaction costs in official institutions (Hugon 1996 – see n. 53). Financial repression therefore leads to this dualism in the financing sector, where the informal sector makes up for the shortcomings of official institutions. This theory holds that it is because real interests rates are negative that credits are rationed, thereby stimulating the emergence of informal financing systems. To solve this problem, it would be necessary to liberalize financing and raise real interest rates, and thus increase the savings of economic agents weighing risk and profitability. The pricing system would then indicate social and individual preferences and utilities as well as the productivity of factors.

Appraisal of the orthodox model It should first of all be pointed out here that econometric studies have not established any direct relationship between the level of interest rates and the level of savings (Giovannini 1985 for developing countries, IMF 1994 for Africa). Neo-structural economists (Eboué 1990) think either in terms of the theory of choice or bring out the savings and investment functions, differentiated according to informal and formal markets. They hold that the effect of an increase in real interest rates on the mobilization of the savings of households would depend on the degree of substitution between bank savings, liquidity, investment in informal financial markets and currency. According to P. Hugon, 'an increase in interest rates can in the long term increase bank savings, retroact negatively on informal savings and positively on informal interest rates'.[55] In Morocco, the low level of the dependence of the economy on the banking sector, and low salaries, are the reasons why savings are often slow to respond to variations in interest rates.

Other more recent micro-economic and neo-institutional studies (Hugon 1995; Servet 1996 – see n. 56) have examined information deficiency and the opportunistic behaviour of economic operators. The studies make a distinction between risk and uncertainty. In a high-risk environment, economic operators would be more likely to examine probabilities and either minimize the risk or transfer it (insurance, diversification of activities, etc.). In an uncertain environment, collateral is of no use; consequently many agents are excluded from the official financing system. The choice is no longer between risk (which can be calculated) and profitability, but between uncertainty (which cannot be calculated) and liquidity.[56] The latter, largely preferred, serves as a shock absorber for the former. We see therefore that one should talk, not of a homogeneous and isotropic environment, but rather of 'of a heterogeneous and anisotropic environment where hierarchies, disparities and polarizations exist'.[57]

The hypothesis of the segmentation of the finance environment requires that we

> take into account the economic rationality of minimizing risk and the strong preference for liquidity, which leads to the diversification of activities and to the short-term importance of social insurance and housing. Informal systems are built around family relations and within solidarity networks. It would therefore be necessary to work less on individuals than on groups and to take their various modes or organization into account.[58]

There are also *ex ante* and *ex post* transaction costs. These may be the costs of identifying partners or management and control costs. Decentralized financing, 'closed' since it involves only people or members of the same group (*tontines*, pseudo-mortgage), can be cheaper than external financing through loans (bank loans).

The informal or decentralized system of financing, which involves personal relations, makes it possible to reduce transaction and intermediary costs for small loans, in spite of the high cost of managing small loans. The economics of conventions can help us to understand informal systems of financing. Since it is now recognized that economic agents have a limited procedural or adaptable rationality, households cannot apply a subjective distribution of probabilities to the entire set of possibilities.

Thus, the ideal does not obtain, but rather the search for a satisfactory situation. In addition to these 'holistic' distinctions, we can propose other more individualistic ones. We can, for instance, distinguish between 'hot' money, involving personal, community and close relations, and 'cold', distant and anonymous money (Bédard and Krapp 1991). A distinction has to be made between individual savings banked through an informal intermediary and a contractual community or forced saving (Dupuy 1988). *Tontines* and pseudo-mortgage practices in Marrakesh belong more to the second category. Methods of financing function more within the framework of a community of voluntary membership than within a community of natural belonging (Dupuy 1990; Servet 1990). Indeed, people choose their *tontines*, lay down the conditions under which they give their houses out on pseudo-mortgage (they would prefer to give out their houses to couples with small families) but they cannot choose their relatives.

How does this apply concretely to those for whom the 200,000 houses are intended? Some of the respondents in the survey were in favour of the setting up of 'homogeneous' groups: indeed, although it is difficult to use the level of income as the factor determining homogeneity (these people have very similar incomes, between 2,500 to 3,500 Dhs per month), other factors such as origin (most home buyers are from Marrakesh, a situation that can facilitate contact), profession (more than 85 per cent of the respondents were civil servants, 40 per cent of whom were primary and secondary school teachers) can be considered as powerful levers for the constitution of social groups and the emergence of associative life.

The experience of *tontines* studied by F. Navez-Bouchanine deserves to be examined. After studying unsanitary neighbourhoods that were rehabilitated by public authorities (construction of utilities, roads)[59] the author found out that it was mainly through *tontines* that the inhabitants built up savings that were later used to pay the required first instalments. Public authorities encouraged this practice, and later the population appropriated it, setting up many other *tontines* on their own, without any external support. As concerns the 200,000 Houses Programme, a partnership between public authorities (which initiated the setting up of rotating loans associations), the population concerned and commercial banks made it possible to mobilize the money needed either to pay the first instalments for the purchase of a house or for the construction of a house. Concerning pseudo-mortgage, it would be necessary to regulate and officially recognize this practice, taking measures to counter the risks that can occur.[60]

Instituting an economics of solidarity The economics of solidarity is witnessing an unprecedented expansion and activity. It is being developed by associations in developing and developed countries, and is proof of the failure of the market and of the state to regulate the economy. Many theories have been put forward (new macro-economics, new micro-economics) to try to 'improve traditional hypotheses from conventional neo-classical theories'.[61] O. Williamson (1985), for instance, observes that market regulation takes place not in a context of certainty but in one of uncertainty. According to him, the economic agent has a limited rationality as a result of limited information and cognitive capacity.

For this reason, the market will not be perfect or ideal and would thus generate transaction costs (information cost, cost of size of market). Where, for example, information systems are deficient, practices (production or financing) based on personal relations can become more efficient. Informal or decentralized systems of financing are sometimes more profitable and more adapted when compared to the extent of risks, transaction costs, cost of mobilization of funds (Servet 1996; Hugon 1996 – see n. 53).

On the other hand, the substantive approach to economics, as suggested by K. Polanyi, comes in reaction to the formal approach of conventional economics. This approach considers that man is not 'a utilitarian atom'; consequently, he is subject to psychological, environmental and social constraints. This approach holds that the analysis of institutions, the influence of social values and hierarchies, has to be integrated into the economy. Economic phenomena have to be interwoven and enshrined in social and symbolic relationships. The concepts of social capital and social networks can be used firmly to establish this substantive approach.

Social norms and the milieu in which one belongs constrain the capital that can be made available. Here we are insisting on the notion of community, which rejects any idea that considers human action as being asocial or atomic. There is a logical relationship between the person (not the individual) and the community to which he or she belongs. An analysis of the social network brings out this double relationship. The network, in essence, involves synergy. The network is complete when its members are interdependent. Its strength and dynamism depend on the extent to which its members have confidence in one another.

A network has not only a social and material capital, but also a symbolic one. It gives the network a specific identity. Members of a network are not members only. They are actors. The factors that build up the social capital are the milieu to which they belong and the level of education. To this should be added subjective competences and the ability to form relationships. The economics of solidarity must have a 'local' dimension. We got inspiration for the 'local' economics of solidarity concept from 'the territorial economics of solidarity' concept proposed by A. M. Alcoléa (1998). We are insisting on the local dimension because, for a development process to be sustainable, it must start from the bottom or from the site, according to H. Zaoua (1996). The economics of solidarity can be considered as a third sector in the sense that local initiatives fall under the purview neither of the market nor of the state. A special status can be granted to actors with social missions. The economics of solidarity can also be a new economic actor (Laville 1999) capable of mediating between many different approaches and forms of co-ordination. Two other paradigms, the economics of grants and the economics of the site, can be highlighted.

Mauss later generalized the notion of symbols in human relationships, taking it beyond symbolic or structural signs. In going beyond the Durkheim opposition between the good and the profane, the individual and the society, Mauss insisted on the inter-relationship between the utilitarian and the symbolical and also between interest and disinterestedness.[62] In this respect, social phenomena become complete, since they become symbols. There is no separation between the individual and the society. As we can

285

see, this concept is anti-utilitarian, but does not go as far as to say that individuals reject selfishness, interest or strategy. The grants paradigm is based on the triple obligation of giving, receiving and rejecting any economic totalitarianism

that places material interests above all social order. It endeavours to transcend the conventional division between methodological individualism and holism. Methodological individualism guides all the actions, rules and the more or less conscious calculations done by individuals, considered as being the sole reality. Holism on the contrary considers that the action of the individual (or groups) only expresses or brings to reality an *a priori* whole that existed prior to it and which in its turn appears as the only reality.[63]

Sitology, as developed by J. P. Dupuy and H. Zaoual, is a dissident theory against the single and totalitarian market approach.[64] Site economics holds that the market breeds chaos and acts as a destabilizing force. According to J. P. Dupuy, it contains a strong dose of panic. On the other hand, the site acts as an economic and social regulator. Based on reciprocity, it is aimed at strengthening community cohesion. It is obliged to adapt itself continuously to the changes in the environment and to protect itself from development 'missiles'.[65]

Conclusion

This study has highlighted four points. First, the chaotic urban planning of Marrakesh can be understood only from a multi-causal analysis that goes back to the origin of the crisis. The housing shortage in Morocco is primarily a policy problem. Instead of responding to the high demand with adequate actions in the supply of housing, public authorities stuck to a few short-term actions that did not have any real impact, particularly as the solutions proposed did not often meet customers' requirements. The proliferation in recent years of unhygienic and clandestine housing is a clear indication of the failure of the low-cost housing policy.

Second, the housing problem in Morocco is a structural one. It is the outcome of the effects of the underdevelopment of the country. Since there is no development catalyst based on greater labour productivity and better capital returns, the vicious cycle, i.e. poverty–lack of qualifications–unstable jobs–unhygienic housing–poverty, will continue to exist. Even in the area of production, the policy of construction by private individuals is archaic because it does not boost productivity.

Third, the role of the state in the production of housing is also at the root of many problems. Instead of a clear distribution of roles between the public and private sectors, the public sector is playing a predominant role in the formulation of laws, rules and regulations, the development of land, construction of houses, rehabilitation of unhygienic neighbourhoods, etc. The outcome is the confusion of roles, inefficiency in the work carried out, high costs, waste of rare resources, and products that do not meet the requirements of customers.

Finally, in addition to the shortage of land and the absence of an industrialization policy for housing construction, the problem of financing, in recent years, has become even more acute. Instead of looking for solutions that recognize the natural coexistence of the official and 'informal' systems of financing, public authorities are acting as if the latter did not exist. And the entire community ends up being the loser. Housing is a precondition for social harmony. An appropriate solution would require not only technical and bureaucratic input, but also political courage and audacity, as these are the only factors that can mobilize and involve all social categories.

Notes

1 The Tensift is a big river that cuts across the Haouz Plain and passes through Marrakesh. The Haouz is a vast depression running from the east to the west and is found between the Jbiletes in the north and the High Atlas in the south.

2 J. Pegurier (1982) *La médina de Marrakesh entre son passé et son avenir des médias (de Marrakesh à Alep)*, Research paper No. 10, Tours, p. 73, cited by M. Mouradi (1999), *Le phénomène des douars spontanés dans l'agglomération urbaine de Marrakesh*, DES dissertation on 'Aménagement et urbanisme', Rabat: INAU.

3 See *Histoire du Maroc* (1982), Paris: Édition Hâtier, p. 89.

4 G. Deverdun (1966) *Marrakesh, des origines à 1912*, vols 1 and 2, Paris: Édition Technique Nord Africaines. 'Indeed, because of the size of the water table in Marrakesh, a new method of irrigation was adopted: interconnected subterranean water reserves, referred to as Khettaras. Today, with the expansion of urban residential areas to where orchards used to be, many housing units are now found directly on top of Khettaras' (information provided by M. Mouradi – see n. 2 – p. 20).

5 See A. Bellaoui (1994) 'Marrakesh: des villes dans la ville', in *Revue Atlas Marrakesh*, No. 2.

6 Diego de Torrès (1988) *Histoire des Chérifs des Royaumes du Maroc, de Fès à Tarudant et autres provinces,* trans. M. Hajji and M. Lakhdar, Casablanca, cited by Deverdun (see n. 4) and by Bellaoui (see n. 5).

7 Lyautey's ideas were implemented by a great town planner, H. Prost, who attempted to apply some of the principles advocated. These included: setting up new towns near traditional ones; separating the two towns with empty spaces; maintaining the traditional and original aspect of the traditional urban structure.

8 See A. Rachik (1995) *Villes et pouvoirs au Maroc*, Casablanca: Edition Afrique-Orient, p. 27.

9 Paradoxically, it was the factories set up to process agricultural produce from the hinterlands that attracted rural labour and led to the massive exodus of the rural population to Marrakesh, resulting in the rapid expansion of slum areas.

10 Recent estimates show that informal labour accounts for more than 60 per cent of the total workforce. This percentage of informal labour is much higher for the more underprivileged category of workers ($\approx$ 90 per cent for children). For more information, consult *Diagnostic de la pauvreté urbaine à Marrakesh* (1998), UNDP/Ministry of Social Development, Solidarity, Employment and Vocational Training, March–August, p. 10.

11 See M. Gheris (1999) 'Espaces de la pauvreté et régulation étatique', Paper presented during the international colloquium in Perpignan, France, 20–22 October.

12 The kingdom was formerly divided into seven administrative regions.

13 A comparison of the distribution, in percentages, of households in the new administrative units (sixteen regions) shows that Marrakesh-Tensift-El Haouz has 10.8 per cent of the total number of households, coming after Casablanca (12.7 per cent). In terms of urban households, out of a total of 2,519,685 households in the Marrakesh-Tensift-El Haouz region, 177,753 households, i.e., 7.05 per cent, are urban. In addition, 39.3 per cent of the households in this region, in 1994, were urban households, as against 29.2 per cent in 1982 (source: Department of Statistics).

14 Mekki Bentahar, 'Vie quotidienne en banlieue marocaine', *BESM*, No. 148–9, p. 55.

15 A. Bellaoui (see n. 5) and M. Mouradi (see n. 2).

16 A. Bellaoui (see n. 5).

17 Ibid.

18 The master plan (*schéma directeur d'aménagement et d'urbanisme*) for the urban development of Marrakesh, SDAU, distinguishes between three generations of unplanned *douars*: the oldest of them, except the Sidi Youssef Ben Ali (SYBA) (in the 1920s) neighbourhoods, surround the new town; the second set is found along the industrial zone and in the periphery of the colonial section to the west of the new town (in the 1940s); the most recent generation is found along and beyond Issil to the west and in the *medina* (after independence).

The SYBA is a clear illustration. In 1955, this *douar* had 2,821 uncompleted houses and 1,768 completed ones, occupied by 2,013 households, representing almost 10,000 persons. In 1994, its population was estimated at 120,000 people. Some ten years ago, this neighbourhood was raised to a *préfecture*, rehabilitated and improved. For further historical information on this neighbourhood, see M. De Leenhee (1970) *L'habitat précaire à Marrakesh et dans la zone périphérique*, Rabat: RGM No. 17.

19 See M. Mouradi (n. 2), p. 85. The author points out that from 1982 to 1998 the population of the *douars* was multiplied by 3.6 per cent, going up from 42,000 to 150,000 inhabitants, an 8 per cent annual growth rate.

20 See M. Gheris (1998) 'Etat, marché et financement du logement au

Maroc: contradiction des interventions publiques', Paper presented during the colloquium 'Europe – Mediterranean, Towards What Kind of Development?', Third World Association, CRERI, University of Toulon, 27–29 May.

21 M. Naciri (1982) 'Les politiques urbaines au Maghreb et au Machrek', IRMC and ERA 1036 / VA / 913, round table conference of CNRS, University of Lyon.

22 Ibid.

23 M. Bentahar, (n. 14) p. 52.

24 'Fonctions des villes urbaines', *BESM*, No. 122, quoted in ibid., p. 53.

25 M. Pinseau (1991) 'SDAU de Marrakesh', report for the Ministry of the Interior, p. 20.

26 Ibid., p. 35.

27 These figures are only rough estimates because it is very difficult to know the exact number of houses constructed. In this respect, see a very interesting study, which critically examined and evaluated the collection and processing of data on building permits. The study first of all carried out a careful census of the building permits granted in 1994 and subsequently tried to verify if the number of these permits, as indicated in the registers of the urban councils, matched the reality on the ground. This was done using a sample of selected building sites. See 'Etude relative à la détermination des flux de production de logements et l'évaluation du système de collecte des données des autorisations de construire' (1996), 2 vols, Ministry of Housing, Department of Real Estate Development, July.

28 Faced with this shortage, the population reacted in various ways: unauthorized construction of houses, increased cohabitation among families, increase in the number of persons per household.

29 Because of the nature of its financing, and the strict conditions dictated by CIH, those who could afford houses under the 200,000 Houses Programme were mainly from the private sector affiliated to the CNSS and employees of local administrative bodies and public administrative services.

30 Buyers had to pay a first instalment of at least 30,000 Dhs to the body selling the houses. We shall see later on that many prospective home buyers could not meet these conditions and for this reason many of them gave up.

31 See M. Gheris (1999) 'Financement du logement et titrisation hypothécaire au Maroc', Paper presented during the UNIMED–FORUM seminar on 'Politics and Economic Cooperation', 29 November–3 December, Aix en Provence, France.

32 See '*La Vie économique*', Friday 17 December 1999, which states that 'many of the unsold houses in some ERACs were constructed under the 200,000 Houses Programme. In other words, it is very difficult to find buyers, even when the houses are inexpensive (not more than 200,000 Dhs)', p. 17.

33 See the study entitled 'Etude relative aux aspects financiers et fiscaux', Groupe Algoe – Promoconsult, requested by the Ministry of Housing, 1997.

34 See the section dealing with the financing of housing in Morocco.

35 State-controlled bodies are now facing serious financial difficulties.

Because of the large amounts of money they owe the CIH, practically all of them are unable to repay the loans they get from the CIH; consequently, the latter has decided to suspend further pre-financing for these bodies until these loans are repaid.

36 Low-cost housing is also financed by the BCP which, like the CIH, received government authorization in 1998 to finance housing. Commercial banks are also allowed to finance low-cost housing, but they have not shown much interest in this activity.

37 This figure is the same for the years prior to 1998. From that year, and faced with the drop in the activities of the CIH, this percentage dropped substantially. It should be pointed out that many banks (Wafabank and BCM notably) are becoming more and more interested in financing real estate development even though they are interested only in luxury real estate.

38 For instance, the CIH had the monopoly to finance Operation 200,000 Houses.

39 A comparative study of Moroccan banks shows that the net financial products of the CIH were far higher than those of the other banks (mid-1990s).

40 ERAC-Tensift, the French acronym for the regional body responsible for the development and construction of the Tensift region (Établissement régional d'Aménagement et de Construction de la région de Tensift), was set up by Dahir No. 172–438 of 21 May 1974. This state-owned and financially autonomous body is under the supervisory authority of the Ministry of Housing. Its activities include the development and sale of plots and the construction of villas and flats houses, either owned by them or commissioned by others.

41 Almost three-quarters of the work by ERAC-Tensift was done in Marrakesh. For the latest figures, see the progress report of the ERAC of 1998, pp. 7, 26 and 32. The number of units under construction since January 1999 can be broken down as follows: 1,182 houses, 8,122 plots, 374 commercial structures and 2,265 units under rehabilitation.

42 A breakdown of products by ERAC-Tensift shows a predominance of plots for private houses (58 per cent), individual houses (13 per cent) and apartments (11 per cent).

43 See La Vie économique of 17 December 1999, p. 17. Other works not falling directly under the responsibility of ERAC–Tensift, but which it carried, include the extending of the national highway from Marrakesh to Agadir over a distance of 2.7km, and the corresponding drainage work, in addition to other works for a total sum of 11.3 million dirhams.

44 See activity report of ERAC-Tensift, p. 11.

45 This figure of 60,000 houses mostly stands for plots that will be developed and sold, further boosting the private construction sector.

46 From discussions we held with town planning officials in Marrakesh and with senior staff of the Agence Urbaine de Marrakesh, we learnt that many waivers were granted to ERAC-Tensift, permitting it to go beyond densities and heights authorized by the town planning document of the city.

47 Moreover, ERAC-Tensift recognizes that 'the urgent nature of the programme and the hasty studies and start of the programme had a negative impact on the progress of the construction work and on the implementation timetable'; see round table discussion on the low-cost housing programme in HAM, evaluation of work done by ERAC-Tensift, 2 July 1999. It should be noted that because of the urgent nature of the programme, there was a lot of precipitation and no synchronization with the other ministries.

48 These were improved semi-finished houses.

49 This study will not dwell directly on the pre-financing problems faced by the bodies implementing the 200,000 Houses Programme. We shall focus more on post-financing problems (loans to buyers).

50 Most respondents stated that they resorted to pseudo-mortgage to enable them to build savings.

51 The law on leasing of houses in Morocco is archaic. It discourages investment in this sector. The *laissez-faire* attitude of the administration and the judiciary makes people afraid to let their houses for fear of losing them. This is the reason why most landlords ask for exorbitant guarantees (the payment of rents for several months as advance).

52 Institutional savings, which stood at 70,755 million dirhams in 1997 as against 56,962 in 1995, account for at most 20 per cent of total investments by non-financial agents. Meanwhile, cash advances and short-term investments account for more than 75 per cent of investment by non-financial agents (Reports from the Al Maghrib Bank, 1997).

53 P. Hugon (1996) 'Incertitude, précarité et financement local, le cas des économies africaines', *Revue Tiers Monde*, No. 145, January–March.

54 A. G. Chandarvakar (1998) 'The role of the informal credit markets', in *Support of micro-business in developing countries*, Washington, June.

55 P. Hugon (n. 53), p. 27.

56 Servet observed that: 'in the south as in the north, because of the adverse selection process, an interest rate considered too high can discourage both loans and savings, as this can be an indicator of the existence of high risk. However, if interest rates were to act as vectors of rationality, it would be difficult to understand the existence of so many cases where the interest rate on savings is zero or even negative. In a tontine, the last persons to receive savings often have a negative interest rate on savings, but more than 2/3 of the members of these thrift and savings groups prefer to be among the last beneficiaries so as to be forced by group pressure to save.'

Further on, he concludes: 'in many African societies, the interest rate cannot act as a compensating factor for the lack or insufficiency of guarantees to make them acceptable to banks; loans are granted and savings made, in most cases, only in an environment of interpersonal confidence: the personal relationships of old, a characteristic of contemporary finance in the West, are somewhat replaced by group relations. The most efficient financial practices are therefore those in which confidence is born of close proximity, and where, consequently, the degree of information is high (or of beliefs recognized as such).' J. M. Servet in 'Risque, incertitude et financement de proximité en Afrique', *Revue Tiers-monde*, No. 145, 1996, p. 48.

57 P. Hugon (n. 53), p. 33.

58 Ibid., p. 35.

59 These are the Hay Moulay Ismaïl and Ank Jmel à Salé neighbourhoods.

60 The proprietor of the house runs the risk of not getting back his house even if he wishes to repay the loan taken. The tenant of the house also runs the risk of not getting his money after leaving the house. The legal basis of the practice should also be clarified.

61 The hypotheses are the following: co-ordination of economic operators takes place exclusively through the market and prices, hence optimization; economic operators react to utilitarian and self-interested concerns; economic rationality is unlimited (considerable) because the economic operator has the information and calculations necessary to take the best decisions.

62 See A. Caillé (1996) 'Ni holisme ni individualisme méthodologiques', *Revue du MAUSS*, No. 2, second quarter.

63 A. Caillé (1997) 'Don, association et solidarité', *Revue internationale de l'économie sociale*, No. 265, quoted by Alcoléa (1998).

64 See A. Akkari (1997) 'L'État dans le marché', *Revue Tunisienne d'Economie*, No. 8, Centre de Publication Universitaire, Tunis.

65 H. Zaoual (1996) 'Le paradigme relationnel des organisations économiques africaines', in Collectif (ed.), *Organisations économiques et cultures africaines*, Paris: l'Harmattan.

References

Alcoléa, A. M. (1998) 'Emergence du développement local solidaire et alternatif en France', conference in Toulon, France, 'Europe – Mediterranean – Whither development?', Third World Association, 28–30 May. Unpublished.

Assidon, E. (1994) *Les théories du développement économique*, Paris: La Découverte. Repères.

— (1996) 'L'approfondissement financier: épargne et crédit bancaire', *Revue Tiers Monde*, No. 145, January–March, pp. 153–71.

Bédard, G. and E. Kropp (1991) 'Development Banking, with the Poor, for the Poor, and by the Poor, New Models for Banking', Eschborn, GTZ OE 404.

Bester, H. (1985) 'Screening vs Rationing in Credit Markets with Imperfect Information', *American Economic Review*, Vol. 75, No. 4, pp. 850–5.

Dupuy, C. (1988) 'Les comportements d'épargne dans la société africaine: étude Sénégalaise', in M. Lelart (ed.), *Les tontines , pratiques informelles d'épargne et de crédit dans les pvd*, Paris: UREf, John Libbey.

Eboué, C. (1990) 'Les effets macro-économiques de la répression financière dans les pays en voie de développement', *Economie appliquée*, Vol. 63, No. 4, pp. 93–121.

Favereau, O. (1989) 'Marchés internes, marchés externes', *Revue Economique*, March , pp. 273–328.

Gentil, D. (1996) 'Les avatars du modèle Grameen Bank', *Revue Tiers Monde*, No. 145, January–March, pp. 115–33.

Gentil, D. and Y. Fournier (1993) 'Les paysans peuvent-ils devenir banquiers?', *Epargne et crédit en Afrique*, Paris: SYROS.

Germidis, G., D. Kessler and R. Meghir (1991) *Système financier et développement, quel rôle pour les secteurs financiers formels et informels*, Paris: OCDE.

Gheris, M. (1999) 'Le financement du logement au Maroc: entre stratégies de l'État et contraintes du marché', contribution to the 51st Congress of the International Association of Francophone Economists, Marrakesh, 30 May–6 June. Unpublished.

— (2000) 'Logement au Maroc: entre le contrôle de l'État et la prise en charge de la société civile', speech to the Caddi Ayad University, Marrakesh, 17–20 February. Unpublished.

Giovannini, A. (1985) 'Saving the Real Interest Rate in LDCA', *Journal of Development Economics*, Vol. 18.

Henry, A. (1991) *Tontines et banques au Cameroun. Le principe de la société des amis*, Paris: Karthala.

Hicks, J. (1974) *The Crisis in Keynesian Economics*, Oxford: Blackwell.

Hugon, P. (1990) 'L'impact des politiques d'ajustement sur les circuits financiers informels africains', *Revue Tiers Monde*, No. 122, April–June, pp. 325–49.

— (1995) *L'Afrique des incertitudes*, Paris: PUF, Collectif.

IMF (1994) 'Effects of Macro-Economic Stability on Growth, Savings and Investment in Sub-Saharian Africa: An Empirical Investigation', Washington, DC: International Monetary Fund.

Laville, J. L. (1999) 'L'économie et le tiers – secteur', *Transversales Sciences/ Culture*.

Lelart, M. (ed). (1990) *Les tontines: pratiques informelles d'épargne et de crédit dans les pvd*, Paris: UREF, John Libbey.

McKinnon, R. (1973) *Money and Capital in Economic Development*, Washington, DC: Brookings Institute.

Perkins, D. W. and M. Roemer (1991) 'Reforming Economic Systems in Developing Countries', Harvard Studies in International Development, Cambridge, MA: Harvard University Press.

Picory, C. L. and B. Geffroy (1995) 'Degré d'intégration bancaire des PME: une approche par l'organization industrielle', *Revue économique*, Vol. XXXXVI, March.

Polanyi, K. (1978) *Trades and Markets in the Early Empires*, Glencoe: The Free Press.

Scannavino, A. (1992) 'Actualité de la théorie de l'intermédiation financière', in E. Girardin (ed.), *Finance internationale, l'état actuel de la théorie*, Paris: Economica, pp. 141–84.

Seibel, H. D. (1992) *Self-Help Groups as Financial Intermediaries: A Training Manual for Self-Help Groups, Banks and NGOs*, Saarbrücken and Fort Lauderdale, FL: Breibenbach Publishers.

Seibel, H. D. and M. T. Marx (1986) 'Mobilisation de l'épargne des ménages par les sociétés coopératives ou les associations autochtones d'épargne et de crédit: étude de cas au Nigeria', in United Nations (ed.), *Saving for Development / l'épargne pour le développement*, New York: UN (ST/ESA/171), pp. 231–48.

Sellami, K. (1994) 'Essai sur les fondements et les mesures du rationnement du crédit. Application économétrique au cas de la Tunisie', Doctoral thesis, Nice.

Servet, J. M. (1990) 'Les tontines, formes d'activité informelles et d'initiatives collectives en Afrique', in M. Lelart (ed.), *Les Tontines: pratiques informelles d'épargne et de crédit dans les pvd*, Paris: UREF, John Libbey.

— (1996) 'Risque, incertitude et financement de proximité en Afrique: une approche socio-economique', *Revue Tiers Monde*, Vol. 37, No. 145, January–March.

Stiglitz, J. E. and A. Weiss (1981) 'Credit Rationing in Markets with Imperfect Information', *American Economic Review*, Vol. 71, No. 3, pp. 393–410.

United Nations (1986) *Saving for Development / l'épargne pour le développement*, New York: UN (ST/ESA/171).

Von Pischke, J. D. (1991) *Finance at the Frontier, Debt Capacity and the Role of Credit in the Private Economy*, Washington, DC: Economic Development Institute, Development Studies, World Bank.

Williamson, O. (1985) *The Economic Institution of Capitalism*, New York: Free Press.

Zaoual, H. (1996) 'Le paradigme relationnel des organisations économiques africaines', in *Organisations économiques et cultures africaines,* Paris: l'Harmattan, pp. 37–45.

Contributors

Mohamadou Abdoul is a historian from Mauritania who works for the Prospectives Dialogues Politiques team of the international NGO Environmental Development Action in the Third World, based in Dakar. His research concerns issues of urbanism, regional integration and transfrontier economies, in conjunction with the OECD, Club du Sahel and ECOWAS.

Abdelghani Abouhani teaches urbanism and political science in Rabat at the University Mohamed V. He has long been involved in several important research networks for the Council for the Development of Social Science Research in Africa, and was a member of the organization's executive committee from 1995 to 2003. Key publications include: *Pouvoirs villes et notabilités urbaines au Maroc: quand les notables font les villes* (2000); *Enjeux et acteurs de la gestion urbaine: redistribution des pouvoirs dans les villes marocaines* (2002); and *Pouvoirs locaux et municipalités dans le monde arabe* (2004).

Dr Victor A. O. Adetula holds a teaching and research position at the University of Jos, Nigeria, where he is presently Associate Professor of Political Science. He has previously served as the Director of the Centre for Development Studies, University of Jos (1998–2001), and also as Senior Program Manager (2001–03) in the Democracy and Governance Office of the United States Agency for International Development (USAID), Abuja, Nigeria. Dr Adetula has researched and published articles/book chapters/ monographs on broad issues of development in Nigeria, West Africa/Africa and Europe. His most recent publication is a co-edited book entitled *Border Crime and Community Insecurity in Nigeria* (2002).

Bénédicte Florin is Maître de conférences de Géographie at the University François Rabelais, Tours. She co-ordinates research workshops on 'Fabriques et pratiques de l'urbain' for the EMAM laboratory and is a member of the network Urbanité et vies citadines (University Aix-Marseille and University Paris X-Nanterre), as well as co-ordinator of the research programme 'Analyse des discours sur les cités d'habitat social. Une comparaison Maghreb-France' (CESHS, Rabat and EHESS, Paris). She has contributed to *Regards Sociologiques* and written *Naqd, Revue d'études et de critique sociale* (2002) and *La réforme et ses usages, Hesperis-Tamuda* (2002).

Mohamed Gheris teaches economy at the Quaddi Ayyad University in Marrakesh. He specializes in the economics of housing and its relation with informal and decentralized financial systems. He is finishing his doctorate on the financing of housing in countries in the Maghreb.

Anna Madoeuf is a Maître de conférences in the Geography Department at the University François Rabelais, Tours. She is also a researcher at EMAM and UMR-CITERES, Tours. Recent publications include contributions to *De l'espace domestique à l'espace privé et de l'espace communautaire à l'espace public* (2005) and *Regards croisés sur le patrimoine dans le monde à l'aube du XXIe siècle* (2003).

Jean Omasombo is a senior researcher at the Africa Institute (CEDAF) in Brussels, as well as a Professor of Political Science at the University of Kinshasa, where he directs the Centre for Political Studies. Key publications include: *Patrice Lumumba, jeunesse et apprentissage politique* (1998) and *République démocratique du Congo: Chronique politique d'un pays en guerre et des trente derniers mois de Laurent Désiré Kabila* (2001).

Edgar Pieterse is Director of the Isandla Institute, an urban development policy NGO based in Cape Town. He is co-editor of: *Democratizing Local Government – the South African Experiment* (2002) and *Voices of the Transition: The Politics, Poetics and Practices of Social Change in South Africa* (2004). He is also a Visiting Lecturer in Urban Studies at the University of Cape Town and the University of Stellenbosch. His current research is focused on urban social movements, the politics of urban integration and insurgent policy responses to differential urbanization.

AbdouMaliq Simone is an urbanist who presently holds joint academic appointments at the Graduate Programme in International Affairs, New School University and the Institute of Social and Economic Research, University of Witwatersrand. He has taught at the University of Khartoum, University of Ghana, University of the Western Cape and the City University of New York, as well as working for several African NGOs and regional institutions, including the Council for the Development of Social Science Research in Africa, the United Nations Economic Commission for Africa, and the United Nations Centre for Human Settlements. Key publications include *In Whose Image?: Political Islam and Urban Practices in Sudan* (1994) and *For the City Yet to Come: Changing Urban Life in Four African Cities* (2004).

Mohammed-Bello Yunusa is head of the Department of Urban and Regional Planning and deputy dean of the Faculty of Environmental Design, Ahmadu

Bello University, Samaru-Zaria, Nigeria. He has conducted numerous studies on non-governmental organizations, rural and urban livelihood strategies, poverty and infrastructure, and published in a number of books and journals in those areas of research.

Bahru Zewde is a Professor of History at Addis Ababa University, author of *A History of Modern Ethiopia 1855–1991* and *Pioneers of Change in Ethiopia: The Reformist Intellectuals of the Early Twentieth Century.* He is also Resident Vice-President of the Organization of Social Science Research in East Africa, and Chairman of the Board of Advisers of the Forum for Social Studies.

Index

Abercrombie, Patrick, 135
Abou Bakr Ibn Omar, 264
Abû Zayd, 79
accountability, 15, 156
Addis Ababa, 13–14; issuing of land
  charters, 126; Italian occupation
  of, 128–30; renamed Shawa, 128;
  shifting city centre of, 120–37
Afizere Cultural and Community
  Development Association
  (Nigeria), 211
Afizere Youth Movement (Nigeria),
  226
Africa, urban projects in, 2–4
African Centre for Democratic
  Governance, 210
African National Congress (ANC),
  146–7, 150, 159; democratic
  constitution of, 147
Agence National de Lutte Contre
  l'Habitat Insalubre (ANHI)
  (Morocco), 263
agency, 154, 161
AIDS see HIV/AIDS
air transport and airports, role in
  shaping settlements, 121, 130–1
'Aîsha, Sayyida, 80, 89
Akawu, Baba, 227
Ake, Claude, 208
Alcoléa, A.M., 285
Ali Ben Youssef, 264
Alî Pasha Mubarak, 69, 76
Amado, George, 68
Al-Amal town, 32
Amin, Ash, 141, 164
amusement parks, creation of, 46
Anguwar Mai Gwado (Nigeria),
  177–205
anti-poverty programmes, 154
Anti-Privatization Forum (South
  Africa), 153
apartheid, unmaking of, 159
Appadurai, Arjun, 155
Arada market, Addis Ababa, 129–30
architectural forms, symbolic values
  of, 42
Ariès, Philippe, 71

associations: local, 17–18, 19; urban,
  250–5 see also ethnic associations
Aswan Dam, building of, 33
Atteya, K., 38
autonomous agency, 148

Bachelard, Gaston, 70
al-Badawî, Sayyid, 70, 72, 86; moulid
  of, 84
Al-Badir town, 32
Baka-zuwa-Jere, Alhaji Garba, 227
Balibar, Étienne, 14
de Balzac, Honoré, 91
bank, universal, concept of, 262
banking laws, 262
al-Bannâ, Hassan, 84
Bayat, Asef, 161
Beall, Jo, 158
Beckman, Björn, 207
Bedoui, Najab Laraichi, 263
Bellaoui, A., 267
Berom Educational and Cultural
  Organization (BECO) (Nigeria),
  211, 214, 215–26, 226, 230
Berom Historical Publications (BHP),
  223
Berom Progressive Union (Nigeria),
  214–16
Berom Women's Association
  (Nigeria), 220–2
Berque, Jacques, 69, 71
Bichi Urban Development Plan
  (Nigeria), 178
bicycle, as transportation, 109, 111–16
Biegman, Nicolaas, 69, 87
Borja, Jorge, and Manuel Castells,
  Local and Global, 148–9
Braeckman, Colette, 97, 100, 107
Bralima company (Kisangani), 104
Brazilianization of suburbs, 139
building activity, irregular, 22
building codes in cities, 177–8
Bûlaq, moulids of, 87
burial arrangements in communities,
  221

cadastral, control of, 22

Cairo: 1956 Master Plan, 31–2;
1970 Master Plan, 32–3; 1981
Master Plan, 33–4, 48; feasts
and festivals in, 68–95; October
1992 earthquake, 34, 35, 52, 60;
public celebrations in, 8–9, 68–95;
satellite cities of, 6–7; urban
policies in, 29–67
Caisse de Dépôt et de Gestion (CDG)
(Morocco), 263
Cape Town, 158, 163; remaking of,
159
cars: as transportation, 113;
ownership of, 191
Case Incis, Addis Ababa, 130
Castelli restaurant, Addis Ababa, 129
Castells, Manuel, 148
de Certeau, Michel, 235
Chih, Rachida, 69
children, sexual predation on, 139
Christianity, 11, 214, 218, 223
Al-Churuq town, 50
cinemas, 46
citizen juries, 146
citizenship, 7, 44; social, expanding
of, 155
city: as laboratory of change, 1;
dynamism of, 23–4; identity of,
158
city centre: as shifting concept,
120–37; dispersal of, 13–14
city development strategy (CDS)
(South Africa), 147, 149
city politics, in Nigeria, 206–34
civil society, 16, 150, 203
Cleaver, Frances, 143
co-operation in cities, 140
co-operatives, 31–2, 34
Cohen, Abner, 208
cohesive local communities, passing
of, 17
community, concept of, 143
community forums, establishment
of, 155
community gardens, 155
community management, 146
community militancy, 140
community organizations, 144
competitive city, imperative of, 158
complexity in environment, 16
Congo, Democratic Republic of, 96,
97
Conrad, Joseph, *Heart of Darkness*, 96

consensus in cities, 140
Coquery-Vidrovitch, Catherine, 238
cosmopolis, 143
cosmopolitan cities, 10–13
Council for the Development of
Social Science Research in Africa
(CODESRIA), 210
Country Women's Association of
Nigeria (COWAN), 230
credit: access to, 220, 251, 252;
controls abolished in Morocco,
262
Crédit Immobilier et Hôtelier (CIH)
(Morocco), 262–3, 271, 272, 274,
279, 281
credit institutions, in Nigeria, 194
crisis, as area of contestation, 143
Crummey, Donald, 121
cultural resignification, 160
culture, meaning of, 158

Dakar, 238, 242
Dar es Salaam, 2
decentralization, 22
deforestation, 125
democracy, 6, 17, 139, 141, 143, 146,
147, 156, 160, 162–5; local, 149
demographic growth, 261
desert: fear of, 39, 59; settlements
in, 33
desert rush in Egypt, 30, 39
development: alternative ways of,
156; control of, 183; politics of,
144
dhikr, 79, 82, 83, 84
diamonds, in Kisangani, 105–9
Diouf, Mamadou, 243
Dire Dawa, 120
direct action, 151–4
discourse, operations of, 158, 162
displaced persons, 229
Dix de Ramadan, 32, 38, 43, 46, 51
Dokotri, Patrick, 214, 215
domestic work: of women, 197–8,
203; survey of, 181
dominant discourse, deconstruction
of, 160
dormitory towns, around Cairo, 51–2
drainage, 32, 183, 184, 192, 193, 195,
202, 236
Dupuy, J.P., 286
Durban, 158
dynamism of the city, 23–4

Index

East India Company (EIC), 99
Economic Interest Groups (GIE)
    (Senegal), 252–4
education, 18, 47, 186–7, 199–200;
    school attendance, 161
Egbe Omo Oduduwa group, 210
Ekeh, Peter, 208, 209, 210
electricity, supply of, 18, 32, 46,
    184, 192, 201, 202, 236, 241, 271;
    tapping of, 161
Eliade, Mircea, 77, 88
employment, hard to access, 3
entrepôt nature of cities, 10
equality: in politics, 14; relation to
    liberty, 163
ERAC-Tensift, 266, 273–6, 278, 281
Eritrea, 128
Ethiopia, revolution in, 132
Ethiopian Airlines, 131
Ethiopian People's Revolutionary
    Party (EPRP), 133
ethnic associations, 206–34 passim
ethnic riots, 164
ethnicity, 11; in Nigeria, 206–34
eucalyptus trees, in Ethiopia, 125, 136

Fahmy, N., 38, 41–2
family: extended, 209; support
    systems, 3
Fanon, Frantz, 153
feasts and festivals, 8–9, 89–91, 252;
    in Cairo, 68–95; in Egyptian life,
    75; in Nigeria, 223; Nzem Berom
    (Nigeria), 222
Federation of Muslim Women's
    Associations in Nigeria
    (FOMWAN), 220
Fez, 265
financial systems in developing
    countries, 262
fire, disasters, 179
fishing, 252, 253, 254; traditional, 251
flooding, 179, 244, 245
Foucault, Michel, 138, 142, 144, 158
Freire, Paulo, 153

Gamâliyya neighbourhood, 77
Gambella, 120
Gandhi, Mahatma, 153
gangs, 139
gated communities, 30
gender: and domestic work, 197–8;
    issues of urban living, 181

general intellect, 9
ghorba, 39, 44
globalization, impact on cities, 148
gold courses, 50
Golf Village (Cairo), 45
Gondar, 121–2
governance: concept of, 142; urban,
    15
government, concept of, 142
governmentality, concept of, 142
grassroots development practice,
    154–7
grassroots organizing, 150
green belts, 48
green spaces, 54
Growth, Employment and
    Redistribution (GEAR) (South
    Africa), 151–2
Guinaw Rail neighbourhood
    (Senegal), 242–3
Gunder, Michael, 150
Gurage people, 130
Gwom, Sen Luka, 214, 222

Habitat (UN), 146, 149
Haile Selassie, Emperor, 122–3, 131;
    coronation of, 127; Silver Jubilee
    of, 132
Hanna, Milad, 42
Haqqi, Yehia, 69
Hârat al-Sukkariyya, 72
Haruna, Alhaji Isa, 227
Hausa-Fulani people, 210–34 passim
Haut Comité de Planification du
    Grand Caire, 32
health care, 242
Helena, Saint, 124
high-density urban area, definition
    of, 177–9
Hillier, Jean, 150
HIV/AIDS, 2, 140
Holston, James, 165
Homeless People's Federation (South
    Africa), 156
household spending, 190
housing, 9, 180; complexity of issues,
    20–3; in Marrakesh, 261–94; in
    Nigeria, 182–3 (types of, 191–3);
    middle-class, 31–2; private, 42,
    48–52, 53; relation to urban
    policies, 29; rights of citizens,
    187; shortages of, 262, 269–70;
    working-class, 31, 34–5

Hugon, P., 282
human rights, 141, 146, 152
Husayn, grandson of the Prophet,
    68; mosque of, 74, 83, 86, 88, 89;
    moulid of, 71, 72, 73, 86, 87; tomb
    of, 76
Hussein, Taha, 69

Ibo State Union, 210
Ibrâhîm Al-Disuqî, 70
identities: concretization of, 15–16;
    making of, 12
Idris, Youssef, 78
Igbo Cultural Association (ICA)
    (Nigeria), 211, 218–19, 225
Igbo people, 210–34 *passim*
illegal occupation of property and
    land, 49
imports into Africa, effects on local
    production, 4
Independent Development Trust
    (South Africa), 156
inequality in urban areas, 138
Infitah, 31, 33, 35
informal sector, 103, 161, 251
informality, 4, 7; concept of, 235–60
infrastructure, investment in, 159
integrated development plans (IDPs)
    (South Africa), 138, 147, 148, 152,
    159; forums, 146
interstitial spaces, use of, 56
Inuwa, Alhaji, 227
Iskân al-Mustaqbal, 34
Islam, 11, 21, 186, 242; and seclusion
    of women, 198, 219–20; in Nigeria,
    219–20 (festivals, 223–4)
Islamic culture, 68–95 *passim*
Israel, war with Arab countries, 32
ivory, trading of, 99, 105
Izala groups (Nigeria), 223–4

Jama'atu Nasri Islam (JNI) (Nigeria),
    223–4
Jassawa Development Association
    (Nigeria), 211, 214, 217–18, 224,
    226, 227, 228, 230
Jewsiewicki, B., 99, 100
Johannesburg, 139, 158; *Joburg 2030*
    report, 139, 149
Johnson, Martin, 126
Jos (Nigeria), 17; 'Cultural Day', 223;
    history of, 212–14
Jos Metropolitan Development Board
    (JMDB), 213

K.N., a university lecturer, 112–15
Kabila, Laurent, 100–1, 105, 107
Kaduna State Planning and
    Development Authority
    (KASUPDA) (Nigeria), 185
al-Kafrawi, Hassab Allah, 37
Khalwatiyya Hasâniyya fraternity, 83
Kisangani, 96–119; collapsing
    infrastructure of, 102–5; ruination
    of, 10–13
Kombe, W.J., 250
Kreibich, V., 250

Lagahar, Addis Ababa, 135
land: collective ownership of, 20;
    complexity of issues, 20–3;
    informalized disposition of, 22;
    nationalization of, 13, 21, 133;
    nature of transactions in, 22;
    opacity of sub-markets, 21; sale
    of, 244; state-owned, sale of, 271;
    urban, value of, 243; *wakf* status
    of, 21
land charters, in Addis Ababa, 126
land rights, 241–2
Lane, Edward, 69, 89
Lebou group (Senegal), 245–6, 252
Leopold II, 96
Les Logements de l'Avenir see Iskân
    al-Mustqbal
liberalization, 4, 33, 35, 262
Lippens, Sergeant, 98
literacy, 18
local authorities, traditional, 245–50
locality, preoccupation with, 6
Long, Norman, 141
Luizard, Pierre-Jean, 69, 87
Lumumba, Patrice, 116
Lyautey, L.-H.-G., 265–6

MacPherson, J.-W., 69, 76, 86, 87
Maffesoli, Michel, 68
Mahfouz, Naguib, 69, 80
Mai Gwado Youth Development
    Association (Nigeria), 192
Manal, a Six Octobre resident, 44
Mangvwat, Monday, 215
Maputo, 2
Marcos, Commandante, 153
marginalization, 13
market gardening, urban, in Senegal,
    242–5, 251
markets, creation of, 55

Marrakesh, 23; housing in, 261–94;
Medina of, 265, 267; splitting of
the city, 265–6
marriage, 194
Marxism, social theory of, 153
Masâkin al-Zilzâl, 47, 52–6
Mato, Mallam Aminu, 225, 227–8
de Maximy, René, 236
Mayeur-Jaouen, Catherine, 69, 72, 86
Mbembe, Achille, 246
Mbole, a *toleka* rider, 115–16
Mbow, Lat Soucabe, 250
memorialization, as reconstruction
of the past, 164
Menilek II, 122, 123, 124, 125
Mercato, market of Addis Ababa
(later Arada), 129–30, 135
methodology of urban study, 180–3
middle classes, 152; housing for,
31–2, 35
migration, 180, 182, 189, 191, 203,
212, 261; in Nigeria, 216–19; to
cities, 11, 20, 33, 43, 268
mobility of urban dwellers, 24
mobilization, social and political,
211, 224
Mobutu, Sese Seko, 101, 103, 106,
107, 113
Morocco, housing in, 261–94
mortgages: market established in
Morocco, 271; pseudo-mortgages,
279–80, 283
Mouffe, Chantal, 163
moulids of Cairo, 68–95; as nocturnal
festival, 78; as inconspicuous
objects, 68–73; Christian and
Jewish, 70; containment of, 86;
criticism of, 85; importance to
fraternities, 84; of the Prophet,
89 *see also* al-Badawî, Husayn,
al-Nabî, Nafisa, al-Rifâ'î, Sakîna
and Zaynab
Mozambique, 2
Mubarak, Hosni, 34
Mubarak Project (Egypt), 34
Muhammad, Mukhtar, 227, 228
multiculturalism, 163
multiple intensities of cities, 9
Mumbai, 155

al-Nabî, *moulid* of, 86
Nadim, Nawal al-Messiri, 72
Nafîsa, *moulid* of, 86

Naipaul, V.S., *At the Bend of the River*,
96, 98
naira, devaluation of, 187
narcotics, use of, 43
Nasserite urban policy in Egypt, 31–2
National Council of Nigeria Citizens
(NCNC), 210
National Council of Women's
Societies (NCWS) (Nigeria), 230
nationalization of land *see* land,
nationalization of
Navez-Bouchanine, F., 284
N'Dahiro, Major, 101
necropolis, Cairo, 76
neighbourhood watch, 155
neo-corporatism, 144, 148–51, 157
neo-liberalism, 251
de Nerval, Gérard, 69
networks, social, 285
new towns: cultural values of,
43; design of, 36; in Cairo,
development of, 30–52; myth of,
35–52; security in, 46
Nigeria: ethnic politics in, 206–34;
urban living in, 177–205
Nigeria People's Congress (NPC), 215
Nigerian Town and Country Planning
Ordinance (1946), 185
noise pollution, 45
non-governmental organizations
(NGOs), 19, 152, 251
Northern Nigerian Non-Muslim
League, 214
Nzem Berom festival, Nigeria, 222

Okri, Ben, 165
Omnium Technique de l'Urbanisme
et de l'Infrastructure (Cairo), 33
opacity of urban life, 3
Operation 200,000 Houses,
Marrakesh, 261–94
ordinary, encroachment of, 161
Osaghae, Eghosa, 206

parks, creation of, 54–5
participation, 6, 146, 149, 152, 156;
experiential importance of, 155
participatory action research, 146
passing of time, 17
payment for services, 19
Pencum Demba group (Senegal), 252
Pencum Senegal group (Senegal),
252, 254

People's Democratic Party (Nigeria), 226
petty trade economy, 110–11
piazza, concept of, 128–30
Pikine, Senegal, urban development in, 235–60
planning discourse 'from above', 29
Plotnicov, Leonard, 212
Polanyi, K., 285
political contestation, development of, 143
political formations, and local economies, 18–20
political sphere, 162–5
politics: representative, 145–8; symbolic, 157–62; urban, towards conceptualization of, 144–65
pollution, 45
polycentrism of cities, 134, 135
Pons, Valdo, 10
poor people: coping strategies of, 177, 179, 180; exclusion of, 37; resources of, 109–16; support systems of, 203
population, growth of, 20, 32, 48
poverty, 179, 195, 235, 266; cycle of, 286
Poverty Alleviation Fund (South Africa), 156
privacy, sacrosanct, 57
private estates, 30, 37 see also housing, private
privatization, 35, 151; resistance to, 139
public: concept of, 5; provisional, 6
public spaces, 54–5; struggle for, 208
public sphere, 162–5

qabale associations, 133–4
Qassem, Abdel Hakim, 69
Qattamiya settlement, Cairo, 34, 50
Quinze Mai town, 32, 33, 37, 38
Qur'an, 75, 82

racism, 164; structural, 163
railway, Djibouti-Addis Ababa, 126
railways, role of, in shaping settlements, 121, 130
Ras Makonnen, 127
regional economies, decline of, 148
regionalization, 248
relational model of urban politics, 138–73

religious associations, 193, 194
rent subsidies, 32
resettlement of slum communities, 22
resource-poor population, 49
retribalization, 208, 231
al-Rifâ'î, Ahmad: moulid of, 86; mosque of, 89
Rimi, Alhaji Abubarkar, 217
roads, 9; 26 July highway (Cairo), 45, 47; building of, 236, 241
Roncayolo, Marcel, 70
Ruqayya, Sayyida, 76

Sa'adî, Sheikh Yûnis, 77
Al-Sâdât town, 32
sacred places, perenniality of, 88
al-Sadat, Anwar, 31
Sakîna, moulid of, 86
Santhiaba (Senegal), 18–20, 238–60 passim
savings and loan associations, 251, 252; in South Africa, 155
Scott, James, 154, 161
Senegal, urban development in, 235–60
Serageldin, M., 38
Serres, M., 8
service charges, boycotts of, 150
sewage see drainage
Al Shakaa, Mustapha, 69
sitology, 286
Six Octobre town, 32, 33, 37, 44, 45, 47, 51; seen as ghost town, 39
Size and Scope of the Non-Profit Sector in South Africa study, 155
slum clearance, 22
slum dwellers' associations, 155
slums, history of, 179
Société générale pour le logement préfabriqué (Cairo), 50
Société Textile de Kisangani, 103–4
social mobilization, 153
social viscosity, 68
solidarity: economics of, 284–6; social, reformulation of, 7
solidarity economy, 23
Sorgerie factory (Kisangani), 104
Sourour, Fathi, 85
South Africa, 2; cities on political agenda of, 138–7; Constitution of, 154
South African Constitution Act (1996), 145

Index

South African National Civic Association, 139
space pathology, 59
spatiality, as means of understanding city, 142–3
spatialization of operational memory, 12
spontaneous neighbourhoods, 30
squatter settlements, 49, 182, 183
stakeholder forums, 148–51, 157; criticism of, 149, 150
Stanley, H. M., 98, 99
Stanley Falls, 99, 101
Stanleyville, renamed Kisangani, 101
state: disengagement of, 250; regulation by, 237; role of, 264 (in city planning, 41; in housing provision and regulation, 34–5, 270, 272–3, 286–7)
Steinbeck, John, *Tortilla Flats*, 90
structural adjustment programmes, 187, 208
Sufi Council (Egypt), 84
Sufi fraternities, 79; numbers of, 74
Sufism, 68, 70
surveillance, social, 7

Tajbakhsh, Kian, 143
Tanzania, 2
Taytu, Empress, 122
territorialization of occupations, 11
Thiaroye-sur-mer (Senegal), 238–60 *passim*
Thrift, Nigel, 141
time: passing of, 17; sacred, 88
Tippo-Tip, 99
Tiv Women's Association (TWA) (Nigeria), 211, 220–1
Tocaia Grande, 68
Todes, Alison, 158
toleka taxis, 111–16
tontines, 251, 252, 279, 283, 284
town, concept of, 68
trade unions, 44, 144, 193, 194, 207; resistance to restructuring, 138
traditional modes of sociality, 1
transgression: acts of, need for, 163, 165; concept of, 138
transportation, 29; infrastructures, 45
Treatment Action Campaign (TAC) (South Africa), 153
Tuhâmi, Sheikh Yasîn, 89

Al-Ubûr town, 32, 33
Umaru, Alhaji Ibrahim, 216
Umm Kulthum, 89
UN Environmental Programme (UNEP), 149
UN International Children's Fund (UNICEF), 178
United Middle Belt Congress (UMBC) (Nigeria), 215, 230
urban change, dynamics of, 235–60
urban development, in Senegal, 235–60
urban living, high-density, in Nigeria, 177–205
urban politics: conceptualization of, 140–4; new, 14–17; relational model of, 138–73
urban public life, 4, 5–17
urban social practices, 4, 17–23
urbanity, new models of, 57–8
urbanization, 2, 11, 13, 20, 189, 195, 237, 240, 241; absence of, 2; definition of, 238; normative, 4; of villages, 203; uncontrolled, 178–9, 235
Uways, Sayyid, 69

Verhaegen, Guy, 108, 110
violence: cycles of, 18; in cities, 140
voice, expanding of, 155

water, supply of, 18, 32, 46, 183–4, 192, 201, 202, 236, 241, 251, 271
White Paper on Local Government (South Africa), 138, 146
wild zones, 30, 46
Williamson, O., 284
women: domestic work of, 190, 203; in community associations, 251; of the hâra, 72–3; organizations of, 20, 193–4, 230, 252; seclusion of, 57, 198, 219–20
women's organizations, 20, 230, 252; in Nigeria, 219–22
working classes, 36 *see also* housing, working-class
World Bank, 149, 242; report on housing in Morocco, 263
'world-class' imperative, 139, 158

Yacoub Al Mansour, 265
Yoruba Community, 211
Yoruba people, 210–34 *passim*

young couples, housing for, 34–5
youth organizations, 20
Yussuf, S., 43

Zambia, 2
Zangs, D.B., 227

Zaoual, H., 286
Zaria Master Plan (Nigeria), 182
Zaynab, Sayyida, 76, 77; mosque of,
81; *moulid* of, 71, 72, 73, 81–2, 85,
86, 87–8
zoning of cities, 29, 35, 36, 37, 177

Index